THE LANGUAGE OF CITIES

The Language of Cities

A GLOSSARY OF TERMS

Charles Abrams

With the assistance of ROBERT KOLODNY

NEW YORK / THE VIKING PRESS

For my grandchildren, Scott, Jason, and Adam

PREFACE

Some seventeen years ago I completed an extensive study of the world's urban land problems for the United Nations, which it subsequently published under the title *Urban Land Problems and Policies*. I had appended a list of definitions which I thought would help guide the reader through the technical jungle of planning and housing terms, but the UN's budget people excluded it in the interests of economy. I made it available over the years to students in my classes at the Massachusetts Institute of Technology, at the University of Pennsylvania, and at Columbia University, and they helped me enlarge it from time to time. By 1967, having accumulated several hundred words and short definitions relevant to housing, city planning, and associated disciplines, I concluded that the definitions had too narrow a focus and that the time had come for a more comprehensive piece of work, for what was known as the "urban problem" had become distended and now encompassed not only housing and city planning, but land economics, real estate, public administration, architecture, social welfare, transportation, public law and government, race, and a variety of other aspects of urban life.

Armed with the planning terms I had collected, I paid a visit to my old friend Louis Winnick of the Ford Foundation, which had previously helped me complete two other studies, and made a modest request to enable me to defray the cost of a research assistant and stenographer. To my consternation Winnick rejected my proposal but proposed a $400,000 grant instead. What he evidently wanted was a "project" entailing the hiring of a team of scholars for the production of a definitive urban dictionary—authentic, scholarly, impersonal, and precisely the opposite of what I was then prepared to do. I rejected the offer but I hope that what I have produced here will be the forerunner for the more comprehensive job Winnick proposed.

This limited glossary aims to do three things: identify some of the most relevant urban terms for the expert and layman; define them simply and accurately, expanding on the definition where clarification is necessary; add some of my personal opinions or biases where I consider them useful and relevant.

Identifying the urban terms proved a perplexing experience, for I found that to exclude was far more difficult than to include. The addition of words and terms seemed endless. Almost every new science, cult, enterprise, and profession (not to mention the literati, hippies, yippies, spacemen, con-men, etc.) had invented and expanded their terms of urban communication. We were experiencing not only a population and a technological explosion but a neological explosion as well; new words, word combinations, and terms were seeking acceptance into the language at every turn. I now see what a large task remains to be undertaken by some scholar with more years ahead than my own and with more research apparatus than my limited effort enjoyed.

Defining the terms in simple language was not difficult, and in many cases I have defined without excessive amplification. I have taken more liberties with my commentaries where I felt an issue had to be explored with something more than a dictionary definition because to understand the urban problem requires more than simply a grasp of the terms. Urban problems vary widely from country to country, and if I have given the book an American emphasis it is because the United States, as the most technologically developed of nations, is being looked to for solutions. It should be noted, however, that the gap between the geographical dialects has narrowed considerably with the growth of literature on urbanization and city planning, the exchange of experts, and the activities of the United Nations and international aid agencies. While the nature of the problem may differ between countries there are many common denominators—all countries, whether developed or undeveloped, are experiencing housing shortages, slum life, migration into cities, competition for land, regional problems, a disparity between income and shelter cost, race or group frictions, crime and violence, urban discontents, and the assumption of governmental responsibilities by cities at the very time that these cities have more and more limited resources for coping with them.

I have consulted other dictionaries and encyclopedias, borrowed from them where necessary, and stolen pitilessly from my own writings where relevant. I found the *Encyclopaedia Britannica,* the *Encyclopedia of Social Sciences,* and the *Unabridged Oxford English Dictionary* particularly helpful.

First, my thanks go to my dear wife Ruth, without whose encouragement I could never have completed this effort. For their faith in this volume and their efforts on its behalf I am indebted to my good friends George Backer and Dwight Macdonald. And I am grateful to a number of people who have reviewed some of the definitions—Professors Lloyd Rodwin, Nathan Glazer, Sigurd Grava, and especially Drs. Otto and Renata Koenigsberger. My appreciation goes also to Betsy Hite, June Greenberg, Barbara Brandt, and Kathy Coon for their clerical assistance. To Harvard University my thanks for providing research and clerical help and affording me the time to complete my work.

My greatest expression of gratitude goes to Robert Kolodny, who has spent many days helping me add, eliminate, check, and correct, and has shared with me those tedious labors which Dr. Samuel Johnson said (in discussing the writing of dictionaries) were needed "to remove rubbish and clear obstructions from the paths of Learning and Genius, who press forward without bestowing a smile on the humble drudge that facilitates their progress. Every other author may aspire to praise; the lexicographer can only hope to escape reproach."

CHARLES ABRAMS

New York City

THE LANGUAGE OF CITIES

abandonment   The relinquishment of ownership and control of property. Property may be abandoned because there are no heirs to claim it or because the owner no longer wants it. Desertion of real property is occurring at an alarming rate in a number of American cities due to vandalism of vacant units, lack of neighborhood safety, and inadequacy of the profit margin. Parts of New York City's Brownsville, East New York, and South Bronx look as if they have been bombed, with an estimated 4000 to 5000 buildings (containing 40,000 to 50,000 units) vacant and abandoned in 1968. Among the structures are perfectly sound, solid elevator buildings built to modern standards in the 1920s. The owners simply stopped collecting rents and disappeared from the scene. The situation in New York City suggests that fear—of break-in, mugging, and fire—plays a more important part in undermining sound areas than age or obsolescence. Once a unit becomes vacant, vandalism occurs, derelicts move in, more units become vacant, fires are started in empty apartments, the streets become less walkable, more vandalism follows, and soon the area takes on the appearance of a ghost city. Philadelphia, Cleveland, Detroit, Baltimore, and Newark have experienced similar phenomena.

Abandoning personal property is easier than abandoning a building. Real property carries with it responsibilities. They cannot be "surrendered" unless there is someone to accept the surrender, and the city will not always assume the responsibility. Nor is the mortgagee usually willing to foreclose, for he thereby assumes the penalties for not keeping a building in repair. Failure to pay real-estate taxes may of course eventually result in a tax foreclosure and a takeover by the city, but this may not happen for years. In this sense, abandonment of real estate can be compared to abandonment of a wife—the obligations continue; one cannot "abandon with abandon." (See BUILDING, DERELICT; ESCHEAT; UNTENANTED HAZARD.)

abortive subdivision. See SUBDIVISION, ABORTIVE OR PREMATURE.

abstract of title. See TITLE, ABSTRACT OF.

acceleration clause   A mortgage provision which gives the lender the option to terminate the loan and demand immediate payment of the balance upon the borrower's default in performing any of his obligations (failure to pay interest or taxes, make repairs, etc.) or upon his commission of certain forbidden acts (demolition of a structure without the mortgagee's consent, etc.). The right to accelerate payment may also be written into other types of agreements. (See MORTGAGE.)

accessibility   The quality of admitting entrance, access, or approach. Without accessibility real estate has little or no value. In the development of the American West by land companies, many lots laid out on the gridiron plan were bought, sight unseen, from maps. When the buyer finally got there he often found his lot inaccessible and valueless.

Aristotle, in the list of characteristics for his ideal city, included access to both the mainland and the sea (and, if possible, all parts of the country equally). At the same time he would make accessibility by the enemy difficult and favored walls for the city: "it should be easy of egress by the citizens and hard for enemies to approach or blockade."

accessory use. See USE, ACCESSORY.

access roads. See ROAD HIERARCHY.

activity rate. See LABOR-FORCE PARTICIPATION RATE.

ad valorem tax. See TAX, AD VALOREM.

adverse possession   The right of an occupant having a color of right (or some basis of a claim) to a particular property to acquire its title from the real owner after occupying it without being challenged for a prescribed number of years (usually a statutory twenty years). To be effectual, the occupancy by the user must be open, continuous, peaceable, under a claim of right and not by permission. A squatter, however, has no claim or color of right to his possession and does not acquire title by the mere fact of occupancy. But statutes of limitations (prescribing the time within which a claimant must sue to enforce his rights) may bar an owner from asserting his right to evict. Moreover, legislation may confer rights upon the squatter he did not have at the time of his original trespass. (See COLOR OF RIGHT.)

Aesopian covenant. See COVENANT, AESOPIAN.

aesthetic zoning. See ZONING, AESTHETIC.

agglomeration In general, a jumbled heap, mass, or cluster; thus an urban agglomeration is a clustering of population that has outgrown municipal or administrative boundaries and has willy-nilly fused two or more separate jurisdictions into one large area of settlement. Agglomeration is both the process and the ungainly result. (See CONURBATION; MEGALOPOLIS.)

agora The market place in ancient Greek cities, and the place of popular assembly. The agora was originally the assembly of the Greek people convoked by the king or one of his nobles; later it became the daily scene of political, religious, judicial, social, and commercial activities. It was an open space either in the city's center or near the harbor and was surrounded by the council house, temples, and other public buildings. Porticos frequently enclosed the agora, and there were statues, altars, trees, and fountains to adorn it. It was the precursor of the modern city center. (See CIVIC CENTER.)

airport city; jet city A city built around an airport and economically dependent upon it. Shannon, Ireland, was one of the first such cities; after the jet age rendered Shannon obsolete as a refueling port for transatlantic flights, industrial settlement was encouraged by liberal tax exemptions. A *jet city,* built around the economy of a jet airport, has been the subject of proposals in both the United States and England. The concept is new but possible and logical. With the journey from airport to downtown often consuming more time than the flight, the activities around a port could accommodate many of the traveler's needs. The land use would include only those that are practical for such a terminal—motels, low-lying factories dependent wholly or partly on air freight, airline offices, banks, shopping centers, and recreational and open-space facilities. Because of the noise problem, the uses must be carefully planned and buildings must be soundproofed.

airport zoning. See ZONING, AIRPORT.

air rights   The right to the use of air space over property owned by another. Air rights are granted for the space above railroad tracks, reservoirs, highways, or other property. Through the erection of a platform over the existing use, additional "land" can, in effect, be created. The air rights can either be sold or leased. Their use is particularly important in cities where land is in short supply. Buying air rights is a highly technical transaction entailing purchase or lease of the land required for the foundation and for access to it. Substantial air-right transactions have recently been effected with railroads, the most notable of which, in New York City, cleared the way for the new Madison Square Garden built over the Pennsylvania Railroad Station. Others include the Prudential Center over the Massachusetts Turnpike in Boston, the four high-rise apartment buildings straddling the approaches to the George Washington Bridge in New York City, and the forty-one-story Prudential Building over the Illinois Central tracks in Chicago.

A virtually uncharted air-rights frontier exists in city property used for schools and other public facilities. Modern school buildings are often no more than three or four stories high. The air space above their costly inner-city sites could be devoted to offices or apartments. Ground space now used for playgrounds could be rented to stores—thereby eliminating the dead areas that render streets dark, unsafe, or underutilized at night, and the playground space could be located on the roofs. Substantial revenues now dissipated in wasted land space could thus accrue to the city.

The federal highway program contemplates the use of air rights in urban areas to replace some of the housing and facilities demolished to make way for new roads. (See JOINT DEVELOPMENT.)

alienation   The voluntary transfer of real property by one person to another.

alley dwelling. See DWELLING, ALLEY.

alteration A change or rearrangement in the structural parts of a building or in its facilities, or its extension either horizontally or vertically. An alteration may include repairs and replacements but is distinguished from them by the fact that repairs and replacements do not entail a change in partitions or in other parts of the structure. Repairs or replacements do not generally require filing of plans or securing of official approvals while alterations do. Changing a house from a two-family to a three-family dwelling may, however, require a city's approval though entailing no structural changes. Approval is also required for the movement of a building from one site to another or its change from one use to another—commercial to residential, for example. (See REHABILITATION.)

amenities The pleasurable or aesthetic, as distinguished from the utilitarian, features of a plan, project, or location. Indoor amenities include places of entertainment, refreshment, assembly, worship, and play, as well as clubs, museums, and cultural facilities; while outdoor amenities include open spaces, green belts, sites for recreation and play, areas of scenic beauty, access to bodies of water, open vistas, and similar blessings.

The term "amenity" is now used so broadly that it can refer to just about anything that makes life more agreeable—from the temperate climate of Southern California to the intellectual climate of Cambridge, Massachusetts. With the increased mobility and affluence of Americans, the "amenities" are coming to have more and more influence on where people, institutions, and industries settle.

amortization The prorated liquidation of a debt over a fixed period, either by payment of the installments of principal into a sinking fund, or by direct payments to the lender or mortgagee. A mortgage is being amortized when it is being paid off in installments. Ordinarily the debt service on a loan includes interest, which represents the cost of borrowing the money, and amortization. Unlike interest, amortization is not a deductible expense for income-tax purposes, being viewed as the periodic repayment of a debt. (See DEBT SERVICE; MORTGAGE.)

annexation The process by which a municipality or other governing authority absorbs surrounding land and brings it under its jurisdiction. The great cities of the United States achieved their present size primarily through this mechanism, which was more commonly used before 1900 than it is today. Acquisition by annexation is now usually only of unincorporated territory. It is accomplished under a special act of the legislature, by action of the governing body where so authorized, or by a combined vote of the electorates concerned. Although Detroit and Los Angeles both annexed substantial territory during the twentieth century, and while there was a revival of annexations after World War II, fringe areas surrounding existing cities now generally resist it either through exertion of political pressures or by "defensive incorporation." The growing problems of the big city have made its neighbors reluctant to share in them. (See CONSOLIDATION.)

annual contribution   A yearly grant from the federal government to local public-housing authorities to enable them to meet their payments on the bonds issued for building projects for low-income families, and to enable them to lease the units at rents within the means of such families. The amount of this contribution is set at the time of construction, and with labor and material costs rising, many authorities are complaining that they will have to raise rents unless the federal formula is amended. (See HOUSING, PUBLIC.)

annuity   A sum of money payable at specified intervals over a prescribed period, for life or in perpetuity. Though it may sometimes be secured by real estate, it is not a rent.

Also, the estimated future stream of payments from a given property. For appraisal purposes, a calculation is made of the present worth of such future payments. This appraisers call the "annuity approach" to valuation. (See APPRAISAL.)

anomie   A condition in which established values and common meanings are rejected or not understood by a group or a society and in which new values and meanings have not yet replaced the old. Anomie is widely held to be a by-product of urban life. Recently the condition has been associated with the rejection of the traditional values by Negro groups and by the young. Emile Durkheim, in his investigation of suicide in 1897, found its chief modern cause in anomie and gave it its name, but the word seems to be a derivative of "anomy," which means "disregard of divine law."

apartheid A South African term for "apartness" or the enforced separation and disenfranchising of the colored races. The term has often been used in exaggerating the extent of segregation between blacks and whites in the United States. (See RACIAL POLARIZATION; SEGREGATION.)

apartment A single room or set of rooms occupied as a dwelling. In general usage, an apartment is rented living space that is part of a multi-family structure, as opposed to a house, which connotes something owned and free-standing or at least with a private entrance. However, the growing popularity of cooperatives and condominiums—apartments that are owned—has left the term ambiguous. (See DWELLING, MULTIPLE.)

apartment, efficiency A small apartment providing the minimum space required for one's habitation. For living purposes it may be neither efficient nor sufficient, but since it uses less space it may be cheaper.

apartment, garden A general term describing low-rise, multi-family housing surrounded by landscaped open space. Usually the apartments are walk-up, and the building rarely exceeds three stories. Garden apartments are cheaper to build than those with elevators and after World War II became a popular housing type on less costly outlying and suburban land.

apartment, high-rise An apartment structure with many floors, vertically designed to achieve a high dwelling density and an economic ratio of land to building cost. High-rise apartments are generally built on high-cost land accessible to or in the central area of a city.

apartment hotel An apartment house containing suites for relatively permanent housekeeping, as well as furnished rooms with dining service for transient guests; sometimes, a furnished apartment house with dining service.

apartment house A building divided into residential suites, usually for rental, where cooking is generally done within the individual units. In Britain, this is called a "block of flats," with each unit called a "flat."

The apartment house is of ancient vintage. Communal occupancy was

known to the Iroquois Indians; in the Roman Empire four-story buildings were common, and even units of six, seven, and eight stories were in
use. During medieval times apartment houses were erected in walled
cities such as Paris and Edinburgh, and they remain one of the main
forms of residence in many parts of the world, particularly where land
cost is high or land is available only at a premium. As metropolitan areas
grow in the United States, pressures are being exerted to liberalize zoning
laws to permit more apartment construction in suburbia.

apportionment   The division of rights or liabilities among several persons in accordance with their respective interests or responsibilities. At a
title closing, rents, insurance premiums, taxes, and mortgage interest will
be apportioned, *i.e.,* credited to or deducted from the sale price as the
computations indicate. Apportionment is also the allocation by the tax
department of responsibility for the payment of real-estate taxes when a
parcel of property is subdivided for acquisition by several owners.

appraisal; valuation   The process of estimating the value of a piece of
property; also the valuation itself. The four main formulas used by professional appraisers that are admissible in court for the determination of
"market value" are: a previous sale of the same or a very similar property; the capitalization of the income derived from the property and its
foreseeable future income; the cost of reproducing the building (replacement cost) less depreciation; some combination of the above methods.

    Appraisers are employed to value property for mortgaging, in condem-
nation proceedings, in the valuation of estates for tax purposes, and in
other cases in which value is a factor. They often testify in court, and
their estimates (given under oath) vary widely with the clients for whom
they may be testifying. But "value" is an elusive concept that defies precise definition, and even the most virtuous appraiser can at best give only
an opinion. Indeed, an appraisal is often the transposition of a psychic
equity into a vested illusion. (See VALUE; VALUE, MARKET; VALUE, USE.)

appreciation   Increase in the value of property flowing from general economic conditions as distinguished from increment due to physical improvements or added investment. (See BETTERMENT; TAX, BETTERMENT;
TAX, INCREMENT.)

apprenticeship The practice of learning a trade or calling through association with a qualified skilled worker. The practice was common in the Middle Ages, when it was thought that neither arts nor sciences could flourish unless those who practiced them gave proof of their proficiency and were part of the guilds. The old apprenticeship system has in modern times been supplanted by training in schools and in universities, but it still goes on in certain industries, notably the printing and building trades.

The current system has come under attack on the claim that the unions with their protectionist proclivities exclude minorities and select favorites as apprentices. When electrical workers are in great demand in urban areas, the unions will import semi-skilled electricians from the hinterlands for temporary work instead of training new workers. The union's explanation is that if it trains too many new workers, there will be a labor surplus when demand slackens. It is also asserted that even when the doors are opened to Negro youths, they are often disinclined to take the low pay of the training period when higher wages lure them elsewhere. While discrimination in apprenticeship continues, time and the shortage of skilled labor may break the barriers, as has already happened in some labor-short operations. Organized pressures by Negro groups coupled with organization of black unions are other developments that may widen opportunities in the better-paid trades.

arcade; galleria A roofed passageway having stores within it and most often leading from one street to another.

architecture, legislative The fixing of styles in design and construction, of location and siting, by legislative restrictions such as overrigid zoning, building codes, regulations governing height, setbacks, and light and air specifications. These are often copied from other codes, though irrelevant to the local environment, and have a tendency to endure far beyond their time. Frequently they protect the vested interests of labor unions or materials producers rather than the public interest. The influence of some of these restrictions on the building product is telling. They narrow the scope of the architect's talents considerably. They are frequently more constrictive than constructive, and while they are intended to, and often do, prevent the building of unsound structures, they as often make a building unprofitable as well as aesthetically offensive. Specifications and regulations promulgated by housing authorities and other public agencies have the same effect and might well be called "bureaucratic architecture."

Building standards need not be standard. Regulations should be accompanied by financial as well as architectural mock-ups to test their practicality before they are enacted. Provision should be made for deviations from the restrictions where safety is not in issue and a better design could be obtained. Legislation that retards prefabrication of parts or the use of more efficient materials and methods should be continuously re-examined and modified as necessary. Building legislation is essential, but legislation that discourages originality and that enforces waste and sterility can be disposed of without sacrificing health or safety standards. (See ARCHITECTURE, URBAN; MOCK-UP, ECONOMIC.)

architecture of discomfort Design deliberately intended to make people uncomfortable. It is exemplified in counter restaurants designed to encourage quick eating and a larger turnover; in hotel lobbies and railroad and bus terminals that supply few seats so as to discourage both loitering and relaxation for the weary; in church pews to effect simplicity and eschew luxury; and in classic museum and palace architecture in which pomp is accorded priority over comfort. An American "comfort station" justifying the name is still to be built.

architecture, prestige Prestige architecture is the design of structures primarily to enhance the prestige of the client or his commercial products. Here, as in price-no-object architecture, cost plays little or no part and may be charged to the advertising budget. Examples are the Lever Brothers, Pepsi-Cola, and Seagram buildings in New York City. Sales of soap, carbonated beverages, and whiskey are considered to be enhanced by the building and its presence on a prominent avenue. Homes built to maintain or enhance the status of their owners also fall within the prestige classification.

architecture, price-no-object The design of structures in which structural cost plays little or no part in the owner's calculations. Its primary objective is to produce a building of beauty, merit, or pomp rather than something economical, and it is exemplified in the great European cathedrals, the Palace of Versailles, and some contemporary buildings in which a well-heeled client has given the architect a free hand in design and specifications.

architecture, speculative The design of buildings to produce maximum profit with minimum outlay. The owner is less concerned with long-term investment than with resale potential. He looks for maximum mortgageability to minimize his investment and requires his architect to produce plans and specifications that will cost the minimum per cube of building. The speculative architect designs multiple dwellings and small homes, though most often the latter are built from stock plans. They may not be the most beautiful but they are cheap, produced in quantity, and meet a need.

Architectural critics and design contests usually judge speculative, prestige, and price-no-object architecture as though they were all in the same class. Yet no judgment can be complete that fails to weigh the "givens" and the limitations conditioning each product. A speculatively built apartment house should be rated superior to a piece of prestige architecture if the architect showed ingenuity by designing something far better than the routine product. At the same time, the architect with few limitations upon his blueprints could well be passed over when his building is not what his budgetary freedom allowed. (See DESIGN CONTEST.)

architecture, urban The profession of designing buildings and other physical additions to the urban environment; also, the physical inventory produced in cities.

The urban revolution has altered architecture's place and character in a number of ways:

(1) The architect's main client is no longer a prince or prelate but an entrepreneur. He is less concerned with "frozen music" than with liquid assets. Urban buildings, once erected for pride, power, or permanence, are now built mostly for profit or sale.

(2) Cities, seeing the surge of speculative firetraps, have imposed codes and regulations. But these have limited the scope of originality. The most ingenious architect often finds his talents frustrated by official requirements under which he can only produce more of the same.

(3) The architecture of the individual home has all but disappeared except for a few mansion folk. "I would have," said Ruskin, "our ordinary dwelling houses built to last, and built to be lovely: as rich and full of

pleasantness . . . with such differences as might suit and express each man's character and occupation, and partly his history." The urban architect, however, no longer designs "ordinary dwelling houses"; they are not built to last, though some do, to the city's dismay; they are too often unlovely, with one looking pretty much like the other.

(4) Architecture as a profession is also becoming architecture as a business with the advent of the industrial designer, who might or might not hire architects; with the conglomerate corporation (one of which has actually bought a large architectural firm); with the industrial corporation, which is producing houses en masse with or without architects; with the mobile-house manufacturers, who are currently producing mobile and immobile units by the tens of thousands; and with the speculative builder, who builds housing almost exclusively from stock plans.

(5) The job of the architect is being increasingly limited to the design of specialized structures such as office buildings, churches, public buildings, and some price-no-object structures for philanthropists, embassies, museums, or commercial establishments looking for a prestige structure that can puff its product.

(6) In other types of design, the architect has been powerless because he has had to accept the general pressure of waste and disorganization in the construction industry and the demands by his client-entrepreneur that every usable inch be squeezed out of the property to produce maximum profit with minimum outlay. The docility of the home-buyer, the indifference to quality of the renter concerned primarily with location and low rental, the absence of a market keenly competitive in quality, the philistinism of public-housing officials, a tax structure that demands the utilization of every utilizable inch—all these give little opportunity for using the architect's endowments.

(7) Until the twentieth century the architect, landscape architect, and engineer performed the city-planning function, and until the middle of the present century city planning was viewed in Europe as a branch of architecture. The movement to make city planning a profession in its own right received its main impetus in the United States, where architecture began to be viewed as only one branch (though still an important one) of the city-planning process. But the multiple aspects of the urban problem began to call for a broader education than the architect received or the universities were offering. A neighborhood designed by an architect could be undermined overnight by social problems that were outside

the architect's frame of reference or his competence. The complex problems of the city—its poverty, slums, racial frictions, and social distortions—have called for a more inclusive education.

(8) Urban renewal, highway programs, and other federal efforts have opened up new frontiers for urban architecture, but few architects have enlarged their horizons. The failure of the profession to broaden its sights has seen engineering firms stepping into the breach and taking on the larger public contracts, hiring architects where needed. The big industrial corporations have simultaneously pre-empted contracts for research in building and in other aspects of the urban problem.

No single profession or discipline is capable of dealing alone with the protean problems confronting the urban world. Whether architecture as presently defined can broaden to meet the challenges of world urbanization depends not only on whether the existing professionals can rise to the challenge, but also on whether architectural education can be reoriented to prepare new architects to cope with its vast potentials. This calls for a major overhaul of the architectual schools—in their teachers, their teachings, and their curricula.

assemblage The merging of separate properties into a contiguous unit generally for a new building or project. It is accomplished by purchase of the individual properties and their transfer into single ownership. Assemblage into larger parcels makes the project more economical to build and often facilitates a better design. The holdout (an owner or lessee refusing to sell) is the bane of the assembler.

Assemblage is a practice requiring cunning as well as persuasiveness. Two of the best examples are the gathering, in more than 140 separate transactions, of some 15,000 acres of land for the new town of Columbia, Maryland, and the assemblage for Tudor City in New York City. Properties were purchased in the name of dummy buyers until the plan became known. Once the true scope of an effort is revealed, higher prices must inevitably be paid. Because of the difficulties in assemblage of city properties, there has been a growing tendency to liberalize the eminent-domain power to force owners to sell. Often properties are acquired by a public agency claiming a public purpose such as urban renewal, after which the property is resold to private builders. (See EMINENT DOMAIN; HOLDOUT; PARTITION ACTION; REPARCELATION; URBAN RENEWAL.)

assembly line; mass production   A production system under which inter-changeable parts or sub-assemblies are brought together into a com-pletely finished product. A conveyor belt is usually used to carry the parts past a line of workers, each of whom performs a specialized task on the product as it reaches him, until it goes on to the final completion point. Mass production is fabrication in quantity to achieve standardiza-tion and low cost per unit.

House building has remained the Cinderella of the assembly-line revo-lution. If the automobile had to be built under home-building's archaic handicraft, few could afford one. However, there are indications of a breakthrough in apartment-house prefabrication in the United States through the building of a plant on the site for the production of stand-ardized parts. A number of such building systems have been successfully employed in Europe. (See AUTOMATION; PREFABRICATION.)

assessment   A levy upon property to defray the cost of a specific im-provement or service, such as a sewer installation. It may also mean the value put upon property for purposes of computing the real-estate tax. Thus an assessment may be *on* property or *of* property. Assessment equalization is the adjustment of valuations where some properties are over-assessed and others under-assessed so as to establish a more equita-ble division of the tax burden throughout an area. A taxpayer may bring an action charging that his property is being unequally assessed in rela-tion to other property within the same tax jurisdiction, and the courts have compelled some cities to reduce assessments on industrial and com-mercial property and increase them on residential property. (See TAX.)

assessment ratio   The ratio, computed for purposes of property taxation, between the market value of property and the value at which it is as-sessed. Thus if the assessment ratio is 1 to 2, a property with a $200,000 market value would be assessed at $100,000. Assessment ratios vary with cities; in some the assessed valuation is close to the market value, in oth-ers it may be a fraction of actual value. (See TAX RATE, EFFECTIVE.)

assessment, special   A charge imposed by a government upon all or upon a restricted group of properties in an area to defray, in whole or in part, the cost of a specific improvement or service. Examples are sewer and street assessments. Payment of the assessment is often spread over a specified number of years. If the improvement benefits the property, it is called an "assessment for benefit." (See TAX, BETTERMENT.)

assignment Transfer of a title, right, or interest in a lease, bond, note, or other asset to another; the one who assigns is the assignor, the recipient is the assignee.

atomic energy Energy released in nuclear reactions; it is more accurately called nuclear energy. Nuclear-reactor plants promise to be the new power source for cities as well as for numerous industrial uses. Their effect on the location of industry as well as on the creation of new industrial communities and the decentralization of existing ones is still an unknown factor in city and regional planning, though it could be significant. It is clear, however, that extreme caution must be exercised in populated areas both in the production of atomic energy and in the disposal of wastes. (See NUPLEX.)

attic "Attic" means "having characteristics peculiarly Athenian"; it came to designate a decorative structure consisting of a small order (column and entablature) placed above another order of much greater height constituting the main façade, usually an Attic order with pilasters instead of pillars, whence the name. It now describes the room or rooms just below the roof of the house, also called the "garret," which meant a place of refuge or watchtower.

authority. See PUBLIC CORPORATION.

automation The process that substitutes self-acting and self-regulating machines for human labor. The term can probably be credited to John Diebold's book *Automation: The Advent of the Automatic Factory* (1948).

With the advance of communications, precision controls were able to spark a sequence of "instructions" that sharply diminished the need for hand and brain, bringing fears of labor surplus and obsolescence of current skills. While industrial production began calling for higher skill levels, workers either were unqualified for the new tasks or could not be easily retrained to perform them. The Negro was the most patent victim. While he was demanding greater equality, there were many jobs going begging because he often was not trained for those an automated economy required, or because he could not accept jobs still open to him in the more menial and ill-paid trades. He had escaped from sharecropping and was at last advancing, but not as fast as he felt he should, and he often manifested his frustrations by violence or by withdrawing from the white community and its offerings.

From Aristotle to Rossum's Universal Robots, the dream of the machine taking over man's work has stirred man's expectations—or haunted him. The pains of displacement of labor by the machine have been chronic in man's history and in the long run he has mitigated them, employed his growing numbers, conquered famine, cut his workday, extended his life span, and enlarged his horizons. But there is no agreement on what lies ahead. One school sees the new technology ending all human conflicts, making the machine the slave of man, doing his bidding, dispensing with his chores, extending his food supply and his leisure hours, increasing his comforts, and opening horizons that will identify not only the earth's unplumbed resources but those of other planets as well. Another school sees man as incapable of using the new technology constructively—in fact, as capable of using it only destructively, no longer controlling the technological forces he has released, but becoming the victim of his own nuclear weapons, his pesticides, his pollutants, his genetic and personality controls; in short, advancing in chaos and heading for the abyss.

It is difficult to be entirely optimistic, for while the prospects for technological progress seem endless, man has not made parallel progress in devising or improving the political institutions that govern him or in controlling the forces that can destroy him. The failure of the United Nations as a control is only the most recent manifestation of this. The easy access to devastating weaponry by national leaders who lack the will or wisdom to control its use is another. Nor is there any evidence of a universal surge of moral spirit concerned with preserving the planet or spreading man's advances. The gulf between technology and ethics remains wide, and political systems based upon acknowledged ethical principles are still to be devised. Until the gulf is bridged, this problem threatens to overwhelm us—and for what man has achieved, he may have to be more pitied than envied. (See ASSEMBLY LINE.)

bail out To throw water from a boat with a bucket (nautically known as a bail) or to parachute from an aircraft to avoid disaster; hence, to emerge from a troublesome business venture with the salvage of the original capital or part of it. One thereby remains above water or escapes from a tough situation. During the depression of the 1930s many mortgage institutions were bailed out by the Home Owners Loan Corporation, and landlords tried to bail out of investments in multiple dwellings by taking all the rent they could before the mortgagee clamped down on them by foreclosure. This is called "milking." Bailing out also describes the process under which mortgage institutions sell their mortgages to the Federal National Mortgage Association, which was set up by Congress to create mortgage liquidity. Big business firms unwilling to tie up funds in building operations have also pressed for bailouts as a condition for investing. (See MILKABILITY.)

backlash. See WHITE BACKLASH.

basement A story in a residence which is partly underground but has no more than half of its clear height from finished floor to finished ceiling below mean finished grade. A basement may be legally occupied under certain laws (where, for example, the rear portion of a back basement is level or near level with the yard). A cellar may not be so occupied except by possessions. The word "basement" is also used to describe a story wholly underground in any type of structure in which it is the lowermost portion. (See CELLAR.)

Bauhaus A school of design established in 1919 in Weimar, Germany, by Walter Gropius, the main emphasis of which was to bridge the gulf between artistic form and industrial production. Gropius believed that industrial production must be the basis of the modern aesthetic, just as handicraft had been the basis of pre-industrial aesthetic standards; that cooperation among design specialists was essential; that the production of good design for the modern era called for a unitary theory of education that would break the schism between the artist and the technically expert craftsman by training students equally in both areas. "Although employing a visual syntax," says Professor James M. Fitch, "the Bauhaus developed a rationale very similar to Sullivan's thesis *Form Follows Function*—i.e., valid form derives from function understood and served." The Bauhaus influence has been apparent in building design, furniture, automobiles, china, and other articles.

beautification The act of improving the aesthetic attributes of the physical environment. In American usage, it is being applied to urban and suburban cosmeticizing, roadside and sidewalk arborization, auto dump concealment, and scenic and historic preservation. Though the term "beauty" is not defined, it seems to embrace a variety of meanings, including venerable, attractive, rustic, pleasing, and picturesque. To beautify can also mean to hide the ugly.

Until the 1960s, the beauty of the American landscape exercised little restraint on the population that urbanized it. Trees were viewed as lumber, and greenbacks rather than greenways ruled the mood. Shrapnel subdivisions leveled hills and converted undulating plains into semi-slums. But it was the automobile that delivered the real blow to beauty. Our road-builders have seized whatever was beautiful and converted it into concrete monotony. As Professor Colin Buchanan of London told the President's Task Force on Beauty, "If you . . . add up the total amount of excruciating ugliness associated directly or indirectly with the motor vehicle . . . it is staggering."

It is no accident that in America the most popular demonstration of beauty (in the sense of "the pleasurable exercise of pure contemplation") has become the beauty contest, and it is some sign of recent progress that the winning specimen has had to say a few words into the microphone to prove she can talk.

The most vocal defenders of beauty are the nature lovers, conservationists, estate owners, and suburban governments. They have concerted their efforts and learned all the gimmicks—zoning, green belts, gerrymandering of land, purchases by dummies, income-tax escapes, and other inducements to keep the home-hungry city dwellers from overrunning their dales and valleys. Their efforts are frequently commendable and they have wrested many a brook and valley from the subdivider. But the over-all problem of land use and land preservation has still to be grappled with.

betterment An increment in the value of private property accruing to its owner because of the public provision of facilities, roads, open spaces, or other improvements. The term is used mainly in England and its former possessions. (See APPRECIATION; TAX, BETTERMENT; TAX, INCREMENT; TAX, SINGLE.)

bid. See TENDER.

bikeway A thoroughfare reserved for bicycles either exclusively or during specially assigned periods. Bicycle travel to work is common in many parts of Europe and in underdeveloped countries, where the bicycle shares the road with the automobile, motorcycle, horse, pedestrian, and even the rickshaw and roving cow. There are bikeways in the United States, but they are mostly limited in extent and are used for recreation rather than for the journey to work. In New York City's Central Park, the Park Commissioner barred traffic to automobiles on Saturday and Sunday and the weekend bikeway gained popularity among many who had never before pushed a pedal. The growing parking problem in big cities could lead to a surge of bicycling to work if bikeways were reserved for it, but so far little support is visible for subordinating the accelerator to the pedal. If sales of bicycles continue to increase, however, we might yet see the growth of a bicycle pressure group pushing for rights-of-way.

binder A receipt for a sum of money paid to a property owner or his agent evidencing a prospective purchaser's willingness to buy the property upon agreed terms. A formal contract is entered into thereafter. If the binder is also signed by the owner and contains all the essential terms of an agreement, it is as enforceable as a contract. Also, an interim agreement under which an insurance company covers a risk (fire, burglary, etc.) pending issuance of a policy. (See EARNEST MONEY; OPTION.)

birth rate The annual number of births per 1000 population in any given area. This is called the "crude birth rate." If allowance is made for differences in the population composition (the rate, for example, for each 1000 women of childbearing age), the measure is called a "refined birth rate." The world population is increasing at the rate of 2 per cent per year, which means a doubling of its numbers in thirty-five years.

Feast and famine are factors in population growth and decline, as evidenced by Ireland, whose numbers reached 8 million by 1845 only to drop by a million during the potato famine between 1848 and 1854 and by another million through the emigration this induced. Today, despite religious prohibitions on birth control, its population is only 4 million. Among the reasons are fewer and later marriages and continued emigration.

Birth rates in the United States, except for the postwar baby boom, have fluctuated with economic conditions. The wealthier the community, it seems, the slower the population growth. In northern industrial Italy, for example, the birth rate is low compared to the agricultural regions of the south despite government encouragement of births and Catholic restrictions on birth control. The anomaly is that population grows with productivity but tends to decrease with affluence. (See CAPILLARITY, LAW OF; POPULATION EXPLOSION.)

black   A word used by a number of Negro leaders and groups as a replacement for the word Negro. Malcolm X referred to Negroes as blacks, and Marcus Garvey's rallying cry was "Black is beautiful." Black militants favor using "black," saying that Negro is a "slave word." "Afro-American" is also acceptable to some. Others insist on being called "Negro" or "colored." The National Association for the Advancement of Colored People uses all the words interchangeably and will not alter its name. The feeling here is that the term "black" would measure Negroes by the amount of blackness and thereby emphasize a "reverse racism."

black capitalism   The theory that the Negro should have a greater opportunity to share the lush fruits of American capitalism and enterprise, that blacks should own and operate businesses, particularly businesses that serve black communities. Although there are some black banks and insurance companies, most such enterprises have been marginal in profitability, stability, and condition. Most are single-proprietor retail and service trades such as hairdressing and barbering, and many of these would be submarginal without their free family labor.

Black capitalism looks to federal aid through the Small Business Administration and other agencies to help Negroes get on their business feet, and to training programs to equip them for competition in the business world. Some private banks also make loans to foster local black enterprises, but these have been on a small scale. The growing disenchantment with owning enterprises in volatile black communities has brought offers to sell by white storekeepers, but lack of training and capital has impeded takeovers. Real-estate ownership and its related opportunities (subcontracting, management, brokerage, insurance, furnished-room operations, etc.) would seem to offer potentials for a breakthrough, since profits can be substantial in the ghetto and many white owners are withdrawing from the field. Easier financing and better training would help considerably, but these have been slow to materialize. Nevertheless, a growing proportion of the real estate in the black ghetto is coming into Negro ownership as white owners are selling out.

black power The rallying cry of a militant Negro movement based on the premise that the deliberate and concerted exercise of black pressures on the white community will gain the black real independence, generate race pride and greater self-respect, as well as win social and economic advances that have been long denied him. The term was probably first used by Richard Wright in his book by that name dealing with Ghana under the rule of Kwame Nkrumah. Subsequently adopted by activist groups, it has acquired many different meanings, including the advocacy of a separate state for blacks. To some, black power has meant a greater black consciousness, independent action, and political organization to put blacks into office, build up black businesses and cooperatives, and gain control of the local schools. To others, it has meant "getting the gun," meeting fire with fire; and to a few it has even justified looting and arson, armed rebellion and guerrilla warfare. But it is now more likely to imply "black pride" rather than "black coercion."

In the wake of the Negro riots of the late 1960s, it was not unexpected that the movement would strike fear into the hearts of the white community, particularly since the views of the most militant Negroes, though often a small minority, received the greatest notice. Black power soon began to confront a white backlash. Moreover, it seemed that black power, by advocating black separatism at the same time as it urged black unity, pressed for a resurrection of the all-but-dead "separate but equal" doctrine, this time with real equality. The hard-fought struggle by some of the older Negro leaders for an integrated society was pushed into the background.

Black separatism, it is felt, means concentrated black political power; the ghetto provides an easier forum for oratory and organization; it also affords protection in numbers against brutality. Desegregation would mean dilution of power and a reversion to subordination. The validity of the various positions remains to be settled by clarification of views, by bringing history and precedent to bear on logic, and above all by events. (See COALITION DOCTRINE; WHITE BACKLASH.)

blight A metaphor from the plant world used to describe that concentration of forces which puts a building or a neighborhood on its way to becoming a slum. A blighted area is one that has deteriorated or has been arrested in its development by physical, economic, or social forces. Overhead subway lines and heavy industries are said, for example, to be blighting influences on residential neighborhoods, as are physical dilapidation and conversion to transient residences. But clear causal relationships between factor and condition have yet to be established.

Statutes generally require that an area be blighted before it is eligible for urban renewal, but what constitutes blight is open to interpretation. The requirement has been liberally construed in many jurisdictions, and the courts usually have been loath to second-guess the agencies. The lines between a viable section, a blighted area, and a slum are fuzzy ones, and they are usually to be found where the public authority chooses to draw them. (See GRAY AREA; SLUM.)

block The segment of a city that is bounded by four neighboring and intersecting streets and not transversed by any roadway meant for through traffic. Blocks come in all sizes and need not be rectangular. They can be bounded by only two streets that intersect twice or three streets that meet at oblique angles.

Because the block is an easily identified and separate chunk of a city, it is often the basic unit for the keeping of records and the collection of statistics. For the purpose of social understanding and political organization, however, the block is frequently defined as the two sides of two separate physical blocks that face onto a common street. (See LOT.)

block-busting The practice of accelerating sales of houses by circulating rumors that unwelcome minorities have purchased or rented houses in the neighborhood and will soon overwhelm it. The block-buster's objective is generally to precipitate a drop in prices and a buyer's market, after which he can purchase the properties himself and resell them to minority families at higher and often inflated prices. He achieves his objectives when he raises fears among the owners and precipitates panic sales and flight. Block-busting can lead to forfeiture of a broker's license, but it is sometimes hard to differentiate between what is block-busting and what is a sincere effort to integrate a neighborhood or break an exclusion practice. (See RACHMANISM.)

block interior The unbuilt-upon land at the center of a city block. This land remains undeveloped usually because of the restrictions on 100 per cent lot coverage. While it constitutes one of the most abundant sources of vacant land in densely developed areas, it is difficult to bring into use. One reason is its long and narrow shape—in Manhattan, for example, a typical residential block interior might be 400 feet long and only 40 to 80 feet wide. Another is the fragmentation of ownership, particularly on a residential block where there may be a different owner for each lot. And it is difficult to find appropriate uses for such land, hemmed in by buildings on all sides and having limited access to the street.

Some imaginative schemes, however, have been carried out in block cores. The Harlem Park Urban Renewal project in Baltimore, for example, has twenty-nine inner-block parks, created by clearing out rear-alley dwellings and other backyard structures from the large blocks and then consolidating the land under a unified plan. Despite the variety of designs and recreational facilities, the project has its critics, and reports are that the parks are not so well used or well kept as expected. But the principle of recapturing this land for more efficient use seems an excellent one. Backyard unification plans have been proposed for slum areas in cities like New York, where the need for even small open spaces and play areas is pressing. So far, however, the only real successes have been in well-to-do areas like Greenwich Village and Turtle Bay, where the large yards and low densities that come with single-family brownstones have made some very handsome enclosed parks possible. There have even been proposals for erecting temporary relocation housing in block interiors, allowing for full-scale demolition and rebuilding of slum housing while the residents still stay on the block. (See PARK, VEST-POCKET.)

"blue-sky" laws   A set of regulations designed to prevent fraud and misrepresentation pertaining mainly to the subdivision of land; these laws call for full disclosure by the subdivider to assure each buyer of a clear title. They take their name from a remark by the proponent of the first such law in Kansas (1911), who warned that some land companies sought to "capitalize the blue skies."

bond, first-mortgage   A bond the payment of which is secured by a first mortgage on real estate. The bond (or its equivalent, such as a note) is generally issued simultaneously with the mortgage, the bond or note representing the commitment to pay and the mortgage representing the security. (See MORTGAGE.)

bond, industrial-development   A tax-exempt bond issued by a public agency to finance the building of a private factory or enterprise. Such bonds have financed the plants of the nation's largest corporations, and much of the investment and risk which they once took under the old private-enterprise formula have now been assumed by municipal corporations. Thus Louisport, Kentucky, with only 610 people and an annual budget of $2300, marketed a $48.5 million issue to finance a private aluminum rolling mill. The bond will be repaid from the rent received. Cherokee, Alabama, with 300 residents, sold $25 million of such bonds to build a chemical plant, and Eufala, Alabama, financed a Holiday Inn in this way. In 1950 only three states permitted their municipalities to sell such bonds; in 1963 there were twenty-seven. The amount of such bonds issued has not only accelerated remarkably but also become acceptable to the same big-time corporations and investment houses whose executives so often complain that the Tennessee Valley Authority and similar public operations are "socialistic."

As more and more private risks are assumed by public agencies, the area of private investment is narrowed. Simultaneously Wall Street investment houses look for more private enterprises they can launch as public operations so that they may issue more tax-exempt bonds and thereby immunize more of the nation's entrenched wealth against federal levy. Socialism is thus coming from Wall Street rather than from the left, and the spread of the device presages a socialism for the rich and private enterprise for the poor. (See SPECIAL DISTRICT.)

bond, public   A bond issued by a public agency. The agency may be the federal government, a state, county, city, township, borough, school or special district, special-purpose authority, or any one of numerous subdivisions of government. A municipal bond is a bond issued by any political subdivision of the state, usually a city. A tax-anticipation bond is a bond issued in anticipation of tax receipts. A special assessment bond is one issued for a special improvement repayable out of earmarked assessments levied on designated persons or property.

Municipal bonds must be issued for a public purpose. They may be general-obligation bonds to which the full faith and credit of the issuing agency is pledged, or revenue bonds payable from specified revenues. They may also be bonds of federal agencies payable out of their own assets and income but having the moral backing of the federal government.

Public-housing bonds are bonds issued by local housing authorities. In the case of federally aided projects, they will be backed by federal subsidies pledged to the authorities.

State and local government bonds usually yield a lower interest rate to the buyer than federal bonds, but they are exempt from federal levy because the states in the United States are viewed as the original sovereignties and the federal government as the states' creation. Since the power to tax carries the power to destroy, the federal government has been held to be unable to tax its creators or subdivisions and instrumentalities. This immunity from taxation has encouraged a steadily increasing stream of tax-exempt obligations for a growing variety of purposes. The purchasers are usually holders of larger aggregations of wealth seeking escape from federal levy.

bond, revenue   A bond issued by a public agency payable from earmarked revenues, as distinguished from a general obligation bond in which the general credit of a city or state is pledged. Revenue bonds have become common devices for financing such public works as water and sewer systems, bridges, tunnels, highways, public garages, and similar improvements. The charges, assessments, or tolls derived from the improvement are pledged to pay the interest and sinking-fund requirements of the bonds. Since the general revenues of the issuing government are not pledged to the bonds and since their security depends on the sufficiency of the earmarked revenues to pay them, they will be priced somewhat higher than general obligation bonds. Defaults, however, are few on well-rated bonds issued by the responsible investment houses.

The reasons a state or municipality will issue revenue bonds instead of general-obligation bonds are unwillingness to pledge the general revenues or inability to pledge them due to legislative limitations on the amount of general revenue bonds issuable, and fear of impairing the general credit by the issuance of too many general bonds.

bond, surety An undertaking by an insurance company guaranteeing performance of an act or agreement by another. It may take the form of a bail bond, guaranteeing the appearance in court of an accused; a completion bond, guaranteeing the completion of a project or building by a contractor; a performance bond, guaranteeing the performance of a specified act under a contract. If the guarantor is a surety or insurance company, a premium will be paid for its guarantee. The company may demand collateral to protect it against loss. Completion or performance bonds are usually required on public contracts.

boondoggling; leafraking Wasteful labor employed in uneconomic work. Both are words of derision carried over from New Deal days to describe some of the less useful work on projects designed mainly to get people off the unemployment rolls.

The Works Progress Administration (WPA), which financed these projects, was set up in 1935 and directed by Harry L. Hopkins until 1938. The WPA was intended to supplement the public works program of the Emergency Relief and Construction Act, then under the direction of Secretary of Interior Harold L. Ickes, who seemed incapable of getting his projects under way. When the result was stagnation and widening hardship, Hopkins moved into the breach.

While not all of his projects were lasting monuments to civilization (nor were they intended to be), many were constructive contributions. They included 116,000 buildings, 78,000 bridges, 651,000 miles of road, and improvement of 800 airports. Among other projects were the Federal Writers Project and the Federal Theatre Project. Some 10,000 pieces of art and sculpture were produced; musical performances averaged 4000 a month. WPA also produced First Houses in New York City, the nation's first municipal public-housing project. Most important of all, 3,500,000 people were put on the payrolls and an over-all total of 8,500,000 people were employed. Because the appropriations for WPA added up to $11 billion, it was criticized by a Senate committee in 1939 and was thereafter curtailed. The agency ceased operations in 1943, but the terms "boondoggling" and "leafraking" have survived in the vocabulary. (See PUMP-PRIMING.)

borings Tests made by running a bore into the ground to determine the nature of the foundation. Since the foundation is often one of the unknowns in the building operation, test borings provide important clues before an investment is made. Underground rock where a basement is needed or a long-forgotten underground stream may turn what is a paying building proposition on paper into a financial flop on completion.

borough plan. See FEDERATION.

boycott The concerted refusal to have commercial, social, or other dealings with any party as a means of making him alter his practices, bring him to terms, or penalize him. It is used in labor conflicts by unions and by nations as sanctions against one another in international disputes. It has assumed an urban relevancy when Negro groups have employed it against firms doing business in the South; against businesses refusing to hire black workers, charging exorbitant prices, or discriminating in the quality of services offered to blacks; and against school administrations and school boards that resist their demands. A boycott is "secondary" when third parties are coerced into joining it. In England boycotting is known colloquially as "sending to Coventry" and was modestly called "exclusive dealing" by W. E. Gladstone.

Boycotting derives its name from Captain Charles Cunningham Boycott, an estate agent, who in 1880 refused to cut rents to levels fixed by his Irish tenants. He had his life threatened, his possessions looted, his food supplies cut off, his fences leveled, his letters intercepted, and his figure burned in effigy. Boycotting was part of the Irish nationalist campaign, and it took 900 soldiers to protect the beleaguered Captain and bring in his crops.

broker   An individual who, for a fee, arranges the purchase or sale of land by acting as intermediary between the seller and purchaser. He may also negotiate loans on real estate and manage and lease property for a fee. In old France the *brokière* broached or opened the cask of wine. In fourteenth-century England there was the love broker, or pimp. Later, a broker came to mean any retail dealer, middleman, or seller of wares. (See COMMISSION; LISTING; MANAGING AGENT; OPERATOR.)

Bronxification   The process of coming to resemble the environment of the Bronx, a borough of New York City. The Bronx has accommodated first- and second-generation immigrants in its five-story walk-ups as well as in small homes and more modern apartment houses. The borough's mushroom growth and individual flavor were not always in favor with outsiders or devotees of finer architecture. Thus "Bronxification" became their term of contempt, embracing not only the people of the Bronx (Jews, Italians, Puerto Ricans, Negroes, etc.), but also the dense and uninspired structures that housed them.

brownstone   A reddish-brown sandstone often used for the facing of row houses built in the big cities during the nineteenth century. It has given its name to these structures, many of which are now highly prized for rehabilitation as modern townhouses.

budget   An itemized statement of proposed expenditures and anticipated receipts of any government, person, or corporation for a defined period, usually a year. The Bureau of the Budget prepares the federal budget that the President submits to Congress. State and local budgets are prepared for presentation to the appropriate legislative bodies. Legislators then generally trim them to suit the pressures of groups or their own notions of where the spending should go. National budgets are now not always balanced by revenues, and borrowing may be resorted to to make up deficits. The sources of municipal revenues are steadily drying up, and the cities are looking more and more to state and federal contributions to balance their budgets. (See CAPITAL BUDGET; CAPITAL IMPROVEMENT PROGRAM.)

buffer zone. See ZONE, BUFFER.

builder; developer One whose occupation is to erect buildings. He may engage in building operations throughout the year or put up a few houses annually as a side line when a profit is indicated. Most builders are small operators, many with offices in their hats, purchasing land only when needed. A builder may be one who builds for his own account or for others, including public agencies.

The terms "developer" and "builder" are often used interchangeably and may be applied to either an individual or a corporation. The former term seems to be more popular, however, and to have more public-relations appeal, for it suggests operations on a large scale.

A commercial builder is one whose sole or principal business is home building rather than the construction of other types of structures.

A contract builder erects houses by prearrangement with a specific buyer or owner—that is, by contract.

Merchant builder is a term applied to the more substantial commercial builders.

builder, operative One who constructs and sells his product as a business, deriving his profits (or sustaining his losses) from resales rather than from holding his inventory for investment. He is the main generator of the home-building machine. Though generally small-fry with an average production line of perhaps ten houses a year, it is he who gets the factories turning out doors, wallboard, and cement. The home-building industry is the bellwether of economic activity, and the operative builder is one of its main activators.

Though small and presumed to be inefficient compared to the tycoon enterprises, the operative builder is more efficient than is generally thought. His overhead is small, he knows the ropes and the intricacies of beadledom, and he can produce a house for much less than can a housing authority. His problem is mainly his lack of capital for on-site mass production (Levitt-style) and for building up a land inventory for continuous operations.

builder, tract One who has bought land for subdivision into lots and who builds houses on them for sale. He applies for the proper rezoning, engages engineers for his utilities, provides for the street improvements, and may either build houses for resale in quantity or build a sample house and others on order. He will also build the commercial facilities and either retain or sell them. In the process he will prepare the contracts and deeds, arrange for handling installment accounts, releases from the blanket mortgage, and the other multiple details connected with development of a tract.

building Any structure having a roof supported by columns or walls and intended as a shelter for persons, animals, or property. Thus a tent, though a shelter, is not a building. A barn is. So is an airplane hangar. An accessory building is a supplemental building incidental to the main building and sharing the same lot.

building and loan association A society (generally incorporated) organized to accept savings and to aid its members in purchasing homes or buildings and improving them. It may also finance other types of building operations if authorized by law. Funds are usually accumulated from members by periodic payments of a fixed sum per share and loaned to the members on the security of mortgages or the stock of the association. In the United States the associations have been attracting savings by offering higher interest rates than are obtainable from banks or government bonds. They earn their profits mostly by making mortgage loans in their localities, garnering the appropriate interest and fees that enable them to pay overhead and dividends. The early building and loan associations actually built homes, but today they are hardly distinguishable from mutual savings banks. They are called "cooperative banks" in Massachusetts, and elsewhere may be known as "benefit societies," "mutual loan associations," and "savings and loan societies."

The associations have developed a language all their own, which includes such terms as "assured investment combination," combining the life-insurance contract with a savings plan; "cancel-and-endorse method," the periodic reduction of principal and interest in units of one share, with the association endorsing the borrower's note and certificate as each note is canceled; "company association," a savings and loan association sponsored by a corporation for the primary benefit of its employees; "equated time," the average length of time an investment has been held by an association; "periodic reduction," in which the borrower makes uniform payments throughout the life of the loan, part of which is applied to interest, the remainder to the reduction of principal—the interest is charged only on the balance; "maturity of shares," in which installment shares mature when they reach their par value and are ready to be repaid to the investor; "gross or lump sum premium," the premium paid by the borrower and deducted from the loan in advance; "free shares," savings shares not pledged as part of the security loan, the proceeds of which are paid to members at maturity or when withdrawn; "pledged shares," shares pledged to the association as part of the security for the loan; "fully paid stock," in which full par value is paid by the member at the time of subscription; "withdrawal value," representing book value of shares at any given time minus charges, if any.

building area   The total area covered by a building, taken on a horizontal plane at mean grade level, exclusive of uncovered porches, terraces, and steps.

building code. See CODE, BUILDING.

building, derelict   A building that is abandoned or becomes victim to the elements so that public action is called for to compel its restoration or demolition. A derelict area or landscape is one that is abandoned, substandard, or unsightly. (See ABANDONMENT; UNTENANTED HAZARD.)

building, detached   A building surrounded by open space on its own lot.

building industry; construction industry   All businesses that share in the receipts of expenditures for construction. At the core of the industry are the builders themselves, including the manufacturers who prefabricate components or whole structures, and the many specialty subcontractors who provide much of the on-site construction work. These firms are served by an enormous range of enterprises and professionals—materials manufacturers and suppliers, engineers and architects, city planners and landscape architects, real-estate brokers, lawyers, surveyors, title-insurance companies, and a wide variety of lending and financing institutions.

Once construction is completed, a whole new sub-industry comes into play—rental and management agents, security services, superintendents, repairmen, and a variety of maintenance workers from window cleaners to charwomen.

By this definition upward of several million firms are involved in the construction industry. A more narrow definition would include only those firms directly engaged in the erection, maintenance, and repair of structures and utilities that are fixed to the land, and whose principal business is construction.

building line   A boundary fixed at a specified distance from the front or sides of a lot beyond which a building cannot lawfully extend.

building loan. See LOAN, CONSTRUCTION.

building restrictions   Limitations on the erection of structures, on the material going into them, and on the way they are to be built. These may be codified, be written into deeds or other instruments, be statutory or contractual. They include restrictions: against erection of any structure whatever; as to the style of architecture, the cost of the structure, the materials, the position of the building on the lot or its distance from the street, its height or depth; on the use to which the building shall be put— *i.e.*, occupancy for residential purposes only or for specified types of enterprises. More recently they have included requirements for parks, parking, and other amenities as a condition for approving a subdivision or street pattern. (See BULK REGULATIONS; CODE, BUILDING; ZONING.)

building site   A parcel of land suitable for building or on which a building may be erected, including all surrounding land allocated to the improvement.

building, speculative   A building erected with a view to its immediate resale rather than to its long-term prospects for investment and income. The term also refers to home-building of the cheaper variety and to the cheaper type of apartment building, the aim of which is to produce the highest immediate return as distinguished from a smaller average return over a longer period. Speculative building of apartment houses is encouraged by the tenant's lesser concern with the durability of the structure than with rent and location. Mortgagees financing such building feel protected by the high net profits and by the amortization payments; they are

generally indifferent to flimsy construction, particularly when their mortgages are secured by FHA insurance. (See "608".)

bulk regulations Zoning or other regulations that, by controlling height,
mass, density, and location of buildings, set a maximum limit on the in-
tensity of development so as to provide proper light, air, and open space.
(See ZONING.)

bundle of rights The sum total of the rights pertaining to property ownership. In the case of real property it embraces the right to quiet enjoyment, the right to sell, to mortgage, to lease, to bequeath, to regain possession at the end of a lease, to build and remove improvements, and to
control the property's use within the law. In short, it describes the scope
of the legal protections granted to property ownership. The bundle may
grow or diminish depending on the nature of the political system and the
social and political pressures bearing upon property ownership. (See
LAND TENURE; OWNERSHIP; PRIVATE PROPERTY.)

bungalow Originally in India a lightly built, single-story house usually
with thatched or tiled roof surrounded by a veranda, hence any house or
cottage of this general type. Its derivation is from the Hindustani word
bangla, meaning "of Bengal." By extension it is now a more or less solidly constructed house for permanent residence, generally one-story
(sometimes one and a half), preserving the low sweeping exterior lines of
the bungalow.

business welfare state. See WELFARE STATE, BUSINESS.

busing, school Transporting some children who would normally attend
an all-white or predominantly white school to an all Negro or predominantly Negro school, or *vice versa,* in order to desegregate both. The plan
has been tried in many northern cities and in some in the South. Many
white and some black parents have objected to the practice, claiming the
right to have their children attend schools in their immediate neighborhoods. As a result, in some jurisdictions it is specifically prohibited by
law.

Even were busing a politically acceptable policy, it could hardly
achieve desegregation in most large cities in the long run, because of the

overwhelming number of minority children reaching school age, the preference of many white parents for parochial and private schools, and the flight of many others to the suburbs. Busing that involved an exchange of students between city and suburban schools would have an impact but poses an even thornier political problem. Busing has nevertheless succeeded on a small scale in several carefully prepared instances, usually where the schools and instruction were of particularly high quality.

bustee   A group of small East Indian mud huts. Bustees are among the worst of slums. They are set on narrow lanes, often no more than a few yards wide, through which the putrefying effluents wind their way past every door. In some bustees one cannot stand or lie down at full length, and it is not unusual to find six persons sharing the earth floor of one hut. About a third of Calcutta's population subsists in such shelters; others prefer bedding down on streets and alleys.

cadastre   A register of a nation's real property with details on each parcel's area, owner, and value.

calibration   The testing and adjusting (usually by trial and error) of the values of mathematical constants in a model, so that results correspond to the known facts of a particular real-life situation. Calibration in a general sense is the checking and rectifying of an instrument such as a gauge or thermometer so as to allow, in graduating it, for any irregularities; the word derives from caliber, the original meaning of which was the degree of social standing, importance, quality, or rank. Businessmen now use the term in the sense of correcting a system; appraisers of real estate have been known to use it in connection with their estimations of value; city planners have drawn it into their language in the sense as first defined, employing it in their model-making. (See MODEL.)

cantonment A collection of temporary structures for the use of military personnel. In India and Pakistan it is a permanent military station often in or near a town or city. These stations occupy valuable land that could be put to better use as urbanization encompasses them. Erected in the days of the British Lancers when proximity to the city was part of the colonial peace-keeping strategy, there is no longer any valid reason for them not to be relocated on less precious but equally accessible land. But the military will not sound retreat easily and in most cases stands its ground against officialdom, squatterdom, and planners. (See NEW-TOWN-IN-TOWN.)

capacity In transportation planning, the capability of a roadway to accommodate traffic, usually expressed in the number of vehicles per lane per hour. Basic capacity is the maximum number of passenger cars that can pass a given point during one hour under ideal road and traffic conditions. (See CHANNELS OF MOVEMENT; DESIGN SPEED.)

capillarity, law of The theory that population rates will decrease when conditions improve. The theory holds that potential parents postpone having children to allow for their own upward social mobility or the advancement of their fewer children. Deriving its name from the capillary attraction of liquids, the theory is ascribed to Arsène Dumont (1849–1902), who dissented from Malthus' more somber theory. Dumont argued that birth rates decline as living standards increase. In urbanized countries, economic growth has outpaced population growth. (See BIRTH RATE; POPULATION EXPLOSION.)

capital budget A statement of proposed public expenditures together with a plan for financing them, usually prepared annually. A municipality's capital budget generally provides for the financing of its schools, parks and playgrounds, public offices, and other non-recurrent expenditures; these may be financed out of revenues, borrowings, or both. (See BUDGET; CAPITAL IMPROVEMENT; CAPITAL IMPROVEMENT PROGRAM.)

capital gain An increase in value of capital invested. Its special significance is in income-tax reporting. Property sold after being held for six months or more is a long-term capital gain, and the federal tax on such gain is usually computed at a rate lower than that on ordinary income.

Property sold after being held for six months or less is a short-term gain, which is fully taxed and does not receive the preferential capital-gain treatment. Though sellers of real estate benefit (when they are not operators with frequent sales), the biggest beneficiary has been the stock trader. (See TAX INCENTIVES.)

capital grant A direct gift of capital from one level of government to another, usually for a specified purpose. In an urban-renewal project, for example, the federal government contributes two-thirds and in some cases three-quarters of the net project cost. The locality is required to raise the additional amount itself.

The term is also used to denote a public subsidy in the form of total or partial extinction of debt. Thus if an advance of a million dollars is made to a public agency and only 60 per cent is required to be repaid, the remaining 40 per cent represents the capital grant. Capital grants were authorized for public housing in its early stages but were later replaced by annual subsidies, which were seen as a means of enlarging the program and as easier for the federal budget to absorb. (See SUBSIDY.)

capital improvement Any substantial physical facility built by the public or any major nonrecurring expenditure of government. The construction of schools, highways, sewer and water systems, the landscaping of a park, the purchase of land for a municipal hospital, the architectural restoration of a city hall—these are all capital expenditures as distinguished from operating costs, which can be expected to recur annually as long as a program or service is offered.

One of the great defects of federal aids to urban areas is that the great majority are limited to capital costs. The much-vaunted federal program for multi-service centers, for example, makes no provisions for the cost of the services housed in a center or even the money to sweep the floor. Often the more capital improvements a city accepts from the federal government, the more impoverished it becomes trying to use and maintain them.

capital improvement program A governmental schedule of permanent improvements budgeted to fit financial resources. A city's planning commission is sometimes given authority to budget the city's program, thereby linking planning to function and giving the commission more prestige and independence. Despite this optimistic effort to strengthen the commission's hand in the city's development, experience has shown that the mayor's support still gives the muscle to the agency he favors. In contrast to the capital budget, capital improvement programs are usually projected five or six years in advance and updated annually. (See CAPITAL BUDGET.)

capitalism   An economic system based upon private ownership and private acquisition of property, including the means of production, with only such governmental interference in the general interest as will not frustrate the entrepreneurial incentive for ownership, production, and profit and the credit mechanisms that foster them.

Capitalism rests primarily on individual and corporate initiative, organization, rationalization, and salesmanship. There has never been a true capitalism in the sense that the individual is given full reign in his economic activities. Government always retains an active place in the system, and even Adam Smith carved out a role for the public in the unprofitable areas. The USSR has countenanced some small capitalist practices by its concessions to cooperative housing, private sale of some agricultural products, recognition of private savings, inheritance laws, and protection against arbitrary exercise of eminent domain. The rights in its bundle of rights are still small compared to those in Western nations, but the latter in turn have also veered from the old formula by increasing the scope of public regulation and acquisition, by assuming functions formerly in the private domain, and by steadily increasing taxation on profits and property.

Most economic systems today are a mixed sort, with their precise nature varying from government to government. Ownership of stock in private corporations has become so extensive in the United States that their operations have become affected with a public interest and are publicly regulated to a degree. Moreover, there has been such an extensive expansion of government power in the United States since the New Deal— with government playing an unprecedented role in the building of public works, credit operations, mortgage insurance, home construction, and other enterprises—that government has substantially supplanted the individual as the exclusive activator of enterprises. The individual's stake and risk have markedly diminished as generators of economic activity. Promotion of the public interest has taken form not only in taxation and regulation, but in the creation of many public and quasi-public corporate mechanisms that operate much like private corporations. Simultaneously, municipalities have built housing for low- and moderate-income groups, garages and parking lots, and factories for entrepreneurs, and have even made loans to the entrepreneurs from tax-exempt borrowings to produce the plants. Similarly, public motivations are present in corporate, individual, and foundation operations, which allocate contributions to or investment in public causes. Often it has become virtually impossible to distinguish between the private non-profit function and the public function.

Ownership is no longer unconditional, private property not always purely private, the profit motive not the exclusive driving force, the credit mechanism not uncontrolled or uninfluenced by government, the means of production not always privately controlled or privately created, the acquisitive instinct not always confined to a concentrated group of owners or managers, the operations of the entrepreneur not unfree of public supervision. Whatever its name or definition, the new system seems to work reasonably well and distributes its dividends widely, with government tending to take up more and more of the slack. The changes in the system have been so dynamic and so rapid that predictions of its ultimate course or complexion would be sheer conjecture. There are too many uncertainties and too many unforeseeable variations. One thing is certain—the older usage of the term "capitalism" no longer describes the system as it presently functions. (See LAISSEZ FAIRE; MIXED ECONOMY; POWER PLANT; SOCIALISM.)

capitalization   The present value of expected future returns from an investment, or the conversion into a capital sum of a property's foreseeable net return. Thus a piece of real estate yielding a net annual profit of $50,000 will be worth $500,000 (its capitalization) if the rate of return is computed at 10 per cent (10 per cent of $500,000 = $50,000, or $50,000 × $100/_{10}$ = $500,000). The term is also used to denote the authorized or outstanding stocks and bonds of a corporation, and the total investment of an owner in his enterprise.

Different types of real property are capitalized at different percentages, depending in each case on the going interest rates for invested capital, the nature of the tenancy, the stability of the net return, the future prospects of the section, and other relevant data.

car pool A form of semi-mass transport in which up to six neighbors share a car to bring them to and from their job sites, reducing the expense of each. The participants must all leave simultaneously or be relegated to other means of transport. Apparently because of the need to accommodate oneself to the pool's schedule, such arrangements are too little used. Cars entering or leaving the nation's major cities during rush hours average less than two occupants, except during transit strikes. Incentive systems have been proposed to encourage pooling by reducing tolls for full cars, but these have not yet been successfully implemented. (See JOURNEY TO WORK.)

CBD An abbreviation for "central business district," *i.e.,* the business core of a city with the major concentration of retail, office, and service functions. It is sometimes referred to as "downtown," though it may in fact be located uptown or midtown. The CBD is the city's principal magnet, its mainstay and principal taxpayer, generating a quarter or more of its local revenues. The CBD is also its office center, the confluence of diversities, the scene of financial and political action, and the source of a substantial portion of its jobs. It is the place where a man can dine with a lady without being accused of having a rendezvous. The cities with a pulsating CBD are generally the cities that thrive; those without one are headed for desuetude.

cellar A story wholly or partly underground and having more than half its clear height from finished floor to finished ceiling below the mean finished grade. Also a place where one keeps his boiler, stores his unused possessions, and, in some cases, his rare wines. (See BASEMENT.)

cemetery A burial place or ground—among the least productive and most tenacious land uses. In modern times the urban cemetery has become the bane of planners and road-builders. When the site was selected for burials, it was usually a good distance from areas of intense habitation but not too far for a visit by the kin. As the city's population expanded, however, the cemetery appropriated space for the dead that could better have been used for the living. In England public crematoria and crematoria societies exhort cremation as an alternative to burial, and public meetings are often convened at which the advantages of one's quick reduction to ashes are expounded—*i.e.,* the time limitation placed

upon graveyards, the high cost of dying, etc. In the United States graveyards are more stubbornly defended and road-builders must often bypass or bridge over them at astronomical cost. Less political resistance
can be encountered in clearing a whole area of the living poor than in
moving a small number of the dead. Paradoxically, if a cemetery holds
out long enough it can again become an asset; ancient cemeteries located
right at the core provide open and "breathing" space in congested city
areas. Only a developer, for example, would favor razing the Trinity
Church graveyard at the head of Wall Street in New York to make way
for a skyscraper. (See NECROPOLIS.)

census An official periodic enumeration of the number of a nation's
people, identifying and recording their conditions, their resources, and
other data. The earliest Roman census aimed to register adult males and
their property for tax purposes, the distribution of military obligations,
and the determination of political status. The British census was introduced in 1801; earlier scientific censuses are credited to France, Canada,
and Sweden.

Though a census enumeration was required in the United States Constitution, it was not until 1850 that scientific census-taking began. Recently, information on housing conditions, economic status, and educational attainment have been added to the census, and the information
obtained has become the factual basis for advancing housing and social
legislation. Although only once in ten years is everyone counted, the Bureau of the Census spends the other nine years digesting and reporting
the decennial results, making interim sample studies, and projecting
trends.

Periodically the census questions have come under attack as an invasion of privacy, and fears have grown that a central data file is imminent,
with a dossier on every American. Planners, on the other hand, usually
find themselves wishing the census-takers had asked more questions and
asked them more often, say once every five years, for they are convinced
that the information is indispensable to rational planning at both the
local and the national levels.

In fact, there is no comparison between the delicacy of the modern
questionnaire and the inquisitorial prying of earlier American censuses.
During Reconstruction respondents were asked to indicate whether they
were white, black, mulatto, quadroon, or octoroon. Enumerators were

instructed to be sure that every person "having any perceptible trace of African blood" be properly classified. Instructions to enumerators regarding the insane in an early census were: "Does this person require to be usually or often restrained by any mechanical appliance, such as a strap, straitjacket, etc.?" With regard to "paupers," the census wanted to know if they were tramps, syphilitic, intemperate, habitual drunkards, insane, or idiotic. The 1890 census contained nearly five hundred separate questions, setting some record for official intrusion into private affairs. (See DEMOGRAPHY; NON-WHITE; POPULATION.)

central business district. See CBD.

central city. See CITY, CENTRAL.

central place theory The theory that cities arise as a response to the service needs of surrounding rural areas and that the location of urban settlements can be understood in terms of the functions they perform for these tributary areas.

certificate of occupancy Official authorization to occupy premises, affirming that the use and conditions of a new building or an existing building undergoing change are consistent with the zoning ordinance of the locality. In jurisdictions with zoning laws, no property can be occupied unless a certificate of occupancy is issued or if the certificate is revoked. (See ZONING.)

cesspool An old device for disposing of sewage from individual dwelling units, utilizing a perforated, buried tank that allows the effluent to seep into the surrounding soil but retains most of the solids. Cesspools are in common use in many parts of the United States but are not considered acceptable under current standards of public health. (See LATRINE; SEPTIC TANK.)

channels of movement The collection and distribution routes along which people and goods pass. These include various kinds of roads and rail lines, terminals and facilities for parking, loading, unloading, and transferring people or goods in transit.

chattels Movable articles of personal property, such as household goods or removable fixtures.

chawls Indian lodging houses, mainly three- or four-story tenements, found in urban areas such as Bombay. The dwelling units usually consist of one room with primitive, communal sanitary facilities serving the crowded occupants.

city A word with many meanings, generally referring to any large or important human settlement. The term is also used to distinguish such areas from the countryside or rural districts. As a legal term it denotes the class of inhabited area with the largest size and most substantial legal powers. In the United States a city is a municipal corporation occupying a definite area, the creature of one of the fifty states from which it derives its powers. The charter issued by the state is the statement of the city's authority. If we accept the definition of President Lyndon B. Johnson in his message to Congress in 1965, a city is the "entire urban area—the central city and its suburbs."

In Great Britain and Ireland the term "city" is the traditional or honorary designation of any one of various places. Originally denoting a cathedral town, the title "city" is now occasionally conferred by royal charter on important boroughs, such as Leeds.

In ancient Greece the *polis* was a city-state, while a Biblical city such as Bethlehem we might describe as a village. The word "city" is derived from the Latin *civitas* ("city-state"); the Latin word for "city" was *urbs*. The French word *ville* comes from people grouping around the villa or manor of the feudal lord. (See HAMLET; MEGALOPOLIS; METROPOLIS; MUNICIPAL CORPORATION; PLACE; POLIS; TOWN; UTOPIA; VILLAGE.)

City Beautiful A term describing an influential movement in city planning during the late nineteenth and early twentieth centuries, emphasizing civic centers, monuments, boulevards, waterfronts, and neoclassical architecture as part of a new urban environment. It was the romantic concept of a period of hope and civic optimism, which faded into history as speculation and the quest for profit became the dominant forces in city development.

city, central As defined by the Bureau of the Census in 1960, the largest city in any standard metropolitan statistical area (SMSA). One or two additional cities can be termed "secondary central cities" if they have at least 250,000 inhabitants or are one-third as large as the largest city and have a minimum population of 25,000. (See STANDARD METROPOLITAN STATISTICAL AREA.)

City Efficient The name given to a movement in city planning and administration emphasizing scientific management, zoning, and public works, particularly highway building. Successor to the civic-design orientation and monumentality of the crusade for the City Beautiful, the movement began after the turn of the century and reached its heyday in the 1920s. During this period experts began to be brought into government, the science of municipal administration was developed, planning was seen primarily in terms of legal regulations on the height and use of buildings, and the way a city worked for commerce, traffic, and officialdom was considered more important than how it looked. Robert Moses has become the archetype of the trained planner-administrator of this era.

city estate The property owned by a city either in public use or rented to private occupants. The term is used primarily in Great Britain and Ireland. (See CROWN LANDS.)

city, floating A city built in prefabricated sections and then towed to moorings at or near the water's edge. The building of floating cities was the subject of a study made for the federal government in 1968 by the Triton Foundation and Buckminster Fuller. It noted that 80 per cent of the metropolitan areas with populations over one million were near bodies of water with adequate depth for shipping and that water depths of 25 to 30 feet in sheltered harbors, lakes, or riverfront areas could support such cities. These would be constructed on steel or concrete platforms with prefabricated components; four-acre pre-built neighborhood units constructed on platforms could each house up to 5000 people. Three to six neighborhoods could be clustered to form floating towns of 15,000 to 30,000 people. Structures up to twenty stories were said to be feasible.

Floating communities are not unknown. Cities on water have been built over offshore oil deposits in the Baku oil fields in the USSR. Hong Kong harbor is lined with boat shelters, a makeshift example of a floating city. Belen Del Peru, a community of houses floated on the Amazon, shifts with the river's currents. Neolithic lake-dwelling communities are primitive examples. The Neolithic houses built on stilts were provided with pitched roofs, walls plastered with clay, fireplaces, and porches. They measured 750 square feet, which would meet FHA specifications, and if built in Miami today could rent for $1500 per season.

city hatred   Hostility or aversion to the city, which sees city life as impersonal, inhuman, and threatening to the moral life of society. It stereotypes the city dweller (noisy, vulgar, crooked, overclever, ambitious, etc.) and often makes him the symbol in America of city life and the target of people's prejudices. Once the Jew was the city symbol, but as many Jews have become suburbanized the Negro has moved into his place. (See URBIPHOBIA.)

city, ideal   The conception of the perfect city for the perfect life. The ideal city has existed only in man's mind, and when his mind roamed free in utopian ecstasy, it was the city that was often closest to his vision of heaven—the Celestial City, the Heavenly City, the City of the Sun, the City of God, and the New Jerusalem. Hell was more often conceived of as a region, and—since it is governed by the most methodical of spirits—it is doubtless a planned region.

The city has inspired hope from the day Cain first constructed one; though but a little distance from the Garden of Eden, there is no historical evidence that even it was ideal. The ideal city presupposes an ideal state, which Francis Bacon described as a community in which science was the key to universal happiness; Tommaso Campanella saw it in his communistic City of the Sun; James Harrington conceived his Oceana on the notion that property in land was the basis of political power. There were many other visions and visionaries, and in a number of instances idealized "communities" were actually built, but most proved to be ordeal rather than ideal cities. Because fifty-four ideal cities in Sir Thomas More's *Utopia* were all to be the same, life in them would have been a bore and few people would have lived in them for long. Diversity appears to be more important than perfection. And if sameness is heaven, there probably would be many a spirit that would prefer London or Paris for a post-mortem sojourn.

The search for the ideal city will nevertheless go on—as it should. It will be sought in new towns, in cities of 30,000 people and of 500,000, in the new suburbs of the great metropolises, and in the New Lanarks of the future. But it is in the vast miscellany rather than in the prototype that the ideal will be found. For what is ideal can neither be one man's concept nor remain a constant. Life can be ideal in a garret for some, or at Walden Pond for others, and as it goes on both the garret and the pond may ultimately prove restrictive. The existence of many forms makes choice possible, and the existence of choice makes the search for the ideal and the ideal city hopeful. Choice, however, implies not only a choice of physical forms and a variety in the types of houses, streets, sites, neighbors, and facilities, but also the existence of institutions and devices that allow men to move about and develop their potential free of unreasonable restraints—free to reject the creations of what some planners see as the ideal. (See UTOPIA.)

city, linear A concept of city form envisioning commercial and service facilities strung out in a narrow belt along or even over a main traffic route. Residential areas might extend on either side of the service strip, served by transverse streets. Major facilities would be duplicated along the strip at whatever interval is dictated by demand. The concept is closely identified with one of its originators, Arturo Soria y Mata, who designed a thirty-mile "Ciudad Lineal" for Madrid in the 1890s, only three miles of which were ever built. Similar developments extending out over the water have been proposed for the future expansion of both Amsterdam and Tokyo.

city manager plan; council manager plan A plan of municipal government under which an administrative official called "the city manager" is appointed by an elected council and given responsibility for managing most of the city's business except perhaps the school system. Policy-making and political leadership in the community remain with the council and mayor. The council passes ordinances, makes appropriations, develops plans for the city's development, and selects and discharges the manager. The mayor, largely free of administrative duties, has more time for participating in the council's deliberations and for politicking.

The city manager plan was initiated in Dayton, Ohio, in 1914 and has proven satisfactory on the whole, but its success has varied with the competence of the manager and the community's political traditions. (See COMMISSION SYSTEM OF GOVERNMENT; MAYOR-COUNCIL PLAN.)

city planning; urban planning   The guidance and shaping of the development, growth, arrangement, and change of urban environments with the aim of harmonizing them with the social, aesthetic, cultural, political, and economic requirements of life. City planning is as old as cities and it has varied with the times, the conditions, and the planners. It may be a product of private action, though it is usually effectuated through the lawful and reasonable manipulation of the regulatory, eminent-domain, and tax powers. Democratic city planning should respect the rights of individuals and their communities as these are consistent with the general welfare of the city, the region, and the nation.

City planning is a profession, an art, a science, a governmental function, and a social and political movement. Because its scope and responsibilities have grown with the growing complexities of urban life, it has become involved with other arts, professions, and sciences in the effort to achieve its objectives. City planning not only concerns urban communities and their relationship to the regions of which they are a part, but seeks or should seek to improve the conditions of urban and suburban life and well-being through sensibly arranging the residential, commercial, and industrial parts of areas; developing each section to standards of space consonant with health and safety; providing good housing at costs within the means of the inhabitants; supplying adequate recreational, educational, and other communal facilities; providing an efficient system of circulation and adequate utilities and public services; identifying the financial resources to fulfill these objectives; creating environments people can live and grow in decently, without unreasonable restraints on the lives they choose to lead. (See PLANNER; PLANNING EDUCATION; TOWN AND COUNTRY PLANNING; URBANISM.)

city, poly-nucleated   A city with a cluster of communities adequately spaced and bounded, as distinguished from a mono-nucleated city or a single large urban concentration. "Twenty such cities in a region," wrote Lewis Mumford, "whose environment and whose resources were adequately planned, would have all the benefits of a metropolis that held a million people, without its ponderous disabilities, its capital frozen into unprofitable utilities and its land values congealed at levels that stand in the way of effective adaptation to new needs."

The poly-nucleated city is the direction in which suburbs have been developing, but the suburbs are set around at least one large city of which they are the satellites. Mumford's thesis presumes that no single larger nucleus is needed and that, if it did not exist already, would not ultimately form out of one of the poly-nuclei. It presumes that all people would prefer poly-nucleation and that none would want a medley of faces and a dense city at the core to serve their needs, afford them anonymity, and a greater range of choice. It presumes also a kind of stabilized series of poly-nuclei in which free entry, free movement, and free expansion would probably be subordinated to the preservation of the poly-nuclei. It assumes, in short, that what is static would also be ecstatic. (See DENSITY; UTOPIA.)

city, satellite   A smaller city on the outskirts of a larger city, independent of its jurisdiction but within its economic and social orbit. Most of its citizens will work in the larger city and depend on it for escape and for some of their recreation, for the purchase of certain goods, for specialized medical treatment or hospitalization, and for other services and facilities not available locally.

A satellite town is usually smaller than a city and larger than a village, located on a city's outskirts and independent of its jurisdiction but within its economic and social orbit. It generally refers to those of England's New Towns that have never become self-contained as originally intended, but have remained dependent on the city for employment, shopping, and services. (See SUBURB.)

cityscape   The urban equivalent of a landscape—the shape a city (or one of its parts) presents to the eye, particularly from a distance. The silhouette of Manhattan's skyscrapers is a familiar example.

civic center   A place in which a city's principal public buildings and civic and cultural institutions are grouped into a unit. The civic center should be more than a scroll for dead heroes plus a cannon fronting on a city hall. It should offer the citizen a central convenience for the transaction of his public business while providing a public demonstration of aesthetic form, dignified planning, and architectural excellence. Civic centers can become a problem, however, if they overreach themselves. When a metropolis's institutions and cultural facilities become too centralized, individual neighborhoods are robbed of the attractions that helped give them life and intercourse with the rest of the city. (See AGORA.)

civic organizations Groups of citizens who associate themselves to further a public cause or purpose. They are numerous in cities and have markedly increased in suburbs. Most are pressure groups, some dedicated to advancing the general good, others to advancing their own good. They may try to keep taxes down or up, press the city to build more public housing or less, protect the school system or change it, sponsor or protect zoning ordinances, support or oppose bond issues, protect civil liberties, keep elections honest, or tackle issues as they arise. The organizations may be Chambers of Commerce, Rotarians, or groups of employees, architects, lawyers, teachers, reformers, social workers, planning officials, scientists, veterans, housewives or their husbands. They may be local, state-wide, or national. They may publish papers, make investigations and surveys, hold forums, or do research. They may also be tax-exempt fronts for special-interest groups or particular industries. Larger organizations have a paid director and staff, but many are letterhead organizations; some exist to counteract the pressures of other groups. When the organizations are not lobbyists, contributions to them are exempt from federal taxation, a benefit without which many could not stay in operation. Unfortunately organizations that might do their most effective work by lobbying in the public interest are deprived of that benefit and direct their efforts to less constructive work so as to maintain the exemption privilege and their fiscal solvency.

Civic organizations act as a buffer between the individual and government—what the individual may fear to do in his own name, he does with the protection of numbers, for he wins anonymity and attains greater security against reprisal. Civic organizations may often be nuisances to officialdom but they are one of democracy's bulwarks.

civil disorder An outbreak of violence characterized by the setting of fires, looting, seizures, vandalism, or other disturbances of the peace. Civil disorders are generally uncivil; they reached into the hundreds throughout the United States in the 1960s and were classified by the National Advisory Commission on Civil Disorders (1968) into three types:

Major—*i.e.,* many fires, intensive looting and reports of sniping, violence lasting more than two days, sizable crowds—requiring the use of National Guard or federal troops as well as other "control forces."

Serious—*i.e.,* isolated looting, some fires and some rock throwing, violence lasting one or two days, only one sizable crowd or many small groups—requiring the use of state police.

Minor—*i.e.,* a few fires and broken windows, violence lasting less than one day, participation by only small numbers of people—requiring the use of only local police or police from a neighboring community.

As used by the Commission, civil disorder is a catch-all term embracing all categories of mass violence in all its degrees. (See CROWD; RIOT.)

civil rights   The rights guaranteed to a country's inhabitants by law. They are distinguishable from political rights, which legal commentators have held to protect citizens, and from natural rights, which are said to be the inherent rights protecting the individual under a presumed "natural law." It is law, statutory or constitutional, that has become the real shield for the protection of people in the United States against incursions by government and by private interests vested with public functions or authority.

The protection of civil rights has had a checkered career in the United States. The ink had hardly dried on the Bill of Rights when the Alien and Sedition Acts gave President John Adams extraordinary powers to deport "dangerous" aliens and political criticism was virtually made a crime. With Jefferson's election, the laws were repealed. Civil rights were fortified after the Civil War, which saw passage of the Thirteenth, Fourteenth, and Fifteenth Amendments supplemented by a series of civil-rights acts the aim of which was to assure the Negro minority the same rights and privileges enjoyed by other citizens. The Supreme Court, however, soon developed a series of doctrines that enfeebled the protections. From 1868 to 1936, Negroes won three tests in peonage cases, but only six of sixteen cases in which they sought federal protection for their franchise or other rights of citizenship; twelve of twenty-one cases in which they sought fair trials in criminal cases; and only two of fourteen in which they sought use of the same facilities as whites in public places, transportation, schools, and housing.

In the period between Reconstruction and the end of World War II there were both gains and retreats. The invasions of the rights of Chinese Americans in the nineteenth century form a dark page in the nation's history; the herding of Nisei into concentration camps during World War II is another, and its ugliness is not relieved by the Supreme Court decision that justified it. But on the better side was the Supreme Court's invalidation of racial zoning in 1917, the striking down of restrictions against children of aliens owning property in 1948, and the ruling against racial covenants in 1948. Thereafter, with the Warren Court, came the decision in 1954 banning segregation in public schools and the decision in 1968 giving life to the post–Civil War law that had long and vainly sought to prohibit discrimination in all private and public sales and rentals of housing.

If the federal government during the New Deal adopted discriminatory policies in housing, the states showed more enlightenment, and by 1962, when President Kennedy signed an executive order outlawing discrimination in federally aided housing, seventeen states, the Virgin Islands, and fifty-six cities had already passed anti-discrimination laws or resolutions. Twelve of the states had banned discrimination in private housing. It was the impetus given by these laws and by the more enlightened Supreme Court decisions that caused Congress in 1968 to enact a fair housing law forbidding discrimination in private as well as federally aided housing.

Civil-rights laws have great value as expressions of the public morality, as educational vehicles, and as protections against discrimination. But they are not self-enforcing. Enforcement, like enactment, depends on official leadership and on public support. When leadership and public support languish, so will enforcement. When they awaken, inactivated statutes come to life and dormant precedents are renewed. (See COVENANT; EQUALITY; FAIR HOUSING LAWS; "SEPARATE BUT EQUAL.")

civil service The non-military servants or paid civil administrators and clerks of a government who acquire their positions by merit rather than political appointment; alternatively, the aggregate of all the government's civil employees who rank below the principal administrators and the elected and judicial officers.

A civil-service merit system is the antithesis of personal and partisan government. The abuses of patronage and the dispensing of colonial positions as sinecures to the favorites of the British King were said to be among the causes of the American Revolution. Yet it was not long before the "spoils system" gained headway in American political life, and in fact it was not until 1883 that a national law guaranteed selection by competitive examination of all appointments to the "classified service" without obligation to make political contribution or render political service. A Civil Service Commission was set up to administer the service. It provides examinations for personnel, investigates applicants for national security purposes, and classifies positions. The merit system has also made considerable headway at the state and municipal levels.

Increasing exemptions from the merit system, however, have modified the original design. But the civil-service system suffers not only from the intrusion of political and partisan considerations but from inherent limitations. Many good people who would accept appointments to office shun competitive examinations; incompetent civil servants can rarely be replaced without an embarrassing and difficult proceeding. There has also been a running battle between adherents to the civil-service principle who want exemptions eliminated and top officials trying to escape its rigidities by appointing people they consider more competent or politically loyal.

Despite its weaknesses the civil-service system has effected a marked improvement over the appointive system and elevated the level of public service. But until the still troublesome issues are resolved and the service demonstrates the superiority of its applicants, the civil-service principle will continue to be flawed. This is particularly true at the local and state levels, where many soundly conceived programs have failed during implementation because of the ineptitude of those charged with carrying them out.

client A term apparently borrowed from lawyers and social workers and now used by planners to describe the group that is to be the beneficiary (or victim) of their work. Determining who the client is, and living with him, turns out to be one of the most difficult tasks in city planning. According to one definition, the client is the fellow who contracts for the work and pays the bills. In this sense, a professional working in a city-planning agency has as his client the planning commission, the mayor, the city council, or all three. Others insist that these are only clients in a narrow sense—that one's real duty is to the city as a whole and the best interests of the public. Advocacy planners claim that the real clients are the residents of the area being planned, and that since the city rarely puts their interests first, they are entitled to their own professional advice and assistance. Futurists and other visionary types claim that generations yet unborn and the society of the future ought to be, but rarely are, considered as clients. And the ecologists take Mother Nature and the ecosystem to be their most important charge.

The man who plans for a private developer has a much easier time in identifying his responsibilities, but even he is admonished to take Nature, the future, the community as a whole, and the public interest into account in developing his plans.

Clearly client analysis is enormously important in determining how to proceed as a planner, but a good deal of ambiguity seems inevitable, and perhaps that is for the best. Often a planner must simultaneously keep several groups convinced that he has their interests at heart or, even better, that their interests coincide. Meanwhile he has a duty to the profession itself and to whatever truths, principles, and ethical codes it has developed over time. (See CITY PLANNING; PLANNER.)

closing Completion of the purchase or sale of a parcel of real estate, at which moment the title to the premises passes by deed from the seller to the buyer and the consideration to be paid is delivered to the seller along with the execution of any mortgages. Usually the parties involved, which may include the buyer and seller, the attorneys for each, a title-company representative, and a representative of the lender, assemble in one place in order to execute the necessary documents simultaneously. Closing costs are costs incidental to completing the purchase of a parcel of real estate—*e.g.,* costs of the title search and insurance, property survey, recording fees, mortgage service charges, etc.

cloud on title. See TITLE, CLOUD ON.

cluster development. See PLANNED-UNIT DEVELOPMENT.

cluster zoning. See ZONING, CLUSTER.

clustration A concentration in one area of a city of enterprises of similar or related character. A commercial cluster can be a concentration of department stores, food marts, second-hand bookshops, insurance enterprises, jewelers, coffee houses, textile and leather merchants, antique shops, art dealers, chandlers, theaters, bargain shops, furniture stores, vitamin markets, stockbrokers, radio and television shops, flower markets, or discount houses. A cluster can be a wholesale or retail center. It can be homogeneous (selling the same wares or services) or heterogeneous (offering similar wares and services but near other clusters offering other types of goods or services). It can be ethnic, like a group of Italian food stores or a Chinatown. Clustration widens the choice of buyers, browsers, and bargain hunters within a compact area. The presence of many enterprises, though selling the same products, has been found to yield more benefit to each business than the competition diminishes. (See LINKAGE; NUCLEATION.)

coalition doctrine A theory holding that the way for the Negro to win his political and economic rights is by forming alliances with liberal labor, religious, and other well-meaning groups, including the liberal wing of the Democratic party, on the grounds that only this method can significantly influence national legislation and speed the Negro's social progress. The groups supporting coalition see separatist efforts as destructive. Some black activists, while not opposing alliances *per se,* charge that coalitionists ally with groups that have never had the total revamping of the society as their central goal. These groups accept the American system and want—if at all—to make only peripheral, marginal reforms, reforms that, it is felt, will not rid the society of racism. (See BLACK POWER.)

code, building A body of legislative regulations or by-laws (usually local) that prescribes the materials, minimum requirements, and methods to be used in the construction, rehabilitation, maintenance, and repair of buildings. (See BUILDING RESTRICTIONS.)

code enforcement Local regulation of buildings and enforcement of building- and housing-code provisions, a principal tool of officialdom to assure neighborhood upkeep. A provision of the Federal Housing Act of 1965 established the authority for "programs of concentrated code enforcement" in deteriorating areas; the federal government will make grants to a city covering much of the costs of planning and effectuating such programs. These costs may include repair of streets and lights, tree planting, and similar improvements. Owners in the designated areas are eligible for rehabilitation grants as well as loans at below-market rates.

Code enforcement has been a bane as well as a blessing. In periods of housing famine it is apt to increase hardship by inviting closing of buildings, thereby reducing the available housing supply. Nor does it ease overcrowding, and when there is a dearth of housing it will intensify it. Yet, judiciously employed, it is a means of securing safety and health and an important device for preserving the housing inventory against neglect and erosion.

code, housing Local regulations setting out the minimum conditions under which dwellings are considered fit for human habitation and putting certain limits on their occupancy and use. Overcrowding, unsanitary conditions, vermin, inadequate heat, and structural hazards are the kind of deficiencies housing codes are designed to prevent or remedy.

cohort-survival method A technique for projecting future population which classifies the population into sex and age groups and applies differential death rates to each cohort (depending on its stage in the life cycle) to determine the number of survivors at the end of a stated interval. Birth rates are applied to women of childbearing age to determine natural population growth. Migration figures are introduced separately as either an addition or subtraction, but once migrants enter (or before they leave) they are subject to the same calculations as to the likelihood of their producing offspring and of surviving. (See DEMOGRAPHY.)

collateral Security for a debt. It is generally pledged to reinforce the personal obligation of the borrower to the lender. Collateral may be in the form of personal property or real estate. In the latter case, the collateral may take the form of a mortgage on the real estate. (See MORTGAGE.)

color-blindness The doctrine espoused by dissenting Justice Harlan in *Plessy v. Ferguson* (1896) that the color of a person should play no part in the dispensation of public benefits. Men are "created equal" and so they should remain before the law. While the old dissent is now the legally accepted view, a strict application of the color-blind doctrine might conceivably limit the Negro's rights at the same time as it establishes them. Black groups are becoming deliberately color conscious and are demanding not equality alone but equality for them as an identifiable group. Moreover, can honest desegregation efforts ignore color in the process of desegregating? Can the pressures for giving the black priority in jobs ignore color identification? Can a commission seeking to ban discrimination against a black overlook it? Can the courts themselves be blind to color as they enforce desegregation in the schools with "deliberate speed?"

It is clear that an accommodation must be made between benign principle and cold reality. Color identification is hardly more inconsistent with democratic principles than the laws that single out war veterans, the elderly, or the physically handicapped. The color-blind doctrine should not mean blindness to injustice and oppression. Its aim is to guarantee rights, not annul them. It simply means that wherever the arm of government appears, whether in the form of regulation, taking of property, or dispensation of benefits, it must move with an even hand. But it puts no restraints in the process upon voluntary ethnic formations or the will of a particular race to live with its own. It is only when the right to go elsewhere is checked, where public power or funds are employed to sponsor or encourage separatism, or where social, economic, or political compulsions operate against the group that law should intervene to protect equality of rights and treatment. (See CIVIL RIGHTS; PHASE PROGRAM; QUOTA SYSTEM; TIPPING POINT.)

color of right A claim upon property which, though not strictly recognized in law, gives some arguable basis for its validity. (See ADVERSE POSSESSION.)

commission The fee or award paid for services to a real-estate broker, agent, executor, trustee, receiver, etc., usually calculated as a percentage of the amount involved in the transaction or the amount received or expended; also, a company of persons set up to perform some public duty. (See BROKER.)

commission system of government A type of city government in which all executive and legislative powers are vested in a small elected board. It is a marked departure from the system of checks and balances that most American cities have adopted from the federal scheme. It was first introduced in Galveston, Texas, following the flood of September 1900, which left both the city and its finances under water. The state legislature, which inaugurated the scheme as an emergency measure, set up five commissioners who, by majority vote, could pass local laws, levy taxes, appropriate and borrow money, and make appointments. The plan was continued permanently and between 1908 and 1914 won acceptance in more than four hundred other cities.

Under the plan, one of the five commissioners acts as chairman, often carrying the title of mayor though lacking a mayor's powers. Administrative functions are divided among the five. This has both strengths and weaknesses; vesting of authority has sometimes brought better people and more efficiency into the city service but has simultaneously diffused responsibility and created frictions when three commissioners ganged up on the other two; though one commissioner may have charge of safety, public finance, or city property, he may be overruled by the majority, and often unwise concessions are made as the price of support. The commission, moreover, is too small to be representative and often too unwieldy to make proper decisions. As a result, adoption of the plan has slowed, major modifications have been made, and the city manager plan has often replaced it. William B. Munro has called the commission a five-headed executive, "a pyramid without a peak," and though he thinks it has prompted municipal reform, it "has proved more successful as a protest than a policy." (See CITY MANAGER PLAN; MAYOR-COUNCIL PLAN.)

communism. See SOCIALISM.

communistic settlements; communitarian societies Communities that order their lives and property communistically in one respect or another. Though communities organized along these lines existed in ancient times, it was the nineteenth century that produced such settlements in great numbers. In the United States there were two main types—one set up by Christian sects, the other established by non-Christians, typically anti-religious or grounded in pure utopian concepts.

The religious societies generally practiced a thoroughgoing communism with incoming members assigning all their worldly goods to a common fund. No wages were paid, but everyone was guaranteed food and care. Founders generally joined in the work; it was their personalities that supplied the mortar which held the communities together. When they died, conflict, indifference, or chaos frequently eroded the communities as well as the founders' hopes. The Oneida and Economy communities successfully sold their goods on the open market; the Shakers were once famed for their garden seed, furniture, and wool products. Some of the experiments had unique aspects and some were far ahead of their time. The Zoarites practiced non-resistance and experimented with community care of children long before it was practiced in Russia or in Israel. The Perfectionist women not only voted but wore short hair, long trousers, and short skirts more than a century before the mini. Celibacy was practiced in some of the communities, despite its inconveniences and tensions.

The founding of voluntary communities is a form of social and political reform common to the American system. Indeed, the earliest American settlements in Massachusetts and Virginia were intentional communities and shared many utopian yearnings. The hippie and dropout communes that have developed in the Far West and rural New England in the 1960s are only the most recent manifestations of a similar impulse. Here, too, the sacred institutions of the larger society—private property and the family—are being deliberately if haphazardly transformed to see if a more satisfying human society can be built. Instead of working for amelioration and reform within the system or revolutionary overthrow of the whole, the communitarian society attempts to create a model of the good society *de novo* and apart from the rest of the world. Depending on its missionary zeal, it may either encourage the rest of the world to follow its example or simply ask to be left alone.

The American settlements of the nineteenth century set few lasting precedents and most were failures, though it would be unfair to assume they were without personal satisfaction and fulfillment for their members. One of the most important spoilers was the competitive social order that was pressing against them and the blandishments it offered the younger generation. Among current experiments, the Israeli kibbutz is held to be one of the most resilient, but even here the hiring of labor is not uncommon, and it is far from certain that the kibbutz will be the exception in the long list of failed experiments. Here, too, not the least of the problems is the competitive order—the urbanized Jews migrating from Europe and the United States are neither willing nor necessarily equipped to love the simple, agricultural, collective life of the kibbutz. (See COOPERATIVE; FOURIERISM.)

community   A group of people living together in some identifiable territory and sharing a set of interests embracing their lifeways. This term has many applications, ranging from a self-contained and self-sufficient peasant community to the "community of man," from New York's "Italian community" to the "community of educated men" at Harvard, from the "community" created by a suburban developer (or his advertising man) to the "community" invoked by the neighborhood militant at a city council hearing. Community, unlike neighborhood, implies more than geographical propinquity—it requires some identification of its members with the area and each other and some self-consciousness as a social entity. A community assumes form and character as its people acquire common interests, experiences, roots, and memories.

The American urban community—with its anonymity, its population shifts and changes, and its ethnic conflicts—resists the designation. Whatever common interests may be identified in it seem vague and fragile, and its elements are often found less in the central city than in the suburbs surrounding it, where a common concern over the school, the neighborhood, the local services, the tax levies, or the fear of invasion by non-whites might be in evidence. The raw elements of a community might be identified as often in one of the lush western mobile camps as in the metamorphic city. Recently, however, publicly aided programs have sought, with some success, to spawn or nourish neighborhood communities that would have a hand in their own improvement. A resurgence of local initiative and political organization has brought signs of rejuvenation to many urban neighborhoods.

Community, finally, is that mythical state of social wholeness in which each member has his place and in which life is regulated by cooperation rather than by competition and conflict. It has had brief and intermittent flowerings through history but always seems to be in decline at any given historical present. Thus community is that which each generation feels it must rediscover and re-create. (See NEIGHBORHOOD.)

community center   A neighborhood building for social, recreational, and cultural activities. The term came into general use about 1915 as a new name for the social center with which the churches and settlement houses had become involved. Initially school buildings were used for adult education and recreational programs. Community houses, churches, and other institutions supplemented the educational centers. Community centers have become more important in suburbs, where recreation is receiving emphasis, but have lost some of their influence in the central cities. As earlier generations of urban immigrants left for the suburbs and central-city church activities declined, many of the privately organized centers weakened. Lately the resurgence of community emphasis among minorities and the growth of publicly assisted programs have given them new strength, particularly in the slums and ghettos where the loss was mostly felt.

community college An institution, usually public, offering college-level instruction, with or without credits, to the residents of a community. The late 1960s witnessed pressures by local minority groups upon locally based colleges and universities to assume the functions of community colleges.

community control; neighborhood control The control of a public facility or service by a local community. Community control gained national prominence in the struggle over the governing of three experimental school districts in New York City in 1968. Demands for neighborhood control often go beyond mere "citizen participation" or "consultation" to the power to allocate resources, set policy, hire and fire, and plan and run programs. While the blueprints for decentralized control vary among neighborhoods and from city to city, at least three powers usually remain with the municipal government—to raise revenues, to set the city budget and its allocation to respective neighborhoods, and to enforce general rules and standards.

The community-control movement is seen on the one hand as a natural outgrowth of the citizen-participation provisions in the Poverty and Model Cities Programs (plus the administrative trend toward decentralization of public services), and on the other as demands for territorial sovereignty and self-government in black communities growing out of the civil-rights and black-power movements. What started as an experiment in public administration and social psychology has matured into a political demand and a movement to be reckoned with. (See DECENTRALIZATION.)

community development A term embracing all those activities and programs designed to strengthen the physical, social, and economic conditions of an area with a view toward making it a more healthful, prosperous, and gratifying place to live, and in the process to develop the community's capacity to help itself. The term was once mostly applied to work in developing countries, especially to efforts relying on local planning and self-help. It is now also used to refer to work in urban ghettos and poor rural communities in the United States and has come to describe that larger enterprise in which urban planners, public-health experts, social workers, economic planners, community organizers, and the like find themselves engaged when they look beyond the traditional bounds of their own disciplines.

community facilities   Facilities used in common by a number of people and often owned by the public, such as streets, schools, parks and playgrounds; also facilities owned and operated by non-profit private agencies such as churches, settlement houses, recreation and neighborhood centers.

community organization   The mobilization of a community to take deliberate collective action to deal with problems affecting its own social welfare or to achieve some broad social change. Community organization (known by its practitioners as "c.o.") can be spontaneous, initiated by local leadership, or undertaken with the prompting of a professional organizer from the outside.

The emphases in community-organization work have undergone changes in the last decades. In the 1930s, with the work of the settlement houses in mind, the *Encyclopedia of Social Sciences* defined "c.o." as "the various activities and programs of social reconstruction built around the community as a social and ecological unit." In the 1940s the American Association of Social Workers identified it as the process of bringing together social-welfare agencies "for the purpose of welfare planning and coordination of efforts within a given neighborhood or community." Emphasis was on integrating the work being done by various welfare agencies, particularly blending that of the established private charities with the government efforts that emerged in the New Deal. Of course both types of "organizing" still go on, but they have been overshadowed in the 1960s by the more activist and militant organizing characteristic of the civil-rights movement and the War on Poverty. Here the principles are to help the residents (usually of a poor area) identify their problems; set up an organized structure within which to operate and work out a plan of action; seek out and develop local leadership; recruit relevant political and institutional support and then pursue their strategy with the most effective means—whether it be registering voters, sitting-in at City Hall, or sponsoring a block clean-up.

There is a crucial difference in mobilizing to get someone else to do something and mobilizing to do it yourself. The first may require pressure tactics and an uncompromising stance; the second usually demands organizational consensus and technical expertise. One source of the poverty program's troubles has been the tendency to carry the organizing skills and tactics necessary for confrontation into the arena of planning and operations.

community participation   The theory that the local community should be given an active role in programs and improvements directly affecting it. Just how active depends on the city's attitude, the community's muscle, and the nature of the program. The local community's role may be consultative; it may be given jurisdiction over a local poverty program; it may be accorded the right to approve or administer model-cities grants in its locality; or it may manage a particular local improvement.

The advantages claimed for community participation are that it spurs greater interest by the local citizenry, gives it responsibility over its own affairs, develops local leadership, and decentralizes central bureaucratic authority into local hands. The city is said to be too big to take on all tasks, and the people in a neighborhood are felt to have a more intimate knowledge of its problems; they are more apt to win cooperation from the local residents, while unruly militants and trouble-makers are kept occupied. One reason there were no riots in New York City during the summer of 1968, says a militant Negro leader, is that "we were too busy." The City's Mayor saw participatory democracy as the road to race peace.

Like all political innovations, participatory democracy has demonstrated its virtues as well as its peccadilloes and venalities. New leadership has been developed in local areas, greater local interest aroused, and more citizen responsibility assumed. Participatory democracy may sometimes acquire the flavor of the town meeting and the cachet of the true democratic process. But it has also demonstrated that bureaucracy and corruption are not confined to city hall, that local groups are not always representative, and that a clique may take command because only a few turned up for the local election. Local vested interests, moreover, have proven harder to dislodge when incompetence has been demonstrated. Discharging a Negro from a position of power has become a ticklish job, particularly if he has acquired a following; a charge of "white racism" is often a sure-fire defense.

Community participation is still in its infancy, and as with all infants the rates of disease and mortality are threatening in the early years. But some preliminary conclusions seem justified. Instead of decentralization relieving the mayor of his burdens, these have increased as he has been called upon to settle a growing number of touchy conflicts. Delegation of authority has frustrated action as often as it has promoted it. Local groups have sometimes proven so stubborn in protecting the interests of their own areas that the interests of the city as a whole have been subordinated. At a time when city problems have become regional in scope and remedy, the fractionalization of functions has invited the fragmentation of power and policy.

The general principle of decentralization can never resolve the concrete riddles of human behavior. The ultimate answer may begin to appear with time and experience. Giving a local group control over a school may fail, where allowing a block group to set up a day-care center will succeed. In the long run each decentralized task must be viewed in its own context, authorizing consultation in one case, supervision or dominion in another, and no authority whatever over what should remain a city-wide responsibility.

community property   Property shared equally during marriage by husband and wife, which usually can be transferred or otherwise disposed of only with the consent of both parties.

commuter   One who travels back and forth between a city and an outside residence, or from a city to an outside work location, to earn his livelihood. Increased suburbanization and the automobile have steadily increased the number of commuters, until it has become the symbol of a special way of life, a subject of contemporary drama and fiction, and a whole new factor in family life, affecting the breadwinner's role as husband and father.

A dominant way of life for a growing proportion of the American people, commuting contrasts sharply with the older European life pattern and with the pattern contemplated for new towns in which workplace and home are within easy distance. Traffic jams, crowded passenger trains, and the hours spent getting to and from one's job have offset much of the gain achieved in the shortening of the work week. The forty-hour week is still fifty hours measured portal to portal, and the ten hours spent on the road or train may be more enervating than the work itself.

Numerous remedies have been proffered to humanize commuting services—more trains and buses, separate bus lanes, lower fares, more comfort, better feeder and transfer services, fringe-area parking, coordination of mass transit with new highway networks, and better land planning to bring housing and work location into line.

But if policy continues unchanged, future generations of commuters will not only pay higher fares but fare worse. Meanwhile, suburban development is stretching farther and farther into the backlands, lengthening the journey into and out of the city and jamming roads and other lines of communication. Some hope for improvement may lie in linking federal highway planning to subdivision planning. This would mean purchase by the road agencies of excess land around the road routes, its planning by a public authority, and its resale to industry and homebuilders for development subject to the plan. But by 1970 the idea had hardly received serious mention. The Department of Housing and Urban Development was still fumbling with regional planning subsidies and other voluntary aids while developments continued their sprawl into the ever-lengthening outlands. (See CAR POOL; JOURNEY TO WORK; TRANSPORTATION.)

company town A community inhabited solely or chiefly by the employees of a single company or group of companies that also own a substantial part of the real estate and housing. It may be unincorporated, be part of a larger, incorporated municipality, or be incorporated as a separate town. Company motivations may be benevolent or merely practical, as when the provision of housing is the only way to attract workers. Motivations may also include stabilization of the labor force; repression of recalcitrance through the added weapon of eviction; or simple profit. Because of opposition by labor unions and reformers, company housing has become increasingly unpopular in the United States, so that even when federal housing assistance made it possible for industry to build planned towns and give their employees ownership under FHA and other programs, industry remained indifferent. A slight stir of interest by industry, however, began to manifest itself in the late 1960s. Enlightened company development of new communities coupled with worker owner- ship could provide one of the most constructive formulas for improving the nation's environment.

In less-developed countries, company housing is still being built. Con- siderable company housing, some of it good, may be found in Japan, the Middle East, South America, and Canada. Some of the new regional or national capital cities, like Chandigarh and Brasilia, could also be con- sidered company towns, where the chief employer is the government. (See HOUSE, TIED.)

compensable regulations   Regulations that place tight restrictions on the use to which private land can be put and that compensate the owner for any drop in value attributable to the regulations. Under compensable regulations, land required for permanent open space is restricted to farming, recreation, or other low-density use. The owner is guaranteed, should he choose to sell, that he will receive an amount equal at least to the value of the land just prior to imposition of the regulations, as deter- mined by a special assessment. The government obligates itself to pay the difference if the actual sale price is lower than this valuation. Though compensable regulations have not been widely tested, they seem attrac- tive devices for guiding development and preserving open space and nat- ural areas. Theoretically they chart a careful course between conserva- tion zoning so restrictive as to be confiscatory, and public acquisition of enormous acreage that can be too costly for the conservation and open- space budgets of most local governments. Land subject to compensable regulations remains in private ownership, continues to yield tax revenue, and requires no public maintenance expenditures. Payment by the public comes due only when a particular parcel is sold, and then only when the sale price is less than the guarantee. (See EASEMENT, CONSERVATION.)

compensatory treatment; preferential treatment   The theory that the Negro (or other minority) should be accorded priorities in education, training, employment, and government assistance to compensate him for past injustices. This is called "discrimination in reverse" by its oppo- nents, who argue that discriminating in favor of a class is discrimination against the unfavored class. They contend that there is no way of know- ing where and when to stop such favoritism and that there are some among the compensated who do not need or deserve it, while there are many whites who also need help. If the priorities were based on need rather than color, would not the same end be achieved?

The argument for compensatory treatment is that a realistic recognition of differences must be made. Special benefits were given to freed slaves, are given to old people and war veterans, and, it is contended, should be given to Negro children in schools to enable them to compete in a post-industrial world. Those so long victimized by discriminatory practices, it is argued, should be made whole against the damage their group sustained. (See COLOR-BLINDNESS.)

compound   An enclosure containing a house or houses as well as outbuildings. In Africa the family compound is the common arrangement: round huts joined by a connecting wall (West Africa); a series of rooms or huts grouped about a courtyard or courtyards (northern Nigeria); a rectangular court with rooms on two or more sides (Ashanti, Ghana). The compound was designed partly for security against thieves, slave raiders, and enemies. The size of the house varies with the customs and wealth of the owners. The compound pattern has won its way into some public housing and new housing developments in Africa, the open center area serving as a place of assemblage and a safer play-space for children. In India the term denotes any plot or property with one or more buildings.

comprehensive plan   An official document adopted by a local government setting forth its general policies regarding the long-term physical development of a city or other area. The plan should be broad enough to include all aspects of a development or redevelopment program as distinguished from sporadic, isolated, or piecemeal planning. It is used interchangeably with the terms "general plan" and "city plan" and is probably most familiarly or notoriously known as a "master plan." (See MASTER PLAN.)

compulsory purchase. See EMINENT DOMAIN.

concentric zone theory   A theory of urban growth, developed by Ernest W. Burgess in the 1920s, that holds that predominant land uses tend to be arranged in a series of concentric circular zones about a city's central business district. The theory seeks to explain the effect of market forces and ecological processes on land-use arrangements in the city. In Burgess's abstract scheme, zones are arranged as follows: (1) central business district; (2) zone in transition; (3) zone of workingmen's homes; (4) white-collar and middle-class residences; (5) commuters' zone. As the city grows, the theory held, each inner zone invades the neighboring outer zone (a process human ecologists call "invasion and succession"), but the basic ringlike structure remains. (See INVASION AND SUCCESSION; MULTIPLE NUCLEI THEORY; SECTOR THEORY.)

concession A period of rent-free occupancy offered as part of a letting. It may be given as a means of inducing a tenant to rent or to afford him an opportunity to prepare his apartment for occupancy. Giving a one- or two-month rent concession instead of lowering the rent proportionately over the lease period may be an advantage to an owner intending to sell because it maintains the higher monthly rent level on the books.

A concession is also a space or a privilege granted to a tenant or licensee for a subsidiary business or service, such as a hat-check concession in a restaurant or a gambling concession at a Las Vegas hotel.

condemnation A term used interchangeably with "eminent domain" to denote the compulsory acquisition of private property for public use with compensation to the owner. In France it is called *expropriation.* Condemnation also denotes the declaration by an appropriate public authority that a property is unfit for use or occupancy and must therefore be closed, vacated, or torn down. When the property is taken for public use the reasonable value of the property must be paid the owner; in other cases, no compensation need be paid. A house may be demolished by the public authority when it is structurally unsafe and the owner fails to do so himself. Whether it may be demolished when it is unsanitary or unfit for occupancy depends upon the laws and rulings of the particular jurisdiction. (See CODE ENFORCEMENT; CONFISCATION; EMINENT DOMAIN; EXPROPRIATION; UNTENANTED HAZARD.)

condemnation, excess The taking by eminent domain of more property than is necessary for a public improvement and the resale of the unneeded portion to private purchasers. The excess land is acquired to effect a more comprehensive planning of the improvement or to secure for the public the increment in value due to the improvement. Because of unfavorable court decisions on its constitutionality and the restriction of eminent domain to the land actually required for the improvement, excess condemnation remained virtually unused until the early twentieth century. It has since been validated by constitutional amendment in a number of states after being first adopted in England and Germany. Liberalization by the courts of the public-purpose concept has dispensed with much of the need for employing excess condemnation. Excess land can now be acquired through other means. If the need for the extra land is incidental to the main purpose or if the land is needed for better planning, it will usually be sanctioned by the courts. (See EMINENT DOMAIN; LEX ADICKES.)

condominium A type of multi-family dwelling or row-house project in which each dwelling unit is owned (and financed) by the occupant but in which the halls, entranceways, and underlying land are owned jointly. It is different from a cooperative, in which residents own an undivided share in the whole. When an individual owns his own unit and pays for it he is not affected by the defaults of other occupants, as he would be in a cooperative subject to a mortgage covering all the dwelling units. The word is derived from the Latin *dominium,* to have control over jointly with (*con*) one or more other persons. (See COOPERATIVE.)

confiscation The seizure of property and its forfeiture or transfer to the state. The term is also applied loosely to any arbitrary or unreasonable action of government in dealing with private property. Confiscation is to be distinguished from the legitimate exercise of the tax, police, or eminent-domain powers. It is authorized, however, in the case of contraband or in the taking of an enemy prize under the international law of war. Property of insurrectionists was confiscated during the Civil War, and the USSR confiscated all private land after its Revolution. (See CONDEMNATION; EXPROPRIATION.)

confrontation politics Political action based on the theory that society can be aroused to its shortcomings and moral failures through activist, tactical improvisations by a small minority, such as sit-ins, demonstrations, challenges to police, and general obstructionism. Prevailing discontents are identified and become the issues around which support is mobilized. By these tactics, it is thought, the weaknesses in the established political system can be exposed and the masses stirred into revulsion or revolt, thereby bringing about the much-needed political and social changes.

The theory (at least the American version) was spawned out of the dissent and despondency accompanying the Vietnam war, the impatience of youth with racial injustice, outworn university practices and curricula, and the general feeling that there was a lack of idealism in capitalist society. In some cases reforms resulted, but often the confrontationists were less interested in winning concessions than in keeping the pot boiling.

Confrontation politicians are intolerant of efforts to achieve reformation through legal means, believe that existing liberal movements and democratic processes are unable to bring about change, and hope, by constant assaults upon existing institutions, to break up the liberal bloc and ultimately pit the left against the right in open confrontation.

Confrontation politics is basically tactics without objectives, strategy without ends. By advocating violence, confrontation politics has invited counterviolence. But the confrontation leadership sees this as sound, as a means of highlighting the savagery of the "law and order" forces. If violence stirs impatience and heats up passions, this is viewed as an advance. If it releases the nation's marginal minds into rabidity, this is viewed as regrettable but unavoidable. If it lends justification to brash counteraction by other irresponsible groups, this is seen as expressive of the harebrained nature of our society.

congested district   An area of highly concentrated occupation or use, so crowded with people, vehicles, or buildings as to impede movement, threaten health, or overload public services. (See DEPRESSED AREA; DEVELOPMENT AREA.)

conservation   The protection of the resources (minerals, water, forests, fisheries, wildlife, etc.) of man's environment against depletion or waste and the safeguarding of its beauty. Also, an urban-renewal strategy that emphasizes the protection of an existing, viable neighborhood against the encroachment of blight; it usually includes improvement of the area's amenities, organization of the residents, and strict code enforcement. (See EASEMENT, CONSERVATION; OPEN SPACE.)

consolidation The absorption of one municipality by another or the merging of two or more municipalities (or a city and a county, two school districts, etc.) to create a single new governmental unit; a technique for enlarging local units to a size conducive to efficient administration. Before 1900 municipal consolidations were accomplished by special state legislative acts, but more recently local opposition has reduced the number to a token, although school-district consolidation has continued apace. In Toronto, Canada, consolidation of thirteen local units was accomplished by provincial order, and in Japan five cities effected a voluntary consolidation into a single city. In the United States, with suburban resistance, the prospects of similar consolidations are dim. (See ANNEXATION.)

constant-payment plan. See LEVEL PAYMENT.

construction industry. See BUILDING INDUSTRY.

construction loan. See LOAN, CONSTRUCTION.

contamination The act of making something impure by contact or mixture with some unwholesome substance. Water, for example, is contaminated when it is rendered unfit for a specified use by the introduction of bacteria, sewage, or any substance dangerous to health. Air may be contaminated by pollutants. Contamination now also refers to interference with communication by noise. (See POLLUTION.)

contract An agreement between two or more persons to do or refrain from doing a particular thing. The consideration for the contract may be "a horse, a hawk or a robe," cash, or anything given, done, or abstained from. Contract was the spur to urban formations and the root of the "contract society," a society dependent on consent in which government's function was to enforce agreements except where enforcement contravened statute or public policy. With these exceptions, contract implies self-regulation and self-assertion, free of the state's unreasonable impositions. Man's move from status to contract was one of his great strides toward freedom and individualism. With the growing complexities of urban society and a welfare economy, regulations and restrictions have multiplied, the authorizations for eminent domain have been extended, and taxation has increased so that the fruits of contract have been cut into. But though contract now operates within a framework of expanded government supervision, the contract operation, except in Communist countries, is still the dominant force in economic development. (See CAPITALISM; SOCIALISM.)

contractor   The party responsible for the construction of a building or a public operation. Plans and specifications are usually part of the contract. The contractor may let out all the subcontracts or, in the case of a building operation, do the carpentry or other portion of the work himself, letting only some or none of the work to subcontractors. Also anyone who makes a contract. (See BUILDER.)

conurbation   An area in which there is a large, unplanned aggregation of urban communities, such as greater London or metropolitan New York. "Each new idea for which we have not yet a word deserves one," Patrick Geddes said. "Constellations we cannot call them; conglomerations is, alas, nearer the mark at present, but it may sound unappreciative." He found conurbation "appreciative," and it may now be found in some dictionaries. (See AGGLOMERATION; MEGALOPOLIS.)

conventional house. See HOUSE, CONVENTIONAL.

conventional mortgage. See MORTGAGE, CONVENTIONAL.

convergence   The coming to the same point of people from different directions or places. It is one of the three elements vital to the successful mating and reproduction of any species of life, of which the two others are "selection," or the choice of a variant in preference to others, and "courtship," or the wooing process.

The urban mechanisms for human convergence have become increasingly impaired, and the opportunities for meeting and mating (or meeting without mating) have diminished. The chances for boy meeting girl (except on campuses) are fewer, and the newcomer to a city may never meet his or her neighbor, much less a suitor. Meetings of course do take place—among dog-walkers, at bowling parties, at art openings, at "singles bars," and via computer-dating, but the opportunities are limited and not always wholesome.

The debutante or coming-out party is known in higher social circles but nowhere else. The church and the "Y" operate to a limited extent for others. The most strategic opportunity for convergence and selection is the college, and many a parent's hopes are raised with the matriculation. But if this filtration point for kindred souls is passed up, no better one will come along easily. Only about 40 per cent of the youngsters eighteen to twenty-one years of age go to college anyway. The rest must either angle in the small provincial pools in which they were reared or head for the difficult waters of the metropolis.

The limitations of city life are a boon to some employers—an advertisement for a stenographer may play up "the young executive." The prospects of an airline stewardess's marrying a passenger are reflected in the lowly pay. The young stenographer who can land a job at the right university has achieved a tour-de-force.

Improvisations to effect convergence after the budding years have budded appear in the form of "28 Clubs." Two pages in a Friday edition of a major metropolitan newspaper will advertise a "reunion" for bachelors and "bachelorettes" only; a "dansant" for "business and professionals twenty-eight and over" with a Saturday get-together that guarantees "equal guys and girls at tables." There are groups for "singles only," "membership clubs," and affairs with "ladies free up to 9 P.M., gents $1.50," and a "young college graduates club, proof of college degree required." An "Indoor-Outing" is offered that promises a "feast on toasted marshmallows" with an option to "have a waiter serve you or find some fair maid or gallant Galahad to do the honors" (the waiter often has the better entree to conversation and may even prove to be the best catch.)

In a big city these meet-marts sometimes work, but their brashness keeps the verecund from venturing. The burgeoning professional house-parties at $3 per head are embarrassing—there is rarely a surplus of males and more of them are apt to be prowlers than prospects. The professional dance studio is big business and costly but, like the dancehall, it holds dubious opportunities. (See HIPPIES; TRYSTORIUM.)

conversion The division of a single dwelling unit into accommodations for multiple households, or the changing of the use of an existing building to another use. Synonyms with varying degrees of difference in the nature of the work include: rehabilitation, renovation, remodeling, reconditioning, reconstruction, rebuilding, alteration, and redevelopment.

Conversion is also a legal term for the unlawful appropriation of another's property.

conveyance The transfer of property from one person to another and the instrument or document by which this is effected. Also, a vehicle for transporting people or goods. (See TITLE.)

cooperative In its widest sense, a form of human organization grounded in the belief that life is best ordered by mutual help rather than by individual competitiveness; more specifically, a combination of individuals organized for buying or selling as a means of increasing the benefits or offering some service to the membership.

Equity, reason, and the common good underlie the cooperative movement. The word is derived from *con* ("with") and *opus* ("work"), or working together, and it was the idea of togetherness that led to the cooperative movement in Rochdale, Lancashire, England, where in 1844 twenty-eight poor flannel weavers and the like got together a small amount of capital to launch a cooperative shop. After paying 5 per cent interest on the share capital, all profit was allotted to the purchasing members in proportion to their purchases. Each member bought at the store and brought in new customers. The store's ownership remained with the members and as business grew other stores were founded on the same principles, which included: giving one vote to each member irrespective of his shareholdings; selling goods for cash and at the going price; distributing the net income above expenses and reserves according to the purchases made; allowing no restriction on membership; permitting only nominal interest on capital invested; setting up a reserve for educational purposes.

The cooperative movement has grown and taken many forms, including store cooperatives following the Rochdale principles, building and credit societies, tenant cooperatives, and industrial cooperatives.

In less-developed areas, there is evidence of cooperation in squatter colonies where joint action is needed for survival and for successful resistance to official intrusion. Cooperation here is often the legacy of rural or tribal relationships or of the extended family.

Labor organizations and civil-service groups have organized cooperatives in housing and stores and, in the United States, have been instrumental in financing some substantial housing ventures.

Cooperatives have been urged for poor neighborhoods as a way to put local gougers and absentee landlords out of business, or at least to give consumers and tenants a decent alternative. So far little has been done to turn existing low-rental buildings into cooperatives, though it is much talked about as a solution to abandonment and disrepair. There has been more experience but only mixed success with cooperative food and furnishing stores and wholesaling operations in the ghetto. (See COMMUNISTIC SETTLEMENTS; FOURIERISM; HOUSING, COOPERATIVE; HSB.)

cooperative housing. See HOUSING, COOPERATIVE.

core house. See HOUSE, CORE.

corner influence   The element of value of a plot of land stemming from its location at the intersection of two streets. In most instances, a corner location adds value. (See "KEY TO THE CORNER.")

corporation   An entity created by law, consisting of one or more persons empowered to act under its name in accordance with its charter. It is a body without a soul but is more enduring than the human body and can be given perpetual duration. Subject to its charter powers, it acts like any individual in making contracts, carrying on business, suing and being sued, borrowing or lending, or going into bankruptcy. The corporation rather than the individual is liable for its debts, but the corporate veil may be pierced and enmesh the directors for fraud or other malfeasances. There are numerous corporate types, including stock corporations with shares held by stockholders; profit and non-profit corporations; charitable corporations; religious corporations; public and municipal corporations; quasi-public corporations (*e.g.*, railroads and utility corporations); federally chartered corporations; and limited dividend corporations.

The corporate concept had its origins in Roman law where a *collegium* or *corpus* consisted of at least three persons who could hold property in common in the corporate name and govern themselves under their own by-laws. Individuals and *corpus* were separate, the *corpus* continuing in existence even when all the members had changed. Public bodies, religious societies, official societies, and trade societies all adopted the corporate form.

The corporation usually comes into being upon filing a certificate of incorporation, which then becomes its charter of powers. This and its by-laws supply the authority of its officers and directors. State statutes regulate corporations as to their dissolution, merger, and other affairs.

The modern corporation grew up with the city and has become the vehicle of big business in the United States. Millions of dollars in bonds and stocks are issued yearly to the public, who share in the profits and losses. The widespread ownership of corporations is one of the phenomena of modern capitalism. The nineteenth century witnessed a slow abdication of state control of corporations, but the widening involvement of the public in corporate stock led to increased government concern. The concern, however, has taken the form of only limited regulation and supervision, primarily of stock issues offered to the public.

The nation's major corporations have their main offices in the central cities where they carry on their managerial and clerical work and often their manufacturing as well. The city is still the primary source of skilled workers, the main market for goods and ideas, the source of contacts, and the seat of business services. It has a built-in consumer market, is more easily reachable by air and other communications, is a central focus for salesmen and buyers, and provides the banking services, subcontractors, and spare parts that industry needs. In an era of expanded government intervention, it also provides more intimate access to officialdom, proximity to import and export licenses, consuls, lawyers, and accountants. Despite the growing inconveniences of city life, few large enterprises can afford to pull up stakes and gamble on recruiting talents in exurbia. If some enterprises do move, they generally look for land on the city's fringe but within its orbit. (See PUBLIC CORPORATION.)

corporation, public. See PUBLIC CORPORATION.

cost-benefit analysis An analytic method designed to evaluate alternative programs in terms of their potential benefits and likely costs, and to aid decision-makers in choosing among them. When this method is applied in the environmental sciences, ideally it weighs the social, ecological, and aesthetic as well as economic factors and takes account of the *indirect* consequences of different courses of action. (See EXTERNALITIES; PPBS.)

cottage A small, one-family house, usually of one story, although it may sometimes have second-floor rooms. Also, a resort or summer house.

cottage, tied. See HOUSE, TIED.

council houses In England and Wales, housing owned by county and borough councils; the equivalent of public housing in the United States.

council manager plan. See CITY MANAGER PLAN.

council of governments. See METROPOLITAN COUNCIL.

court An open area partly or wholly bounded by building walls or enclosures. In some undeveloped areas it is the central open space of a compound. As used in zoning, an open, unoccupied space bounded on two or more sides by the exterior walls of a building or by the exterior walls and lot lines. (See PATIO.)

covenant An agreement between two or more persons, often written into a deed, to do or refrain from doing certain acts. It aims to achieve by agreement much of what zoning does by ordinance and may go further—as when owners agree to have certain types of roofs, passageways, and green spaces, or to support common services.

The restrictive covenants of the 1930s and 1940s were designed to prevent the sale of houses in white neighborhoods to Negroes and other minorities and were held legal but judicially unenforceable. (See DISCRIMINATION, FEDERAL HOUSING; FAIR HOUSING LAWS.)

covenant, Aesopian A discriminatory housing covenant written into a deed or other instrument in language that may be legal on its face but that is actually designed to exclude people of certain races or colors. Such covenants may prescribe excessive lot sizes that are relaxed for the "right" people and enforced for the "wrong" ones; they may require membership in a club as a condition for buying into a development or contain other devious exclusionary requirements. The covenants get their name from Aesop, a Greek slave and writer of fables, who peopled his stories with animals to mask his real intention of writing about men. (See DISCRIMINATION, FEDERAL HOUSING; FAIR HOUSING LAWS.)

coverage   The proportion of the net or gross land area of a site taken up by a building or buildings. Coverage regulations are rules prescribing the percentage of the lot that may be covered by a building.

creative federalism. See FEDERALISM, CREATIVE.

critical-path method   A way to improve efficiency by scheduling or re-scheduling the individual steps in a project to obtain the most efficient operation. It gives a name to an old but unchristened practice. It aims to find the bottlenecks or constraints and to test different allocations of work and resources so as to cut down on the total time required and achieve the best performance. The critical path is the chain of tasks that determines the minimum time the total work package should require. The technique can be utilized to help cut the time span in a public operation such as urban renewal, just as it does in a private business operation. (See REHABILITATION, INSTANT.)

crowd; mob   A group of individuals gathered together so closely as to press upon one another. A crowd at a cocktail party or art opening is entirely different from a street crowd. The street crowd is an urban phenomenon, with a personality of its own, the product of a dense population brought together fortuitously by incidents, accidents, curiosity, or other stimuli. The sociologist adds another factor—*i.e.*, the psychological influence upon its members of the mere fact of their physical proximity.

A crowd may be expressive (as at a revival meeting), active (*i.e.*, pushing into a closing subway door), passively curious, or fun-loving. A crowd that is a bane to the police may be a boon for a candidate. It may cheer or jeer, applaud, or remain mute as at a funeral. Excitement adds electricity to crowds, and if the current stirs anger the crowd may be converted into a mob—*i.e.*, a crowd given a purpose and bent on lawless action. Indications are that mass media accelerate crowd formation and increase its volatility. The media highlight violence as entertainment and communicate the prevalence of mob action, thereby touching it off epidemically. The word "mob" is clipped from the Latin *mobile vulgus*. (See CIVIL DISORDER.)

Crown Lands; Crown Estate   The lands vested in the British sovereign in his or her public capacity and administered by the Crown Estate Commissioners. Government buildings and land occupied by the armed forces are excluded. The largest Crown Estate was administered by William the Conqueror at whose death the Estate accounted for a quarter to a third of the landed wealth of the kingdom. The holdings are now estimated at up to 300,000 acres and include both ancient possessions and some more recently acquired. Neither the reigning monarch nor the Crown Estate Commissioners enjoy the revenue, which is paid into the exchequer for public use. Crown lands also existed in former colonial possessions such as Ghana and were turned over to the new governments when the colonies attained independence. (See CITY ESTATE.)

cubic contents; cubage   The actual cubic space enclosed within the outer surfaces of the outside walls and contained between the outer surfaces of the roof and six inches below the finished surfaces of the lowest floor. The cubic contents include the dormers, penthouses, vaults, pits, enclosed porches, and other enclosed portions of the building, but exclude courts or open light shafts, outside steps, cornices, parapets, open porches, or roofed open galleries (loggias).

cubing   Determining volume in cubic feet, yards, meters, etc. "Cubic foot cost" is the total cost of a building divided by the number of cubic feet it contains. Cubic foot cost varies for each type of building as well as for buildings in areas differing in climate, wage rates, standards, etc.

cul-de-sac   A passage or place with only one outlet, such as a dead-end street or blind alley. Brilliantly used for residential access in Radburn, New Jersey, to keep the noise and danger of through traffic away from the houses and small children, cul-de-sacs have now become part of the stock-in-trade of suburban developments. (See RADBURN PLANNING.)

cultural pluralism   The theory that people's welfare can best be served by preserving and strengthening rather than blending cultures and ethnic characteristics. It would encourage marriage within each group and educate children in their own group's language and traditions. Also, a state of society in which diverse groups coexist in relative harmony.

Cultural pluralists do not reject all forms of assimilation but maintain that assimilation can take place through a common language, in education for citizenship, in associations, and in common causes without sacrificing the values of the separate cultures. Religious pluralism, they point out, has long existed in the United States. Influential Negro groups have pushed for retaining a black identity, which is an acknowledgment of pluralism.

Others, however, see cultural pluralism as a threat to equalitarianism, as another word for segregation and even a step toward apartheid. They want housing projects integrated and schools attended by both white and black children. (See MELTING POT.)

curb level The officially established grade of the curb fronting the midpoint of a lot.

curtilage A small court or yard attached to a house and forming one enclosure with it, or so regarded by the law; the area of land occupied by a dwelling, its yard and outbuildings.

cutcha A term used in India meaning "temporary" or "makeshift." When the word is coupled with housing or building, it denotes structures generally made of sun-dried brick or mud as distinguished from *pucka,* or *pukka,* meaning "more permanent and solidly built"—of stone, brick, or mortar.

day-care center A facility for taking care of children during their parents' working hours. Day care has become an important social service in urban areas, particularly for fatherless households. Expansion of such facilities is advocated by those eager to get mothers off the welfare rolls and into jobs. Others regard this as callous economizing and disastrous to child-rearing in families already missing one parent. There is, however, a good deal to be said for a voluntary program that would allow beleaguered mothers respite from their children and a chance to get work and circulate in the adult world. Many regard a well-run day-care program as a valuable educational and socializing experience for young children.

daylight factor   A factor evolved by British town and country planning authorities as an indicator of the level of interior natural lighting; it is based on a ratio between the daylight available inside a building and the total light available outdoors under an unobstructed sky.

dead land. See LAND, MARGINAL.

debt limit   A constitutional or statutory limitation placed upon the borrowing capacity of a government. With a municipal or other local government, the limitation may be a specified sum, a fixed percentage of the assessed value of its real estate, or a sum arrived at by some other formula. These debt limitations have particularly troubled the big cities. Urban social problems multiply, educational needs, pensions, and payrolls rise, while revenues dry up. To meet these swelling commitments, the cities have resorted to elaborate but legal devices for evading the debt limitations, such as the use of authorities and special districts with their own borrowing powers, or revenue bonds repayable out of special taxes.

Between 1946 and 1966 the taxes of local governments increased more than threefold per capita. In their resort to borrowing, gross local debt during the same period rose from $14 billion to $77 billion, a fivefold jump. Meanwhile federal debt increased only from $269 billion to $319 billion. On a per-capita basis local debt in that period rose nearly four times, while federal debt actually dropped about $300 per head.

Debt limitations on cities are like appeasing one's hunger by tightening one's belt. Nor will loosening the belt help. The only answer—and one that is being evaded—is for the federal government to assume directly the burdens the cities can no longer carry themselves. This does not mean more pilot housing programs, poverty assistance, and urban renewal, valuable as these aids are, but the direct assumption by the federal government of the major costs of education, safety, health, welfare, and administration. In short, an obsolete revenue system needs adjustment to the realistic needs of an urban society. (See BOND, REVENUE; PUBLIC CORPORATION; SPECIAL DISTRICT.)

debt service Periodic payments of principal and interest made on a mortgage or other evidence of indebtedness. The debt service on a home is the largest of the owner's carrying charges, accounting generally for more than 50 per cent of the monthly costs. (See AMORTIZATION; INTEREST; MORTGAGE.)

decentralization The transference of authority—legislative, judicial, or administrative—from a higher level of government to a lower one or to the people. It is distinguishable from "deconcentration," which is the delegation to a subordinate officer of the capacity to act in the name of his superior without actually transferring authority.

Decentralization and deconcentration are used also to denote the dispersing of population, industry, and business from a central to a wider area. Dispersal is sometimes a deliberate attempt to achieve greater efficiency, convenience, or amenity. When it is not planned it often results in waste, sprawl, and hardship for those left behind.

decentrists A group of urban theorists who believe in thinning out the dense cities and dispersing businesses and people to smaller places. The group includes, among others, Lewis Mumford, Clarence Stein, Henry Wright, and Catherine Bauer, who contributed the word to the language. Ebenezer Howard, author of *Garden Cities of Tomorrow,* was the decentrists' intellectual and spiritual predecessor. (See DENSITY.)

decision theory A body of general propositions dealing with the process of making rational choices (particularly by complex public and private organizations) and defining the limits of rationality in decisions governed by uncertainties. (See GAME THEORY.)

dedication A setting aside of land for some public use by an owner or developer and its acceptance for such use by the public. Land may have to be dedicated for a road, park, parking lot, or other common use as a condition for the approval of a plan by a local planning board or authority.

deed A written instrument under seal by which an estate in real property is conveyed by the grantor to a grantee. The deed may be a full covenant and warranty deed, a bargain and sale deed, or a quit-claim deed; the first two of these documents carry varying guarantees as to the validity of the title conveyed, and the last carries none at all. (See TITLE.)

deed, full covenant and warranty A deed containing five covenants by the seller: a covenant of seizin (or lawful possession); a covenant guaranteeing quiet enjoyment (free of molestation, disturbance, or claims); a covenant against any existing encumbrances; a covenant of further assurance (that the seller will execute any further necessary assurance of title to the premises); and a covenant of warranty (that the seller will forever warrant the title to the property conveyed). Some full covenant and warranty deeds contain a sixth covenant warranting that the seller has not previously done anything himself to impeach the title he conveys. Prospective buyers naturally demand full covenant and warranty deeds while prospective sellers resist giving them. A compromise may then be reached through a reduction of the warranties.

deed, quit-claim A deed in which the seller transfers only such title as he may possess. It carries no warranties of title or other guarantees, and the purchaser must rely on his own title search for his legal security. The quit-claim deed is sometimes given by persons with a dubious interest in a parcel. It forecloses their claim to it, if in fact any existed. It is also often given in the ordinary purchase, though a careful lawyer for a buyer will want a full covenant and warranty deed or at least a warranty that the seller has himself done nothing to mar the title.

deed, tax A deed given by the city or other taxing authority to the purchaser of a tax lien placed on a defaulting property; the lien is foreclosed when the owner fails to pay it, after which the tax deed is delivered to the purchaser. There are professionals in the field whose business is to trade in tax liens.

default Failure to meet an obligation (such as a mortgage payment) when due. (See ACCELERATION CLAUSE; DEFICIENCY JUDGMENT; DELINQUENCY; EQUITY INSURANCE; FORECLOSURE.)

deficiency judgment A judgment for that part of a debt secured by mortgage which is not realized in the foreclosure sale of the mortgaged property. Thus if a $10,000 mortgage is foreclosed and the proceeds realized from the foreclosure sale are only $7000, the mortgagee may have a deficiency judgment for the $3000.

In the depression of the 1930s, when foreclosures were taking place at the rate of a thousand a day, the injustices of deficiency judgments caused public concern. A home worth $8000 with a defaulted mortgage of $10,000 would be sold to the mortgagee, who was the only bidder at the foreclosure auction, for as little as a dollar. The mortgagee would then enter a deficiency judgment for $9999, which represented the difference between his bid and the amount of the mortgage debt. He might then resell the house for $8000 but still retain the judgment against the owner for $9999. To correct such inequities, some states enacted laws limiting the defaulting owner's liability to the difference between the actual value of the house and the mortgage amount irrespective of the bid. The laws of many other states, however, would still permit this practice.

delinquency The act of falling, or condition of being, behind in the payment of some obligation, such as taxes or installments on a mortgage. (See DEFAULT.)

demography The study of population and population change. The basic interests of the demographer are the size, composition, and distribution of peoples. Once thought of as simply a matter of births, deaths, and other vital statistics, demography now records patterns of marriage and divorce, consumer expenditures, educational attainment, and distribution of wealth. Demographers are the source of a mass of other information vital to understanding urbanization and the problems that beset urban life. (See CENSUS; POPULATION.)

demolition The razing of a structure either as part of a redevelopment scheme, or because of dangerous conditions or obsolescence, or to make way for another improvement. A public authority may demolish a house where the house is found to be unsafe and the owner fails to do so after notice. Recent statutes and decisions authorize the demolition of vacant, uninhabitable structures. The right to demolish a grossly unsanitary structure, however, is far from clear. (See BUILDING, DERELICT; CONDEMNATION; UNTENANTED HAZARD.)

denationalization. See DESOCIALIZATION.

density The average number of persons, families, or dwellings per unit of area (acre, square mile, etc.).

The density issue has been one of the main sources of intellectual conflict among planning theorists. Among those who have favored small low-density developments have been Ebenezer Howard, Sir Patrick Geddes, Lewis Mumford, Clarence Stein, and Sir Raymond Unwin, who popularized the theme "nothing gained by overcrowding." Jane Jacobs and others have challenged the thesis. "Dense concentrations of people," says Mrs. Jacobs "are one of the necessary conditions for a flourishing city diversity. This means a dense concentration of dwellings on land." She properly draws a distinction between high density of dwellings and overcrowding of dwellings, conditions often lumped together and deplored, which are neither the same nor equally deplorable. Only overcrowding can be flatly labeled undesirable. "The desirable density," she insists, "cannot be set arbitrarily at so many families per acre. Right amounts are right amounts because of how they perform." The absurdity of viewing high population density as bad and low density as good is illustrated by Cambridge, Massachusetts, whose houses stand on generous, well-treed lots but whose population density per square mile is the third highest in the nation. Barbados, described as the densest area this side of mainland China, is still filled with sugar plantations and did not have a single multiple dwelling in 1968.

Net residential density is the density of the building site.

Gross residential density is the density of the building site plus traversing streets, alleys, and drives, and one-half of bounding streets and one-quarter of bounding street intersections.

Neighborhood density embraces the area that contains not only the buildings and the plots they cover, but all the necessary services and facilities in the vicinity, including schools, churches, shops, playgrounds, other amenities, and land taken up in streets. (See DECENTRISTS.)

depreciation Loss in value of property due to all causes, including functional and economic obsolescence and deterioration. Also, the provisions in federal and state tax laws that allow, for tax purposes, the writing-off of a percentage of a building's acquisition cost or construction cost (exclusive of the land) during its economic life.

Theoretically, a structure may never suffer physical depreciation—witness the Pyramids. In fact, a building may appreciate in value while it is being depreciated on the books. This happens when the replacement cost, or building value, exceeds the actual cost. A building may also depreciate at a faster clip than the depreciation rate allotted to it by the tax collector, as in the case of a cinema theater in a neighborhood in which television becomes the favorite. Because there is no way of determining the precise rate of depreciation (particularly the obsolescence factor), the federal tax collector generally allows a yearly fixed rate of 2 to 5 per cent, depending on the type and age of the building. On a new building, for example, 2 per cent may be allowed annually for the building and 4 per cent for the equipment in it. The owner may deduct such depreciation each year as an expense on his income-tax form.

The federal income-tax law allows a building owner to make his own choice of depreciation rates between a "straight line" basis (i.e., a fixed rate throughout the building's life) and a "double-declining balance" basis (i.e., taking a larger depreciation in the earlier years and a declining rate in the later years). When a building is fully depreciated, such income-tax deductions cease. However, if the owner sells a fully depreciated building, the buyer may set a fresh depreciation base for the building and take his deductions anew.

Depreciation has become an important factor in investment, and the terms "net after taxes" and "take-home pay" have replaced "gross income" and "gross earnings" as the measure of a sound venture. The terms "20 per cent tax free," "capital-gains deal," "depletion allowance," "deductibles," "high depreciation factor," and "tax shelter" dominate the language of business and shape its incentives. With a tax system that in the 1960s lopped off up to 48 per cent of annual corporate profit and up to 70 per cent of a tycoon's annual intake, entrepreneurs have focused on building investments as yielding the highest return that can actually be pocketed. The right choice of the depreciation rate (i.e., "straight line," "double-declining balance," "150 per cent," or "sum of the digits") may make the difference between big gains, little gains, or no gains at all.

Depreciation, one of the factors in the game of profits, applies to machinery as it does to real estate. Moreover, the tax benefits allowed to real estate are relatively small compared to those allowed to oil drilling and tax-exempt municipal-bond purchases. (See ECONOMIC LIFE; OBSOLESCENCE; TAX EXPENDITURES.)

depreciation acceleration A tax incentive designed to encourage new construction by allowing a faster write-off during the early life of a building. This usually constitutes a tax advantage during the building's first twelve years, at which point it might make good business sense to sell to another investor who can begin depreciating the building anew. Accelerated depreciation has become a favorite recommendation for encouraging investment in slum and ghetto areas. It is a hidden subsidy and a very substantial one. (See SUBSIDY.)

depressed area A section of a country or city whose people are either unemployed or live at a level near subsistence; in England and Wales, an area subject to severe depression, unemployment, or destitution as defined by special legislation (in which the name becomes "special area"). In the United States an area officially designated "depressed" (as measured against specific standards of destitution) becomes eligible for a wide variety of special federal programs. (See CONGESTED DISTRICT; DEVELOPMENT AREA.)

desegregation. See INTEGRATION.

design-concept team A group of experts who plan a highway project. The first such team was assembled in 1967 to study the Baltimore links in the interstate highway system. For the first time it was officially acknowledged that road-building entails more than simply running a bulldozer through neighborhoods to make way for more automobiles. The concept team was charged with considering the social, economic, and aesthetic implications as well. There were such issues as the displacement of residents and the provision of new housing for them, the selection of a route that would least disturb existing neighborhoods, preservation of areas adjoining the route, and the use of "joint development" to create new facilities and centers along the highway. In short, what was thought to be needed was not only a highway but a new "design concept" that was to consider the road's effect on people as well. There is of course a long distance between concept and fulfillment, and concept teams are not always popular with state road commissions; but, considering the callousness of the highwaymen in the past, the conceiver of the concept deserves credit for his efforts to insinuate conscience into highway-building. (See JOINT DEVELOPMENT.)

design contest   A competition for the best design of a building or project carrying an award of some sort to the winners. Public agencies have employed the device for proposed housing and urban-renewal projects, and some private companies have found it useful for publicity or prestige in connection with their office or commercial buildings. The prize usually includes a contract to design the project.

A jury—generally composed of esteemed architects or planners, an official, and perhaps a builder—wander around a room filled with the submissions, striking down the losers until they are confronted with the more promising residuum, at which time opinions may become irreconcilable and a vote will end the agony.

Opinions differ on the value of design contests. The negative view is that the best practitioners do not deign to enter them; that submissions give too much emphasis to building design and too little to the other relevancies such as site planning, materials, specifications, and financial considerations; that the winning design does not always represent the best work even of the contestant; that the winner is not always the most expert in implementation; that the submission is only an outline concept, the validity of which can be judged only in detailed plans.

In the case of Title I submissions by urban renewers, it is said that the cost of a good submission may run up to $50,000; many who have become involved swear they will never compete again. They argue that the winning design is not necessarily the one that will be translated into mortar and that the award is only the first step in a renegotiation skirmish that eventuates in major modifications. Here, too, the winner may not be the most expert in the difficult implementation that must follow.

Arguments in favor of the design contest are that it brings out the unique plan and gives hope to the ignored young who rarely get a crack at a good project. The variety of submissions, it is said, also educates the inflexibly unimaginative official who would otherwise employ a hack because he knows him or has dealt with him before. Competition, it is argued, challenges favoritism.

Though the design contest is often a chore for the sponsor, an occasional one will season his dull diet; and while a contest sometimes invites a volley of criticism, it may produce a wholesome exception to architectural mediocrities. Having gone through the ordeal once, moreover, the official agency may never venture it again, so the contest cannot do much long-range harm. (See ARCHITECTURE, URBAN.)

design speed Theoretically, the highest speed at which vehicles can safely travel on a road when weather is good and traffic moderate. It is determined for any given highway according to considerations of the course, design of curvatures, super-elevations, sight distances, etc. (See CAPACITY.)

desire line A transportation term denoting a straight line drawn between the origin and destination of a trip. It is not necessarily the actual route of a journey (which has to follow the existing road system) but symbolizes the need or desire to make the trip. When put on a graph, desire lines summarize the data collected by an origin-destination survey. The composite width of the lines connecting the same points or zones indicates the demand for movement in particular corridors and the proportion of total trips likely to occur in each. (See ORIGIN-DESTINATION SURVEY; TRANSPORTATION PLANNING.)

desocialization; denationalization The sale or other disposition of a public enterprise to private interests. Examples in the United States are the disposition of the public domain and the more recent disposition of the Federal National Mortgage Association. Just as there has been socialization of some things in the United States and in Europe (public housing, utilities, land), there has been some desocialization in the USSR, where home-grown products are now retailed by the farmer and where a growing proportion of the housing is being bought for cooperative ownership. The old Marxian concept was that with the socialization of all enterprises, the state would "wither away," but with complete socialization it might not have a place whither to wither to. (See CAPITALISM; SOCIALISM; WELFARE STATE, BUSINESS.)

detribalization The fading or dissolution of tribal ties, customs, and loyalties due to contact with a new culture or environment, particularly the urban environment. Urbanization in Africa and elsewhere in the world's hinterlands has been one of the main forces challenging the ancient tribalisms and bringing new conflicts and contrasts: between barter or trade-in-kind and money economies; between human cooperation in meeting life's challenges and the specialization of function that accompanies industrialization; between animism and the missionary's crucifix; between old established ethics and those imported from more acquisitive societies; between sharing and individual savings; between tribal conventions and imported governmental systems; between the political demands of the rising central state and the village, chief, elders, tribe, and individual. The old system of gift that once carried its own dignity confronts the interdictions against bribery in the new order. Furthermore, the task of setting up an independent civil service confronts the nepotistic inclinations that derive naturally from tribal fealty. The old reverence toward the chief is converted by some into a faith in the omniscience of a new prime minister. What would be looked upon as the loyal opposition in British politics is sometimes confused with a hostile tribe. The shift from village to city or from tribe to family as the basic social unit has effected a mutation in ways of life that had stood fast for more than a millennium.

Tribal life itself may seem as strange to a Western visitor as polygamy or animism. Yet the ancient tribal structure is a proved social and political organization with its own culture, traditions, rituals, and loyalties. Its cooperative features would win the admiration of the most committed utopians. An orderly life has been built around communal ownership and communal effort—whether setting the sprawling fishnets and pulling them in laden with herring or gathering food and fuel from the soil. In a precarious environment that few "civilized" men could endure, the primordial tribe has held its members together for centuries in simple dignity.

developed area   An area of land on which site improvements such as grading and utility installation have been made and buildings erected. The term is also used to distinguish an economically developed country like the United States from an underdeveloped or developing country like India or Liberia. (See LAND, IMPROVED; LAND, RAW.)

developer. See BUILDER.

development area A term in England defining (under the Distribution of Industry Act, 1945) an area to which government guides new industry to relieve "congested districts" and to provide a better economic balance within the country. Development areas were originally classified as "depressed areas" and thereafter as "special areas." (See CONGESTED DISTRICT; DEPRESSED AREA.)

development plan A plan required of every local planning authority under Britain's Town and Country Planning Act of 1947. The term is practically synonymous with the earlier "master plan." Each authority must survey its area, submit a report of the survey, and file a plan showing how its land is to be used and the stages by which its development will be brought into effect. The development plan, among many other details, must also designate land that should be compulsorily acquired. The term in the United States refers generally to any plan of development.

development rights The rights to develop land (as distinguished from ownership of it) transferred to the British Government by law in 1947, payment for which was to be made out of a "global sum" of £300 million. The proposal was made in an extensive report for the government by a commission headed by Lord Uthwatt. The law was found to be administratively cumbersome, and major modifications followed. (See UTHWATT REPORT.)

devise A gift (particularly of real property) by will.

discrimination The unfair treatment of a person or group as compared with others. It is not wrongful to discriminate unless in doing so one denies to others the equality of treatment one expects for one's self. While race, religion, color, creed, or origin are the main criteria of discrimination, they are not the only ones. Wrongful and often illegal discrimination occurs on account of age or sex, and law may widen the scope of the proscriptions.

Anti-discrimination laws exist in a few countries, including England and the United States, and a number of national constitutions contain provisions against unfair treatment of minorities that are respected more

in the breach than in the observance. (See CIVIL RIGHTS; FAIR HOUSING
LAWS; PREJUDICE; SEGREGATION.)

discrimination, federal housing   Discrimination by federal housing agencies, now unlawful. From 1935 to 1949 racial and religious discrimination was exhorted by the Federal Housing Administration and made a
condition of FHA housing assistance; the agency insisted on social and
racial "homogeneity" as the price of its insurance. In its official manuals
the agency urged the "prevention of infiltration," warned against "adverse influences" such as "unharmonious racial groups," and pressed the
use of a "model covenant" against occupancy by "persons of any race
other than ———," with the acceptable race to be inserted as agreed to by
the FHA. Methods were described for enforcing "homogeneity," exclud-
ing "undesirables," and preventing "mixed neighborhoods." FHA also
advocated the use of deed restrictions to bar occupancy by "undesirable" minorities and described the nuisances to be guarded against—
"stables and pig pens," hills, ravines, high-speed traffic arteries as well
as occupancy by "undesirable" minorities. It urged "artificial barriers"
to accomplish segregation and exclusion. FHA was not the only
federal agency to discriminate. Similar practices prevailed in the Home
Loan Bank System and the National Housing Agency.

Almost two years after the Supreme Court outlawed the enforcement
of the racially restrictive covenant (1948), FHA finally and grudgingly altered its policies. But in the fifteen years of federally sponsored discrimination millions of homes in thousands of American neighborhoods were
erected with government sanction of racial exclusion. The patterns have
persisted despite the shift in federal policy resulting from President John
F. Kennedy's executive order barring discrimination in federally aided
housing and from the Civil Rights Act of 1968. But at least a federal policy reminiscent of the Nuremberg Laws has been relegated to the ar-
chives of history where, it is hoped, it will remain. (See CIVIL RIGHTS;
DISCRIMINATION; FAIR HOUSING LAWS.)

discrimination in employment   The differential treatment of people when
they are hired, advanced, or discharged on the basis of race, creed, color,
religion, or national origin rather than qualifications. The discrimination
may favor or disfavor one group as against another. It is not illegal *per
se,* but it is illegal when forbidden by statute and when a right is set up in

favor of the victim. Discrimination may be practiced against a person by outright refusal to hire him, openly or subtly; restricting his housing opportunities in the employment area; refusing him the opportunity to apprentice; denying him equal access to education; refusing him proper counseling services or misdirecting him; refusing to license him where a license is required; an employment agency's refusal to recommend him for a job; and a union's refusal to provide him with membership.

There are state and federal laws prohibiting discrimination in employment. Though diminishing, such bias still functions sufficiently to be among the causes of inequality of status and opportunity for blacks, Puerto Ricans, American Indians, Mexican-Americans, and to a more limited extent for other minorities.

district. See CONGESTED DISTRICT; SECTION.

domicile The place where one has his permanent residence and to which, if absent, he intends returning. *Domus* is the Latin word for "house" and supplies the root in many languages. (See DWELLING; ESTABLISHMENT; HOUSE; SHELTER.)

dormitory town. See TOWN, DORMITORY.

doubling up The sharing of dwellings by two or more families. It is reported that in the earlier days of New York's Chinatown as many as three shifts of workers would occupy the same bed, each for an eight-hour stretch. The sheets were "never cold" in what is probably the most extreme prolonged instance of doubling (or tripling) up on record in the United States.

drafting The art of graphic representation, especially of the plans for structures or cities.

drafting, legislative Preparation of bills for submission to a legislative body for debate and action—the work of a legislative drafting department or of an individual. A bill generally takes the name of the legislator who introduces it, although the wording and content of many bills are the work of the draftsman rather than the sponsor. This is particularly true for complicated legislation, which often emanates from an unknown specialist in a government department.

A monument might well be erected to the "Unknown Draftsman," for though England's statutes are said to be "made by the King, the Lords and the Commons," it is the draftsman who is their rightful parent. It is he who reduces the statesman's generalizations to language, and it is upon his misplaced comma or imprecise word that many a kingdom, life, or estate has hung. The Ten Commandments, of course, were written by God. But who can cite the true author of the Code of Hammurabi, the Statutes of Labourers, or the myriad laws hidden in vellum but speaking the will of the world's parliaments?

dummy; straw man   A person who stands in for another in a transaction in which he has no real interest. One type of dummy is the man who buys property for another, the disclosure of whose identity might raise the price. Another is the person working for a title-examination company who, for a fee, signs the bonds on mortgages, thereby assuming the real owner's liability in the event of default. After taking on obligations running into the millions, he periodically goes into bankruptcy to relieve himself of his debts. Another type is the record owner of slum property. Unwilling to assume the hazards of prosecution, the true owner designates someone he can trust to hold the property for him, often taking an unrecorded deed from the dummy and recording it only if and when necessary. Dummies may also be employed by debtors who want to conceal their assets. Dummy officers of corporations are common, particularly when a corporation is first organized. The dummies are usually workers in the lawyer's office who resign shortly after the first meeting. They are dummies for convenience in contrast to dummy officers who stand in for the real parties-in-interest for the purpose of concealment.

duplex   A suite in an apartment house that has rooms on two floors; in England the word is "maisonette." Duplex is also used in the United States to describe a two-family or semi-detached house.

dwelling   A structure designed or occupied as the living quarters of one or more households, usually equipped (in the more developed areas of the world) with cooking, bathing, toilet, and (where necessary) heating facilities.

A "dwelling unit" (d.u.) is a room or group of rooms providing complete living facilities for one household. (See DOMICILE; HOUSE; HOUSING UNIT; SHELTER.)

dwelling, alley A rear house facing an alley. Such dwellings have been classed as unfit for living (in Washington, D.C., for example), but since they are off the main street and quiet they have often been converted into studios and expensive living quarters. The rear houses backing upon the Washington Square mansions in New York City, for example, though once used only for horses, are now stable real estate.

dwelling, multiple Generally a building composed of three or more dwelling units, usually having common access, service system, and use of land. As defined by the Multiple Dwelling Law (1929) of New York State, such a structure has at least three families or more living independently of each other and doing their own cooking on the premises. The term was introduced in this statute, which pioneered important advances in housing legislation. (See APARTMENT.)

dwelling, seasonal A dwelling intended for seasonal rather than year-round use. A beach house or a ski lodge is an example. Seasonal units are often harnessed into year-round use in times of housing shortage.

dynametropolis A metropolis exhibiting continuous and dynamic growth. It is a Doxiadian neologism. A dynametropolis, says Constantinos Doxiadis, may, "in addition to its major urban areas, contain examples of all types of settlements, including agricultural and nomadic."

dynapolis A dynamic city. It is a nonce-word coined by Constantinos Doxiadis and used by him in his frequent writings on cities.

earnest money   Money paid as a binder on a contract of sale. Until the thirteenth century an earnest was a payment made to secure the seller's forbearance from selling to anyone else. The payer of the earnest was free to withdraw by forfeiting the payment, and the seller was free to default upon paying a sum double the amount (or more by some laws). The buyer's right was equivalent to the modern option with liquidated damages for failure to exercise it. Among merchants and in real-estate transactions this has now lost currency in favor of the binding commitment— provided of course that all the terms of sale are set forth in the binder agreement. (See BINDER; OPTION.)

easement   An acquired right of use, interest, or privilege (short of ownership) in lands owned by another, such as an easement of light, of building support, or of right-of-way. Easements are often acquired by highway departments because they entail smaller payments than would be required for outright purchase, yet satisfy a road's land requirements. They may be permanent or limited in time dependent upon the easement agreement.

easement, conservation   An easement acquired by the public and designed to open privately owned lands for recreational purposes or to restrict the use of private land in order to preserve open space and protect certain natural resources. Flooding easements, water-access easements, hiking- and riding-trail easements, and easements not to build are among the common forms. Some easements are negative in that they give the holder the right to prevent the landowner from using his land for specified purposes, such as erecting a billboard or cutting trees. A water-access or hiking easement is affirmative, however, giving the public rights to the use of lakes, streams, trails, and so forth. (See COMPENSABLE REGULATIONS.)

easement, scenic   The grant by a landowner to a road agency of the right to use his land for scenic enhancement. The easement, which is usually bought by state road commissions for the planting of greenery, bars the owner from changing the use or appearance of his land without the agency's consent. Scenic easements are sometimes purchased for all land viewable from the road but more often for particular strips along the way.

ecology   The study of the interrelationships among living organisms and their environments. As a branch of the biological sciences, ecology is concerned with the way plant and animal species distribute themselves and how they adapt to one another and to their total environment. The high degree of complexity and mutual interdependence that characterizes the natural world has suggested analogies to students of the city, who have borrowed a number of terms and concepts from ecology to describe   urban   processes.   (See   ENVIRONMENT;   PHYSIOGRAPHIC DETERMINISM.)

ecology, human   Most broadly, the study of the relationship between man and his environment. When it focuses on the urban environment, it is the study of the spatial distribution in a community of people, groups, and institutions; the relationships among them; and the changes that come about in the distribution through adaptation, competition, and accommodation. Just as patterns of development in the natural world occur in a series of phases—a certain balance among inhabitants is achieved, this equilibrium is upset by some change or intrusion, and a new balance is subsequently achieved—so human communities are held to develop and evolve over time and in space. "Urban ecology" and "human geography" are other terms for the same essential discipline. (See INVASION AND SUCCESSION.)

economic base   The sum of all activities that result in the receipt of income in any form by a city's inhabitants. The economic-base theory holds that the future growth of a particular city or urban region can be reasonably predicted through an analysis of its economic base. The theory distinguishes between basic economic activities, which create goods and services for export, and non-basic or service enterprises, whose products serve only the home area and result in no additional income flowing into the city from outside. The theory argues that the basic industries are the key to a city's economic growth: increased exports bring added income, which encourages capital expansion, which brings the need for added manpower, which increases the need for more local service industries whose additional employees themselves create an increased market for services, and so on. Economic-base analysis has its critics and has been attacked in its most rudimentary premises, but as the simplest technique for analyzing the structure and operation of an urban economy, it continues to be one of the basic tools of practicing urban planners.

economic life   The period during which it is more profitable to keep a building in use and in repair than to scrap or reconstruct it. Put another way, it is the period during which a building has value in excess of its salvage value. The economic life of a building is to be distinguished from the rate of depreciation, the latter being an arbitrary rate allowed by government, whereas a building's economic life, while relevant in fixing the depreciation rate, may be longer or shorter, being measurable by its actual usefulness to the owner. A building may be fully depreciated for tax purposes and still have long economic life. (See DEPRECIATION.)

economic rent.   See RENT, ECONOMIC.

economy house.   See HOUSE, ECONOMY.

economy, mixed.   See MIXED ECONOMY.

ecumenopolis   The city of the future, which, with the open land (and water) surrounding it, will cover the whole earth as a continuous and universal settlement. The term was coined by Doxiadis. "Ecumenopolis, which mankind will have built 150 years from now, can be the real city of man because for the first time in history, man will have one city rather than many cities belonging to different national, racial, religious or local groups, each ready to protect its own members but also ready to fight those from other cities. At the present time ecumenopolis, because of its physical extent, structure and form, will consist of many cities, large and small, interconnected into a system of cities. Ecumenopolis, the unique city of man, will form a continuous, differentiated, but also unified texture consisting of many cells, the human communities." At the end of the twenty-first century, says Doxiadis, ecumenopolis will have a population of twenty to thirty billion people and will operate as one organism.

educational park A large school center composed of consolidated or clustered schools with shared facilities and designed to achieve a racially and economically heterogeneous student population. The educational park was conceived as one of the devices for eliminating school segregation not only within a city but between the city and the suburbs. The economy of scale, it was thought, would facilitate quality education and, by achieving economies, make possible more individualized education as well as the greater use of educational technology. Parks of 100 acres capable of serving up to 20,000 students have been proposed for the larger cities.

efficiency apartment. See APARTMENT, EFFICIENCY.

effluent Liquid sewage discharged by a collection network, various treatment units, or a treatment plant; also, the liquid, solid, or gaseous product discharged or emerging from a process.

An effluent standard is the maximum allowable amount of specific pollutants in discharged sewage as established by regulating agencies to achieve desirable stream standards. (See SEWAGE TREATMENT.)

ekistics The science of human settlements. The word was originated by Constantinos Doxiadis, who has given the name to a book and a magazine and to the Athens Centre of Ekistics. He writes: "Ekistics, although directed at human settlements, is obliged to include large parts of the problem of production. . . . It must include an even greater part of the problem of transportation, . . . and finally it must cover the total aspect of residence and the shells of human settlements. . . . There are many functional aspects of space which can just as well be covered by other disciplines. It is, however, the role of Ekistics to cut through them and provide the synthesis necessary for an approach to problems of terrestrial space within human settlements." (See CITY PLANNING.)

emergency shelter. See SHELTER, EMERGENCY.

eminent domain The right of a government to acquire private property for public use or benefit upon payment of just compensation. It is an attribute of sovereignty and is eminent in the sense that it is paramount. While the line between police power and eminent domain is a fine one, the essential difference is that in the latter the property is taken for actual public use or benefit. In England (where it is called "compulsory purchase"), determination of the legality of the public use and the nature of the compensation is a legislative function. In the United States this is subject to judicial review. The terms "eminent domain" and "condemnation" are used interchangeably in the United States, although condemnation is also applied to the demolition by public authority of a dangerous structure where no compensation is paid and the condemned property is not actually acquired.

Eminent domain can be exercised by all three levels of government in the United States, but it must be within each of their prescribed prerogatives. The city, for example, may acquire property for schools, public housing, public buildings, streets, transit, courts, prisons, etc.; the state may acquire property for roads and other purposes, many of which are similar to the city's; the federal government, as a limited sovereignty, may acquire property only for those purposes the Constitution authorizes. Since federal powers have broadened considerably, so has the federal exercise of eminent domain.

Eminent domain followed a somewhat different development in the United States than in other countries. The nation was largely developed by private interests—railroads, bridge companies, private irrigation districts, utility companies, and the like—which were frequently given the acquisition power by statute. The practice has continued, although most exercises of the power are now by public agencies. Another characteristic has been the more liberal exercise of the power by states and cities. Land in the United States was plentiful, widely owned, and, like any other commodity, freely exchangeable for cash. People lacked the deep attachment to the site that was characteristic of Europe; nor did land-ownership carry as much prestige. This attitude has carried over to the present day, when the public purposes for which property may be taken include many that were formerly viewed as unauthorized. The one ethic with a claim to universality, for example, has been that the property of one person could not be forcibly taken simply to be turned over to another. Yet this is close to what has been authorized in urban-renewal operations, where private property is taken in the name of slum or blight clearance or better planning and resold to private interests for such redevelopment as high-cost housing, private garages, parking lots, shopping centers, and the like. The courts have been liberal in such authorizations because eminent domain, unlike the tax and police powers, is the one public power affording compensation as a concomitant of its exercise. The desperate need for rebuilding cities has been another factor.

Whether cities or states can take open land by eminent domain for new towns is still an undetermined question. It is a frontier legal issue on which the character of the nation's future physical development will hinge. But if it is an instance of road-building, park development, or other acknowledged public purpose the courts are likely to approve. (See CONDEMNATION; CONFISCATION; EXPROPRIATION; POLICE POWER; PUBLIC PURPOSE; URBAN RENEWAL.)

enabling act Legislation authorizing cities, governmental agencies, and sometimes private groups to carry out an undertaking or project; for example, the state statute empowering a housing authority to build, manage, and finance public housing.

encroachment An unauthorized extension of a building or part of a building upon the land of another. Depending on its seriousness, and on whether it has been authorized or acquiesced in, it may or may not justify a rejection of the title by a prospective purchaser.

encumbrance An interest or right in real property that diminishes the value of the property subject to it, but does not necessarily prevent its conveyance to another. Mortgages, taxes, and judgments are encumbrances (also known as liens). Restrictions, easements, and reservations are other types of encumbrances. (See LIEN; MORTGAGE.)

endogenous; exogenous Terms borrowed by city planners from botany, where endogenous means "growing or proceeding from within" while exogenous means "having external origins." In planning, the terms are used to distinguish variables that are part of the system and are more manipulable by the planner from those that are of external origin and largely beyond his control or calculation, though affecting his plan. The annual capital budget of a municipality for which he is planning would be an endogenous factor (his recommendations would influence it); congressional appropriations for national housing and urban-development programs would be an exogenous factor.

entail   The limitation of the inheritance of land to a specific line of heirs so that the land can never be legally transferred. The object of entails is to preserve estates in the hands of successive and cohesive generations of the same family. It was a concomitant of feudalism and disappeared in many countries following the French Revolution. Entailing land was inconsonant with the leanings toward freehold ownership of the Founding Fathers and is against public policy in the United States, where the disposition of land is limited to no more than two lives in being. (See FEUDAL TENURE; LAND FRAGMENTATION; PRIMOGENITURE; REPARCELATION.)

entrepreneur   One who assumes the risk and management of a business. With reference to housing, the entrepreneur is usually the initiator and organizer of the building process. The term was originally used as an alternative name for "employer." Adam Smith used the word "undertaker" (now a live entrepreneur engaged in burying dead ones). John Stuart Mill expressed regret that the French word "entrepreneur" had not won entry into the English language. It has since been naturalized and generally accepted.

environment   The sum of all external conditions influencing the growth and development of an organism. Also, all that is apart from and surrounds an observer or something being observed. A distinction is commonly made between the natural environment (air, water, trees) and that made by man (a room, a street, a city). Urbanists, who used to be primarily concerned with the improvement of the man-made environment, have become increasingly concerned with the dislocations caused in the natural one. Studies suggest, for example, that cities can change climates, contribute to droughts and flooding, pollute air and water, disrupt delicate systems of interdependence among flora and fauna, and contribute to a host of other ecological disasters only now being guessed at. (See ECOLOGY; PHYSIOGRAPHIC DETERMINISM.)

equality   The state of being equal in legal, political, economic, and social rights and status. An older and broader definition would include parity in dignity, rank, and knowledge. The doctrine of equality holds that the resources and devices of a country should be directed toward equalizing the condition of *all* its people, in their ability, achievement, and excellence. It rejects equivalence as a substitute, viewing this as a sanction of separatism. It supports the premise that it is the environment in the broadest sense that elevates or subordinates men. Since government has now intervened to manipulate that environment in housing and neighborhoods, in social, educational, recreational, and other facilities, it follows that government has assumed a substantial portion of the responsibility for eliminating any appearance of inequality that is the consequence of environment or public default. Government now has duties and in performing them must help bring people toward a more equal posture in the society by use of every relevant and practicable facility at its command.

Inequalities are emphasized with the expansion of urbanization. Here government has greater obligations than it has assumed to date—to strive for more equal opportunity among its citizens; to assume the responsibility nationally for improving education and health where the beleaguered cities can no longer do so; to eliminate poverty by supporting those who cannot raise themselves out of their lowly status; to improve the environment that impairs the chances of those depressed by it; to intervene with its vast resources wherever the private mechanism falters or fails.

It is not an easy road to travel, but if the objective is identified, the commitment made, the purpose pursued, and the proper means provided to implement it, the prospect of fulfillment in the democratic, technologically developed nations will be better than elsewhere. Yet there will still be no assurance, when full equality is achieved, that man will be happier or that it will thereafter endure. (See CIVIL RIGHTS.)

equity The value of property above all mortgages, liens, or charges; also, that amount which an owner or investor has or must put up from his own funds above what he borrows in order to complete a purchase. Equity is what a home purchaser puts up out of his own savings and what he, unlike a renter, builds up as he pays off his monthly costs. It is both the first requirement and one of the main incentives for home-ownership. (See LEVERAGE; OWNERSHIP.)

equity insurance The insurance of homes against foreclosure due to the owner's death, illness, or unemployment. For odd reasons, a nationally sponsored program of equity insurance has never received the approval of the federal government, with the result that many owners lose their homes when unemployment or misfortune disables them from paying installments of interest, principal, or taxes.

The principal hazards in home-ownership are unemployment and curtailment of income. In 1962 these were the reasons for defaults for 35 per cent of all FHA borrowers and about 40 per cent of Veterans Administration borrowers. The second most important factor was "death or illness in family."

Equity insurance would be a proper use of the federal insurance function and make both the ownership and mortgage structures sounder in the long run. Additional protection against the death of the breadwinner might also be given through ordinary life insurance or through cheap savings-bank insurance, as in Massachusetts and New York. Homes with conventional mortgages could also be insured, subject to approval of the risk and the fixing of an appropriate premium. If the insurance were issued on mortgages given by savings and loan associations, these societies would be sounder operations and the Home Loan Bank System would be spared the embarrassment of bailing them out whenever they are confronted with multiple mortgage defaults.

An insurance fund protecting the owner would benefit the government by preventing a large-scale loss of homes, a deflationary movement, and a capital depreciation due to a glut in the home market; dispensing with the need for huge federal outlays all at once; making federally chartered mortgage institutions sounder operations and cutting down on federal advances to them by the Home Loan Bank System; making owners less inclined to drop their homes when values are down; saving the government major expenditures in repairs, foreclosure charges, and resale costs upon repossession. (See DEFAULT; DELINQUENCY; FORECLOSURE.)

equity of redemption   The right of a mortgagor, upon paying the arrears of principal, interest, and costs, to recover his real property, which by the terms of the mortgage became the mortgagee's property upon his default. Redemption rights may also exist in long-term tenancies unless waived. The equity of redemption is generally defined by statute. When favoring the defaulting owner with too many rights, it is apt to discourage mortgage lending.

equity, sweat   The interest one acquires in property by contributing his labor or services instead of his money. Contribution in labor or services is permitted under certain federal housing programs, such as Section 235 of the 1968 Housing Act, which is designed to facilitate home-ownership by low-income families. The required down payment of $200 (or 3 per cent of family income) can be paid either in money or equivalent labor.

equivalent elimination The elimination by demolition, rehabilitation, or repair of a number of unsafe or unsanitary units equal to the number of new public-housing units built by any community. Made a requirement in the U.S. Housing Act of 1937, it induced considerable demolition of slums—often accentuating housing shortage, overcrowding, and higher rents in the residual slum inventory. (See HOUSING, PUBLIC.)

escape hatch. See URBAN ESCAPE HATCH.

escheat The reversion of property to the state by reason of lack of heirs or of a lawful proprietor.

escrow A deed, money, or property put in the keeping of a disinterested third party pending performance of obligations specified in the escrow agreement.

establishment The place where one is set up for one's business or residence, including furniture, grounds, and fittings; also, an institution or place of business with its fixtures and staff.

estate The property in land that a person possesses in aggregate. It often also includes the personalty as well. If the possessor dies, it becomes known as the "decedent's estate."

Euclidean zoning. See ZONING, EUCLIDEAN.

eviction Ouster of persons from occupancy of a property. Eviction proceedings represent the legal process for the recovery of property by virtue of a paramount right recognized by law or for a default for which eviction is authorized. Eviction of occupants is now also effected to make way for urban renewal, public housing, roads, or other public improvements. (See RELOCATION; SOLATIUM.)

exception. See VARIANCE.

excess condemnation. See CONDEMNATION, EXCESS.

exemplary school; magnet school A model school with model programs designed to attract students of varying racial and social characteristics, induce middle-class white families to remain in the city, induce others to return, and provide better opportunities for a common educational experience for city and suburban school populations. Such schools are planned to serve all the students in a small city or draw them from diverse sections of a larger city.

exogenous. See ENDOGENOUS.

Experimental City One of many conceptualizations of the ideal city, with a tentative location in Minnesota or the Great Plains. The prime mover of the project has been Athelstan Spilhaus, financed by substantial federal research money. He envisioned a self-contained city with a population not to exceed 250,000 that would employ all the technological advances and innovations, such as computer-controlled transport pods, underground services, "symbiosis of industries," and reuse of wastes including derelict automobiles. Spilhaus viewed present cities as obsolete ("we need urban dispersal, not urban renewal"), and hoped his experiment would be the progenitor of a new kind of livable environment free of congestion, fumes, dirty water, and noise. A Comsat-type (but non-profit) corporation would build and operate the City. "Experimental City would be far enough from urban areas so that it can develop self-sufficiency and not be hampered by the restrictive practices of a dominant neighboring community."

Existing experience suggests difficulties in the self-containment theory and in population limitations. Planned cities seem to function best when near larger cities. People living in planned cities seem to like them provided there is an unplanned city nearby. If there is none close at hand, an unplanned one will probably be created on its periphery. This casts some doubt on the practicality of an isolated city in an isolated environment. There is also considerable doubt about the prospects of limiting growth if and when growth asserts its demands. As with all such ideas, modifications will have to be made when the ideal is translated into brick and mortar. The Experimental City, if ever built, will not be an exception.

expropriation   The action of the state in taking or modifying the property rights of individuals through the exercise of sovereignty. The term is often used to describe eminent domain but might also be used to describe a more confiscatory taking. (See CONDEMNATION; CONFISCATION; EMINENT DOMAIN.)

external economies   The benefits businesses derive from the independent activities of other businesses, or advantages that accrue to them without their having to change their organization, internal structure, or outputs. A stock exchange generates the need for offices, banks, lawyers, printers, and many other skills and services, which, of course, a variety of other enterprises are free to use. Firms of the same character or dependent upon one another for sales, supplies, and services similarly generate external economies.

externalities; side effects; spillovers; repercussion effects   The indirect consequences, for those other than the direct beneficiaries or targets, of a course of action. Externalities may be good, bad, or both, and they are very important considerations in setting public policy. An analysis of the side effects of a private action may suggest some form of restriction or incentive, depending on whether the side effects are desirable or deplorable. Much of the recent anti-pollution legislation is based on increased understanding of the spillovers of modern industrial processes and motor transport.

The examination of externalities in public programs is also important and often much more complex. For example, an analysis of a highway-building program might show that congestion and travel time between suburbs and central city would be cut and that retail sales in downtown stores would increase—in other words, that the program would fullfill its objectives. On the other hand, the poor families uprooted to make way for the road might be paying an enormous and disproportionate cost for the added convenience and profit to others. Enlightened public policy would modify the highway program or at least strive to compensate the losers out of the increased welfare to the gainers. (See COST-BENEFIT ANALYSIS; FALL-OUT; PPBS.)

extraterritorial powers; extraterritoriality Powers a city is permitted to exercise beyond its own boundaries. Extraterritoriality is a departure from the standard doctrine that the powers of a municipal corporation are limited by its borders and cannot be exercised outside them. In most cases extraterritorial authority is either expressly conferred by state legislation, or it may be inferred from other powers and duties. States are fairly liberal in permitting the exercise of proprietary powers (which include doing business, holding and operating a variety of property, and providing services) outside local borders. But the grant of extraterritorial *governmental* powers (such as planning, zoning, and establishing subdivision regulations) is almost always limited to adjacent and unincorporated territory. Extraterritoriality is an attractive means of rationalizing local government because it requires little governmental reorganization. But it is hedged in by a variety of statutory limitations, and its effective use is rare.

One overlooked and apparently untested use of such powers would help break the housing Mason-Dixon line. While there are virtually no precedents, there is some reason to believe that the courts would sustain a city's right to build housing outside its boundaries for its low-income households. Cities have long owned considerable suburban property in the form of cemeteries, quarries, reservoirs, parks, and the like. Indeed, many used to own poorhouses and workhouses in the hinterlands, where they sheltered and at the same time isolated the poor of an earlier age. Doubtless an experiment along these lines would encounter obstructionist zoning, taxpayer suits, and eminent-domain proceedings, and of course a state legislature could expressly deny such powers, taking them out of the hands of the courts. Still, direct construction or purchase of housing by the city or one of its agents deserves to be tried as one possible device in the arsenal needed to open the suburbs to the city's poor, both black and white.

exurbanite A person of the upper-middle class who lives in the semirural areas beyond the suburbs but who works in the metropolis. He is viewed as conforming to the standardized social and cultural routines that characterize his class. The word was coined by A. C. Spectorsky.

exurbia The area beyond the more heavily settled suburbs of a city, distinguished by higher-income commuters, class consciousness, and exclusiveness.

Fair Deal   The term used by President Truman to characterize the program he presented to the 81st Congress in 1949. The program called for higher taxes, curbs on inflation, more housing, and other reforms. It was during the Truman administration that racial egalitarianism was spurred. The postwar atmosphere engendered by the United Nations Charter, the Supreme Court decision outlawing enforcement of racial covenants, the Report of the President's Committee on Civil Rights, and the Truman order to FHA to cease its discriminatory practices gave impetus to a drive against racial discrimination in housing, which reached a higher tempo during the administrations of President Kennedy and President Johnson. (See GREAT SOCIETY; NEW DEAL.)

fair housing laws   City, state, or federal laws forbidding discrimination in the sale, rental, or financing of housing. State and city commissions are usually set up to administer the laws following a prescribed procedure. When a complaint is filed an investigation is made, after which the complaint is either dismissed or "probable cause" found of discriminatory practices. If cause is found, an effort is made to have the owner accept the excluded person as well as stop his discriminatory procedures. If this fails, a public hearing will be ordered. If, after hearing testimony, a finding of discrimination is made, a court-enforceable order is entered. Public hearings are infrequent because most cases are either settled or dismissed.

The fair housing laws have proven effective in jurisdictions in which they have been properly enforced. There is also some educational value in putting the government on the side of fair play. But while these laws have opened up some housing to minorities, they have proven no complete solvent for either discrimination or segregation. The minority influx into the central cities has radically altered the racial composition of neighborhoods and schools; many among the minorities prefer to remain in the ghettos rather than challenge the white areas; the influx of non-whites has accelerated a white flight from central-city neighborhoods into suburbs, where the principal discriminatory practices have now taken root. Subtle devices such as zoning laws and other abuses of the police and eminent-domain powers are employed to discourage the entry of minorities or to dislodge them from established footholds. The low incomes of many non-whites, moreover, disable them from competing for the better housing in the suburbs even when such homes are opened to them. Fair housing laws can operate successfully only when there is a dual program—one to bar discrimination and another to build ample housing within the means of the minority groups, but such housing programs in 1968 were little more than token efforts.

The federal Fair Housing Law can be helpful if properly enforced and if coupled with an adequate federally aided housing production program. It represents an inversion of policy from the direct encouragement of housing discrimination by FHA and the Home Loan Bank System during the 1930s and 40s. Whether it will also achieve equality of access to housing will depend largely upon the fluctuations in public and official attitudes and their effect on the enforcing agencies. (See DISCRIMINATION, FEDERAL HOUSING.)

fall-out   The ancillary incidents of a transaction or program. Its derivation is from the airborne particles of radioactive and other materials resulting from an atomic explosion. In its derivative meaning, the incidents may be good or bad; in the original sense, they can only be bad. (See EXTERNALITIES.)

family   A group of two or more persons related by blood, marriage, or adoption residing together. For the purpose of housing or planning analysis, they must be living together to constitute a family. The term is commonly used interchangeably with household, but strictly speaking a family is only a type of household, for single individuals living alone and unrelated persons living together are also grouped under this category. A nuclear family encompasses the immediate family (husband, wife, and children), while an extended family includes grandparents and collateral relatives.

The extended family has been losing ground steadily with urbanization. The old sprawling house that sheltered eight or more members and several generations has given way to the three-bedroomer for the younger couples and the efficiency apartment for the older folks. In the more developed countries suburbanization has extended the distance between them, while in the less developed countries, detribalization and the growth of cities have severed their once strong ties. In Lagos, Nigeria, one can still find a family unit of as many as eighty in a single house, but even here the construction of a large suburban development in Sure Lere has begun to fragment the old tribal pattern that sought to re-establish a foothold in the cities. In the United States, as incomes have doubled, families have undoubled; the professional baby-sitter has replaced the mother-in-law; and with the increase of mobility and migration, the distance between relatives has widened. The mobile house, the movement of the elderly to warmer climates, extensive shifts from one house to another (a family moving on the average once every five years), accelerated desertion of the cities for the suburbs by younger families, the shifts of work opportunities, and increased incomes have all contributed to a severance of old family ties. (See HOUSEHOLD; LIFE CYCLE.)

FAR. See FLOOR-AREA RATIO.

farm population. See POPULATION, FARM.

feasibility study A survey to determine the practicality of an enterprise before a commitment is made. It is often undertaken in advance of urban renewal and other federally assisted projects.

Federal Housing Administration (FHA) The Federal Housing Administration was created in 1934 to insure mortgages on residential property. FHA does not lend money or build housing but insures loans made by private lending institutions for housing construction, rehabilitation, and purchase. The agency was conceived during the New Deal depression period as one of the pump-primers for home-building, but it has survived as a prop for lending institutions and builders. Its operations, sustained by insurance premiums and investments, have been a main force in the development of suburbia. More recently, its other activities have included programs to assist low- and moderate-income families to obtain decent accommodations. Competition from the savings and loan associations, offering liberal loans without insurance premiums or red tape, has reduced its role in private building operations. It has been argued that FHA insurance has little effect in reducing interest rates on the average home and that, except where its operations serve a social function, it has little justification for existence. (See COVENANT; DISCRIMINATION, FEDERAL HOUSING; EQUITY INSURANCE; "608.")

federalism, creative   A term implying a kind of constructive but vague joint venture between the federal government and the states, in which federal purse, power, and prestige would be employed through the states to advance the general welfare.

"Marble-cake federalism" is the mixing up of functions among the theoretically separate levels of government. The term is ascribed to Morton Grodzins but has been modified by Daniel P. Moynihan into "wedding-cake federalism," a multi-tiered system of bureaucracies and governmental units surmounted by the President, with federal funds providing the icing.

federation; borough plan   An approach to city governmental reorganization that assigns area-wide functions to an area-wide or metropolitan government and leaves local functions to existing municipalities (sometimes the municipalities are enlarged in territory and called boroughs). In Canada, both the Toronto and Winnipeg areas have adopted this form of government. While advocated by many, no federation plan has ever been adopted in the United States, although the urban county and multi-purpose special district are somewhat similar in that they provide a clear separation between area-wide and local functions. (See METROPOLITAN COUNCIL; METROPOLITAN SPECIAL DISTRICT; URBAN COUNTY.)

fee   Ownership of the title to real property. (See FREEHOLD; LAND TENURE; OWNERSHIP.)

feedback   Originally the returning by a computer of part of its output to be reintroduced as input, particularly for purposes of correction or control (or that portion of a system's output or behavior that is fed back). Feedback also means the continuous automatic furnishing of data dealing with the output of a machine to an automatic control device so that input can be adjusted and mistakes corrected. Feedback has now broadened in usage to include any communications network that produces action in response to an input of information and includes the results of its own action in the new information by which it modifies its subsequent behavior.

The planner uses feedback when he modifies programs as implementation begins and experience is gained. Planners get another kind of feedback when they plan for a local community without giving it some say or announce a program without clearance at the top.

fee simple The largest possible estate in land, of indefinite duration and inheritable without limitation; what is commonly meant when the word "ownership" is used. (See FREEHOLD.)

fee tail An estate of inheritance limited to one particular class of heirs of the person to whom it is granted. (See ENTAIL.)

feudal tenure The numerous types of land-ownership common during the feudal period in England. These have left their mark on the English law of property to this day, though whatever survived of these forms in America was abolished after the Revolution.

When William the Conqueror asserted the right of conquest over Harold's land, many of his followers could not speak English and wanted to return to Normandy. Many did so by renting to others the English land awarded to them for their military services. The government placed numerous "burdens" on the land to maintain control—*i.e.,* fealty, wardship, homage, marriage (a lord's right to prevent a tenant's daughter from wedding an enemy), relief, primer seizin, aids, fines for alienation, and escheats. Other minor types of tenure included tenancy-at-will, tenancy-at-sufferance, dower, curtesy, gage (mortgage), and elegit (a creditor's right to take over half the debtor's land). Tenancy-at-will, dower, curtesy, and mortgage are still known in England and the United States.

The feudal system was modified by the Magna Carta and thereafter, but the respect for land-ownership, despite changes in rights and forms, has survived. Indeed, some of the 999-year leases made at the time of William the Conqueror are still in effect and some are now being negotiated for renewal. (See ASSEMBLAGE; ENTAIL; LAND FRAGMENTATION; PRIMOGENITURE; REPARCELATION.)

FHA. See FEDERAL HOUSING ADMINISTRATION.

filtering   The theory that a unit of housing goes through a gradual decline, which makes it available to successively lower income groups until it becomes unlivable and is replaced. Thus, additions to the high-priced housing stock would cause high-income families to shift to the more desirable new housing, leaving their present units available; the surplus housing would bring a price decline, and the vacated housing would then become available to the income group next in line. In this fashion, each income group would move one notch up the housing spectrum, and the housing vacated at the lowest level would ultimately be demolished. Espousers of the theory argue that subsidized housing for the poorer families is unnecessary—the market, left to its own forces, would take care of everybody.

The filtering theory assumes that there is a fairly high interchangeability among housing units and that there would not be enough housing demand at each price level ready to absorb the newly vacated housing and thereby keep up the prices. However, there has been a continuous demand for nearly all grades of housing in most countries for many years, and this checks most filtering. Market forces tend to keep supply at a level closely matching demand. When a surplus in any income class appears, housing construction generally stops and so does filtration.

With the surge of Negroes into the central cities, however, considerable filtration has occurred—not because of additions to the high-rental stock but because of a rapid exodus to the suburbs and panic movements by whites. Here it may be noted that decent, used housing often becomes available to the low-income black families at rents or prices within their means. (See HOUSING-MARKET ANALYSIS.)

financing, permanent   A long-term mortgage loan on a building recently completed. Permanent financing is not permanent (though it may seem that way to the indebted party) but only long-term. It generally follows the temporary financing (or construction loan) made during construction, which it pays off at the closing.

A builder of an apartment house who needs money to pay his subcontractors during the building operation may arrange his financing in one of three ways: by securing temporary financing through a building loan advanced to him serially as the building goes up and paying the advances off with a long-term loan secured upon completion; by arranging a combined building loan and permanent mortgage so that he will receive serial payments during construction and the balance upon completion, at which time the loan moneys are converted into a term mortgage; by arranging long-term financing before he builds and, on the basis of the take-out available to him upon completion, securing temporary financing. (A take-out is the agreement by the long-term mortgagee to pay off the temporary financing).

Permanent or long-term financing may run anywhere from five years to thirty or forty. In the longer-term mortgages, the amortization payments will generally be enough to retire the mortgage, leaving no balance at the end of its term. (See LOAN, CONSTRUCTION; MORTGAGE; REFINANCING; TAKE-OUT.)

flat In British usage, a suite of rooms on one floor forming a complete residence. It is the equivalent of the American apartment; an American-style apartment house is a "block of flats." In England, "apartment" means a single room. (See APARTMENT.)

floating city. See CITY, FLOATING.

floating zone. See ZONE, FLOATING.

floor area, gross The sum of the total areas of the floors of a building measured from the exterior of walls or from the center line of walls separating buildings. Usually included in the calculations are basement space, the area taken up by elevator shafts and stairwells at each floor, attic space eight feet or more in height, floor space in penthouses, balconies, mezzanines, and accessory buildings except those used for off-street parking. Commonly excluded are cellar space, attics of less than eight feet, space used for mechanical equipment, and any exterior stairs.

floor-area ratio (FAR) A formula for regulating building volume using an index figure that expresses the total permitted floor area as a multiple of the area of the lot. For example, a ratio of 2 on a 10,000-square-foot lot would permit a two-story building with 10,000 square feet on each floor, or a ten-story building with 2000 square feet on each floor, or a variety of similar combinations, with the total floor area not exceeding 20,000 square feet. Of course, economic and design considerations as well as zoning requirements (particularly setback and coverage regulations) limit the options in the actual situation. Some zoning ordinances offer a bonus in the FAR for reduced lot coverage in order to encourage more open space.

foreclosure Legal proceedings to deprive a mortgagor of ownership rights because of a violation of the mortgage terms, such as an unpaid obligation. Foreclosure is usually followed by sale of the property to recover the debt. Cities can also foreclose properties and sell them to recover unpaid taxes. (See DEFAULT; DELINQUENCY; EQUITY INSURANCE.)

Fourierism A nineteenth-century social movement based on a blueprint for the reorganization of society conceived by François Marie Charles Fourier. In Fourier's scheme, population was to be grouped into phalansteries, each composed of some four hundred families, who were to live in a common building, work at farming or handicraft, with all profits going into a common purse; talent and industry were to be rewarded, and no one was to be allowed to remain indigent or lack enjoyment of certain luxuries and public amusements. Fourier envisioned a social order governed by pure reason. He saw waste in competitive organization and great savings in community kitchens, common living quarters, and cooperative buying. In this he is credited with being the father of cooperation. Fourierism was disseminated in the United States, where several colonies were established, including the famous Brook Farm. (See COMMUNISTIC SETTLEMENTS; COOPERATIVE.)

freehold A form of tenure of real property equivalent to fee simple; what is commonly meant by full ownership, including the underlying land; also, the estate itself. (See FEE; FEE SIMPLE.)

friction of space A phrase embodying the idea that any movement is costly because it is restrained by gravity and physical friction and because it takes time. In order to overcome distance one has to expend time, energy, fuel, endure discomfort and delay, etc. Planners and economists have found it convenient to summarize these quantifiable and nonquantifiable costs under this term. Friction of space plays an enormous role in the location of uses and activities in relation to the land and to one another. Thus a manufacturing concern may locate near a supply of raw materials, near its labor force, near its customers, near the environmental amenities valued by its executives and their wives, near a convenient means of transport, or in a location that simultaneously minimizes the aggregate cost of transportation to all of these. Theoretically, it locates in order to minimize the friction of space. (See GRAVITY MODEL; LINKAGE.)

frontage The front part of a building or lot; also, the extent of the front —for example, the footage running along a road; also, the land between the front of a building and the street.

front money The money an applicant for a government project must show to demonstrate his ability to proceed. It may not and need not be his own. Front money may also mean the seed money to pay some of the initial expenses of a transaction by a non-profit corporation or other party, its purpose being to get the wheels turning. End money is a reserve earmarked for use if project cost exceeds estimates. (See SEED MONEY.)

galleria. See ARCADE.

game theory A branch of information theory applied to the solution of various decision-making problems. It analyzes the choices to be made in situations of conflict or competition and takes into account the actions of the other side(s), which it assumes will be rational and based on that group's own goals, resources, and information. It entails a strategy for maximizing gains and minimizing losses within given limitations. It is used extensively by military and business circles and occasionally in city-planning circles.

garden apartment. See APARTMENT, GARDEN.

garden city; green-belt town "A town," as defined by the British Garden Cities Association, "which is planned for industry and healthy living of a size that makes possible a full measure of social life but not larger; surrounded by a permanent belt of rural land, the whole of the land being in public ownership or held in trust for the community."

Also, the planning concept first formulated by Ebenezer Howard, author of *Garden Cities of Tomorrow* (1902). His formulation of an ideal new community had three principal characteristics: public ownership or control of all land, in order to determine land use and prevent speculation; a careful design of the whole city, including determining its optimum size, to make it economically and socially balanced; a belt of permanent farmland surrounding the city.

There was nothing novel in the idea of building new towns, but Howard had the distinction of propagandizing the idea when it was needed. Not only did he shape the concepts, but he advanced them into actual demonstrations. "Town and country," said Howard, "must be married and out of this union will spring a new hope, a new life, a new civilization." A new hope there was, though a new life can hardly be ascribed to it, and a new civilization is still a long way off. The first garden city was built at Letchworth and the second at Welwyn near London.

general welfare A Constitutional abstraction meaning the public interest. The term created rifts among the Founding Fathers, baffled political scientists, invited judicial evasions and contradictions, and has remained one of the unresolved issues in American politics. Whether the federal government has the power to act broadly to resolve urban problems, regulate the many interstate operations in the burgeoning economy, implement regional planning, create a federal police force, condemn land for housing or for new communities, are only some of the unsettled issues.

One of the most troublesome questions facing the Founding Fathers was whether the welfare clause was an independent clause authorizing the new federal government to act for the national good or a mere qualifying clause authorizing expenditures exclusively under the enumerated powers that preceded it (interstate commerce, war, post roads, etc.). On the side of the strong and independent federal welfare power stood Hamilton and Monroe. Their view was reinforced by Judge Story's conception of what had actually happened at the Constitutional Convention. Holding the more constricted position were Madison and Jefferson, and later Presidents Polk, Pierce, and Buchanan.

Whatever may have been in the Founders' minds, all were convinced that the states would remain the dominant power in the centuries ahead. Jefferson left the Convention content in the thought that the new federal government would be little more than a department of foreign affairs, while Hamilton dolefully conceded that the peoples' affections toward their own states would soon make them indifferent toward the infant nation. The feeling that the state was supreme persisted during the century that followed. "Many people in France," wrote Tocqueville, "imagine that a change of opinion is going on in the United States, which is favorable to a centralization of power in the hands of the President and the Congress. I hold that a contrary tendency may distinctly be observed."

Even after the state-secession thesis had been shattered at Appomattox, Lord Bryce, while acknowledging a well-defined division of responsibility between the two great levels of government, thought Jefferson had not been unrealistic in comparing the federal government to a foreign affairs department. An American, he wrote, "may, through a long life, never be reminded of the federal government, except when he votes at presidential and congressional elections." Yet if Tocqueville and Bryce were to return for a look at America's political system today, they would be startled to find that the bucolic America envisioned by Jefferson has shrunk to a small remnant of its original design. The federal government is the dominant government in the federal-state-local trinity. Yet its power to do what it ought is unclear, particularly in the area of urban affairs.

Whatever functions the federal government assumed were under the spending power—not because it had the legal right to spend for operations outside the enumerated powers, but because the courts had ruled that a taxpayer had no standing to question the government's spending. But when the federal government sought to condemn land for housing in Louisville, Kentucky, during the New Deal, it was challenged, and in fact in 1935 the courts restrained it from that condemnation. It was partly this judicial curb on federal power that influenced the decentralization of housing and urban-renewal programs, which were put into the hands of the cities. Under the formula evolved, the federal government lent and subsidized (where its right could not be questioned), while the cities condemned land for housing and other programs under their health and welfare powers (which carried the regulatory and eminent-domain powers with them).

How far the courts would go today toward making an all-inclusive definition of the federal welfare power remains an open question. Can the federal government acquire land in a state for regional planning? Can it acquire land and build housing in a suburb that excludes Negroes? Can it enforce a federal building code? Can it build as well as finance a new town? Until these and similar powers are legislated and tested, the definition of "general" and "welfare" will remain an enigma. (See JUSTICIABLE; POWER PLANT.)

geomorphic Resembling the earth in form. Geomorphic planning or geomorphic housing describes designs or forms resembling or fitting into the pattern of the landscape on which the development is built. Machu Picchu in Peru is a classic illustration.

gerrymander The division or redivision of a voting area in a way that gives an unfair advantage to one political party over another. Its etymology draws on the surname of Elbridge Gerry, Governor of Massachusetts, and the last two syllables of salamander (for the shape of Essex County as redistricted in 1812 during his administration). Since the Negro migration into cities, gerrymandering has been employed to diffuse black voting power. Gerrymandering has also been employed to preserve open space or frustrate land acquisition by subdividers.

ghetto Originally (principally in Italy) the quarter of a city to which Jews were restricted, but now broadened to include almost any area in any country inhabited by an impoverished minority. There are five possible derivations; the *Oxford English Dictionary* gives preference to the Italian *borghetto* (borough). Though the term is used most often to describe an area in which constraints function against the occupants, there have always been voluntary as well as compulsory ghetto formations. Rudiger, Bishop of Speyer, in 1084 tried to attract Jews to the city and thereby "add to its honor." He granted them the right to their ghetto, where "they might not be readily disturbed by the insolence of the population." Here, though there was no political duress, social duress still operated.

In the United States, as elsewhere, the compulsions affecting ghettos vary, but many ghettos are still voluntary, the minority consciously electing to live unto itself, attend its own churches, and have its own neighborhood associations. Harlem in New York City is referred to as a black ghetto, but there are both compulsory and voluntary aspects in the area's organization. There is in fact strong black support for such concentrations on the ground that black political strength is centered there and that it has many aspects of a community. In the background, however, there are also strong restrictive forces to contain the Negro and therefore an interplay between compulsion and voluntarism in most black neighborhoods. The ghetto is not always a slum, nor the slum always a ghetto. (See FAIR HOUSING LAWS; GRESHAM'S LAW OF NEIGHBORHOODS; HOUSING, GHETTO; MELTING POT.)

givens A colloquialism used by architects, city planners, and engineers to describe the preconditions to which they must conform in carrying out a contract. They may twist and turn in their recommendations and plans but only up to a point—their final product must respect the givens, *i.e.,* the contractual limitations or specifications that bound discretion and limit the scope of originality. Also, those conditions in the physical, political, economic, or social environment considered immutable or not subject to manipulation. (See ENDOGENOUS; PARAMETER.)

GNP. See GROSS NATIONAL PRODUCT.

goal; objective; plan; program; project; schedule; scheme; target A goal is the end result or ultimate accomplishment toward which an effort is directed. Although often used synonymously with "objective," "goal" implies the cessation of effort upon fulfillment, while "objective" includes that which must be immediately attained *and* that which is ultimately attained. A city may set objectives for a stated maximum of population and project a city beautiful for its future, but the mayor will also set goals for specific schemes or programs.

"Plan" and "program" have side meanings, implying proposed methods of action or procedures, as in a "Five Year Plan." "Program" also implies a design for the orderly achievement of certain ends that may be part of a general plan. "Schedule" emphasizes the importance of the time element and, like "target" (derived from archery and ballistics), implies a commitment. "Project" is like "scheme," but the latter suggests imaginative scope and a careful ordering of details, while "project" is now used for specific undertakings. "Scheme" in the United States also has the connotation of an underhanded plot or a crafty deceit.

goal, operational A goal or objective stated in such terms that its achievement can be measured. Because human aspirations are frequently intangible or unquantifiable, operational goals are imperfect surrogates for what people and planners are really after. Even an ostensibly concrete goal like eliminating substandard housing runs into thorny problems of definition: what is standard? Bringing all housing up to code requirements might be an acceptable operational goal. The advantages of establishing quantifiable objectives are that progress toward their realization can be measured, costs per unit can be calculated, and programs can be improved accordingly. (See PPBS.)

grade The rate of ascent or descent in the land's surface. A grade is generally calculated: as a percentage of horizontal distance (a 10-percent grade is a grade of 10 feet in 100); as a rise or fall of so many feet in a given horizontal distance (a grade of 50 feet in a mile); as a ratio (1 on 4, meaning that for every 4 horizontal feet there is a rise of 1 foot).

The term is also used generally to indicate that there is a change in elevation in the surface of land (particularly around improvements)—in other words, that the land is not perfectly flat. When the elevation and the changes in elevation of the center line of the street are officially set, this becomes the established or street grade.

grade separation The separation at different levels of two intersecting roads, by bridge, tunnel, or underpass, so as to permit the roads to cross without obstructing free traffic movement on either. (See INTERSECTION.)

grading The entire activity of moving and shaping the earth; the arrangement of the surface of the land to suit human purposes. More specifically, to grade land is to reduce it to a single level, a series of levels, or an evenly progressive ascent or descent.

grandfather clause A provision in a number of southern state constitutions that excluded from voting those whose ancestors were ineligible to vote in 1860. It was invalidated by the United States Supreme Court in 1915. The decision was the prelude to the invalidation two years later of municipal residential segregation ordinances. (See ZONING.)

grant-in-aid A subsidy by one public body to another. (See CAPITAL GRANT; SUBSIDY.)

grant reservation Reservation of federal or state funds for a grant to be made in connection with a specific project, such as renewal of an urban area.

grantsmanship A talent for getting grants, subsidies, or contracts for research or experimentation. Federal funds available for these purposes have swelled, and so have the number of applicants, public and private. Grantsmanship requires knowing where the funds lie waiting, how to apply for them, and how to get the top dollar out of the job. Subsidized research—good, bad, and unnecessary—is no longer reserved for the universities or the scholars. It has also become the bread of big enterprise, with lush contracts awaiting those with grantsmanship.

Grants are also made by foundations to public agencies, non-profit groups, educational institutions, or individuals, but foundations are more circumspect than the government and harder to tap. Among the big foundations, policies gravitate with the executive director or his equivalent. Under less dynamic directors, recommendations may originate at the staff level and then receive formal approval at the top. If the director is of the headier variety, he may originate the types of grants himself, based on his own special notions or biases, and his staff will simply nod.

Grants and grantsmanship are still virgin fields for investigation. Among the subjects deserving study are the uses and abuses of tax-exempt foundations, the subterranean uses of foundation money to promote the private or political ambitions of its influential donors, and the abuses of foundations set up as fronts for lobbies or business interests. The techniques of grantsmanship have only recently come to entrepreneurial notice, and it is possible that the universities and scholars who have thus far enjoyed most of the benefactions may be left far behind as grantsmanship is recognized to be one of the profitable areas of enterprise.

gravity model A representation of human, economic, or functional interaction postulating that the force of attraction between two areas of activity is a function of the size or strength of some pertinent variable in one (population, number of jobs, square footage of retail space, or trip ends), and that it is inversely related to the intervening distance over which the interaction must take place.

The equation, derived from one of Newton's formulations, assumes that certain human functions are analogous to operations in the physical world. While this is probably not strictly true, the gravity model has proved reasonably accurate and useful for many planning purposes. (See FRICTION OF SPACE.)

gray area A blighted area or one the city designates as blighted. (See BLIGHT.)

Great Society The goal of the domestic programs launched and expanded under the administration of President Lyndon Johnson. His was the first to put a primary emphasis on the problem of cities. In his State of the Union message in 1965, he proposed that "we launch a national effort to make the American city a better and more stimulating place to live in. . . . The Great Society asks . . . not only how fast we are going but where we are headed."

That the Great Society was only middling in its accomplishments was due not to paucity of measures but to paucity of funds for social needs because of the Vietnam war. No more than its predecessors, the New Deal and the Fair Deal, did the Great Society come to grips with the problems of cities. The nation had successfully weathered the transition from agricultural to industrial society but had not coped with the urban revolution that came in its wake. The main reason was that the federal government had become the chief recipient of the nation's revenues while the central cities were losing their better-paying taxpayers at the same time as they were being required to bear the rising burdens of poverty, slums, social stress, education, ill health, and crime. Until these urban burdens are more directly assumed by agencies of the federal government, the sores in American city life will continue to fester. (See FAIR DEAL; NEW DEAL.)

green belt A wide band of countryside surrounding a city on which building is generally barred, usually large enough to form an adequate protection against objectionable uses of property or the intrusion of nearby development. The concept is of British origin, and while its early aims were the preservation of amenity, husbandry, and recreation, its later objective has been to contain the city and channel future growth beyond it. In England most of the belt is privately owned. The term has a less restricted meaning in the United States, where it loosely describes almost any kind of green space. In communities beset by fear of minorities, the green belt sometimes turns out to be the barrier separating the black belt from the white belt.

The green-belt concept has its roots in the British countryside. Buckingham House in London bore the motto *Rus in urbe* (the country in the city) while Lord Lanesborough's house at Hyde Park Corner, now St. George's Hospital, was inscribed

> It is my delight to be
> Both in town and country.

Even when the factory blackened the brickwork, the British still respected their parks, squares, gardens, and lawns, and when London's planners had to grapple with population growth, green spaces colored their blueprints. Ebenezer Howard saw the green belt as the townsman's countryside. Sir Raymond Unwin in 1932 proposed a green girdle accessible to London's people, which he wove into the developed areas. Britain's planning acts were "Town and Country Acts," and a "Town and Country Ministry" administered them.

In the late 1920s the government ordered a study of an agricultural belt around London primarily to bar expansion around its periphery (a concept running back to the time of Elizabeth I, who banned all new building within three miles of London's limits). Following the 1938 Green Belt Act, some 38,000 acres of land were either bought or controlled. After the Barlow Commission Report in 1939, there were a number of proposals to disperse London's population. Sir Patrick Abercrombie's plan in 1944 called for a series of concentric rings with a green belt five miles deep separating the city and its suburbs from the countryside. New towns beyond the green belt were expected to take care of the overspill. The Town and Country Planning Act of 1947 thereafter conferred broad powers to freeze the green belt. Any owner building within the belt had to apply for permission. There were many administrative problems and modifications, but the green belt appeared secure. The concept was applied to other cities, where its purposes were: to check further growth of urban areas; to prevent neighboring towns from merging; and to preserve the special character of towns. Recreation and amenity were now incidental.

Whether the green-belt principle has worked is a subject of controversy. Its integrity as open space has been preserved, but as a device for containing London its success is open to question. London has grown, the pressures on the belt are reaching the bursting point, and some of it is already more gray than green. William H. Whyte has attributed its failings to lack of access. "People must be able to do things on it or with it—at the very least to be able to look at it." Birmingham's green belt is also being pressed hard for development, and even the more ardent preservationists are ready to surrender part of the belts to maintain the rest intact.

In Copenhagen the green belt runs through the city and has survived. In Japan the London-style green belt was found impractical as a means of containing Tokyo and was abandoned. In the world's less-developed areas green belts would become anchorages of squatters—in the Philippines even a central city park was taken over.

In the United States—where large green spaces are unsafe at night—pressures have mounted to convert them into housing plots and other uses, and though some belts, like Rock Creek Park in Washington, D.C., survive, small parks are being favored because they can be better policed. (See AMENITIES; BETTERMENT; OPEN SPACE; OVERSPILL; UTHWATT REPORT.)

green-belt town. See GARDEN CITY.

Gresham's Law of Neighborhoods The theory that just as bad dollars drive out good dollars, so people of the wrong race, complexion, or status will drive out good people and drive down property values. The theory was adopted by real-estate theoreticians and texts and formed the basis for the discriminatory Code of Ethics governing members of the National Association of Real Estate Boards up to 1950; and it underlay the thinking of officials in the FHA, the Home Owners Loan Corporation, and other housing agencies.

In Homer Hoyt's *One Hundred Years of Land Values in Chicago* (1933), a hierarchy of ethnic groups accepted by real-estate men as affecting values was listed from the most to the least favorable: (1) English, Germans, Scots, Irish, Scandinavians; (2) North Italians; (3) Bohemians or

Czechs; (4) Poles; (5) Lithuanians; (6) Greeks; (7) Russian Jews ("lower class"); (8) South Italians; (9) Negroes; (10) Mexicans. Hoyt later amplified his theory to show that in the structure and growth of American cities there was a general tendency for the formation of fairly homogeneous residential sectors, and a similar tendency for upper-class sectors to deteriorate when "inharmonious" groups penetrated them.

The theory was challenged in other studies, including one by Lloyd Rodwin, who saw Hoyt's conclusions as based on questionable assumptions and an *ad hoc* theory of class structure, which assumed that locations were selected for class attractiveness and all other considerations ignored—including the functional adequacy of established environments that might be attractive despite the presence of other groups.

Area studies have shown that values may rise, fall, or remain constant with the entry of minority families. The statement that one race or group inevitably affects price favorably or unfavorably disregards an entire complex of relevant factors—the social and economic status of a minority at the time; its numbers in relation to the numbers in the majority group; the latter's social and cultural level; the minority's capacity for social improvement and assimilation; the size of the city and the physical condition of its neighborhoods; the pattern of minority distribution in the city; the nature of the current minority stereotype; the type of social and educational leadership and maturity; the social and economic role of the minority; and the relation between the groups in employment and wage levels. (See DISCRIMINATION, FEDERAL HOUSING; SECTOR THEORY.)

gridiron plan   A pattern of streets that from the air looks like a gridiron —that is, based on right-angle intersections and parallel sets of roadways. A gridiron plan takes little account of natural topography and tends toward monotony and the waste of natural amenities. In 1811 it became the plan for New York City because "it was the cheapest to build." In a city like San Francisco, however, the matter-of-fact imposition of the gridiron becomes inspired town planning, providing magnificent vistas and hair-raising street grades.

gross national product (GNP)   The total annual monetary value of all final goods and services produced in a country. The GNP includes wages, private spending and government spending, useful and useless services, money paid to doctors, lawyers, fortunetellers, and the TV sets they buy with it, money spent for clearing slums and creating them. It is the economist's measure of national productivity. If in 1970 the GNP of the United States exceeds what it was in 1969 by x dollars, say the economists, it indicates "progress"; if it drops, we must worry.

The GNP has its defenders and critics. Some of the critics say that government spending should not be included and that taxes in fact limit rather than increase production. Others question the inclusion of wasteful or unsocial spending and call for a new measure of "gross national disproduct" to add up our national deficits such as air and water pollution, unremedied decay, vandalism and violence, and the social defaults responsible for them. They then also call for a "net national product" to subtract disproduct from product.

This the GNP proponent answers by saying he is an economist, not a social worker; he deals with the satisfaction of human wants and needs that are paid for by people; he should not be making value judgments as to what is good or bad; this should be left to St. Peter. Despite its inability to subtract, GNP has won a firm foothold as an economic yardstick.

ground rent. See RENT, GROUND.

groupers   A number of persons, usually single, joining together to rent a house or apartment and sharing the rent and upkeep. Groupers are encountered mostly in resort areas, where they are often unpopular with the established residents and where zoning laws frequently aim at preventing occupancy by persons who are not part of a family unit. Group occupancy is also common in university areas, where students combine to rent an apartment or house. By doubling up, they are often able to pay high rents, thereby competing with established residents. The competition for dwelling units as university enrollments increase has intensified town-gown conflicts and heightened the pressures for occupancy codes and, in some areas, rent control. (See TOWN-GOWN PROBLEM.)

guaranteed annual wage   A contract formula in the building trades based on a yearly, instead of a weekly or hourly, rate of pay in consideration of a guarantee of year-round work. A guaranteed annual wage has been proposed frequently as a method of bringing down the costs of labor on public housing and other public operations. By guaranteeing the building trades continuous work, labor would receive more per year while the public operations would enjoy lower construction costs. Though it makes sense, the unions have not taken kindly to the proposal, partly because they fear the lower rates will nibble at their wage levels and wipe out their hard-won pay increases.

guide lines   A general statement of policy without very specific details. Also, a form of city planning under which the planning authority lays down general principles, to which private development must conform, without defining precisely what may or may not be built or how. With zoning laws and building codes, the developer knows how his plans should be drawn and what he may build; guide lines, on the other hand, are so general that the planning commission becomes the final authority on which plans do or do not conform. A case in point is that of the Puerto Rico Planning Commission, which, following a surge of speculative construction, issued guide lines for all future construction. Building all but ceased because the builders could not tell what they could build without consulting the planning commission at every turn. As interpretations were made for the perplexed architects and investors, building slowly resumed.

   Guide lines leave virtually all power of decision to the planning authority and may serve as an interim device until a sufficient number of interpretations effect a clarification of what the authority has in mind, or, better still, until specifications are written which amplify them into a comprehensible code. Otherwise guide lines give little guidance.

halfway house.   See HOUSE, HALFWAY.

halfway housing.   See HOUSING, HALFWAY.

hamlet   A small rural center, usually not exceeding 250 residents, which contains the basic commercial, educational, and religious facilities required by the surrounding area. Sometimes it is nothing more than a small group of houses clustered together. It is what urban Americans like to refer to as a wide spot in the road. (See CITY; TOWN; VILLAGE.)

hardware programs; software programs Hardware programs are those entailing physical changes made to the environment, such as urban renewal or mass transit. Software programs, though they may include incidental investment in hardware structures, are concerned primarily with improvements in social organization, education, employment, health, and welfare.

Haussmannization The opening, straightening, and widening of streets, coupled with extensive rebuilding, after the fashion of Baron G. E. Haussmann's rebuilding of Paris in the mid-nineteenth century. It implies a drastic approach to replanning with more consideration given to the character of the ultimate product than to property or individual rights. Paris's present appearance is largely due to Haussmann, who widened old streets and boldly cut new ones. The term was used by the United States Supreme Court in upholding the zoning power.

headway The time span between the arrival of successive buses, trains, or other units of mass transit; in other words, the scheduled frequency of service. During rush hours on a heavily traveled city street, bus headway may be less than a minute; at midnight the same route may have a headway of fifteen or thirty minutes. (See TRANSIT, MASS.)

height zoning. See ZONING, HEIGHT.

heliport A landing and take-off field for helicopters. In England it is sometimes referred to as an air-stop.

high-rise apartment. See APARTMENT, HIGH-RISE.

highest and best use. See USE, HIGHEST AND BEST.

hinterland The outlying area or region surrounding a city or cities. It once referred to "the back-country or the area in back of the coastal region." The hinterland of a metropolis may consist of the "area of commutation" and the "trade area." The towns of the hinterland tend to become feeders for the metropolis, supplying it with food and raw materials as well as some finished products. With suburbanization and the movement of industries to former hinterlands, the hinterland in its old sense is disappearing.

The term is of German origin and became prominent in 1883–1885 when Germany insisted on the right to assert jurisdiction over the hinterland territory lying inland from those parts it had occupied on the African coast. Large areas were claimed by other colonial powers under what came to be known as the "hinterland doctrine." (See CENTRAL PLACE THEORY.)

hippies Mostly white youth, largely sprung from the middle class, who have rejected their parents' ways, standards, and values and have dedicated their days to living, loving, and sharing. Some joined the movement because they were alienated from society or because the society from which they withdrew failed to inspire their interest. They were referred to as the "flower children" and the "first generation of American gypsies." They derived their name from the jazz term "hip" or "hipster," not because they were aware and sharp, but because they were "unhip," or the equivalent of "hippie." The hippies took the disparaging word and gave it honorable usage. Some call the hippie movement a subculture; others call it a movement, cult, culture, or pseudo-religion. Though hippies are non-religious they express values not unlike the religious— *i.e.,* love for all humanity, rejection of material wealth, and sackcloth in dress; even marijuana and other drugs have been defended as if they were sacraments.

The hippies made the big-city street their confluence and place of meeting—Sunset Strip in Los Angeles, Haight-Ashbury in San Francisco, and the East Village streets and parks in New York City. They were mostly misunderstood, sometimes tolerated, and more often scorned. Driven from the streets by other minorities, by the police, or by disillusionment with their society and its mores, some drifted back to suburbia; others cut their beards and hair and went home, got jobs or married; others held on to their hopes and illusions as before.

Though much has been written on the hippie phenomenon, one of the missing commentaries is on the activities of meeting and mating in these youth movements, whether hippies or yippies, civil rights, draft resistance, or the anti-war campaign. It should be said that the hippie movement, like the others, supplied a purpose, cause, or pretext that gave youth the right, the opportunity, and the freedom to meet and mate. The city was failing as a context for bringing people together, and just as young communism and the Spanish Loyalist movement of the 1930s supplied an "honorable cause" for coming together, so did the hippie movement—adding its element of universal love, flowers, and the "trip." Perhaps someday urban renewal will be more broadly defined; not simply as the demolition of buildings, but the renewal of the human spirit, the provision of space for social assemblage, and creation of better devices for the young to meet in an expanding arena of wholesome opportunities. (See CONVERGENCE; URBAN NOMAD.)

hire purchase Rental with an option to buy. Also, a practice under which real estate is rented with installments of principal added to each installment of rent; when a sufficient amount of principal is paid, the tenant must then exercise the right to buy or forfeit his principal payments. It is a practice now prevalent in ghetto areas, in which property is often sold at twice its value to poorer folk who are attracted by the small initial down payment. (See INSTALLMENT CONTRACT; OPTION; OWNERSHIP.)

holdout An owner who refuses to sell property necessary to the assemblage of a site for some new public or private use. (A lessee can also be a holdout when he refuses to sell his interest in such property.) The holdout is seen either as a lonely hero standing up for human rights in the face of the heartless bulldozer, or as a crank making a futile stand against progress or the inevitable. Some of course stand pat out of calculated greed, speculating that they will get more in the end. But the holdout often has legitimate reasons for his refusal. Sale of his property at the market price may force him to pay more than a quarter of the money he gets as income tax. His attachment to the property may be deep, or he may be running a business on the property that is worth more than the property itself. If he is a home-owner, the cost of comparable new housing may be more than he is offered for the old, and because of his age or the general rise in interest costs he may be unable to command favorable mortgage terms in the current market.

A classic holdout is a bar on 48th Street and Sixth Avenue in New York City. It was the one parcel that the Rockefeller interests were unable to obtain when they put together the site for Rockefeller Center. (See ASSEMBLAGE.)

holistic Emphasizing the organic or functional relationship between parts and wholes (as opposed to atomistic). Holistic planning attempts to see its subject (be it a neighborhood, city, region, or nation) as a single integrated system of mutually interdependent parts. (See ECOLOGY; PHYSIOGRAPHIC DETERMINISM.)

home A term that once held sentimental connotations for the family but is now frequently used interchangeably with "house." (See MOBILE HOME; SHELTER.)

home, mobile. See MOBILE HOME.

home rule In the United States, the arrangement under which municipalities are allowed to frame their own charters and regulate their own affairs. Elsewhere, it refers to all types of local or regional self-determination, as in Ireland, where home rule is synonymous with independence from Britain.

Cities may be guaranteed home rule by statute or constitution, the latter being preferred, owing to the caprices of state legislatures. The granting of lush franchises to utility and transport companies in the mid-nineteenth century and the domination of the cities by the state legislatures aroused local indignation and ushered in the home-rule movement. Home rule derived its logic from the increased complexities of urban government, the feeling that state legislatures are indifferent to the city's problems, and that local and state politics should be separated.

The motivations that prompted home-rule enactments a century or more ago were, however, different from those of today. Today the same home-rule privileges wrung from the legislatures by the once powerful cities are being asserted by the new suburbs against these cities. Suburbs resist central-city expansion; as more and more of the middle and upper classes settle in the suburbs, political power passes to them while the home-rule principle shields them against the central city's efforts to annex them. Simultaneously the state, which should be intervening in the rationalization of metropolitan problems, remains aloof in the name of preserving the home-rule shibboleth. (See DECENTRALIZATION.)

homestead A portion of land in an unsettled area granted by the government to a settler for development as a farm. Homesteads were a primary influence in the movement westward by America's nineteenth-century pioneers. Also, a place where a family makes its home—including the land, house, and outbuildings.

hostel A lodging place; one of a series of supervised shelters used by young people on hikes and outings (youth hostels); a lodging place in underdeveloped areas somewhat like a camp, which is made available by the government to approved travelers.

house A building for human habitation. The term is usually applied to a single-family dwelling.

"House," "home," "hearth," "roof," "floor," "oven" are all of Germanic origin. "House" is related to the verb "to hide." "Home" is linked to the "ham" in Birmingham and Gotham. "Roof" comes from the Anglo-Saxon *hrof,* or "top." A shingled roof derives from the Latin *scindo,* meaning "split" or "cleave." "Wall" comes from the Latin *vallus,* meaning "stake" or "palisade," while "chimney" is derived from the French *cheminée* and the Late Latin *caminata,* or fireplace, and further back from the Greek *kaminos,* or furnace. "Pantry" has its ultimate source in *panis,* "bread," and until the seventeenth century was the closet in which bread was kept. "Parlor" comes from the French *parler,* "to speak," and was the room set aside for conversation. The "drawing room," popular during the sixteenth and seventeenth centuries, was actually the "withdrawing room," to which the ladies retired while the men sipped, smoked, and told stories tall or trifling. "Window" comes from the Scandinavian *vindauge,* formed from *vindr,* meaning "wind," and *auga,* meaning "eye," or the eye for the wind, or wind-eye, and ultimately "window."

A detached house is one standing by itself on its own plot.

A semi-detached house is one of a pair of houses joined together and forming a unit by themselves.

A frame house is one constructed with a wooden framework covered with boards.

A row house is one of a continuous row of houses built according to the same or nearly the same plans and with similar fenestration and architectural treatment; also, a house sharing party walls with its neighbors in a row of similar houses. Row houses are sometimes called "terrace houses."

A boarding or rooming house is a place, often originally a one-family house, in which furnished rooms or apartments are let by the day, week, or month to lodgers. The boarding house is distinguished from the rooming house by serving meals.

A bordello was a "little house" in its earlier usage but now designates a house of prostitution.

house, conventional A house constructed element by element at the site, as opposed to one that is prefabricated or built by "systems," or a mobile home.

house, core The central or basic part of a dwelling to which further improvements can be added by the owner. A core-house program is a low-cost strategy particularly suited to meeting housing problems in underdeveloped countries. Core houses are built by either the government or the owners and expanded as earnings permit. Experience has shown that ownership is essential to encourage extension of the core.

No single type of core can be uniformly applied to all countries and all climates. Each country, in fact each region, may call for a particular design. These include: a one-room core for small families in very poor countries; a two-room core to be expanded horizontally for a growing family; a core that can be added to vertically; the row-house core, the front and rear of which are expandable; and the core built as part of a compound. There are also cores composed of subdividable rooms, and warm-climate cores composed simply of a roof, supports, and a floor to be walled in by the occupant. In the frontier period of American settlement the core was an underground room later built over. (See HOUSING, SELF-HELP; MUTUAL-AID CONSTRUCTION; ROOF LOAN.)

house, economy A house of about 600 square feet once promoted by the Federal Housing Administration as a "solution" to the shelter problem of lower-income families. After qualifying such houses for FHA insurance and encouraging their building, FHA became disillusioned with the product and reverted to higher standards.

In 1968 FHA again manifested an interest in what was now called a mini-house—a two-bedroom house designed to sell for under $7000 (a three-bedroom version cost about $1000 more). The first two-bedroom minis, built in Phoenix, Arizona, measured 720 square feet and were quickly sold. Despite this initial success, it is doubtful that the mini-house will be an answer to the housing problem. Experimentation with the mini-house as a core house on a suitably sized lot does, however, offer some possibilities.

house, halfway An institution that provides a sheltered and transitional environment for persons emerging from mental institutions or prisons and helps to ease their return to society.

household A family or one or more persons living in a dwelling unit with common housekeeping arrangements. The housekeeping arrangements, and not the relationship of the members, are the basis for the Census Bureau's definition of this statistical unit; a single person living alone, a group of unrelated people rooming together, and a family with twelve children are all considered households.

A group of persons living in a residence that is not considered a dwelling unit—an army barrack, a fraternity or rooming house—is a quasi-household. (See FAMILY.)

houser One who specializes in the study of the housing problem and the means of alleviating it.

house, tied A historical term for a house owned by an employer and occupied by his workers. Often the tenant pays only nominal or no rent, but his wages are adjusted accordingly. The boss's position as employer-landlord enabled him to evict a recalcitrant worker and to fight union organization. If a plant was located in an isolated area, particularly in a one-industry company town, and the worker was discharged, he had no alternative but to move, for he would soon be evicted. The company would generally assert it had room only for its active workers.

The tied house has taken a variety of forms: the shotgun cottage with three rooms, railroad style, in southern mine and mill towns; the tall frame structure of New England with one or more families on each floor; the single or double board-and-batten frame house of the mining regions; the square hip-roofed cottage of the West; and the semi-detached row house or the apartment building put up where land was limited or costly. Whatever the type, they were generally uniform and dreary.

The tied house may be built out of paternal benevolence or self-interest. In the former case, the houses are better and the facilities for schooling, playing, and praying are generous. The American worker, however, does not usually like to work in his boss's plant, walk on his street, play in his park, ail in his hospital, beg God's forgiveness in his church, and rot in his cemetery. Employers, sensing this disaffection, now often sell the housing to the workers.

In Asia and Africa the worker welcomes a company house and the tied shelter will be accepted, as in the Bibiani gold mines of Ghana or in Osaka, Japan, with gratitude. But in Latin America, an oil-company study has indicated that the worker wants: his own home; a house that suits his tastes and is in a location of his choice; neighbors of his own choosing whether or not they are company employees; roots in the community, with a built-in economic stake for the future; a measure of freedom without dependence on his employer; the dignity associated with the rights and responsibilities of citizenship.

As a result of these findings at least one company, Standard Oil, has veered toward building houses near its South American installations and then selling them to workers. A more recent development in this part of the world is the rise of savings and loan associations set up by employers to provide mortgage loans to workers.

With the birth of the Federal Housing Administration and the workers' ability to buy homes with only small down payments, employer-built housing should have boomed in the United States. New towns backed by seed capital, know-how, and initiative should have spread from coast to coast. The reluctance of employers to enter the housing field, coupled with the unsavory reputation of tied houses, prevented this—and thus prevented what might have been a wholesome and much-needed contribution to the American environment. (See COMPANY TOWN.)

housing In the most general sense, shelter inhabited by man.

housing association A non-profit organization of citizens set up to advise on or criticize official housing policy, provide technical and financial advice in carrying out housing schemes, further housing reform, promote housing legislation, or do several or all of these things. In the United

States contributions to these associations are exempt from federal income tax provided the associations avoid lobbying for legislation or do so only occasionally. This limits their effectiveness in the area in which they can be most influential.

housing authority A public body, generally corporate, empowered to provide and manage housing, especially for lower-income groups, to clear slums in connection therewith, to issue bonds, and in general to function as the operating unit of a city, county, or state in carrying out a public-housing program. Most housing authorities are set up by cities though chartered by the states. Some also carry out urban-renewal programs. All depend on federal subsidies, though a few also operate with state or local funds in state and local programs. (See HOUSING, PUBLIC.)

housing code. See CODE, HOUSING.

housing, cooperative Dwellings built, operated, or managed by a voluntary, nongovernmental association of persons who pool their resources to secure the dwellings, usually on a non-speculative or non-profit basis. The cooperators may be stockholders in a corporation in which title is vested and from which leases are obtained, or beneficiaries under a trust agreement with title being vested in a trustee. Sometimes the term is loosely applied to a project in which some of the services or facilities are cooperative. In the United States, special dispensations make cooperatives attractive, notably income-tax deductions for the cooperator's proportionate share of interest and realty taxes. Not all cooperators cooperate, and most are more interested in the financial and practical advantages of the housing than in the spiritual agglutination ascribed to cooperation by some of its advocates. Housing cooperatives failed in the United States when first instituted and suffered during the depression, but they inspired Swedish formations that have flourished. They are now extensive throughout Scandinavia and Holland and have now made great strides in the United States. They have also taken substantial hold in the USSR despite its extensive state-built housing.

Cooperative housing has the best chance of success when there is an experienced guiding hand and a mechanism for stimulating cooperative organizations, buying land, arranging the financing, and resolving disputes that may arise among non-cooperating cooperators. (See CONDOMINIUM; COOPERATIVE; HSB.)

housing, ghetto Housing in an area inhabited by an ethnic or racial minority. Not all ghetto housing is bad, and some ghetto neighborhoods are well kept and stable, particularly where there is a high proportion of home ownership. A slum ghetto is created when those of a single ethnic minority group live not only in a ghetto but also in bad housing.

The typical characteristics of slum-ghetto housing are: signs of marked neighborhood deterioration that have long been evident; many buildings lack the basic amenities; repairs either are not made by the owners or are not worth making; lending institutions have rated the area as out of bounds for mortgage investment; little or no investment in new building is ventured; tax arrears are higher; garbage collection, building inspection, street maintenance, and other city services are poorer, and schools, hospitals, and recreation facilities are inferior; building values are lower in relation to rents; the proportion of occupants' incomes allocable for rent is higher; both the land and the buildings are overcrowded.

The mass exodus of whites from the central areas of many American cities has made considerable good housing available at low purchase prices. When the property is owned by the occupant, whether he be black or white, it is usually well kept. Where it is rented to the occupant, the tendency toward deterioration and poor upkeep by owners is greater. (See GHETTO.)

housing, halfway Partly finished housing which the owner has been unable to complete owing to lack of financing. Halfway housing is common in the less-developed countries where hundreds of roofless houses dot the cities. The owners can continue building only as their earnings accrue, and they often take years to finish their structures, sometimes never completing them. A United Nations mission in Kenya suggested a financing scheme under which owners could get a government loan to complete the unfinished houses after they had been enclosed or were about half completed. A roof-loan scheme in Ghana, under which loans were made by the government for roofs, doors, and windows, resulted in thousands of homes' being completed. (See HOUSE, CORE; INSTALLMENT CONSTRUCTION; ROOF LOAN.)

housing, in-fill Housing built on scattered sites, usually only a few lots wide, in a built-up section of a city. The sites are vacant either because the structures formerly on them were demolished or because they remained undeveloped when the adjoining buildings were erected. Because vacant land is scarce in most cities and because empty lots are often makeshift garbage dumps and eyesores, numerous proposals have been made for in-fill housing, including prefabricated units of standard size. The high cost of building new housing a few units at a time and the inability of many inner-city families to pay for them have limited the number of in-fill houses. Some vacant lots have been used for small parks or playgrounds. (See HOUSING, VEST-POCKET; PARK, VEST-POCKET.)

housing, leased public. See PUBLIC HOUSING, LEASED.

housing, limited-dividend Housing that receives subsidies in the form of tax exemption and mortgage credits at below-market rates in consideration of which the sponsor limits the net return on his investment and submits to regulation by a public agency. The first limited-dividend housing corporations were authorized in New York State in 1926. Since then other limited-dividend operations have been made possible under federal legislation, in which dividends and rents are regulated by contract with the FHA, which retains a portion of the issued stock for the purpose. To induce investment, FHA is liberal in its mortgage insurance.

There were few private operations at first, and most of the earlier ventures were undertaken by cooperatives and unions interested in providing homes for their members. But there has been a recent surge of such operations by entrepreneurs. One reason is that the fee allowed for building exceeds out-of-pocket cost. The difference when invested in the operation enables the builder to earn 10 to 12 per cent on actual dollar investment. Another reason is the favorable depreciation element in a period of high federal tax rates. Since the mortgage money (often obtained from the city or state or with the backing of FHA insurance) is substantial and the actual investment small, the paper deductions that can be taken are plentiful. This "loss" can be deducted from profits in other operations. More non-profit and cooperative ventures have also been undertaken recently under various limited-dividend statutes.

housing, luxury Housing built for the upper-income group. With rising interest rates and construction costs, many large cities are finding that private developers are willing to build only luxury housing and that the rest of the market requires some form of subsidy.

housing market That arena of exchange (be it a section, a city, a region, or a nation) in which rents, prices, sales activity, housing availability, and other details of the residential situation are determined and in which comparisons can be made and conclusions drawn as to conditions and the forces that affect them. The housing market is not a bourse like the stock or commodity exchange, in which there is a long and short side and a quotable bid and asked. Functions of comparison and substitution are more difficult and less perfect in housing than in other markets, partly because no two buildings and no two sites are identical, each having its own factors of location, convenience, amenities, and neighborhood; partly because the housing market is composed of many small buyers and sellers each trying to create his own terms; and partly because the typical buyer enters the market only once or twice in his lifetime, and thus has little knowledge or experience on which to base his decision.

housing-market analysis The detailed examination of present and future trends in the supply of and demand for housing within a given area. Essentially, a housing-market analysis sets out to compare the number of households now or in the future with the inventory of units that currently exist or are likely to become available. It is then possible—by arranging the households according to income, size, and preference for owning or renting, and by matching this distribution with the supply of available units in each size and rent or value category—to forecast unmet demand or surplus in each segment of the market. Scarcity in one part of the market does not preclude surfeit in another. It would not be unprecedented to find, for example, an overabundance of luxury units co-existing with a marked shortage of low-income rentals.

Sophisticated analysis involves careful delineation of the market areas, accurate economic and population forecasting, sensitivity to consumer trends and attitudes, knowledge of the dynamics of the local construction industry and the mortgage and land market. Market estimates may be undertaken to examine the soundness of a single proposed project or to chart a future housing program for a whole metropolitan area. The most extensive program of analysis is carried out by the Federal Housing

Administration, which periodically gauges the soundness of the mort-gage market in various localities to guide its insurance operations.

Market analysis is also done for office and commercial space as well as other types of development. (See FILTERING.)

housing-market area A geographic area within which dwelling units are closely substitutable one for another—that is, which contain all the units that are likely to be considered potential housing accommodations by the resident population. (A house in Boston is clearly not in the market area of a Philadelphia family, but a house in Camden, New Jersey, or Bucks County, Pennsylvania, might well be.) Since determining what are acceptable housing alternatives is a subjective process, the delineation of area boundaries is often difficult, but the location of the breadwinner's job usually receives the greatest weight in the identification of such an area. With the maximum acceptable journey to work setting the outer limits of the family's possible residence, other considerations such as cost, type of tenure, neighborhood characteristics, shopping conven-ience, availability of suitable educational facilities, and other amenities come into play.

In one sense, every unit in a given metropolitan area is in the same housing market. For study purposes, however, there are numerous sub-markets defined by differences in location, cost, size, style, etc. (*i.e.,* the rental market, the market for new homes, the luxury market). Further complicating the analysis is the obvious but often overlooked fact that one unit need not be closely similar to another to be highly substitutable. A family might well be torn between a new house with the latest appli-ances near a new school and an equivalently priced older house that has more room, a larger yard, and "character." The consumer's willingness to trade off one set of attributes for another complicates the work of the analyst, but it is what makes a market.

housing, open-occupancy Housing that is available to all races and groups without discrimination and free of exclusionary restrictions. An open-occupancy law proscribes such practices, while an open-occupancy policy provides for freedom of access to such housing as a practice. (See FAIR HOUSING LAWS.)

housing project A planned residential development consisting of a building or group of buildings, including land, utilities, and other facilities, that provides shelter and related services for a fairly large number of families. It is often used interchangeably with "public-housing project." With the development of large public-housing undertakings or "self-contained projects designed to create their own environments," the housing project has acquired the connotation of something big, impersonal, and institutional. One hears the saw, "Where is the architect who can design a housing project that doesn't look like a housing project?" More recently the vest-pocket or small housing project has appeared, as well as projects providing single-family homes.

The old-style, massive project in public housing, typified by those in New York City and Chicago, was one of the principal reasons for the decline in popularity of the public-housing program. One of its main defects was its forbidding appearance. It was originally justified as being able to resist the intrusion of surrounding blight, and thus help to upgrade the area around it. It did neither, partly because of the rigid cost restrictions of federal legislation, partly because of the lack of imagination and the bureaucratic set-ups of the authorities, partly because of pressure to provide quantity rather than quality, and ultimately because it paid little heed to the larger economic and social needs of the tenants. (See HOUSING, PUBLIC; HOUSING, VEST-POCKET.)

housing, public   A term used in the United States to describe housing built and owned by a public agency for eligible low-income families for whom private enterprise fails to provide. "Low-rent housing," "low-cost housing," "municipal housing," and, in England, "council housing" are terms often used synonymously. Public housing was first introduced in the United States during the early New Deal as part of the Emergency Relief and Construction Act; it was undertaken as a federally sponsored and federally built operation. In 1937 the United States Housing Act decentralized the program by authorizing federal loans and subsidies to local (mostly city) housing authorities, which would borrow funds and build and manage the housing projects. The Act provided for the elimination of slum dwellings equal to the number built, required a partial tax-exemption contribution by the cities, and set construction-cost limits on the dwelling units and rooms.

Leased public housing is housing leased by a private landlord to a public housing authority for rental to eligible families. Units may be newly constructed, rehabilitated, or existing so long as they meet code standards. The owner is required to provide management and maintenance and must accept occupants from the authority's list, but in return he has a guaranteed income and need make no allowance for vacancies.

The leasing program has become very popular with many big city housing authorities because it opens an enormous potential pool of public housing, eliminates the red tape and delays of new construction, minimizes neighborhood opposition, avoids the aspect of the "housing project," and more or less integrates the publicly housed tenants with the surrounding section. It is finding less favor in Washington, however, because program approval requires almost immediate disbursement of funds, unlike the conventional program where the major costs to the federal government do not begin for two or three years.

No-cash-subsidy public housing is a New York City program under which its housing authority issues tax-exempt bonds for the financing of low-rent housing construction, with the city guaranteeing the bonds and giving the authority substantial tax exemption. Because there is no annual cash subsidy provided (as in federal- or state-aided projects), rents are higher than in ordinary public housing but still well below the market rents for new units.

Turnkey public housing is housing built by private developers for purchase by local housing authorities and operation as part of their normal inventory. The aims of the program—known as Turnkey I—are to accelerate public-housing production, cut down on bureaucratic bottlenecks, and reduce project cost. Under the approved procedure the private entrepreneur hires his own architect, draws his own development plans, arranges for his own construction financing and subcontractors. He must produce a project satisfactory to the authority. The housing authority gives the builder a "letter of intent" under which it agrees to purchase the completed project if it meets specifications and other terms of agreement. Since the letter of intent is not absolutely binding, a large supply of good faith is involved in the transaction. Where public bidding is required by law the private builder may not even ask for a letter of intent and has to build on a handshake. If the authority rejects the project the builder will try to find an alternative use for his building.

There are two other types of turnkey public housing: under Turnkey II private firms or the tenants themselves are hired to manage the housing projects; Turnkey III involves coupling turnkey building with giving low-income families ownership of the housing built. (See EQUIVALENT ELIMINATION.)

housing, self-help Housing built by the owner. The self-help may be total or partial, with the owner doing what he can and hiring skilled workers to do the more difficult tasks such as wiring and plumbing. In Korea, for example, the government builds about two-thirds of the house and the owner completes the rest. Self-help is the world's most common form of construction, and whether it is organized self-help (arranged and supervised by government, a church, etc.) or squatting (which is illegal self-help), it is supplying more shelter in the underdeveloped world than all other public and private housing programs combined. Organized self-help operations have encountered difficulties because of lack of experience, high administrative costs, long delays due to the full-time employment of the beneficiaries, and inability to obtain mutual cooperation. Some organized self-help operations have nevertheless succeeded and are justified where they have also resulted in the training of the beneficiaries for building work. The more rural the environment, the more likely is the prospect of success in self-help. Programs are invariably troublesome where workers have full-time jobs. The worker is apt to do neither job well; he comes in tired when he reports for his regular job, worries about whether the rains are eating away at his foundation, and makes frantic calls to his wife when he should be earning his pay.

Ownership of the land is indispensable to all self-help operations, for no one should be expected to produce well on someone else's land. This applies to total or partial self-help and organized or spontaneous operations. (See HUMAN NIDOLOGY; MUTUAL-AID CONSTRUCTION; SQUATTER.)

housing shortage A condition of the housing market in which the supply of livable dwelling units is insufficient to meet demand or need. A housing shortage is short of a housing famine. A housing shortage can exist even where there is a numerical surplus of houses over households—unless there is a significant percentage of vacant units at any given time, prospective buyers and tenants will have an inadequate selection to choose from, costs will go up, and mobility will be inhibited. "Housing shortage" is a much misused and abused term, particularly by officialdom, whose efforts to relieve housing deficiencies have been lumped together with slum clearance. But for a housing shortage there is nothing that slum clearance can do that cannot be done more efficiently by an earthquake. With a slum surplus the slum dweller has at least the element of choice and mobility. But if slums are cleared and there is no alternative housing, the displaced slum dweller simply doubles up in the slum residuum, where overcrowding and excessive rentals exact a more grinding toll.

By the year 2000, when a good portion of the earth will be celebrating the second millennium of the birth of Christ (delivered in a stable during a housing shortage), the world's population is expected to double. The only reasonable expectation is that there will still be housing shortages in most parts of the globe and that more nations, not yet ready to heed the Sermon on the Mount, will have devices far more effective than urban renewal for clearing slums. Perhaps the tendency of world urbanization will make all nations vulnerable to devastation and therefore more reluctant to employ their awesome prerogatives. Perhaps they will then find the resources for the more mundane purpose of sheltering souls. (See INFRASTRUCTURE; OVERCROWDING.)

housing, substandard   Shelter that is below the acceptable standards of a particular society. Like the word "slum," the term defies precise definition. What is substandard varies with the period and the country. In Singapore public housing may shelter eight persons in a new one-room "standard" unit; in Hong Kong a room in a nine-story walk-up may be standard. In the United States substandard housing is what the official agency designates as substandard, and when so designated it may be acquired for urban renewal or a slum-clearance project.

The U.S. census provides an official measure of housing conditions, but it has no criteria for defining standard and substandard neighborhoods. (See SLUM.)

housing, temporary   Housing built, in response to some temporary or emergency situation, to last for only a short period of time. It is one of the ever-recurring illusions that temporary housing is temporary—it always seems to hang on long past its allotted life. This proved to be the case with the temporary housing built after both World War I and World War II. Another illusion is that temporary housing is cheaper than permanent housing. The temporary housing built for returning war veterans by New York State cost up to three times as much as permanent housing.

One reason is that temporary housing is not built according to traditional methods known to the workers and the contractors. It requires innovation and deviation from customary routines. Though built of less durable materials, it calls for a kind of "custom building" entailing familiarity with new types of materials and strange specifications.

housing unit   As defined by the Census Bureau for the 1960 census, a housing unit is a house, an apartment, or other group of rooms, or a single room occupied or intended for occupancy as separate living quarters —*i.e.,* when the occupants do not live and eat with any other persons in the structure and there is either direct access from the outside or through a common hall, or a kitchen or cooking equipment for the exclusive use of the unit's occupants. Trailers, tents, boats, and railroad cars are included in the inventory if they are occupied as housing units. (See DWELLING; SHELTER.)

housing, vest-pocket   Small housing projects erected on relatively small plots, most often built by public-housing agencies. The argument for them is that they do not displace many families, can be used to fill in the unused spaces left by abandonment or demolition of buildings, and can be designed to fit the surrounding area. The main argument against them is that they are costly to build and manage.

housing, war   Housing built during wartime for war workers and personnel. During World War I, housing was considered a social rather than a war problem, and though the United States entered the war in April 1917, it was not until October of that year that the Secretary of War realized that lack of housing facilities was "sufficiently extensive to menace the quick preparing of ships and war materials." Two corporations were empowered to build housing, the United States Housing Corporation and the United States Shipping Board. This was the first government-sponsored housing program in the nation's history. After the war the government's war-housing stock was liquidated.

The lessons of World War I were forgotten in World War II. Failure to grasp the importance of housing led to its neglect during the elaborate defense preparations in 1940 and resulted in delays, frustration, and conflicts until the administrative machinery was drastically overhauled. Rent controls were imposed for the first time in 1942. In five years the government program produced less than two million units.

HSB The Hyresgasternas Sparkasse-och Byggnadsforening, or National Association of Tenants' Savings and Building Societies, a Swedish housing cooperative organized in 1923 by a group of consumers who needed housing. The guiding hand was that of Sven Wallander, who received his inspiration from seeing the "progress" of American housing cooperatives in the 1920s. Most of these later went under, but not before Wallander had launched his highly successful venture in Sweden.

The cooperative is organized on three levels: "daughter" societies, which own and operate housing projects and cooperative apartments in which their members live; "parent" societies, which initiate the formation of the daughter groups and perform centralized bookkeeping, banking, and purchasing functions for these lower-level groups; and the "national office," which performs architectural, engineering, planning, and financial functions for the local groups; it also undertakes to support business enterprises that operate the banking, manufacturing, prefabrication, planning, and design services required by the participant societies. (See COOPERATIVE; HOUSING, COOPERATIVE.)

human nidology The study of the human nest and of human nest-building. Birds, fish, reptiles, amphibia, invertebrates, and some mammals have the nest-building instinct, but man seems not to. African termites are considerably more adept at structural building, while the hammerhead stork can erect a huge nest of mud and sticks covered by a roof as much as six feet across, and strong enough to bear the weight of a man, without ruffling a feather. The beaver is an extremely competent engineer, and his tools and instincts are born with him.

Only when one man learns how to build from another can he provide a livable nest for his kin. In rural life he must know how to get the roof over his head or perish. In the cities he reveals himself as a fumbling amateur and must hire a professional who has acquired the skills. One has only to see the millions of squatters and homeless sleeping on the streets of Asia and Latin America or bedding down in cardboard shacks or scrap to see the contrast in skills between *Homo sapiens* and other vertebrate and invertebrate nest-builders.

Man's lack of nest-building instinct seems to confirm his descent from the ape. When he shifted from the arboreal to the terrestrial life he could only move into a cave. When he extended it with a covering of animal skin he took an early step toward civilization.

The anthropomorphous ape has built temporary platforms, the orang-utan has blanketed himself with leaves, and a baboon has been known to cover himself with a straw mat to avoid the sun's heat. "In these several habits," says Darwin, "we probably see the first steps towards some of the simpler arts, such as rude architecture and dress, as they arose amongst the early progenitors of man." (See HOUSE, CORE; HOUSING, SELF-HELP; MUTUAL-AID CONSTRUCTION; ROOF LOAN.)

human scale That combination of qualities that gives man's works an appropriate relationship to man's size and feelings. The architect Ya-masaki, when he was asked why he designed two 110-story buildings for New York City's World Trade Center instead of one 220-story building, reportedly countered that he wanted "to keep it in human scale." Great height and bulk are thought to be the prime destroyers of human scale in cities, and the continued construction of sunless valleys of concrete to be widening the gap between man-size and man-works; but even sky-scrapers can be designed so as to enhance rather than diminish man's sense of grandeur and importance. Besides, great vertical densities con-tribute to human scale in other ways—by making mass transit more fea-sible and by helping to shorten the work journey. The answer lies in sen-sitive design and site planning, and in the provision of compensatory retreats for refuge and contrast.

ideal city. See CITY, IDEAL.

igloo An Eskimo house. It is not usually made of snow, though one may still see snow igloos in Canada. In Alaska, the igloos are small frame houses without insulation or sanitary facilities. Many are one-room shacks 10 feet by 10, some of them built in banks of earth or rocks for warmth and strength. A family of five or ten will be found living in one or two rooms. A typical house in less-isolated Bethel, Alaska, consists of one room made of driftwood, lumber, plywood, or logs; in the smaller villages it is apt to be of poor frame construction, drafty, and a menace to health. These conditions contribute to the very high rates of infectious diseases among the Alaskan natives.

imageability That quality in a city or any of its components which will evoke a strong image in the observer. "It is that shape, color, or arrangement," says Kevin Lynch, "which facilitates the making of vividly identified, powerfully structured, highly useful mental images of the environment. It might also be called 'legibility,' or perhaps 'visibility' in a heightened sense, where objects are not only able to be seen, but are presented sharply and intensely to the senses." (See LEGIBILITY; PATHS.)

improved area; improved land. See LAND, IMPROVED.

improvement Any physical addition to land that increases its utility, beauty, income, or value. Not every improvement automatically improves the environment. An improvement may offer utility and income without beauty or beauty without income. The rare improvement is the one with utility, income, value, *and* beauty. (See CAPITAL IMPROVEMENT.)

improvement trust Principally in the Far East, a public body created to improve land, provide housing, or remedy overcrowding. It may also engage in other activities, such as opening up new traffic routes; buying land, replanning it, and reselling it; operating a sawmill or concrete-block plant as an incident of its other functions; developing suburbs and providing parks and open spaces. It may have the right to borrow funds and sometimes to levy taxes, much like municipal authorities in the United States. The purpose is to give the agency independence from bureaucratic routines; often, however, such an agency is too far removed from official scrutiny and in some instances has been abolished in favor of an agency under direct government control. The device was mostly employed and is still in active use in what were once the British colonies.

income That gain or recurrent benefit (usually in the form of money) which proceeds from labor, business, or property. Gross income is the income derived from property before expenses, while net income is the portion of income remaining after paying interest, taxes, and operating costs.

income property Property owned, acquired, or improved to provide a monetary yield to the owner.

increment tax. See TAX, INCREMENT.

industrial park; industrial estate An area zoned and planned for varied industrial uses and developed and managed as a unit, usually with provision for common services for the users. Many industrial parks have been built on vacant land along the major transportation routes of the nation's metropolitan areas to accommodate industrial activities requiring large tracts of land, having heavy-goods movements, or needing high-capacity transportation and industrial water and sewer services. Industrial parks range in size from under a hundred acres to more than several thousand. Like shopping centers, they have played a substantial role in the suburbanization of American life.

Some industrial estates have been built in underdeveloped countries, where inducements of cheap land and tax benefits have been given to attract industry, promote economic growth, and relieve unemployment.

in-fill housing. See HOUSING, IN-FILL.

infrastructure The basic equipment, utilities, productive enterprises, installations, and services essential for the development, operation, and growth of an organization, a city, or a nation. The permanent military installations and facilities of the North Atlantic Treaty Organization, for example, constitute its infrastructure.

The term is frequently used in the determination of investment priorities in underdeveloped countries. One school of economists holds that a poor country should not spend much on assets for immediate consumption but should focus on infrastructure and other assets that advance productivity—roads, railways, power plants, factories, machines, and better seed and livestock. Use of limited resources for such things as housing, it argues, consumes the funds needed for productive development. Another school argues that poor countries, in their eagerness to raise production levels, must not ignore or subordinate investments in their people and thereby affect labor efficiency.

A principal issue remaining in dispute is whether a poor country should expend money for housing. World Bank economists have consistently opposed it. In Israel, however, where the population doubled between 1949 and 1957, an enormous housing program did not halt economic progress and probably aided it. In the late 1940s the war-torn countries of Europe planned not only for housing but for new towns as part of their over-all recovery programs, and the allocation of vast amounts of capital to this did not impede their remarkable growth thereafter.

Building homes is "economic" in that houses in less-developed areas are often small production centers—for the tailor, dressmaker, or storekeeper. Housing also plays a major role in stimulating employment, directly and indirectly; it activates other industries and adds to local purchasing power. Whether "social" or "economic," it is a wise expenditure simply in terms of balanced growth. Because of the prevalence of extensive unemployment during the formative period of a new nation, a properly organized housing program that uses a maximum of domestic materials could be the principal means of employing people productively. In 1963 about half the unemployment in some of Ghana's cities was among construction workers. Yet these cities were experiencing a severe housing shortage.

Housing also fosters savings and the development of other industries (such as building-materials manufacture), and plays a dominant part in the capital-formation process. It is essential to keep factories functioning that produce materials for all types of construction and productive enterprises. Where housing is built—whether commercial, self-help, or squatter—the public investment is fixed in the vast network of public utilities and facilities. Providing the housing and utilities from the start may therefore be wise in the long run, particularly if the transportation routes are planned simultaneously.

There are only a few countries that have not been forced into housing programs by extensive squatting and the breakdown of legal processes. These events have made the debate on the role of housing as infrastructure largely academic.

installment construction Piecemeal, progressive construction of a dwelling as the resources of the owner-occupant permit. It is common where the general income level inhibits extensive home-building, where the climate permits occupancy in an unfinished dwelling, where methods of shelter construction can employ the skills of the average family, and where financial institutions have not yet developed mortgages or other forms of time payments for housing. Where mortgage systems exist, housing is built complete and paid for in installments; in less-developed economies housing is built in installments as earnings accrue. Until mortgage systems are developed for financing complete construction, installment building will continue to play an important role in housing in the less-developed world. (See HOUSING, HALFWAY.)

installment contract   Purchase of real estate with installment payments; upon default, payments and the right to acquire the property are forfeited. Installment purchases of real estate are more often a danger than a benefit. Poorer families, particularly minorities, agree to buy homes at twice their value because of the attractiveness of the small down payments offered under this type of ownership. After paying substantial sums and finding themselves unable to pay the balance due, would-be owners often lose both the house and the equity they have built up. Practices vary between localities. In some cases the deed is placed in trust pending the making of the required payments up to a certain percentage of the asking price, after which the buyer takes title subject to an inflated mortgage. In others the purchaser takes possession under a rental arrangement, which requires him to pay an installment of principal toward the purchase with each rent payment. If he defaults in the installment payment he remains as a tenant with no other rights. If he pays a sufficient number of installments he takes the property subject to a mortgage, usually a loaded one.

Installment contracts are also made for the purchase of furniture, television sets, automobiles, and clothes, with heavy interest charges usually added to the purchase price. (See HIRE PURCHASE; OPTION; OWNERSHIP.)

instant rehabilitation. See REHABILITATION, INSTANT.

integration; desegregation   The elimination or prevention of segregation in public or private facilities by the commingling of the segregated group with others. Also, the state of being thoroughly mixed or randomly distributed. Desegregation is the act of breaking up a pattern of segregation.

The segregated group may be blacks or other minorities, the poor, or the elderly.

Racial integration implies an acceptance of non-segregated patterns by the commingled groups, and a stabilized neighborhood or school. A neighborhood of whites and blacks is integrated when neither is uneasy and both are free of the threat of domination by the other. To achieve integration, or prevent resegregation, it may be necessary for the public authority to be color-conscious rather than color-blind; to desegregate "with all deliberate speed" as directed by the United States Supreme Court calls for identification of groups and a deliberate and well-motivated effort to attain a stabilized pattern.

Neighborhood integration may take place in safe and socially solvent communities, with good schools and services, in which there is no fear of loss of social status or of a decline in property values. It can take place in an open society in which every individual is free to make his own choices and in which there are ample facilities from which to make such choices and no exclusionary devices to prevent this. Integration becomes difficult where the minority chooses self-segregation, opposes a planned integration in new neighborhoods and in housing projects, or where it moves into a neighborhood in such great numbers as to stir an exodus by the other group. For example, in cities where the proportion of black children is high, the public schools almost inevitably become predominantly black, since many of the white children are withdrawn to private or parochial schools.

Black leaders have divided on the issue of integration with whites. Many want separation and see political advantages in it. They want control of their own segregated schools, government programs, and services. Black pride, black power, and black capitalism are the new themes. (See CULTURAL PLURALISM; INVASION AND SUCCESSION; QUOTA SYSTEM; SEGREGATION.)

interest　The charge made for the use of money, usually computed as a percentage of the principal on a *per annum* basis. Interest has become an important aspect of urban life—in mortgaging property, in buying goods on the installment plan, in borrowing to finance public utilities and urban improvements, in financing production and sales, in encouraging savings, and generally in conditioning the entire credit system on which modern capitalism rests.

Interest and amortization (or debt service) account for about 50 per cent of the carrying charges on a home. The other fixed charges—insurance and taxes—account for another 20 per cent.

The payment of interest and the security of the depositor's savings are the two main reasons motivating bank savings deposits, but in less-developed countries interest alone is often an insufficient inducement, for many of the people distrust banks or are chary of disclosing their possessions. Mortgage money is almost impossible to obtain in less-developed countries, and interest rates exacted by private lenders range from 14 per cent (considered low) to more than 100 per cent. (See AMORTIZATION; DEBT SERVICE; LOTTERY; MORTGAGE; USURY.)

intergovernmental agreements Agreements between two governmental bodies for the performance of a function or service benefiting both. They are made between nations and between subgovernments within a nation. When made between nations, they have been expressed in the form of conventions, treaties, protocols, or contracts. Such agreements were known as far back as the sixteenth century, and commercial or political-marital contracts were known long before. Today the contractual form is also by lease, franchise, compact, or international agreement. With the expansion of international aid programs, loans for road-building, industrial development, and other forms of assistance between countries have become the subjects of intergovernmental agreements. Aid to Latin American nations for housing and for the development of savings and loan associations followed the Alliance for Progress, and some housing aid has been extended elsewhere under such agreements.

Interstate agreements within the United States have been made for the operation of ports and river basins, for the control of air pollution, for sanitation operations, for the development and maintenance of parks and bridges, and similar concerns. The line between federal jurisdiction and the jurisdiction assumed by an interstate compact has still to be drawn. Interstate compacts may be carried out by a newly created interstate agency or authority. This has its limitations as well as advantages: freedom from public control but amenability to pressures exerted by the state legislatures. Complaint has been made, for example, that the Port of New York Authority's autonomy has given it too free a hand in its operations; at the same time pressures exerted by the New Jersey legislature forced it to take over the bankrupt Hudson Tube, thereby giving the Authority justification to build two 110-story office buildings (the World Trade Center) in downtown New York City as a means of balancing its losses on the Tube. Its ability to borrow cheaply through tax-exempt bonds for the building operations and to condemn private land and displace the tenants, as well as its decision to rent offices in competition with private office buildings, has been called unfair competition and an abuse of public power. The courts, however, have upheld its action. (See PUBLIC CORPORATION.)

interlocal cooperative agreements Intergovernmental agreements by which two or more local governments exercise a function jointly, or by means of which one local community contracts for the performance of a service by another governmental unit. In general these agreements broaden the geographic base for planning and for administering governmental services, and economize on the costs of services.

Joint agreements between municipalities have embraced such matters as health, public works, schools, fire and police protection, water supply, sewage disposal, tax collection, traffic control, transportation, airport operation, cemeteries, libraries, public markets, and planning. These can be made formally or informally, and when formal pursuant to either a special act or a general law.

Cooperative agreements among local governments have expanded considerably since the extension of federal aid for regional cooperation. Most such agreements have been between smaller cities and suburban governments, where there was mutual benefit or a sense of urgency (as when lack of a fire station in a new suburb threatens the citizenry and their insurance rates). More recently counties and school districts have become important parties to such contracts. Some counties collect a municipality's taxes on a fee basis; joint school districts can often save money, provide better schools, and help fill classrooms.

intersection; interchange The point or system of roadways where two or more roads cross and where allowance is made for the interchange of traffic between them. An exchange point at grade is commonly called an intersection. When roads cross at different levels, the system of interconnecting roadways allowing for exchange is usually called an interchange. On major highways, grade-separated interchanges are essential for maximum safety and efficiency of movement. Interchanges are also the places where motels, gas stations, shopping centers, and discount houses mushroom into planless developments. As the most familiar type of interchange, "cloverleaf" is often used as though it were a synonymous term. In fact, however, there are many types, including the "trumpet," "flying Y," "four level," "diamond," "split diamond," "jug handle," and "centrifuge." (See GRADE SEPARATION.)

invasion and succession Invasion is the interpenetration or displacement of an existing population or type of land use by another that is different in economic, social, cultural, or racial characteristics. If it results in the departure of the former residents or uses, it is called a succession. The terms are borrowed from ecology, where they are used to describe similar processes in the plant and animal world. Though the word "invasion" has won its way into sociological usage, it carries the implication of a sudden and troublesome intrusion, as by an enemy. The process is not always sudden, however, and since people have a right to seek their living space wherever available it should hardly be called an invasion; "influx" may therefore be a better word.

Succession applies not only to population movements but also to all social and cultural changes that population movements produce. The sociologist applies the term to migrations of people, and also to diffusion of ideas, techniques, artifacts, changes in spatial locations and in group or individual occupations. (See ECOLOGY, HUMAN.)

investment guaranty program A federal program for inducing private enterprise to invest, with federal guarantees, in the less-developed areas. Most guarantees have been made for Latin American investments and have accelerated since the Castro take-over in Cuba. The Agency for International Development, which administers the program, has emphasized development of savings and loan associations and housing construction. In 1968 guarantees for housing totaled $550 million in Latin America. A premium is charged for the guarantees, which may cover a specific risk or extended risks (the latter include the risks of war, nonconvertibility of currency, and expropriation). Interest rates on housing loans have been made at as little as $\frac{3}{4}$ of 1 per cent, running up to about the rate prevailing for federal borrowing. The rate the house-owner in Latin America paid was about 14 per cent *per annum* in 1968. Most of the loans have been made to middle- and upper-income families with few to the rank and file. This has been justified by its administrators on the premise that the middle- and upper-income groups are the more politically vocal among the population and should therefore be catered to.

jerry-building Speculative housing constructed with poor materials and workmanship for a quick profit. Thus anything jerry-built is a shoddy job. The term has no connection with anyone named Jerry or his building firm but was probably derived from "jury," meaning "for temporary use," usually in an emergency.

jet city. See AIRPORT CITY.

joint development The use of a highway or other transportation corridor for residential, institutional, industrial, and commercial development. Under the joint-development concept, the Department of Transportation, working through state road commissions, cooperates with other federal agencies in putting needed development on air rights over new roads or on the margins of the right-of-way. There are no special powers or additional monies authorized for this program, and so far there have been only minor concessions in the department's willingness to pay for some development costs out of the Highway Trust Fund. Most of the cost of platform building and other such construction must come from established federal, state, and city programs.

The effort to complete the urban miles in the massive interstate highway program has given increasing prominence to the joint-development concept. It has been championed as a means to replace houses and shops torn down for the road; to gain sites for needed facilities that would otherwise cause additional displacement; and to humanize the highway itself, disguising it so that it fits into the urban fabric. (See AIR RIGHTS; DESIGN-CONCEPT TEAM.)

journey to work The daily trip to and from work. It is usually centripetal in the morning and centrifugal in the evening. It embraces the whole exercise: walking to and from the bus or rail station in good or bad weather, waiting, lining up for the ticket, changing vehicles, standing in crowded cars, hurrying and growing tense for fear of being late, and the fatigue upon reaching the destination. (The auto commuter must be equally intrepid, for he faces traffic jams both coming and going, and the difficult search for a costly place to park.) The mode of travel is usually inconvenient, often harrowing. Carrying people to and from work is often viewed as a losing operation by the transport companies, and comfort doesn't go with the customer's ticket. It is the dead not the live freight, that keeps the railroads going.

In less-developed countries the journey is negotiated by foot, on bicycle, and less often by mass transport. In India the man-drawn rickshaw supplements transportation for those who have the rupees. In the Philippines the wartime jeeps function with relative efficiency. In the more-developed countries the journey is made less often by bicycle, more often by automobile, bus, or rail, with mass transport steadily giving ground to the automobile (although there are signs that mass transport may be staging a comeback).

Between 1950 and 1958 use of public transport in the United States fell from 17.2 billion to 9.7 billion rides, and by 1960 public transport was used by only 16 per cent of urban workers. In smaller cities the use of public transport is as little as 2 per cent; in Boston, New Orleans, Newark, Jersey City, and Philadelphia the percentage ranged from 25 to 44 per cent. The New York metropolitan region headed the list, with public transport accounting for half the work journeys. The automobile (including the car pool) has become the dominant conveyance. In 1966 about 67 per cent of employed persons in metropolitan areas went to work by car —but there was no automobile in 60 per cent of the families with incomes under $4000, or for half of all Negro and elderly households. Meanwhile the concentration of cars on the road has become one of the nation's main headaches—the Long Island Expressway is described as "the world's longest parking lot." The growing dissatisfaction with the auto journey and its melancholy prospects for the larger metropolitan areas has spurred a search for better mass transport.

The journey to work touches upon people's well-being; it affects city planning, road and housing policy, the economy and way of life in general. Portal-to-portal pay raises production costs, and the consumer must absorb these. A worker traveling an hour each way consumes the better part of a month in travel each year of his life. Much of the gain achieved by shortening the work week has been lost by the extension of the work journey. A British report found that "traveling . . . can hardly fail to have adverse effects on health and to result in fatigue [and] loss of energy. . . . There can be little doubt, too, that these adverse effects on the workers are reflected in no small measure on their efficiency and output, and, in turn, on the employers' cost of production."

Cutting down on the work journey has been one of the main aims of Britain's New Towns program. In Dublin, Ireland, parents complain that their daughters often stay away from home because of the difficulty of travel to the outlying housing projects where they live, particularly at night. In the new town of Ciudad Guyana, Venezuela, where the steel mill pays the transportation costs of workers, it has been estimated that the difference in cost per ton of steel between workers living 4 to 6 kilometers from the plant and workers living 15 kilometers away represents 1 per cent of the average selling price per ton of steel and 7 to 10 per cent of the expected net profit on the average ton sold. In the United States poor people cannot reach suburban jobs. In 1968, for example, it cost a resident of Central Harlem about $40 monthly to commute by public transport to a factory in Farmingdale, Long Island. In Watts, Los Angeles, and other areas, special bus systems have been introduced, but only to make the poor man's journey to work possible, not necessarily comfortable. American conveyances are more crowded than a squatter slum, but the human aspects of the journey to work receive little mention and even less attention from policy-makers. (See CAR POOL; COMMUTER; TRANSIT, MASS.)

justiciable   Subject to the jurisdiction of the courts. A justiciable interest is an interest in a litigation that gives the litigant a standing before the court. Thus a taxpayer has a justiciable interest when he questions a city's expenditure, but he has been held not to have one when he questions an unlawful or improvident federal expenditure; his interest is held to be too remote and minute. This immunity from suit gives the federal government freedom to spend for purposes far removed from its enumerated constitutional powers. As long as the government uses its spending and not its regulatory or eminent-domain powers, it can spend for any purpose.

key money   A cash payment (over and above rent or other charge) made to secure possession of a dwelling unit. In areas that lack a mortgage system payment of key money to owners and builders is common and provides part of the building or investment capital. Key money is also paid to tenants in possession, and in home-hungry and rent-controlled areas it may amount to a ransom. (See OWNERSHIP.)

key tenant. See TENANT, KEY.

"key to the corner"   The lot adjoining the corner lot, so called because its acquisition may be necessary to compose a profitable plot. As such, it may command a higher price than a comparable interior lot. (See ASSEMBLAGE; CORNER INFLUENCE.)

labor-force participation rate; activity rate   The proportion of a given population or group that is economically active in the sense of working for wages. The rate may be expressed as a percentage of the total population, as a percentage of those over the statutory school-leaving age, or as a percentage of a single age-sex group (such as males aged twenty to thirty). In the late 1960s the labor-force participation rate has hovered around 40 per cent of total in the United States, which generally relies on relatively fewer of its citizens to produce the goods and services it consumes. Comparative figures from Japan, Germany, and the United Kingdom run to 46 and 47 per cent. Of course the proportion of economically active persons is higher among men than in the population as a whole (well over 50 per cent in the United States).

laissez faire   A theory of government in which almost all economic activities are left to the play of private operation with as little government interference as possible. The theory was the maxim of French free-trade economists of the eighteenth century but is generally associated with Adam Smith's *Wealth of Nations.* Smith, however, did not exclude the need for some public operations—*i.e.,* those that would not be profitable for the entrepreneur. (See CAPITALISM.)

land   Generally the solid portion of the earth's surface. Also, a particular territory marked off by natural or political boundaries, or the ground owned privately or publicly. In real estate and planning it is that portion of the earth's surface that is the situs for an improvement, as distinguished from the improvement itself.

Land, since the dawn of history, has been the primary source from which man has taken the things he needs for existence and progress, for life on the lower margin and for the life of luxury. It produces the food that feeds him, the materials that clothe him, the wood, stone, and iron that house him, the fuels that warm him and that he has transformed by his arts into energy to serve him in a thousand ways.

Land is the subject, the problem, and the *terra incognita* of city planning. Unsolved problems involving land are many. Is society best served by private or public ownership of land? How far should it be regulated and taxed? What should be the public and private spheres of interest? How dense or how spread out should its development be? To what forces—the automobile, the pedestrian, man, or nature—should priorities be given? What measures should be taken to preserve and control the air above it, the water below it, the foodlands being engulfed by cities in the poorer countries and the recreational spaces being pre-empted in the richer nations? Will the land be able to feed, clothe, and house the seven billion people that will inhabit it by the year 2000? Will law and order collapse as people swarm into the cities of Asia, Africa, and Latin America and seize land because land policy has failed or does not exist? Will the contest for *Lebensraum* be resumed? Is there in fact a land surplus, with the problem being the proper planning, utilization, and distribution of the land? Shall we see more land wars or, if industrialization can be managed and hunger appeased, might there be a rational urbanization that would redirect man's drives from the extensive emphasis of the agricultural world to an intensive expansion within the borders of each nation, thereby removing one of the historic causes of wars?

Inlying land is located within easy distance of a city center.

Outlying land is at a distance from the city center.

Peripheral land is land lying at the border of a community.

Urban land is land located within an urban area. This definition must be imprecise, for urban, suburban, and even rural land have now come within the urban orbit and may be viewed as urban. If, for example, we accept President Johnson's footnote definition of the city in his 1965 Message to Congress as "the entire urban area—the central city and its suburbs," suburban land, including farmland located in the suburbs, is also urban land. If, however, we pay homage to jurisdictional boundaries, a distinction between urban and suburban land would be maintained. (See PUBLIC DOMAIN; PUBLIC-LAND OWNERSHIP.)

land bank   A stockpile of publicly owned land; the result of a program under which a government buys land and holds it for future use as needed. Accumulating land reserves for subsequent development has long been the policy of some European states. It has also been urged upon the United States, which from its early days sold public land rather than have it be owned by the government. Land banks can be useful in planning development and are often established in countries where eminent domain is unpopular or difficult. They require an entrepreneur's skill to determine what and when to buy, when to sell, and how much to pay. Banking land takes taxable land from the tax rolls. Accumulation by a public agency may force up the price of private land—as happened in Israel. In less-developed nations government-owned land is also a target for squatters.

The term also refers to a real bank, such as the federal Land Banks of the United States, or, in Europe, a banking institution that issues notes on the security of landed property. (See PUBLIC DOMAIN; PUBLIC-LAND OWNERSHIP.)

land development   The improvement of land with utilities and services, making the land more suitable for resale as developable plots for housing or other purposes. A land developer is one who develops land for sale or use.

land fragmentation   The division of landholdings through distribution or descent into parcels too small for economical use. In Europe primogeniture and entailment of land concentrated ownership until the French Revolution brought a counter-trend with its own faults—*i.e.,* the division of land from generation to generation until parcels were too small to be economically developed. In France consolidation of uneconomic holdings has been introduced in the hope of eliminating some of the by-products of fragmentation. One of urban renewal's main purposes is to assemble fragmented land and redevelop it into more practicable plots. (See ASSEMBLAGE; ENTAIL; FEUDAL TENURE; LEX ADICKES; REPARCELATION; URBAN RENEWAL.)

land hunger   A craving for land ownership; also, a dearth of sites for development. Land hunger is particularly noticeable in underdeveloped countries where considerable land may be publically owned but not distributed or utilized and where large areas of land may be withheld from use by speculators. Lack of access to sites is another cause of land hunger. But generally the progress of nations is retarded not by insufficiency of land but by its improper or inadequate utilization. There are few countries that should actually suffer from land hunger, particularly in an urban age in which man takes up little room for his needs. The highest population densities per square kilometer in 1966 were in the following countries:

Monaco	15,436	Bahrein	323
Singapore	3,293	Belgium	312
Malta	1,005	Republic of Korea	295
Barbados	570	San Marino	291
Mauritius	407	Japan	267
Netherlands	371	Lebanon	237
China (Taiwan)	356	West Germany	232
Maldive Islands	339	United Kingdom	225

It should be noted that Germany, which once complained most about its need for *Lebensraum,* is far from being the most land hungry of nations.

Though 70 per cent of the people in the United States are city dwellers, they occupy only 2 per cent of its land. (The population per square mile in the United States is about 60.) But while there is no shortage of land for urban man, there is a need for planning and for rationalizing the competition for the land in and around the city cores as well as on the city's periphery. (See LAND POOR; LEBENSRAUM.)

land, improved Raw land that has been provided with sidewalks, water, sewers, and other basic facilities in preparation for residential or industrial development. It sometimes also describes land with structures as well, but usually refers to land with utilities only; land with buildings and utilities would be called a "developed area." (See DEVELOPED AREA; LAND, RAW.)

landlord One who owns and leases real property to a tenant. In England the lord was once also the landowner, but by about the sixteenth century the term was already acquiring its extended meaning. The presence of "lord" in the word was prestigious in England but out of tune in the United States; nevertheless the term came to be accepted as a matter of course by courts, lawyers, and laymen. Today it carries a disparaging note, and landlords prefer to call themselves owners, builders, etc. "Landlady" is the female of the species. "Slumlord" has also now won its way into the language. Landlord was once a figure of speech for God ("the great Landlord").

land, marginal Land at the edge of, or surrounding, a city or metropolitan area; also, land of such poor quality or location that the cost of farming it or putting it to some other use is hardly covered by the expected returns. Marginal land will not be used at all until some change (rising returns, technical advances, public subsidy, or the like) makes it likely that the income will exceed the cost of development.

Marginal urban land is city or suburban land the development of which barely warrants the investment of capital.

Marginal agricultural land, or land at the margin of cultivation, if near to cities, is the land that should be used for housing, industrial, recreational, or other urban uses. Too often it is the fertile paddies and fields bordering on cities that are sacrificed to the steam shovel as population pressures grow in the less-developed countries. Some of this land might be planned as green belts or for homes with small garden plots.

Dead land is one of the American city's painful and growingly insoluble problems—hundreds of abandoned lots without an economic use, not even for single-family housing or parking lots. Building costs, taxes, and the price of money would result in a product cost exceeding product value even if land cost were zero. Urban dead land is the most eloquent exhibit against the classical theory that city land value is ever on the rise. (See ABANDONMENT; UNTENANTED HAZARD; URBAN FRINGE.)

landmark   A fixed object used to mark a boundary; also, a prominent feature of a landscape or cityscape that is the emblem or symbol of a place and that helps the traveler to know where he is, such as a capitol dome or a church steeple; also, spots or structures particularly valued because of their historic or cultural interest—a good architectural specimen, a place in which one of the Founding Fathers slept, or a group of handsome houses that a community thinks should be preserved for posterity.

Landmarks legislation designed to save such structures has been enacted both in Europe and in the United States. In the latter it has taken a number of forms. One is the creation of private philanthropic corporations that buy up landmark buildings and restore them or resell them subject to restoration requirements. Another is the increasingly popular law that restricts an owner from changing the façade of the building without a landmark commission's consent; it also provides that the demolition of a building may be delayed until the commission has had the opportunity to arrange in some way for its purchase or preservation. (See PATHS.)

land-office business   A rush of business in very large volume. In the nineteenth century the United States set up offices to allot government land under the Homestead Act. The rush to file claims at these offices led to the adoption of the phrase to describe any kind of sudden business activity. It is also applied to the private sales of lots by subdividers who use Madison Avenue methods to lure prospects into buying up the hinterlands sight unseen.

land, parcel of A lot or group of lots considered as a unit and generally in single ownership. (See PLAT; PLOT.)

land policy The policy of a government with respect to its land. It may take a number of forms, including deliberate inaction or laissez faire; inducement by subsidization or other benefits; persuasion of enlightened property owners or industrialists to build or act for the public betterment; regulation of private development; direct government undertakings; or joint public-private ventures.

The motivations that spur nations to adopt a land policy include: control of speculation; provision of housing; prevention of squatting; elimination of slums; rebuilding of devastated or derelict areas; achieving more equitable holding of land; development of hinterlands; deconcentration of the denser cities; enhancement of the country's or city's beauty; management of industrial settlement; stabilization of rising rents and land costs; regional rationalization; improvement of family life or increase or lowering of the birth rate; provision for minorities, the aging, large families, refugees, or other special groups; stimulation of employment and economic activity through building; providing accommodations for port, railroad, or dam employees; checking inflation due to rent rises or worker demands for housing allowances; generating more tax revenues; encouraging cooperative development; rationalizing agricultural production and distribution; creating an appropriate urban-rural population balance. In many cases the motivations will be multiple. In all cases land planning and development policies should go together.

In the United States land policy is made by every level of government having jurisdiction over its land. The federal and state governments have exclusive jurisdiction over their respective public domains but are joined by myriad local governments in acting upon private property within their respective jurisdictions through regulation, taxation, and eminent domain. This differs from most other countries, where the national power is predominant. The federal government acts primarily through its spending power and through state and local governments, rather than directly, in relation to private holdings. (See TAX, USE.)

land poor Having all or most of one's capital invested in land and therefore lacking the liquid funds with which to develop the land or to support oneself. The term also describes a tiny area with a dearth of land to accommodate its needs, such as Gibraltar (three miles long by less than a mile wide) or a city like Hong Kong. (See LIQUIDITY.)

land, raw   Land available for building but lacking improvements or utilities. Quoting prices for raw land and improved land as though they were comparable is a common error. One often hears attacks against "quick profits" in land speculation, when in fact the land prices may have gone up because sewer or other improvements were made. The cost of raw land in the United States normally is no more than 5 to 15 per cent of total home cost, and even its reduction would do little to ease the problem of housing cost. This is not the case in the world's underdeveloped areas, where land may be 50 per cent or more of the capital cost of a house.

Another common error occurs in the quoting of land cost on land improved with an occupied building that is to be demolished for a new structure. The land cost in this case includes not only land improvements made over the years and paid for by the owner (and the city), but the cost of demolition and the destruction of a real and capitalizable income. (See DEVELOPED AREA; LAND, IMPROVED.)

land reclamation   The construction of dams, canals, pumping systems, etc., to bring irrigation water to arid, semi-arid, or subhumid lands. Land is being reclaimed in the western United States as well as in Israel, Egypt, and other countries of the Middle East, India, Mexico, Peru, and the Soviet Union. Irrigation of dry lands was practiced by the Indians before Columbus in what is now the southwest United States. Reclamation is also undertaken with soils that are salt-affected, swampy, strip-mined, eroded, or infertile.

land registration   The recording of deeds, mortgages, and other instruments in a public office to evidence one's rights in real property and to protect against fraud and other questions affecting the title to, or interest in, such property.

In primitive countries and in tribal areas, ceremony and publicity attend a transfer of land. Passing a handful of earth, breaking a branch, or some other act performed in public manifests a conveyance of title. In Ghana it might be accompanied by a "dash" of gin to celebrate and make the memory secure. But as memories fade or witnesses die litigation begins, and in Ghana land litigation has been called the second largest industry. Considerable urban land remains unimproved because tribes might not have followed procedures necessary to effect a lawful conveyance. Registration is a better protection than the symbolic act or the warranty deed with nothing more.

Land registration in the New World began in the Plymouth Colony in 1626 and in Virginia and Connecticut in 1639. Today deeds are recorded *pro forma*. Though title passes on the delivery of the deed, the recording gives a legal priority to the grantee; failure to register gives subsequent parties who deal with the property in good faith superior rights. An unregistered deed may also be ineffective against creditors of the former owner who had no notice of the conveyance. (See CADASTRE; TITLE.)

land tenure   The holding of land or the right to hold it. The word "tenure," derived from the Latin *tenere,* "to hold," has its origins in feudal days when land was held from another and not owned absolutely. Land tenure in England has been a continuous process, and though owners' rights have been modified by statute from time to time (to maintain beauty, control development, protect tenants, etc.) tenure has been uninterrupted, as manifested by some 999-year leases made at the time of William the Conqueror now being negotiated for renewal. The English system is unique, however. While the outward formalities of landlord and tenant have been preserved, the absolute right to own has been modified considerably. Rent controls, death duties, considerations of sanitation and health, and regulation of development rights have destroyed some of land tenure's ancient privileges. Market rents on commercial properties are respected, however, in contrast to Ireland, whose history is a long and painful struggle with landlordism of all sorts. Here laws have all but wiped out the old fee owners, and rents under long-term expiring leases have been fixed at one-sixth of current value, and even this has been protested as too high.

The United States from its beginning favored alienation of the public lands, and the individual land buyer wanted no restraints on his property. But with urbanization the public has become more concerned about how tenure is being managed. Local governments now regulate how the land may be used and through zoning can reduce value to a fraction of its former worth or, by liberalizing its use, elevate it into a fortune. What one may or may not build is closely supervised, and taking of private property for public use is virtually unrestricted if the statute declares that the taking benefits the public. One reason for the policy is that, in contrast to England and the Continent, land has never been unique or special; migration was frequent and land was viewed as convertible into cash and duplicatable by another purchase.

In the Soviet Union all land is owned by the state, but rights of tenure exist in security of possession, rights of inheritance, and protection against expropriation with assurance of compensation for the taking. (See FEE; FREEHOLD; OWNERSHIP.)

land, underemployed A site ripe for development that is not being utilized for its best purpose. It may be farmland suitable for a subdivision, an armory that should make way for an apartment house, or stores that should be replaced by a tall office building. The motivations that keep land underemployed (also underdeveloped or underimproved) include: land speculation, inability to finance the improvement, unwillingness of an owner to sell, an unmarketable title, a leasehold with too short a term to warrant an investment in a new improvement, or inability to acquire an adjoining plot that would make an improvement economic.

In the United States another reason is that under the tax laws an owner who sells a building that is fully depreciated keeps only 68 to 75 per cent of the proceeds after paying his capital-gains tax; if he has a prime property, he considers himself better off mortgaging the property for 70 per cent of value and keeping the net income. This is one of the obstacles to acquiring property by negotiation in urban-renewal areas. If, however, the property is taken by eminent domain, the owner need not pay the capital-gains tax if the compensation is invested in other property within a year.

In some countries a multiplicity of heirs makes it difficult to obtain consent to a sale. In Dublin, Ireland, prime land remained saddled with obsolete buildings because the original 299-year leases were about to expire. In New York City rent controls and the unwillingness of tenants to move without ransom compensation keep many properties underdeveloped. In Singapore one small office tenant demanded $100,000 for possession and succeeded in preventing construction of a major bank development.

land use The employment of a site or holding so as to derive revenue or other benefit from it; also, the delineation by a governing authority of the utilization to which land within its jurisdiction may be put so as to promote the most advantageous development of the community (such as designation of industrial, residential, commercial, recreational, and other uses under a master plan).

There are five ways in which public power is employed in land-use control: prescribing land use—*i.e.*, designating the way land may or may not be developed (*e.g.*, zoning, building restrictions); preventing misuse of land that might injuriously affect the interests of the community (*e.g.*, preventing slum construction or unnecessarily intense development); preventing the abuse of land (*e.g.*, preventing abortive subdivisions, cut-over lands); regulating the non-use or disuse of land (*e.g.*, taxing to enforce development, clearing unmarketable titles, restraining owners of occupied dwellings from discontinuing their use, escheat); guiding the reuse of land for more appropriate purposes (*e.g.*, urban redevelopment, slum clearance, rehousing).

In the United States controls must be reasonable and are reviewable by the courts. In England it is Parliament alone that determines the reasonableness.

Land use that is inconsonant with its surroundings and that adversely affects the value of other properties in its vicinity is called "inharmonious land use." (See PUBLIC PURPOSE; USE, MIXED; ZONING.)

land-use plan The official formulation of the future uses of land, including the public and private improvements to be made on it and the assumptions and reasons for arriving at the determinations. A land-use plan is not to be confused with the land-use map, which describes how the land and buildings are or have been used; or with the zoning plan, which regulates use, density, coverage, bulk, etc.; or with the master plan of which it is often a part. The land-use plan projects private and public land uses and is usually prepared simultaneously with the highway and street plan. These two plans lay the groundwork for the master plan.

The land-use plan serves as a guide to official decisions in regard to land acquisition for public purposes, as well as to private decisions on the location of shopping centers, residences, and industry. It is also a guide to decisions on zoning, subdivision controls, urban renewal, and future capital-budgeting requirements. For some years land-use planning has been one of the major functions of city planners, and in the public's mind it is often synonymous with city planning. It is, however, only one of the many types of urban planning. (See CITY PLANNING; MAP, OFFICIAL; MASTER PLAN; ZONING.)

land-use survey A survey of the uses to which land is put in a particular area, usually summarized both in map form and statistically, that shows developed and vacant land, streets, parkland, public buildings, etc. Acreages are often summarized in terms of percentages for the developed portions and for the area as a whole. (See SURVEY.)

lane A narrow way intended to carry a single line of moving persons or vehicles. It is usually either marked off or physically separated from adjacent lanes. On a highway all lanes in both directions are counted; thus a six-lane highway is one with three lanes in either direction.

A reversible lane is one which may be used by vehicles operating in different directions at different times, switching at specified times to accommodate peak flows.

latifundium A large landed estate. Its derivation is from the Latin *latus,* meaning broad, and *fundus,* meaning estate. Latifundia are still prevalent in South America, where the carry-over from the haciendas and the large agricultural estates in the old Spanish tradition prevails. Though 60 per cent of all Latin Americans are employed in agriculture, almost 80 per cent of the cultivatable soil in 1968 was still in the hands of 5.5 per cent of the landowners. Such large holdings are exceptional in the United States, the most notable urban example being the Irvine Estate near Los Angeles County, with almost a thousand acres of very valuable land within the urban orbit. Rural land holdings are often much more extensive. While the average number of acres per farm in the United States was only 151 in 1930, it has grown steadily, rising to 360 in 1964. Mechanization has been heading American farm tenure from the old family-size forty acres to the ranch-size holding.

latrine A primitive toilet made by digging a ground-hole for the deposit of family stools. It is safe and serviceable if sufficiently separated from the source of drinking water. While practical on the farm, it may be a bane in a squatter village, where entameba are transmitted from stools or conveyed through the drinking water. (See CESSPOOL; SEPTIC TANK.)

laundromat; washateria An emporium for the on-site renting of washing machines. It is an urban product of automation. The housewife, for a fee fed to the machine (together with soap and bleach), can irrigate and dry the family linen, woolies, panties, and undies while resting, reading, or gossiping. The laundromat is found in neighborhood shopping areas and in housing projects and may include dryers, spinners, coin changers, and other vending machines. It has some of the drawing power of other water magnets, such as waterfalls, fountains, wells, swimming pools, and spas —providing opportunity for social concourse with a neighbor while the water performs its miracles. With the concealment of rivers and water-courses by roads and buildings, the laundromat may ultimately be the last vestige of the aqueous on the urban scene.

leafraking. See BOONDOGGLING.

lease A contract by which one rents land or buildings to or from an-other, generally for a term of years and for a fixed rent. Leases of apart-ments are generally for short terms—one to five years—while leases of land may run for as long as ninety-nine, particularly when the tenant in-tends to put up a costly structure. Long-term leases are highly complex instruments with provisions often covering fifty or more pages and con-taining particulars as to rent, methods of financing, remedies for default, provisions dealing with fire, renewals, and a host of other clauses.

The owner is called the "lessor" and the tenant the "lessee." If the les-see rents to another, the latter is called a "sublessee."

A leasehold is a tenure by lease, or the land leased.

A form lease, printed by a stationer from some approved document and containing an abundance of protections for the landlord, is usually signed *pro forma* by the tenant, who relies more on the statutory and cus-tomary protections for his relief than on the printed clauses. (See RENT; SUBLEASE.)

lease back An arrangement by which the owner sells his land, build-ings, or both to an investor and simultaneously takes back a lease on the very same property. The seller-lessee has many rights he enjoyed before as owner, since his new lease is generally long-term with adequate provi-sion for renewal, while the investor has a more conservative investment that no longer requires his management. The arrangement may be prompted by tax advantages to one or both parties or by the attractions to the seller of the cash received for the sale of the fee. Insurance companies have been the most recent purchasers of such properties; they buy the underlying land, leaving its development and operation to the former owner, now their lessee.

lease, net   A lease under which the tenant agrees to pay, in addition to rent, all the expenses of the property (real-estate taxes, insurance, and repairs) except the mortgage debt service of the lessor. Net leases are usually made on commercial and industrial properties. Since the lessor's receipts are all his own (except for income taxes and mortgage charges), properties with net leases are salable to investors looking for a safe, conservative return. This is particularly true where the lessee is a triple-A tenant (a tenant with the highest rating), in which case the value of the property may be anywhere from thirteen to twenty times the net rent, depending on the length of the lease and the going rate of interest.

lease, percentage   A commercial lease providing for rent based on a percentage of gross receipts. The percentage varies with each business, generally being lowest for chain food stores and discount houses and highest for garages and parking lots. The lease generally also provides for a minimum rental. The following are examples of estimated percentage ranges for a few types of enterprises. These are by no means standard and vary with area, changes in conditions, and in the types of merchandise that are handled.

Enterprise	Percentage of Gross Sales Paid in Rent
automobile parking	35–60
motion-picture theater	$12\frac{1}{2}$–15
book and stationery store	8–10
bar and grill	7–9
supermarket	1–$1\frac{1}{2}$

Lebensraum   Living space, or room to move about and function. Adolf Hitler turned the word into a slogan of conquest, proclaiming that Germany's future was "wholly conditional upon the need for space . . . a larger *Lebensraum* . . . a rational relation between the number of people and the space for them to live in. . . . The fight must start here. No nation can evade the solution of this problem." His solution was simple—he reduced the population density. Without passing on the ethical aspects of conquest and carnage as tools of urban planning, the fact is that in 1940 Germany was less densely populated than England, Wales, the Netherlands, and other parts of Europe.

The fear of land shortage has persisted for centuries, and some of history's most celebrated thinkers have shared it. That urbanization has altered the picture is still not fully understood. There may ultimately be a shortage of food lands for the burgeoning population, but there is no shortage of land for urban uses. It is not land shortage *per se* that is the problem today, but the appearance of land shortage as a result of the competition for the central land in and around the world's great cities. (See HOUSING SHORTAGE; LAND HUNGER.)

legibility In Kevin Lynch's usage, the ease with which the parts of a city can be recognized and organized into a coherent pattern. A legible city is one whose elements are visually robust and can be easily conceived of as a whole. (See IMAGEABILITY; PATHS.)

legislative architecture. See ARCHITECTURE, LEGISLATIVE.

leisure Time free from established routines of work and duty and used for relaxation, diversion, recreation, social achievement, or personal development. Motivations distinguish leisure from non-leisure; writing a glossary may be relaxation for an easy pen and an umbilical strain for a stubborn one; such writing may be part of one man's leisure and of another's livelihood.

The eight-hour day and the five-day week, as well as early retirement and longer vacations, have extended the leisure hours for those Americans who do not consume it in moonlighting or in the journey to work. Leisure time may be home-centered, community- or group-centered, individualized, or institutionalized. The TV screen and suburbanization have made more leisure activities home-centered at the same time as TV's advertisers have sought to lure the homebody into the urban and exurban money stream of packaged leisure activities.

The "leisure class" is no longer confined to the lucky few with time and money on their hands. The Protestant ethic, which made a virtue of hard work, industriousness, and frugality, has been subordinated to the union ethic of less work time, longer vacations, and more coffee breaks. The time won for leisure has simultaneously increased the periods of boredom, which the victims have sought to offset by driving a car or a golf ball; playing bridge (forty million players, with fifty million decks of cards sold each year in the 1960s); bowling (thirty million bowlers); and boating (seven million boats).

The time for leisure has made room for the art of conversation, but a growing number of substitutes have made conversation unnecessary. Boiler-room music at the discothèques dispenses with the need for conversation among the younger set, while television has taken over in the parlor for the rest of the family.

With the need to maintain the morale, loyalty, and good spirit of workers, a growing number of employers sponsor leisure activities, and some unions vie with them in setting up camps, clubs, and socials.

Leisure is not all leisurely. Loaded briefcases make the journey home with executives and businessmen, while politicians and obstetricians hardly expect unbroken respites. Some executives look on their work as a welcome escape from their leisure. Many retired people take flight from their leisure to resume work. To others, the weekend party is more harrowing than the job.

About a third of our married women are gainfully employed while the rest consume much of what was once leisure time in taking children to and from school, attending PTA meetings, bringing their husbands home from the station, and doing household chores once performed by the mother-in-law or the now vanishing servant class. With suburbanization, often the mother-in-law is no longer on hand to fill the gaps.

In short, leisure is being destroyed at the same time as it is being extended. Leisure is not always pleasure. It can be exhausting, costly, or wasteful. Social scientists could render a public service by devoting their leisure hours to more intensive study of its proper uses. (See JOURNEY TO WORK; RECREATION.)

level payment; constant-payment plan　An arrangement in a financing transaction under which the same fixed sum is paid periodically for debt service throughout the term of a mortgage. As the mortgage is reduced and the interest due becomes less, the amount of amortization is increased to the extent of the reduction in the interest, resulting in the level payment. As the mortgage approaches maturity the amortization becomes the main item in the level payment. The alternative arrangement is a fixed amortization payment throughout the mortgage term with diminishing amounts of interest paid periodically until maturity. The declining payment was the customary arrangement before the 1930s and is still the practice in some mortgage transactions. For the ordinary homeowner the constant-payment plan has the virtue of spreading his burden evenly over the term of the loan and giving him a fixed sum around which he can plan his budget and future expenditures. (See AMORTIZATION; DEBT SERVICE; MORTGAGE.)

leverage The employment of a smaller investment to generate a larger rate of return through borrowing. For example, a person buying property for $1,000,000 which yields $80,000 after deducting all operating expenses and depreciation is getting an 8 per cent return free of mortgages. If he raises a $700,000 mortgage at 6 per cent interest (costing him $42,000 annually in interest) his net yield would be $38,000 ($80,000 less $42,000), or more than 12 per cent on his remaining equity of $300,000. Leverage is what makes it possible for banks to function—*i.e.,* they accept deposits at an interest rate lower than on the loans they make.

Lex Adickes A replotting law (named after Mayor Adickes, who first proposed it in Prussia in 1902) under which land is compulsorily pooled and replotted in order to eliminate small and awkwardly shaped plots. The policy was followed in West Germany after World War II during the reconstruction of war-torn areas. Reconstruction associations combined the plots of numerous owners and after reconstruction returned to them their proportionate share of the land. (See ASSEMBLAGE; ENTAIL; HOLDOUT; LAND FRAGMENTATION; PRIMOGENITURE; REPARCELATION; URBAN RENEWAL.)

license A permit or privilege given by an official agency that authorizes the recipient to do something or carry on some trade or occupation for the duration of the license. An official license is not a franchise. The main purposes of licensing are to regulate operations that need supervision in the interests of community health, welfare, or safety; register activities or businesses; pass on the legality of certain operations in advance; and collect revenue for general or other purposes. Practicing law, medicine, or real-estate brokerage; marrying; running a restaurant, pool parlor, theater, dance hall, barbershop; carrying a pistol; operating a liquor store or drugstore—these require licenses in many jurisdictions. There has in fact been a steady tendency to license activities that in former years were operable without a license. Licensing may be invoked when the public concern asserts itself as the result of some highly publicized abuse. Assassinations, for example, have brought pressure for licensing of guns.

In real property, the law of license involves a different conception. Here it is a mere authority to enter upon the land of another for a temporary purpose and to do a particular act upon the land. Laying a telephone wire, opening a door in a fence to permit escape in case of fire, permitting installation of a cigarette machine or a coin-metered washing machine to convenience tenants, are examples of such licenses.

lien   A charge or claim upon real or personal property for the satisfaction of some debt or duty. A mortgage is one type of lien upon real estate; a tax on real estate is another. A mechanic's lien representing an unpaid charge to a contractor, materials dealer, or architect is a third; this may be filed by one whose work or materials has improved the property and serves notice upon any prospective buyer or lender that there is a claim made, which, if sustained, will be a charge upon the property regardless of any change in ownership. A lien may be discharged by successfully litigating the claim or by bonding it to the extent of the claim. The bond (generally of a surety company) guarantees that if the claim is sustained the indemnifier will pay it. (See ENCUMBRANCE; MORTGAGE; TAX LIEN.)

life cycle   The stages through which a family and its members pass, beginning typically with marriage and the establishment of economic self-sufficiency; followed by childbirth and child-rearing; maturation of the children, during which the family attains its maximum size; establishment of independent households by the offspring; retirement by the parents; dotage; the death of one of the partners, and the final dissolution of the household with the death of the second. This, of course, is an idealized example, and there are many variations, but analyzing the progress of a family unit in this way reveals how its needs, particularly for housing and access to recreation and community facilities, change over time. It highlights how ill equipped most cities, suburbs, and even new towns are to accommodate the family through the life cycle, and it helps to explain the increasing segregation within metropolitan areas of the very young and very old households from those in the middle years. (See FAMILY.)

limited-dividend housing. See HOUSING, LIMITED-DIVIDEND.

linear city. See CITY, LINEAR.

linear programing As used in planning, a mathematical technique for determining the optimum allocation of limited resources (such as capital, manpower, or facilities) to obtain a particular objective (such as a maximum tax revenue or minimum congestion) when there are alternate ways of employing the resources.

linear system A circulatory pattern for a transportation system generally consisting of a single line or parallel series of lines. It works well where traffic flows run between two points instead of to or from a single dominant point or a number of diverse points. Railroads, trolley-car routes, canals, rural roads, and service-strip developments along highways are examples. (See RADIAL STREET PATTERN.)

linkage A relationship between two or more establishments that is characterized by frequent interaction, particularly the movement of persons or goods. Where movement is heavy, establishments tend to locate near one another. Uses that are next door to each other may not necessarily be linked, and linked units may be distant from one another, taking advantage of advanced communications and transportation technology to keep up the relationship. Nevertheless linkages and the costs of overcoming distance are still the prime factors in the locational decisions of urban establishments.

Linkages can conveniently be broken down into three types: between dominant establishments (as between a dress manufacturer and a department store); between a dominant operation and a subordinate concern (as between the dressmaker and the sewing-machine repair shop); or an ancillary establishment (the barbershop or luncheonette serving the personnel of the dress manufacturer, the repair shop, and the shoppers).

The relationships expressed by the linkage concept are key ones in ex-

plaining clustration. Planners who have not heeded linkage requirements—the need for face-to-face contact, ready access to up-to-date information, cheap and quick movements of goods—have been responsible
for destroying once viable centers or have seen shiny new ones emerge
stillborn. (See CLUSTRATION; FRICTION OF SPACE; LOCATION THEORY,
INDUSTRIAL.)

liquidity The state of having cash assets or those easily convertible into
cash. It is the opposite of being "frozen," "tied up," or land poor. A main
problem of land developers and builders of new communities is that after
buying the land they cannot find the wherewithal to finance land improvements, the liquid assets having often been spent in the early stages
of the development. If land or home sales are sluggish the developer may
be ripe for the bankruptcy court. Illiquidity may then lead to liquidation.
(See LAND POOR; MORTGAGE MARKET.)

listing Placing properties for sale or dwelling units for rent with brokers. Multiple listing is a system in which real-estate brokers list all
properties for sale or rent with one another. If any broker with whom the
property is listed sells or rents the property, the commission is divided as
agreed between the broker who originally listed the property and the
broker who sold or rented it. (See BROKER.)

loan, construction A short-term loan to a builder that finances construction and precedes permanent financing. Partial advances are made as
and when parts of the building are completed, pursuant to a construction-loan agreement. (See FINANCING, PERMANENT; MORTGAGE.)

loan servicing The administration and collection of monthly mortgage
payments from home-owners and other borrowers, usually by a bank,
mortgage broker, or real-estate company acting for itself or as agent for
the mortgagee. Servicing agents sometimes place the mortgage with an
investor, then perform the servicing function for him. For the agent's fee,
the holder is relieved of the need for maintaining accounts and collec-
tions and for following up on delinquencies such as tax and interest defaults. Use of banks to service mortgage paper has often been urged on
the government as a more efficient and cheaper way of servicing its col-

lections than working through the bureaucratic government agencies themselves. (See DEBT SERVICE; MORTGAGE.)

loan-value ratio   The proportion a mortgage loan bears in relation to the value of the property mortgaged. The range may vary from two-thirds of appraised value by an institution on commercial property to 90 per cent for a loan on a home by a savings and loan association, and up to 100 per cent in the case of a mortgage loan by the government on a non-profit undertaking. Of course in situations thought risky by lenders, such as deteriorated areas with classic homes in the early stages of a renovation boom, loans may be for only half or one-third of value when they can be procured at all. (See MORTGAGE.)

lobby   A passage or hall of communication, as in the British House of Commons and in the United States Capitol. The derivation is from old German *lauba,* meaning "a shelter of foliage." The word then entered the Latin of the Middle Ages as *lobia,* and in the sixteenth century was adopted into English as "lobby," meaning a covered walk.

   Lobby also refers to the people and interests who frequent the lobbies of a legislative house to transact business and influence legislation and public policy. Lobbying has been practiced from America's beginnings, when in 1786 Manassah Cutler promoted his land scheme by sharing profits with influential congressmen.

   Lobbying is not evil *per se,* and virtually every interest of national importance has its paid representative in the capital of the nation and often in state capitals and city halls as well. Some lobbyists are former legislators with connections and know-how; a few represent civic groups; most represent private interests. Honest argument as well as deception and coercion are among the tactics employed. Efforts to legislate the lobby out of existence have proven futile, and registration of lobbyists is as far as the United States has gone in regulating the practice.

   The word is used in a different sense in England, where it refers to the lavatory. It might be said that in England a lobby is where a legislator fixes his unmentionables; in the United States it is where the unmentionables fix the legislators.

local public agency (LPA)   An official body empowered to contract with the federal government for assistance in carrying out urban-renewal projects and certain other federally aided efforts. In most cases the LPA is a specially created local body, such as a redevelopment agency or housing authority, but it might also be a state, county, municipality, or other governmental body.

location theory, industrial   The study of the motivating forces that govern the location, dislocation, and relocation of industries. The subject is crucial to nations dependent on growth, to nations whose economies are still in thrall to agriculture, and to cities having unemployed populations or threatened with industrial exodus.

There is much which calls for the updating of nineteenth-century theories of industrial location. The shift to electric power has freed industries from the tyranny of the belt-line, and the internal combustion engine has diminished dependence on the railroad. Location near a large consumer market may have more advantages for an industry than cheap electricity, subsidies, or advantageous freight rates. Not only wage rates but the severity of regulatory legislation may determine whether an industry will settle in a particular country (for example, Bolivia's social, labor, and tax laws, which put heavy burdens on any operation employing more than five workers, have been enough to discourage almost all large-scale operations). Vague laws requiring employers to furnish travel accommodations or portal-to-portal pay in a new city like Ciudad Guayana, Venezuela, will head entrepreneurs toward the established cities where the transportation problem is the worker's own. Labor strife and unreasonable demands by unions and labor syndicates will hardly draw industrial investment, while clarification of labor laws can do much to encourage it. The social climate in a particular area may be more influential in attracting talent than the pay—it is the executive's wife who is becoming the new sphinx of the trade routes, and the availability of good schooling, shopping, beauty parlors, restaurants, and similar attractions may make the difference between getting the executive or losing him. The general interest, attractiveness, and safety of a community will have much to do with an industry's settling and staying in it; drab, isolated towns will draw neither the investor nor the executives, nor will they attract skilled workers upon whom the success of ventures so often depend.

Political stability or instability is also a prime factor. While certain industries still need proximity to water for power, atomic power may alter such needs, bringing power to bauxite instead of bauxite to power. Availability of air-conditioning is sparking industrial interest in countries where climate was once a retarding factor. Education and training are equipping people once thought to be unemployable. Tax-exempt bonds issued by cities and hamlets, the proceeds of which are being used to build plants and lease them at low rents to industries, have increased the migration of major American companies to once unindustrialized hinterlands. The movement of the American middle class to suburbia has sent major industries after them, for the suburbs now have clerical skills and minor executives in addition to cheaper land. Urban-renewal operations have made in-city land available to some industries that were once looking outward. Airport shipping has opened up new possibilities and, where aided by tax exemption or other inducements (as in Ireland), has stimulated industrial interest.

In sum, new forces are conditioning industrial and entrepreneurial motivations. These motivations change also with political shifts, population shifts, and shifting theories that were once the gospel of capitalism and socialism. (See FRICTION OF SPACE; LINKAGE.)

lot The atomic particle of city building—the smallest subdivision of land or of a block in which cities are sectioned, its size varying with the locality. It may also describe a parcel of vacant land or one with a building or group of buildings in single ownership.

A corner lot is a parcel of land at the junction of two or more intersecting streets, and a corner building is a building erected on such a lot.

An irregular lot is a lot with irregular dimensions, one deviating in metes and bounds from the standard.

An interior or inside lot is a lot that is situated between the corner lots on a street.

A through lot is an interior lot with its ends fronting on two parallel (or approximately parallel) streets.

The lot line is any line separating one lot from another. (See BLOCK; PLOT.)

lottery An arrangement by which a public agency, operator, or entrepreneur contracts with a number of persons, in exchange for a prescribed fee or payment, to pay out money prizes or other rewards to those selected by a process dependent on chance.

The lottery is a more respectable device than is generally believed. The distribution of the Promised Land among the Twelve Tribes of Israel involved a decision by drawn lot. As a source of national revenue, the lottery was introduced in England as far back as 1569 and continued in use there until the 1920s. A lottery helped pay the Virginia Company's colonial expedition, and lotteries were partly responsible for financing the establishment of Harvard, Columbia, Dartmouth, and Williams colleges in the United States. The abolition of lotteries in England and the United States was inspired by corruption and counterfeiting of tickets; but after much debate the lottery has recently won public sanction in New York State.

Some nations, like Ireland and Australia, employ or permit lotteries for the benefit of hospitals, and some conservative churches are not above using this method to raise funds. In Colombia the beneficiaries are not only hospitals but old people, who are given housing. Lotteries have a long and uninterrupted history in Central and South America and in several European countries, and even England has readopted the lottery idea for recent public bond flotations.

Lotteries are sometimes used to promote savings in less-developed countries. Turkish banks have offered houses as prizes to attract depositors. While objections to lotteries exist (one argument is that they make people rely more on luck than labor), the stricture against use of the lottery to draw savings is without much force. The benefits of savings are retained, and thrift rather than speculation is encouraged when the gamble is the inducement to save.

LPA. See LOCAL PUBLIC AGENCY.

lunch In ordinary usage a midday meal, but in entrepreneurial language a vital urban institution in which contacts are made firm, deals made, information obtained, and differences ironed out. Lunch clubs are major amenities for executives in dense business sections, while luncheonettes are where a meal is wolfed down by the help. The paucity of decent restaurants for the stenographers *et al.* has begun to worry downtown planners, real-estate men, and employment agencies, though little evidence of corrective action has as yet appeared.

luxury housing. See HOUSING, LUXURY.

managing agent A person or corporation managing real estate for an owner. The managing agent operates the building, makes repairs, lets the units, and collects rents, remitting them to the owner minus his charges. Managing agents are usually real-estate brokers and often insurance agents as well. (See BROKER.)

map, base A map showing the essential natural or man-determined features of an area. It is used as the starting point for many planning and design operations. Base maps, since they record relatively permanent facts, are reproduced in quantity so that information that is constant from one use to the next need not be redrawn each time analytic material has to be recorded or proposed changes and additions are developed.

map, official A map showing anticipated streets, open spaces, parks and play spaces, school sites, and such other information as the law directs. It is the prospectus of a city's intentions to acquire specific sites for public purposes, giving the locations and extent of the facilities to be installed or changes to be made, particularly street widenings, street extensions, new parks, schools, and other contemplated improvements. It puts developers and other private interests on notice as to the municipalities' plans for site acquisition. The official map is usually recorded and may show existing street rights-of-way and public properties as well as those contemplated. It is not to be confused, however, with a master or comprehensive plan, which embraces a much longer time period and private as well as public development. (See LAND-USE PLAN; MASTER PLAN.)

map, reference Mapped information on the city and its environs. The maps may be engineering, topographic, census, zoning, insurance (showing structures), highway, or tax, or other types of maps used for reference. The original information may be derived from aerial photographic mosaics, windshield surveys, engineering studies, combined subdivision plats, or other sources. These maps are an important source of information for the planning department in subdivision work, site planning, preparation of official maps, and the numerous other aspects of public operations.

map, time-contour A map on which the contour lines connect points of equal travel time from a specified central point, given a particular mode of transport. The line indicating places from which the same time is required for reaching the central point is called an "isochrone." (See TRANSPORTATION PLANNING.)

market value. See VALUE, MARKET.

mass production. See ASSEMBLY LINE.

mass transit. See TRANSIT, MASS.

master plan, city plan A comprehensive, long-range plan intended to guide the growth and development of a city, town, or region, expressing official contemplations on the course its transportation, housing, and community facilities should take, and making proposals for industrial settlement, commerce, population distribution, and other aspects of growth and development. It is usually accompanied by drawings, explanatory data, and a prefatory *apologia* explaining its limitations. Few aspects of the city-planning process have aroused more controversy than the master plan. Conceptions of what it should be run the gamut from the futurama down to the simple zoning scheme. No master plan can be fulfilled specification by specification in face of the ever-recurring changes caused by industrialization, population shift, traffic increase, suburbanization, and periodic political undulations. Nor should this be expected. At best it is the official embodiment of a hope.

The dangers in the proffering of any comprehensive master plan are: public reaction that it will cost too much (the tendency is to consider the costs as an immediate lump-sum expenditure); mobilization of the opposition (each person affected joins others affected by part of the plan); the difficulty of altering it once compromises have been made and public approval secured; the tendency of any plan to become obsolete owing to the supervention of unanticipated changes and circumstances.

While advocates of the master plan will condition their blueprint with precautionary notations about "flexibility," "priorities," and "changes when dictated by circumstances," their conditionings will tend to be ignored or forgotten in the furor that generally accompanies the presentation.

Despite all the perils, master plans deserve venturing and exposure if for no better reason than that they disclose the lucubrations of officialdom and at their best plot a bold course in a sea of trouble. A master plan is an act of political gallantry, and master planning an art in search of the golden mean, between the generalization that will obscure it and the specificity that will defeat it. (See COMPREHENSIVE PLAN; LAND-USE PLAN; MAP, OFFICIAL.)

mayor-council plan   A form of city government in which the legislative and executive functions are separated and both are in the hands of elected officials. Of the basic types of municipal rule in the United States, the mayor-council plan is most closely analogous to the federal system of checks and balances. Its critics claim that it forces political considerations to the fore and makes efficient administration and comprehensive planning impossible. Its apologists insist that there is no way to take the politics out of politics; the mass of evidence is on the defenders' side. (See CITY MANAGER PLAN; COMMISSION SYSTEM OF GOVERNMENT.)

megalopolis; megapolis   The greater urbanized area resulting from the gradual merging of many metropolises and cities into one great urban agglomeration. Ancient Greece had a city by the name, and a contemporary meaning was given it in 1961 by Jean Gottman in his book *Megalopolis.* The subject of this book, the northeastern United States coastal region lying between Portland, Maine, and Norfolk, Virginia, is the most striking example of such an area. It is characterized by enormous urban, suburban, and metropolitan growth producing an almost continuous string of cities.

Megapolis is used synonymously with megalopolis but was originally a nonce-word used by Sir Thomas Herbert, the seventeenth-century English traveler-author, to describe a chief city. (See AGGLOMERATION; CONURBATION; METROPOLIS.)

melting pot   A term applied to the large cities of the eastern seaboard, emphasizing their capacity to assimilate foreign immigrants into the American mainstream. Recently debunkers of the melting-pot notion have shown ethnic groups to be tenacious in sticking together even after discriminatory bars have been lowered. They point out that much less mixing has occurred than is popularly thought and that our cities are still simmering with group conflicts and unassimilated differences. (See CULTURAL PLURALISM.)

metayage; sharecropping   Cultivation of land for an owner who receives a part of the produce as compensation. It exists in some provinces of Italy and France and in the United States. A somewhat remote adaptation in urban terms is the percentage rent paid by a tenant for commercial property. (See LEASE, PERCENTAGE; RENT.)

metes and bounds   A means of describing the location of land by defining boundaries in terms of directions (courses) and distances from one or more specified points of reference. It is the method for describing a city lot in contrast to the usual description of a farm through landmarks or monuments. Metes and bounds describe the dimensions of the lots in almost all deeds conveying urban property. (See MONUMENT.)

metropolis   The chief city of a country, state, or region. The word derives from the Greek *meter,* meaning "mother," and *polis,* meaning "city" —*i.e.,* the mother city. Also used generally to denote any large city. "Mediopolis" has been coined for a medium-sized city, but civic boosterism has prevented the word from gaining currency. (See CITY; POLIS.)

metropolitan area   An area in which economic and social life is predominantly influenced by a central city, to which it is linked by common interests though not often by common policies. The metropolitan area may have one city or more as well as outlying districts or satellite communities. No physical or legal boundaries mark its borders, but roughly speaking these are the outer limits of commuting to or from the central city. (See STANDARD METROPOLITAN STATISTICAL AREA.)

metropolitan council; council of governments   A voluntary association of the elected public officials from most or all of the jurisdictions in a metropolitan area, set up to improve understanding and coordinate joint action on mutual problems. The first such council was set up in Detroit in 1954. The device has been called a "toothless tiger," and operating in the metropolitan jungle it has proven clawless as well. Occasionally a council may press for legislation at the state and federal levels, but only the state can give it its bridgework. Otherwise progress can be expected only through voluntary cooperation, which is forthcoming only when it serves the interests of all and challenges the vested interests of none. (See INTERGOVERNMENTAL AGREEMENTS; INTERLOCAL COOPERATIVE AGREEMENTS.)

metropolitan special district   An independent unit of government created to perform on a metropolitan scale what are ordinarily local government functions. It is generally a limited-purpose district with service rather than regulatory functions, such as operating sewage and water systems, parks, airports, etc. Because it is not bound by the usual budgetary and other restraints of local governments, it can operate more freely; because it poses no major political threat to established entities, it can carry on without too much political meddling. Because problems that cross local boundaries have proven intractable under the older governmental forms, such districts have grown in number, and often in effectiveness. (See FEDERATION; INTERGOVERNMENTAL AGREEMENTS; INTERLOCAL COOPERATIVE AGREEMENTS; PUBLIC CORPORATION; SPECIAL DISTRICT.)

migration   Movement from one place of abode to another (especially from one region or country to another), usually with the intention to settle. (See MOBILITY.)

milkability   The ability of a rental property to allow its owner to extract substantial gross rents in anticipation of defaulting on his mortgage. During the depression many apartment houses experienced milking of rents by owners. Though the gross rents were substantial, the properties yielded little or no net profits; therefore where mortgage interest and taxes became due every six months, the owner could pocket the rents before the mortgagee could declare the default and have a receiver appointed. Many properties were actually bought by speculators for their milkability value alone. Properties in depressed neighborhoods are still candidates for milking. The mortgagee may refuse to foreclose for fear of assuming the responsibilities of ownership. (See ABANDONMENT.)

mixed economy   An economic system with a variety of ways in which government acts in relation to its economic activities. It may be by abstention (giving business free rein with little or no restriction); persuasion (prevailing upon business, out of self-interest or benign motivations, to do something it would ordinarily not do); regulation (restriction of enterprise in the interest of health, welfare, or safety); inducements (giving subsidies, guarantees, concessions, loans, favorable tariffs or tax concessions to stimulate investment); direct operations (government building of roads, schools, housing, etc.); participation in public-private joint ventures (dual government and private mortgage companies, savings and loan associations, or organizations of the Comsat Corporation type); allowance of regulated monopolies (franchises to utility, transportation, or other corporations with an exclusive right to operate subject to prescribed conditions); encouragement of cooperative enterprise (credit cooperatives, housing and farming cooperatives); provision for non-profit corporations (housing corporations operated without profit or eleemosynary corporations); partial socialization or desocialization of enterprises as needs or defects appear or political pressures demand.

Mixed economies may lean more strongly toward one type of government action than toward another. If, for example, the emphasis is on direct operations, the trend is toward socialism; if the emphasis is toward abstention, the trend is more likely toward laissez-faire capitalism. If there is excessive regulation, capitalistic investment is discouraged. Most governmental systems are mixed, with an increasing tendency in capitalist economics to regulate or fill the gaps—through subsidies, socialization, or other means—left open by traditional profit-motivated operations. (See CAPITALISM; LAISSEZ FAIRE; SOCIALISM.)

mobile home; trailer   A manufactured house equipped with kitchen, toilet, and other amenities that can be moved by attaching it to an automobile or truck. The industry says that in 1968 mobile homes accounted for 75 per cent of all new United States housing selling below $12,500 and for more than a quarter of total new single-family sales. The houses vary in price and quality from the cheaper $5500 models to the de-luxe types selling for as high as $50,000. Some are as wide as 25 feet. Factory-built modular units of recent vintage come complete with furnishings, appliances, and other amenities and when de-wheeled can be stacked to form multiple dwellings. "Double wides" are two units bolted together to form a single dwelling of standard size and roof design, and are beginning to challenge the conventional home-building industry. The mobile-homes industry has made the greatest strides in the industrialization of housing, and some mobile homes, though far from seemly, are being permanently fixed to sites.

Mobile homes are occupied by a variety of people—including run-of-the-mill home-buyers, mobile-home enthusiasts, members of the armed forces, vacationists, transient workers, students, and elderly folk. In 1968 young married couples comprised about 50 per cent of the market, while retirees accounted for 25 per cent. About 65 per cent of eligible home-buyers are said to earn less than $8000 a year. Mobiles may be the family's sole home or a secondary one. They are also being used as temporary housing to accommodate tenants pending rehabilitation of their permanent quarters.

Mobile parks rent sites to mobile home-owners or, to persons requiring both, home and site together. The parks range in size from a few lots to extensive acreage equipped with plumbing and electrical connections as well as swimming pools and other community facilities. Stays may range from short periods to several years. The mobile house and park have their problems, not the least of which is opposition from the surrounding community. The fear of an added burden on local school systems, the threat of an alteration in the political balance, the unaesthetic quality of mobile slums, and the general impact on communities of a new and transient population—all play a part in the opposition.

A trailer is a smaller mobile shelter more often used for camping and outings.

mobility The ability or readiness of persons to move from one place or status to another. In economics it is the relative ease with which the elements of production—labor, capital, and land—move from one industry or business to another in response to changing patterns of cost, demand, and technology.

High physical mobility is characteristic of Americans, approximately one in five of whom have changed their place of residence every year since 1948, when the Bureau of the Census began keeping track. Nearly two-thirds of these moves were short—within the same county—and in some texts "mobility" is used to designate only local moves of this kind, with "migration" reserved for moves between counties, states, and regions.

Social mobility is the movement of individuals or groups from one social position to another, affecting their habits, values, and cultures in the process. Vertical mobility is the ascent or descent of an individual or group from one position to another. When the movement represents an advance it is considered upward mobility. It may be economic—the passage up-scale from poor to middle class to upper class, or down-scale; occupational—the passage in relation to occupational strata (dishwasher to chef); or socio-political—as a rise from the log cabin to the White House or from peonage to power. "Mobility," says P. A. Sorokin, "makes the social structure elastic, breaks caste and class isolation, undermines traditionalism and stimulates rationalism." (See MIGRATION.)

mock-up   A scale model of a building, machine, or other apparatus assembled for the purpose of study, sampling, teaching, or testing. (See MODEL.)

mock-up, economic   A hypothetical financial run-through to test the practical validity of a tax law, zoning ordinance, or other action designed to improve standards or give incentive to constructive private activity. Though such realistic tests are highly desirable, they are not often used. Thus the aesthetes continue jacking up building standards but never hear the rasp of a trowel. Nor will they, until either a system of subsidies or a decline in building costs bridges the gulf between balance sheet and aspiration. (See FEASIBILITY STUDY.)

modal split   The relative breakdown in the use of particular modes of travel for a specific type of traffic. For example, in a given city, the modal split might show that 60 per cent of schoolchildren walk to school, 30 per cent use a school bus, and 10 per cent are driven by parents.

mode of transportation   The means of locomotion. It may be animal-propelled (foot, hoof, hand; bicycle or rickshaw); mechanically powered (private car, bus, taxi, subway, trolley, tram, railway, hydrofoil, ferry); or propelled by the elements (wind, air pressure, tide, or gravity). Also, the type of transportation used by a traveler or for a commodity in transit.

model A synthetic representation, patterned after an actual or proposed product or system, created to test alternate formats or predict behavior. It may be in physical form, as in an architectural model (iconic), or in the mathematical form of an equation (symbolic), or it may use one set of properties, such as the electrical current flowing along computer circuits, to represent a real-world set of properties, such as the flow of water in a large sewage system (analog).

Efforts are being made to create mathematical models of urban processes, such as the growth of new residential developments. The most sophisticated models so far developed have been in transportation planning, where the enormous quantity of data involved and the predictability of traffic behavior encouraged their early development. (See MOCK-UP; SIMULATION.)

monument A tree, graveyard, river, stone, or other permanent object demarcating property lines. In a contested issue as to who owns a particular piece of land, monuments prevail when courses or distances as set forth in deeds or other records show otherwise. (See METES AND BOUNDS.)

moratorium The official suspension of legal remedies against debtors; also, the period of time during which a debtor has a legal right to delay meeting his obligations. It is usually proclaimed or enacted in time of great financial distress to give debtors a breathing spell in which to arrange their affairs and meet their obligations. A freeze placed on all development or alteration in an area pending completion of an over-all plan is also called a moratorium.

A national bank "holiday" or moratorium was declared in 1933 in the United States, and the collapse of the Krueger interests in 1932 led to a moratorium in Sweden. A moratorium on mortgage foreclosures was declared in New York State during the depression. A moratorium is an impairment of the rights of contract, and in the United States may be declared only during an emergency period and may continue only as long as the emergency lasts. (See RENT-CONTROL.)

morbidity rate   The number of instances of a specific disease for a unit of population (per thousand or per hundred thousand) in a given area during a given period. The index may also be computed for certain age groups or specific classes of the population. It measures, among other things, the specified duration of a disease, the degree of disability, symptoms, causes, and consequences. There are many varieties of morbidity records, including reports of communicable diseases; hospital and clinical records; insurance, industrial, and school records; surveys of the prevalence of illnesses; records of the incidence of illness accompanied by continuous observation of its course.

Although the debate continues among epidemiologists, planners, and others as to whether urban life injures mental and physical health, the correlation between ill health and urban poverty is clear. High morbidity and mortality statistics can be expected in areas with low income, poor housing, and high rates of dependency.

mortality rate; death rate   The annual number of deaths per thousand population in any given area. The rate may be computed by age group, by specific class, by sex, and by locality of dwelling. The mortality trend has been continuously declining in the United States and other developed nations. Attitudes have changed as a result—a man of fifty is no longer "old," a single girl of twenty-four is no longer a spinster, and a professor retired at sixty-five from one university can get a job at another. (See BIRTH RATE; POPULATION EXPLOSION.)

mortgage   A legal instrument to secure a loan by making it a charge on the borrower's property so that if the debt is unpaid when due, the creditor may foreclose, have the property sold, and get paid the amount outstanding from the sale's proceeds. The creditor is the mortgagee, the debtor the mortgagor.

The conditions written into the mortgage setting forth the rights, obligations, and liabilities of the parties include: the amount due and the length of the mortgage period; the rate of interest and the time for payment of principal; the agreement to pay, the obligation to keep the property insured, not to demolish the building without the mortgagee's consent, to pay taxes and assessments, to keep the property in repair, to certify the amount due upon demand; and a number of other protections in the event of default, such as the right to appoint a receiver.

A piece of property may have more than one mortgage. The second (in time or right) of a series of two or more mortgages is more precarious than the first. Should there be a default on the first, foreclosure will wipe out the second mortgage unless the second mortgagee steps in to cure the default. If there is a default on the second mortgage, the second mortgagee may foreclose and take over the property, subject, however, to the first mortgage. Second-mortgage loans usually charge higher interest rates than first, but they may also be taken back by a seller of property as part of the purchase money.

Mortgage practices vary from state to state: in some the mortgagee still reserves a power of sale in the deed, while in others the mortgagor retains the full title until he is wiped out. Foreclosure laws vary from the simple and summary to the cumbrous. Under the common law, the mortgage involved an actual conveyance of the property subject to redemption if the debt was paid. The common-law mortgage was adopted in a number of states although the courts have often intervened to prevent a summary forfeiture without a judicial sale.

A mortgage system is one of the key factors in a nation's development. In its absence building lags, extortionate interest rates are common, and homelessness, squatting, and slums are the rule. The development of savings is substantially accelerated by a mortgage system—people will save for a home more energetically than they will for other desires. Savings and home-mortgage loans are the two items responsible for the growth of savings and loan associations, housing cooperatives, and mortgage banks, as well as for the expansion of a housing-construction industry.

A mortgage system functions only when adequate protections are accorded to the mortgagee, when savings are available for relending, when titles are clear and secure, and when there is sufficient experience to operate the system.

There is a whole inventory of legal instruments connected with the mortgage, including:

Mortgage bond or *note,* the primary instrument evidencing the debt for which the mortgage is the collateral.

Assignment of mortgage, when the mortgage is sold.

Satisfaction of mortgage, evidence of the payment of the mortgage.

Mortgage participations, issued to shareholders in a mortgage.

Mortgage subordination agreement, executed when a first mortgage is made a second mortgage or when an owner leasing property to a lessee allows the lessee to borrow on his fee to help pay for an improvement.

Collateral bond, executed by a co-guarantor of the bond and mortgage or by a subsequent owner when the prior owner has him share the responsibility on the existing bond and mortgage.

Estoppel certificate, an acknowledgment by an owner to the mortgagee or mortgage purchaser of the amount due on the mortgage, that the mortgage is valid and has no defenses against it.

Stockholders' certificate and certificates of officers, required to manifest the agreement of a corporate owner to the execution of a mortgage.

Leasehold mortgage.

Construction-loan agreement, building-and-loan mortgage, in which payments are advanced as and when construction proceeds until the building is completed, at which time the debt is either paid or is converted into a long-term mortgage.

Extension agreement, an agreement by the mortgagee extending the mortgage.

The term mortgage is derived from the French *mort* meaning dead and *gage* meaning pledge—*i.e.,* the pledge dies when payment is made. (See AMORTIZATION; COLLATERAL; COMMON LAW; DEBT SERVICE; INTEREST; LOAN, CONSTRUCTION.)

mortgage, balloon   A mortgage that leaves a substantial amount unpaid upon its termination. It is to be contrasted with a self-liquidating mortgage on which nothing is due at maturity, the amortization in periodic payments having been calculated so as to retire the mortgage on the due date.

mortgage, blanket   A single mortgage covering a number of parcels of property. Any one of the parcels may be released from the mortgage lien, generally when a partial payment is made. After a developer has bought acreage and executed his mortgage on the land he might sell individual lots, which are still subject to a blanket mortgage on the entire acreage. Here the buyer of part of the acreage is in danger, since a default on the blanket mortgage will wipe out his holding with the others. The knowledgeable buyer obtains a release from the blanket mortgage before he pays for his lot.

mortgage, chattel   A mortgage placed on chattels. (See CHATTELS.)

mortgage, conventional   A mortgage secured through normal channels and not insured by the Federal Housing Administration or guaranteed by the Veterans Administration.

mortgage-insurance premium   A percentage charged annually on the declining balance of the principal of a mortgage to insure the mortgagee against loss. The going rate in the United States is $\frac{1}{2}$ of 1 per cent. FHA insures mortgages both on multiple dwellings and on homes, and a private corporation, the Mortgage Guaranty Insurance Corporation, has also been organized to insure mortgages. The FHA premium is paid with monthly mortgage installments and is designed to cover losses and make FHA self-supporting. The FHA insurance system has worked brilliantly, and FHA has built up surpluses from premiums running into the hundreds of millions of dollars. But this has been due more to the continuous rise in real-estate values than to the fact that the premium charge conformed to standard actuarial policy.

The elements of an actuarial formula for an insurable risk require: a statistical measurement of the probability of a risk happening on the basis of known experience; a hazard that belongs to a class large enough to conform to the theory of probability; the possibility, however remote, that the hazard will cause personal and direct loss to the insured; that the premiums paid for the risk come from a sufficient number of exposed individuals so that there will be money enough to make good the loss arising on any one transaction.

The federal mortgage-insurance scheme fails to conform to these actuarial criteria. Neal Hardy, former FHA administrator, has testified that "both the nation and FHA have been fortunate in the postwar period that no recession between 1937 and 1960 was of such magnitude as to result in major increases in foreclosures, although increases in defaults have consistently occurred in recession periods." In short, the FHA administrator added, as long as property values were rising, there was little danger of loss. A real test of the FHA formula can be made only during a sharp economic downturn.

mortgage market   A colloquialism describing a condition in which mortgage money is available. When mortgage money is lacking one says, "There is no mortgage market."

The secondary mortgage market makes possible the purchase and sale of home mortgages and provides liquidity to the lenders. The liquidity element has spurred mortgage lending by institutions. The most important agency facilitating a secondary mortgage market has been the Federal National Mortgage Association (originally a federal agency and now a privately owned and financed corporation), which is designed, among other things, to buy and sell insured mortgages. It buys them when the mortgage market is tight and sells them when it loosens up. Its aid is primarily to lending institutions, not individuals. (See LIQUIDITY.)

mortgage, open-end A mortgage that allows the mortgagor to borrow additional amounts for improvements subsequent to the original loan and to repay them over an extended amortization period.

mortgage, straight-term or standing A mortgage, usually for amounts less than on amortizing mortgages, that calls for no payment on principal during the term of the mortgage, the full amount coming due only at the end of the term.

motel A hotel that provides guests ready access to their cars as well as their rooms. Motels are generally along automobile roadways or at airports, but are being seen also in cities. The derivation is from *mo*torist plus ho*tel.*

"Mrs. Murphy" A colloquialism for the operator of a small rooming house. The lady came into prominence during the debates on anti-discrimination laws in housing as a representation of the little investor struggling to earn a livelihood by taking in roomers. It was felt that placing a compulsion on her to take in all comers was going too far. She won an exemption in the Civil Rights Act of 1968. (See FAIR HOUSING LAWS; HOUSING, OPEN-OCCUPANCY.)

multiple dwelling. See DWELLING, MULTIPLE.

multiple nuclei theory A concept of urban growth holding that a community's major land uses tend to group themselves around several distinct centers. Such centers might include the central business district, a railroad terminal, or a major university. The nuclei may be historic, remaining intact as the city fills in around them, or new concentrations emerging as the city spreads (such as a major outlying retail center). The concept was first propounded by R. D. McKenzie and more fully developed by Chauncy D. Harris and Edward L. Ullman in the 1940s. (See CONCENTRIC ZONE THEORY; SECTOR THEORY.)

municipal corporation A body politic generally created by the people of a locality pursuant to state law and invested with subordinate powers of legislation designed to assist in the civil government. It regulates and administers such of its own local and internal affairs as state statute permits. The term is generally synonymous and used interchangeably with "municipality." As the creature of legislative power, it may also be created by the state for specific purposes without the consent of its constituents.

A municipal corporation may be dissolved, just as it was created, by state legislation, unless the state constitution provides otherwise. Under its charter it may tax, spend, borrow, regulate, and exercise eminent domain for any of its granted purposes.

In recent years it has become useful for large-scale developers to form municipal corporations, since federal tax exemption on bonds issued by them cuts interest costs on borrowing. The borrowed funds are used to finance streets or utilities in what is, for all practical purposes, an ordinary speculative real-estate development. California and Texas are among the liberal states in which this type of municipal corporation has flourished. Here the public purpose is harnessed to the private interest. (See BOND, PUBLIC; CITY; HOME RULE; SPECIAL DISTRICT.)

municipal private-development corporation A private corporation organized by a municipality to aid it in carrying out a development function. It may be a membership or stock corporation but is usually non-profit. It has no more power than any other private company and may not condemn land or issue tax-exempt bonds. But with the recent trend toward federal financing and subsidizing of private corporations, its effectiveness as a device for implementing local public functions has grown. Its organization is not dependent on legislative authorization or hampered by civil-service restraints.

The Philadelphia Housing Development Corporation, for example, was financed by a $2 million appropriation from the city treasury and a federal poverty grant to cover some of its administrative costs. It was empowered to buy houses, sell them, and create mortgages for low-income families. As a private corporation, it was thought, it could move with greater speed and efficiency in the private market. The New York Port Authority has formed a private corporation to buy land so as not to disclose its identity, and the New York City Housing Authority organized (but did not use) such a corporation in its early days under its power to hold stock.

The municipal private-development corporation can be the private arm of the public body. It can be useful in connection with road development by buying land at the interchanges for various purposes; it can build non-profit or other types of housing for displaced families; it can help implement a public plan or improvement in numerous ways. The public powers of planning, condemnation, and tax-exempt financing might in proper cases be used by public agencies to help implement and finance the developments undertaken by the corporation.

Because the device is new, some questions remain. Is it an evasion of public control and responsibility? Can a taxpayer question a city's· use of public power or funds for such a corporation? Is it an illegal delegation of power? Will it open the door to unrestrained abuses or corruption? Can it operate outside city boundaries when its parent is confined within them by charter? Can it be subjected to civil-service requirements when supported by public monies? As yet there have been few tests of these issues; nevertheless such corporations are proliferating. (See EXTRATERRITORIAL POWERS; PUBLIC CORPORATION.)

municipality A town, city, or other district having powers of local self-government. Its powers are generally provided either by specific charter or by state statute.

mutual-aid construction Building homes with the aid of friends, tribesmen, members of the family, or special groups organized for the purpose. It is usually an organized self-help operation in which a group of workers are taught certain building skills while building homes some of which will be their own. The workers are usually not told which houses they will get so that they will not loaf or skimp on other houses while taking special pains with their own. Mutual aid has not proven so successful a strategy in developing countries as self-help housing, core housing, or land and utility projects. According to one report from Japan, the cost of entertaining the helpers more than wiped out the anticipated savings. (See HOUSE, CORE; HOUSING, SELF-HELP.)

mutual savings bank A depositor-owned savings bank the net profits of which are distributed to the depositors periodically in the form of interest or dividends. The bank is operated by officers and their staffs, who pay the operating costs, set up reserves, make investments, mostly in first mortgages, and act under the supervision of state banking officials.

Mutual savings banks, among the important sources of funds for home purchases, are quasi-cooperatives. In practice, however, the policy-holders and depositors have little say in company affairs. At elections management will almost always hold enough proxies to perpetuate its control. (See COOPERATIVE.)

necropolis A dying or dead city. Also a city of the dead, such as Thebes or Memphis in ancient Egypt. The term is used by Lewis Mumford to compare ancient cities that have fallen away with many cities that are currently decaying. "When a city has reached the megalopolitan stage," writes Mumford, "it is plainly on the downward path." Necropolis is the final stage.

The necropolitan view of the city's destiny has gained more headway in recent years. "The age of the city seems to be at an end," says Dan Martindale in his introduction to Max Weber's *The City*; the same theme is played by Scott Greer in *The Emerging City*, by Kenneth Boulding in *The Meaning of the Twentieth Century*, by York Willbern in *The Withering Away of the City*, and by Melvin Webber, who attributes the city's "demise" to "the internationalization of society generated by the knowledge explosion." There is an American bias in all these gloomy forecasts, much of it colored by the emigration of the middle and upper classes to suburbia and the poverty that is and has always been centered in the city. What the necropolists fail to see is that the American city, though harboring the poor, is actually growing and becoming more important in society—provided the city is defined realistically. That our bizarre form of government makes it possible for a hamlet on the city's fringe to call itself an independent government and shut itself off from the city should not obscure the fact that it is part of the flesh of the city and part of its growth.

The present era is the age of the city, an era witnessing the city's most dramatic advance in human history. The city is burgeoning in Europe and in the poorer countries—the world drive is toward the city, and the migration to the cities is one of the phenomena of our time. That the major growth and development in the United States is occurring in or around the old city cores is not new—its cities have always spread outward as their population grew. The only difference is that today political pressures prevent the central cities from expanding and absorbing the peripheral areas as they once did. (See CEMETERY.)

neighborhood   A local area whose residents are generally conscious of its existence as an entity and have informal face-to-face contacts and some social institutions they recognize as their own. They may or may not have a formal neighborhood organization. There is no clear line between a neighborhood and a community. Sociologists, however, say a community has a socially conscious population working together as a body to meet its common needs and objectives. Often the term "neighborhood" is used to mean nothing more than the geographic area within which residents conveniently share the common services and facilities in the vicinity of their dwellings.

Urbanization is no stimulus to neighborhood conglutination. The city's high population densities, its anonymity, the transience of its residents and their heterogeneity are some of the drawbacks. In the city, moreover, one does not always make friends among neighbors, but is apt to become involved with people and interests in many parts of the city.

There is some semblance of community interest when a special neighborhood interest is challenged, as when a landmark is threatened or a jail or incinerator is proposed for a residential district. There is also some tendency toward community in the ghettos as a result of poverty and model-city programs, which have sponsored formation of local organizations and a common view of the city or other parts of the city as a common enemy.

Home-ownership encourages neighborhood identity because the families have a stake in their investments, maintain a stronger interest in the local school, and generally remain longer in the area than tenants. When an owner improves his home with a tree, a porch, or a fresh coat of paint, this activity has a contagious quality and may inspire similar improvements along the street.

The way neighborhoods become communities may be noted in squatters' settlements. Squatters often come from the same region; they have a common aim (*i.e.,* not to be disturbed by the authorities); they depend on cooperation to build paths and maintain them and to bar or regulate the settlement of newcomers moving in on the prize. They also develop political cohesion in their efforts to have the authorities legalize their tenure. On the other hand a neighborhood having the best housing may still lack the ingredients of a community. (See COMMUNITY.)

neighborhood control. See COMMUNITY CONTROL.

neighborhood unit A scheme for the "family life community" developed by Clarence Arthur Perry for the *Regional Survey of New York and Its Environs* in 1929. Perry sought guide lines for the organization of the urban neighborhood and found one in the principle that the elementary school, parks, playground, churches, and other neighborhood institutions should be within walking distance of each residence. In his scheme, heavy and through traffic were to be routed along the boundaries of neighborhoods and kept out of interior areas used by pedestrians and served by a street system proportioned to its reduced vehicular load. About 10 per cent of the area would be devoted to parks and open spaces. Local shopping districts were to be placed at the crossroads between neighborhoods. From three to ten thousand persons would make up each neighborhood—depending on the number required to support a typical grade school. Perry's theory had a political as well as a planning purpose—the grouping of neighborhood institutions on a central common was meant to foster a rich associational life.

The debate generated by Perry's ideas—centering on whether self-contained neighborhoods are a viable planning unit or a realistic urban ideal—periodically revives. One of its current reincarnations is in the argument over neighborhood control. (See COMMUNITY CONTROL.)

neotechnic period. See PALEOTECHNIC AND NEOTECHNIC PERIODS.

net The remainder after all deductions are made. Hence net income is the income from a property or enterprise accruing to the owner after payment of all the operating charges; net price is the price paid after all deductions, allowances, and discounts; net profit on a sale of property is the excess of selling price over cost less brokerage and other expenses; net yield of a bond is the annual income accruing to the bondholder from the date of acquisition to the date of sale or maturity based upon his cost and expressed in terms of a percentage of his investment; a net lease is a lease under which the tenant pays all operating charges and real-estate taxes except debt service on the mortgage—sometimes minor repairs such as a roof may be reserved for the owner, while in other cases the owner is responsible for structural repairs. A net net, or triple net deal is real-estate vernacular which generally means the same as net lease but adds emphasis.

New Deal The political philosophy and programs initiated during the administration of Franklin D. Roosevelt. The New Deal was designed primarily to relieve unemployment and promote national economic recovery through pump-priming operations. It launched public works, social security, farm support and relief, direct unemployment relief, old-age pensions, unemployment insurance, and a new monetary policy—among other innovative programs. Many of these policies have survived in extended or modified form.

The New Deal's public-works program included a public-housing experiment in cities, which was decentralized by the United States Housing Act of 1937. The Federal Housing Administration through its mortgage guarantees became one of the main instruments for the development of the suburbs. In all, some thirty agencies emerged, most of them offering aid of one kind or another to real estate—to home-owners burdened with debts; to mortgage-lenders looking to be bailed out of their soured hold-ings; to home-builders looking for financing; to farmers needing hous-ing; and to savings and loan associations seeking credit and more con-fident depositors. Although the main problems existed in cities, the urban problem was highlighted only through emphasis on the slum prob-lem, and it was Senator Robert F. Wagner rather than President Roose-velt who gave slum clearance and public housing their driving impetus.

The race problem received no mention or emphasis as part of the New Deal; Roosevelt spoke of the "one-third of a nation" that was poorly housed but put no special accent on the black poor. The FHA in fact discriminated against rather than in favor of the Negro. So did the Home Loan Bank System.

The New Deal was nevertheless a revolution—it turned the nation toward a welfare society by changing the limited national sovereignty, assuming virtually unlimited power to act on the nation's social and eco-nomic problems. (See FAIR DEAL; GREAT SOCIETY.)

new town Any new, large-scale development planned to provide hous-ing, work places, and related facilities within a more or less self-con-tained environment. More specifically, an English term for a town con-structed along garden-city lines, under the New Towns Act of 1946. Some twenty-eight new towns with populations ranging from 20,000 to 100,000 were built or in process by 1968. They are settlements of con-trolled size, with green country as a background, and, though not solely a British patent, are said to be one of Britain's most substantial exports.

New towns have been going up since the dawn of history. They are being currently spawned in one fashion or another wherever population presses, in countries as big as the United States and as small as Israel or Singapore. Some lessons have now emerged. An ultimate population of at least 100,000 is needed to support a new development, and the bigger it is or the closer its link to a region, the better the chance of its success. Private enterprise should not be excluded as a participant in the pro-gram; an exclusively socialist enterprise may please idealists but is no guarantee of paradise. Public land-ownership, while feasible in some places, is unworkable in others, particularly in countries where the indi-vidual urge for ownership is strong and where politics would play havoc with a publicly owned inventory. New towns cannot depend on a single industry or even a few—they develop better when workers are not confined to jobs in the town but where there are other opportunities for them in nearby settlements. Building new towns requires time, patience, and plenty of money.

The equivalents of new towns have been built in the United States ever since Washington, D.C., was first planned. Most were private developments, some of them company towns like Pullman, Indiana, built by the railroad-car manufacturer George M. Pullman. During the Roosevelt administration the Resettlement Administration launched three green-belt towns (Greenbelt in Maryland, Greenhills near Cincinnati, and Greendale near Milwaukee), but these were never completed. The Department of the Interior built Boulder City in Colorado, and Norris, Tennessee, was built by the TVA. Recently the new-town initiative has returned to private hands, the two most celebrated examples being Reston, Virginia, and Columbia, Maryland.

The key to building new towns in the United States is land acquisition by a public agency. This could be done as a by-product of the federal highway program or by setting up an Urban Space Agency (URSA) comparable in capitalization to NASA. Since the moon's land is presently unfit for settlement, at least a portion of NASA's money might be diverted toward developing a few needed sections of our troubled planet. (See COMPANY TOWN.)

new-town-in-town A development on acreage located within a city, as distinguished from a new community developed on open suburban or rural land. The idea, popularized during the Johnson administration, was to develop large in-city tracts or plots occupied by army and navy installations no longer needed as such, obsolete airfields, railroad yards, federal surplus land, and similar acreage, for housing, commercial or industrial facilities, or a combination of these. The proposal had only limited value because of the reluctance of the military to give up its holdings; because few holdings of appreciable size remained in the larger cities; also, the growing racial problem deterred the resolution of what the developments would be like; many of the sites were poorly located, and either lacked adequate financing or could not be marketed. New-towns-in-town might nevertheless be possible in smaller cities, on platforms over railroad yards, and in isolated instances where a present use is no longer urgent.

Also the staged reconstruction of existing city neighborhoods to bring them some of the quality, facilities, and amenity associated with new-town developments that are started from scratch in virgin territory. A national program encouraging the creation of new-towns-in-town with populations of 50,000 to 100,000 was put forward by planner Harvey Perloff in 1966. His proposal criticized the piecemeal approach to redevelopment and held out the possibilities of an urban community "conceived as an integrated and harmonious whole," not unlike the planned new town. (See CANTONMENT.)

noise Sound without value; any unwelcome sound. In law it is defined as an excessive, offensive, persistent, or startling sound and is classed as a nuisance. The polyphony of noises has become one of the more annoying elements of city life. The crow of the rooster has given way to the jet engine and automobile horn. The crowding of people on land has made the backyard the sounding board for radio, television, and air-conditioners. Inside an apartment, knocking radiators, flushing toilets, and the pitipatation of children's feet are added to the score as it reaches its exacerbating crescendo.

What is pleasant to some is noisome to others; a bell signaling a church marriage will be noise when it interrupts a play. Noise can be measured in decibels but there is no way of measuring annoyance—a backfire may shatter one man's eardrum and be of little concern to another. But generally noise has one or all of five effects: it annoys, prevents sleep, disturbs conversation, impedes work efficiency, damages hearing.

Traffic noise holds top rank in the number of people it agitates. Aircraft noise is more intense, and although the exposure time is considerably shorter, it has brought more complaints and more official concern. A hush park composed of batches of noise-absorbent trees has been suggested for airports. The trailer truck is the most notorious land-bound oppressor, generating as much as 90 decibels, while other trucks—with their orchestration of exhausts, engines, transmissions, brakes, horns, chains, and bumping cargo—run a close second. Although trucks are most disconcerting when giving a nighttime solo, during the day their annoying noise is augmented by buses, motorcycles, sport cars, passenger automobiles, building construction, jackhammers, industrial noises, metal garbage cans, lawn mowers, whining air-conditioners, and radios.

Retreating indoors, one copes with the orphan of the technological age—the modern apartment, with its cooling, plumbing, disposing, and automated appliances. Light-frame construction, inferior workmanship, and poor acoustical design accentuate noise conduction, but the high cost of sound-insulation bars improvement except, perhaps, in the plusher areas. It costs from 2 to 10 per cent more to put up a sound-insulated building than a noisy one, and the market is usually so competitive that the increased cost may rob the builder of his profit.

The curbs on noise are not yet at hand. The National Bureau of Standards has conducted little basic or applied experimental research in architectural acoustics, while industry invests most of its research funds in product development and least in acoustical control. A few manufacturers have quieted air-conditioners, however, and produced acoustical tile and wall material, but most packaged products have developed no major acoustical improvements.

In 1968 the Federal Council for Science and Technology reported that the over-all loudness of environmental noises was doubling every ten years and that the number of workers experiencing noise conditions unsafe to hearing is in excess of six and possibly as high as twelve million. Besides loss of hearing, noise has been known to cause cardiovascular, glandular, respiratory, and neurologic changes. A German study has shown a high incidence of abnormal heart rhythms in steelworkers exposed to high noise levels. In other cases there have been personality disorders, complaints of extreme fatigue, impaired tactile function, and sexual impotence. The most serious economic losses have not been charted—the cost of the unremitting headache, the costs of shifting people from one neighborhood and job to another in search of quiet, and the costs of annoyance, sickness, inefficiency, and other by-products of the new hardware.

One view is that creating these new types of hardware is itself a primary goal and that man will ultimately adapt to it or cope with its effects in remedial ways of some sort. The other view is that man is fouling his environment and planting the seeds of his eventual downfall. In this view noise is poison and further intrusions should be halted. In all this, the spatial approach to noise pollution—i.e., planning future neighborhoods so as to isolate them from roads, airports, and other noise sources—has not yet been seriously explored. The true test of public concern and public policy will come with the advent of the supersonic plane.

nomadism The repeated shifting of habitation by people in quest of subsistence or a more hospitable environment. A nomad is a person who moves from place to place as a way of life. Semi-nomads are people who move seasonally but have permanent homes for a part of the year. Nomads include gypsies, Eskimos, other wandering herdsmen and hunters, and itinerant groups of various sorts. They may be tribal or group-organized, families or individuals. They may be transient farmers using slash-and-burn methods as they move from field to field; they may be tinkers or strays.

Gypsies (who call themselves "Rom" in Europe, "Dom" in Syria, and "Lom" in Armenia) are culturally isolated nomads with their own customs and rituals, often making their appearance on roadsides or wherever temporary anchorage is possible. In Poland, Lithuania, Hungary, and Venice they were once placed in the charge of a native nobleman or gypsy lord who taxed them in return for protection.

Urbanization has affected nomads in a number of ways. They have become a problem in Europe, generating a number of official reports on how to deal with them. Nomadic groups of Irish descent, operating as tinkers, junk collectors, and horse-traders, can be seen on the outskirts of Dublin, traveling in colorful gypsy wagons. Attempts have been made to regulate and settle them in fixed shelter and educate their children. There are an estimated fifteen hundred gypsies in Britain, who seem to have survived the order by Queen Elizabeth I to leave or be executed. They appear in lines of broken-down trailers and trucks, carrying scrap or other discards with them. The children live in squalor, and fewer than one in ten has gone to school. Some of the old prejudicial folklore about gypsy practices survives—"passing the evil eye" and child-stealing—but there are also justified arrests for drunkenness, damage, and theft. It was estimated that two hundred sites with water supply and garbage-collection facilities would be needed to accommodate Britain's gypsies, but some local authorities take the easier course of simply driving them off. Gypsies can be seen in the larger cities of the United States, where some are mobile and some settled. Some tell fortunes, hire themselves out as musicians or performers, and become more sedentary though retaining their customs and group solidarity.

Federal programs have had a marked impact on Alaskan Eskimo nomads. Eskimos once moved from place to place in search of fish and game or shifted locations because of flooding or discontent. The Nepaskiak natives, for example, are a centrally based community that ranges seasonally to exploit the local environment. But with welfare and educational programs, and with the loss of much of their hunting lands, many of their settlements have become semi-permanent. Fixed housing programs, the pressures of churches, federally supported village school programs, and the need for a permanent address to qualify for federal assistance are all tending to stabilize settlements. Stabilization and population growth, however, are bound to increase competition for the available fish and game needed for subsistence.

Another by-product of urbanization is the appearance in the central cities of nomadic young people. They hitch their way from city to city and share, beg, or forage for survival. And despite efforts to dislodge the homeless man, migrant and vagrant, through urban renewal and other clearance programs, they can still be seen in the skid rows of the cities. Secondhand trailer-slums are increasing along roads and on the city outskirts, with their occupants ready to move whenever and wherever a subsistence is available. (See HIPPIES; MOBILITY; SKID ROW; URBAN NOMAD.)

non-conforming use. See USE, NON-CONFORMING.

non-white A term used by the Bureau of the Census to designate non-Caucasian persons or groups. Although the non-white population of the United States consists of a number of racial groups, including Chinese, Japanese, and American Indian, the vast majority in this category are Negroes (92 per cent in 1960). In some cities and regions a higher percentage of non-whites are Negro than in the nation as a whole, so it is easy to see why the terms tend to be used synonymously—if not accurately. Since the Japanese and Chinese tend to have higher educational, economic, and occupational status, when they are lumped in with Negroes, the statistics inflate measures of the Negroes' progress and well-being.

nuclear complex. See NUPLEX.

nucleation The clustering of people, enterprises, and institutions at or near a dominant center. The derivation is from the Latin *nucleare,* meaning "to become like a kernel." Nucleation is apt to occur where there is a dense development of tall buildings, a financial center, a market, a shopping center, theater section, or other magnet. (See CITY, POLYNUCLEATED; CLUSTRATION; LINKAGE; MULTIPLE NUCLEI THEORY.)

nuisance An interference with the enjoyment and use of property, or a source of discomfort or annoyance to people in the use and possession of their property. The law acknowledges two classes of nuisance: public (or common) nuisance, which touches the public interest; private nuisance, which destroys or injures an individual's property, interferes with its lawful use and enjoyment or with his enjoyment of what is his common right. Both have multiplied with city life and with the encroachments of urban activities upon people's lives.

Whether a nuisance is or is not a nuisance is a question of fact—*i.e.,* whether the annoyance is such as to interfere materially with ordinary human comforts. The remedy for a public nuisance is by summons, indictment, summary proceedings, or abatement; for a private nuisance, by injunction, action for damages, or abatement. By abatement is meant the termination of the nuisance by legal action.

In nuisance litigation the courts are actually laying down some of the rules for land-use planning. In a New York case in 1907 (*McCarty v. Natural Carbonic Gas Company*), in which the court restrained a corporate owner of a factory that was burning soft coal and releasing smoke, soot, and dust from its chimneys, the rule laid down was: "The law relating to private nuisances is a law of degree and usually turns on the question of fact whether the use is reasonable or not under all the circumstances . . . a use that is reasonable under one set of facts would be unreasonable under another."

In determining "reasonableness," the factors to be considered include: the extent of the harm done; the nature of the harm involved; the social value the law attaches to the type of use or enjoyment invaded; the suitability of the invaded use or enjoyment to the character of the community; and finally how burdensome it would be for the person affected to take measures to avoid the harm.

nuplex; nuclear complex An industrial complex envisioned for the future in which industry would be clustered around a nuclear reactor producing cheap power. Garbage would be processed into usable materials (thanks to low-cost energy), and everything would be automated, efficient, compact, and clean. Air and water would be kept unpolluted. The vision of nuplexity has been projected by Chairman Glenn Seaborg of the Atomic Energy Commission.

Small clusters there will probably be, but since nuclear power can be carried over long distances it is by no means certain that the nuclear era will usher in industrial clusters like those characteristic of the steam age. Industry is more likely to be scattered (though not too far from the city) and will be looking for plenty of parking space and probably for small private airports. Where industrial clustration does occur, its motivating force is more likely to be the need for personal contact, proximity to consumer markets, government offices, executives, and skilled labor, and the opportunity for a daily escape from the complex to a simplex. (See ATOMIC ENERGY.)

"O and D" survey. See ORIGIN-DESTINATION SURVEY.

objective. See GOAL.

obsolescence The process that outdates a structure or product physically, functionally, or socially and thereby impairs or destroys its usefulness. The process may be speeded by changes in technology, style, or consumer demand. It need not be, however, for what is old is not necessarily obsolete; a house built in colonial times may be more functional and more beautiful than one built a year ago, depending on its location, its spacing, its personality, and whether it can be "deobsoletized" with a reasonable expenditure.

The most pervasive force causing a building's obsolescence is the obsolescence of the neighborhood of which it is a part, and a city will obsolesce in both its neighborhoods and their buildings. It is probable that a growing number of smaller cities will face desuetude in the years ahead because of creeping obsolescence.

Besides physical wear and tear, a structure may obsolesce as the result of a sudden departure of, say, a main department store, an adverse neighborhood change, or an emigration of a major industry.

Obsolescence and depreciation are important to property owners from the standpoint of their income taxes. For tax purposes these are coupled and a single rate embraces both. The rate may range from 2 to 5 per cent, and the deduction is made whether or not depreciation and obsolescence actually occur at that rate. (See DEPRECIATION.)

occupancy rate The number of persons per room, per dwelling, or per household. The occupancy rate is an important figure for determining housing need and density. Occupancy and over-occupancy have been correlated with mortality, morbidity, contagion, crime, juvenile delinquency, and other visitations. (See OVERCROWDING.)

old-town greys. See TWILIGHT ZONE.

100-per-cent area The hub of the central business district commanding the highest rents, receiving the greatest pedestrian traffic, and usually tenanted by the most thriving commercial enterprises. The area can generally be identified by the presence of a main department store, with a Woolworth store or its equivalent nearby or adjoining. Other chain stores hugging this precious area help draw customers. The 100-per-cent section tapers off into the 80-per-cent section, and this to the 60-per-cent section, and so on until the stores blend into the "schlag" stores, which trade in cheap merchandise for less finicky customers. Women, as the main spenders, make or break the 100-per-cent area, and the concentration of the good store space is explained by their susceptibility to shopping fatigue. The shift from shoes with French heels to the square-toe, low-heel pump and the oxford may have affected merchandise sales and rental values.

Although big city stores still hold their own, most 100-per-cent sections have been seriously challenged by the suburban shopping center, where a lady can park and buy all her goods and goodies without doing violence to her footgear. Thus the old 100-per-cent section of Newburgh, New York, is deserted, and much of it has gone back to the tax collector. In Hackensack, New Jersey, store rentals have descended to a sixth of their peak levels.

One of the main objectives of urban renewal (originally intended to clear slums) has become the salvage of those 100-per-cent sections. If main highway routes can be run into these sections, as in New Haven, it could help them compete against the crop of regional shopping centers. But the slow pace of renewal operations, the lack of parking space, and the resistance of city storekeepers to change are encouraging continuance of the suburban shopping trend. (See SHOPPING CENTER.)

open-occupancy housing. See HOUSING, OPEN-OCCUPANCY.

open space   That portion of the landscape which has not been built over and which is sought to be reserved in its natural state or for agricultural or outdoor recreational use. Open space also describes parks, squares, yards, courts, and other urban spaces not covered by cars or buildings, but with the advent of federal open-space programs it has come to refer mainly to the larger spaces coveted by developers and others seeking to exploit available land. Open space is being sought for roads and utilities, shopping centers, factories, roadside inns, airports, week-end retreats, billboards, and cemeteries. With 80 per cent of the nation's homes going up on the city's outskirts, thousands of shrapnel subdivisions are pre-empting land wherever a contiguous plot can be acquired.

With another hundred million people to be added to the American population by the year 2000, a campaign by real-estate owners, nature-lovers, and suburban governments has been mounted to salvage the open space. It has taken form in the gerrymandering of land, tax-exemption gimmicks, subsidy schemes, purchases through dummies, "spoiling devices," zoning, and other techniques. The beautification program sparked by Mrs. Lyndon Johnson gave impetus to open-space preservation, and federal grants up to 50 per cent of acquisition cost made substantial acquisitions economical. Open-space programs are worthy if placed in the context of over-all population needs, but in segmented form they are sometimes little more than special-interest efforts by estate-owners and suburbanites to thwart acquisition of land needed for housing, airports, and other necessities of the urban age. (See PARK.)

operational goal. See GOAL, OPERATIONAL.

operator   A professional real-estate dealer who buys primarily for resale rather than for investment and income. The distinction between "operator" and "investor" is important, for the operator's profits derived from sales are rated as ordinary income for tax purposes and can therefore be taxed at as much as 70 per cent; while the investor's profits from sales are taxed as capital gains (provided the property sold has been held more than six months). Buyers of real estate therefore try not to trade too often and to have income represent a substantial part of their profits. (See SPECULATION.)

optimum The best or most favorable. In city planning an optimum scheme is the best under the circumstances. It does not propose the best of all possible worlds but the maximum combined performance with minimum inconvenience to those affected. The optimum road system may not eliminate all congestion at peak hours because it seeks also the minimum human displacements, tries to respect a sound area or an important monument, or pays homage to the dead in a cemetery by bypassing their graves.

To optimize a scheme is to find that version which has the maximum combination of benefits and minimum combination of costs. Mathematical techniques have been developed to aid in optimization, but these can be used only if the costs and benefits can be quantified. Otherwise the optimum is ultimately a matter of judgment.

option The exclusive right, for an agreed period, to purchase or lease a property at a stipulated price or rent. Options are used in various ways in housing and planning. Property is optioned, when possible, by public agencies in large-scale assemblages for urban renewal, public housing, or other public improvements. One purpose of the option is to tie down properties without major outlay until all the other elements of a deal or project are at hand.

A favorite device for the exploitation of minorities is the lease-option device under which a family rents with an option to buy, paying with its monthly rent an installment toward the purchase. The property may be put in trust until the stipulated installments are paid, or the seller may hold title until all or most of the payments are made.

Options are also used in commercial transactions. They may be provided in a lease or in a separate instrument. There is also the option to renew a lease. Long-term leases often contain options to renew every twenty-one years for an agreed rent or for a rent that is a percentage of appraised value. An option may be sold unless otherwise stipulated. To be valid, it should set forth its principal terms as in a contract of sale. Since it is unilateral in obligation, there is no liability on the part of the option-holder should the option lapse, unless otherwise provided. (See BINDER; EARNEST MONEY.)

origin-destination survey ("O and D" survey) A traffic-study technique that systematically samples the movement of people, vehicles, and goods in a given area with a view to determining where they begin and end their journeys, the purpose of the journeys, the modes of travel, the elapsed time, and the land use at origin and destination. Other information of interest (public attitudes and preferences, use of leisure time, etc.) is often collected simultaneously. Methods of obtaining information include home interviews, telephone inquiries, mail questionnaires, and roadside interviews at a cordon line. Since the sampling rate may run from 1 to 10 per cent, a competent "O and D" survey is a sizable and expensive undertaking, but it is the *sine qua non* of intelligent transportation planning, since it provides the basic data on existing movement patterns. Such surveys are usually dependable except in special situations—in Amsterdam, Holland, for example, drivers gave inaccurate information when heading for the red-light district.

overcrowding Too many persons living in too few rooms or too small an area. In the United States an occupancy ratio in excess of one person per room is considered overcrowding, but standards vary considerably across the world depending on cultural factors and housing resources. In 1957 three-quarters of the households in Hong Kong occupied less than a full room, yet these households averaged 4.7 persons.

Crowding has been held responsible for numerous social evils—ill health, delinquency, excessive sexual stimulation of the young, lack of privacy and quiet, and exacerbation of family tensions, to name a few. The housing problem was once thought to be synonymous with the crowding problem, but as overcrowding has disappeared as a serious factor in more developed economies, other factors have come to the fore. In the developing world overcrowding can sometimes be considered a sign of progress, for it implies that the people are at least housed. (See DOU-BLING UP; HOUSING SHORTAGE; OCCUPANCY RATE; STREET SLEEPER.)

overspill A word used by British planners to describe the overflow of population from a large city to its outskirts or to new towns planned to receive it. Sir Patrick Abercrombie's plan of 1944 for Greater London assumed that while the city's population would stabilize or decline, there would nevertheless be overspill, which he sought to accommodate in new towns beyond a five-mile-deep green belt.

ownership The exclusive right to occupy, sell, bequeath, or mortgage property. Absentee ownership is the holding of property by a person or persons not living or working on the premises and not regularly present to oversee its use or maintenance.

Partly as a consequence of world-wide rising land costs and the universal competition for sites, new forms of ownership have made their appearance in both the developed and developing worlds. These include:

Equity ownership. The ownership of property subject to mortgage. While a mortgage system is essential to facilitate the purchase of land and homes at ever-rising costs, it effects a virtual division of the title between the mortgagee (representing the superior interest) and the owner's claim (or equity interest). The equity continues unimpaired only as long as the owner can avoid default.

Contract land-ownership. Here the purchaser agrees to buy land by installment payments, hoping ultimately to pay for it out of earnings. Rising costs have extended the contract payments for prolonged periods. Even when payment is completed, the owner is still faced with borrowing to build a house. Often lacking the funds to build, he puts up a shack from makeshift materials. Sometimes after starting his building, he runs out of money with which to pay for the roof. Ultimately the mortgagee, the weather, or the taxing authority succeeds to the property.

Statutory ownership or *tenancy.* In this case the government has passed laws to protect the owner against foreclosure in deflationary periods, to allow a tenant to remain in possession, to reimburse him for any improvements, or to protect him against rent increases. In these cases a statute modifies or redefines what has been a contractual relationship. Rent-control is the most common example.

Key money (Schlüssel Gelt) tenancy. With the costs of land, homes, and rent rising, key money tenure has grown up in many underdeveloped countries. A premium is paid for the right to acquire possession under a tenancy. It is also often paid to tenants as the consideration for "selling" a rent-controlled apartment.

Building ownership. Because land prices have run ahead of purchasing power, a person desiring to erect a building leases the land instead of buying it. Upon expiration of the lease, the building generally reverts to the landowner unless laws or the contract provide otherwise.

Squatter tenures. The growth of squatting has produced many new and unorthodox forms of tenure, including squatting in which the government or the private owner tolerates possession by the squatters. A type of squatting-at-will may arise when the squatter agrees to pay periodic stipends to the owner for the right to remain. When such land is needed for other purposes, the squatter may be speedily evicted. He may resist eviction by threats or bring pressure on the government for protection against ouster.

Cooperating or sharing devices. The inability of a single family to secure a house has given rise to mutual agreements under which several families join together to build or buy one. Cooperation for mutual aid of various kinds is not new, and its features have appeared in village economic life in China, India, and Russia and in primitive societies. It has incorporated some of the aspects of cooperation that took shape in Britain and France in the 1820s and some of the devices of the private-enterprise system including stock ownership. Other forms include ownership of the individual apartment (condominium) under an agreement to contribute to the upkeep of the building and the common grounds.

Mobile ownership. Under this form of tenure the building is not affixed to the land but remains personal property and may be moved by the building owner when the landowner demands possession or a rent that the tenant cannot afford. The number of mobile tents and houses, as well as demountable units, has increased because of migrations, hostility to minorities, landlessness, uncertain economic prospects, and social conflict. In the more developed countries mobile living, which has its earliest roots in nomadism, is becoming a chosen way of life for many.

Hire purchase (tenancy with option to buy). This device is employed by government to enable poorer families to rent until they have accumulated reserves or made a specified number of payments. The system gives the tenant hope of ownership and encourages him to improve his house and make repairs. It is also employed by private operators in real estate, often with less scrupulous intent.

(See BUNDLE OF RIGHTS; FEE; FREEHOLD; LAND TENURE; PRIVATE PROPERTY; PUBLIC-LAND OWNERSHIP.)

package plant A factory-made, compact, transportable facility such as those developed for water purification, sewage treatment, or power production. The package plant still to be invented is one for the simple and cheap disposal of human wastes. A truly inexpensive and mass-produced chemical toilet would be a greater contribution to the world's cities than any other single technical innovation.

paleotechnic and neotechnic periods Two periods of the Industrial Era, named to correspond with the Paleolithic and Neolithic periods of the Stone Age by Patrick Geddes and adopted by Lewis Mumford, his disciple. Just as the Paleolithic produced only rough stone and the Neolithic chipped and polished it skillfully, it is said, so the two stages of industrialization move from the more primitive to the more socially conscious. The paleotechnic period, according to Geddes, saw the harnessing of technical forces to the narrow ends of private gain, with the sacrifice of human values and considerations. In urban terms the chief result of this was the production of slums and the squalor and debasement of the working class. (Getting drunk "is the quickest way of getting out of Manchester.") In the neotechnic period, which is still emerging from the orientations of the older period, Geddes saw an increasing realization that larger social goals must be served by the technical forces at society's command. This was reflected in preoccupation with better city design, town planning, parks and gardens, health, beauty, and well-being.

parameter A variable that can be kept constant while the effect of shifting other variables is investigated. Though employed largely in mathematical calculations, the word is used freely in experimentation of many kinds, including simulation for planning and housing operations to test traffic, density, and other factors on given land areas.

Also, those boundaries, constraints, or outer limits that are immutable or taken to be so in analyzing and dealing with any situation. Thus one speaks of planning within certain parameters, such as an expected population, the anticipated tax revenues, or one's understanding of the key political limitations. (See GIVENS.)

parcel of land. See LAND, PARCEL OF; PLOT.

park An open area, usually landscaped or left in its natural state, intended for outdoor recreation and the general enjoyment of nature. The distinctive feature of a park, as opposed to other recreational areas, is the opportunity offered for passive recreation—sitting, walking, and watching. Parks may contain playfields (large areas marked off for outdoor athletics), playgrounds (areas containing recreation facilities for children of preschool or elementary-school age), playlots (space and facilities for small children), golf courses, swimming pools, camping grounds, etc., but none of these facilities alone would make a park. Parks can be as small as the empty lot next door and as large as Yellowstone. (See OPEN SPACE; PARK, VEST-POCKET.)

park, educational. See EDUCATIONAL PARK.

park encroachment The appropriation of parkland for non-recreational use or actual development. Urban open spaces are a constant temptation to cities needing space for schools, housing, and other facilities, and frequently they have succumbed, particularly when a park is centrally located. Yet it is just here that parks are most indispensable and hardest to replace. Since few cities have sufficient parkland to begin with, it is best to resist encroachment no matter how persuasive the need or noble the objective. In some urban-renewal and highway projects park space has been taken in one place with the promise that an equal amount will be created in another. Carefully planned, this can result in a more equal distribution of urban open space as well as space for needed facilities, but the trade is often of an area still in its natural state for another that has to be restored. Once developed, land can rarely be returned to its original condition.

parking The temporary storage of vehicles between trips. Off-street parking is storage in garages, driveways, or lots specifically set aside for idle vehicles. Putting a car at the curb on a public right-of-way is on-street parking. Where there is insufficient parking space, back-ups in streets and excessive hunting for parking spots can result, fouling the circulation system. Curbside parking takes up lanes that could be given over to traffic or retrieved for the pedestrian, and creates a safety hazard by hiding a small child until he has already darted onto the roadway. Off-street facilities take up space that could be available for other uses in land-scarce cities.

The city's parking problems are not due simply to the increasing number of cars in use but to the fact that demand piles up at certain hours and in certain key locations. Municipal garage systems are one answer, as are requirements that apartment houses and institutions provide 100-per-cent off-street parking. But there is evidence that such facilities attract additional traffic. Improvement and extension of mass transit, combined with large parking depots on the city's periphery, may be more to the point. Recently transportation planners have become impressed with the argument that parking is one of the most unproductive of all land uses and that at a trip's end a vehicle should be sent back where it came from or recirculated by turning it over to other users. Sharing and retrieval may be the long-range solution, the opening phase of which can be seen in car-rental systems.

Loading is a special category of the parking problem. Here the vehicle is not moving but is in use, depositing and/or receiving passengers and goods. This requires close proximity to the destination or source, and extra maneuvering space for large vehicles. (See TRANSPORTATION TERMINAL.)

park, vest-pocket A park or playground built on a small plot. Vest-pocket parks are often erected in built-up areas on vacant or abandoned lots. While they have advantages, city park departments are often opposed to them because of their high maintenance costs. Vest-pocket parks are sometimes in private ownership for the exclusive use of the surrounding residents. (See BLOCK INTERIOR.)

partition action   An action in equity between two or more persons having a joint interest in the same real estate for its division among the
parties; where a division cannot be effected practically, a sale of the
property is ordered and the proceeds of the sale are distributed to the
parties.

The partition action becomes prominent in cases where the descent of
real estate to multiple heirs makes it difficult to sell, mortgage, or improve the property. In Dublin, Ireland, for example, a strategic parcel
long ripe for redevelopment may have as many as a hundred interests,
making it virtually impossible to assemble for a more rational development. The property is often left to decay, making partition or public acquisition the only remedies.

Another use of the partition action may be possible in the future for
the better development of parcels adjoining each other and owned by
different interests. A single lot can and often does frustrate a vital private
development. If one of the parcels is a slum or holds back a major improvement, an appropriate statute could authorize an action in the nature of partition either to compel the issuance of shares in the assembled
parcel or, where this is rejected by the parties or impractical, to compel
the sale of the property and the distribution of the cash proceeds to the
owners. This may raise a constitutional issue, but if an imperative need is
shown, the courts are likely to sustain the legislation. Provision should,
of course, be made for full compensation to owners and tenants. Their
rights have too often remained inadequately protected in the renewal operation, which in a sense is a form of assemblage and a sale of fragmented parcels for a more adequate use. The same policy should be applied to smaller parcels as to the large renewal operations. (See LAND
FRAGMENTATION; LEX ADICKES; REPARCELATION.)

party wall   A common wall between two adjoining buildings used for
common advantage. The row house offers a typical example of its use,
which is often to lower costs. It may be paid for by the two owners or the
owner of the two lots may build it for both. A party wall, though most
often centered, may be entirely on one lot. It is often built and maintained under a recorded agreement. The main purpose of a party wall is
to support the buildings, but either owner has the right to demolish his
own structure. Party walls are often regulated by building codes, and in
San Francisco, which still winces under the memory of the great fire,

builders complain that the party-wall provisions are too onerous. Generally either party may extend a wall or elevate it, but the use must be for both parties and the work must not threaten the adjacent owner's building.

paths, edges, districts, nodes, landmarks Kevin Lynch's breakdown of the elements of a city that give it its visual and conceptual identity in the minds of a resident or a visitor—in his *The Image of the City* (1960).

Paths are the city's circulation routes; everything from a highway to an alley, an elevated line to a canal, comes under this rubric. For many people paths are the predominant element in their image of a city, for they observe their surroundings while moving through them, and along pathways the city's other elements are arranged and related.

Edges are linear elements we either do not use or do not consider as paths. Shores, walls, railroad cuts, edges of developments are examples. Edges may be more or less penetrable barriers, which close one region off from another, or they may be seams along which two regions are related and joined together. Although not so powerful an element as paths, edges are important organizing features.

Districts are medium to large areas of a city each distinguished from another by a set of common characteristics—similar building types, activities, population, land use, degree of maintenance, topography, etc. In our mind's eye we enter into and leave districts as we move about or traverse the city. When they identify themselves quickly upon entry they help us locate our relative position within the city and to some extent help to organize the city as a whole when seen from outside.

Nodes are the central points in any complex or system, and in Lynch's usage they are the central points of reference in a city—the "intensive foci" to which or from which we see ourselves moving as we travel. A node may be an intersection of paths, a small or large square, a transportation junction where one changes modes. Or they may be nothing more than concentrations of a particular kind of physical structure or use, such as the street corner in a residential neighborhood where one finds clustered the grocery, the candy store, and the bar and grill.

Landmarks, like nodes, are points of reference within a city, but unlike nodes they cannot be entered into or transversed. For the most part they are fairly simply defined physical objects—a church spire, city hall, bridge. There are also local landmarks—the sign, storefront building, or tree that gives clues to persons familiar with a place as to their location and the distance to their destination. (See IMAGEABILITY; LEGIBILITY.)

patio   A courtyard of a house surrounded by low buildings or walls. The word is of Spanish origin. Also, a paved area adjoining a house and used for outdoor living. Spanish-American houses enjoy inner courts open to the sky, and Washington Irving in the *Life and Letters* compiled by his nephew (1863) wrote of "patios planted with orange and citron trees and refreshed by fountains"—a rarity in 1970 when every buildable inch in the city seems to be consumed by structure. (See COMPOUND; COURT.)

payment in lieu of taxes.   See TAX, PAYMENT IN LIEU OF.

peak hour   For any given road, that exasperating sixty-minute period of the day during which everyone tries to get to the same place at the same time, *i.e.,* when it carries its maximum volume. Usually the morning or evening rush is the time of the peak hour. The peak-hour load is the amount of traffic carried by a given road during this period. (See CAPACITY.)

Peckham Centre   A settlement house with health care, built in the 1930s in the Peckham district of South London, which a family could, for a small charge, join and in whose activities all the individual members could participate. While improved health was the founders' main aim, they felt that recreation must go along with it. The center's principal feature was that it catered to the family as a unit—a nursery was provided where the infant would be cared for while the parents could play cards on the balcony and the children swim or play ball. Another important feature was the swimming pool, which could be seen from the balcony and which dominated the center upon entry. Activities went on above the pool, but the presence of water and water activity served as a magnet for the eye (much the same as the swimming pools of Miami do).

pedestrian   One who walks to negotiate distances. A pedestrian island is an island, section, or planned space reserved for walking and walkers— Old Dubrovnik, Venice, and Fire Island are examples; in its more pedestrian use, it is also an elevated slab in the middle of a street designed to be a refuge for persons crossing. Pedestrian malls are promenades either in a park or in a planned area reserved for strolling. Pedestrianism, though defined as "an addiction to walking" (as well as a walking exercise), is hardly an addiction since walking is natural to the species, in contrast to driving or flying. Pedestrianization should be a term for converting roads to walkabouts or bringing about more space for walking by deliberate scheme.

A walkable city is a city holding interest for pedestrians and encouraging walking, browsing, and taking in the scene—London, Paris, or New York City, for example, but not Los Angeles. Though there are many walkable cities abroad there are few in the United States, and they are becoming fewer with the influence of the automobile on neighborhood development. Despite this and the surge of recreational forms and gadgets, walking still holds second place in people's recreational choices, and in cities of a million or more almost half the population walks for summer pleasure. A national survey in 1967 showed that from 1960 to 1965 the amount of summer pleasure-driving increased only about 8 per cent while walking for pleasure increased 82 per cent.

The more sensitive renewal schemes provide walking malls—San Francisco's Market Street project has a twenty-block mall, and Philadelphia is considering a similar scheme. Despite the importance of pedestrianism, however, no city had (as of this writing) appointed a Commissioner of Pedestrians to guard the walker's prerogatives against the incursions of the Traffic Commissioner, or to provide ways of linking walking to mass transport. Designing promenades and no-way streets, raising downtown sidewalks to second-floor levels free of auto traffic, would help redeem cities for its forgotten strollers. Part of the billions spent annually for highways could well be diverted to walkways. Pedestrian planning is still a frontier in the new world of wheels, fouled air, curb cuts, and death-dealing streets. (See STREETWALKER.)

peppercorn rent. See RENT, PEPPERCORN.

percentage lease. See LEASE, PERCENTAGE.

performance standard zoning. See ZONING, PERFORMANCE STANDARD.

phase program Any program that envisages change in stages or phases; in particular, a program for preventing and eliminating segregation in public-housing projects by controls on occupancy and by redistribution of tenancies to obtain a more balanced racial mix. The term was used by the New York City Housing Authority, which identified four types of projects: those occupied predominantly by non-whites, which the Authority thought could be better integrated by increasing the number of whites; those occupied by non-whites and Puerto Ricans, which required more white non-Puerto Ricans; those occupied predominantly by whites, which should have had more non-whites; and projects with extensive Puerto Rican occupancy calling for their redistribution into other projects.

The Authority felt justified in adopting the phase program because it thought school segregation as well as segregation in the projects themselves was undesirable and that white applications were being discouraged in the minority-occupied projects. The chairman of the Commission on Human Rights dismissed a complaint charging that the program was discriminatory and sustained the Authority. He held that under the statute the Authority's duty was to prevent segregation as well as be "color blind," that prevention of segregation required identification by color and that where there were two principles in apparent conflict, the motivation of the Authority was determinative. The motivation, he found, was to avoid segregation. One of the Commissioners of Human Rights in a later unsolicited opinion called the practice an illegal quota system. Which of the two holdings is consistent with law has still to be finally determined. (See COLOR-BLINDNESS; DISCRIMINATION; HOUSING, OPEN-OCCUPANCY; INTEGRATION; QUOTA SYSTEM; TIPPING POINT.)

physiographic determinism A theory that the natural elements of an environment should be respected in planning and given priority consideration in arriving at policy determinations. Landscape architect Ian McHarg has been preaching its gospel. Forests help prevent floods, he says, soils produce food, marshes are the spawning grounds of fish and birds. But marshes are the first to be filled, streams culverted, farms subdivided, forests felled, flood plains occupied, and wildlife destroyed. Nature should have priority in the planning; the aquifers, slopes, wetlands, and the rest of nature's assets should be preserved in any development plan. Build on the plateaus and leave the valleys open. A somewhat similar theory applicable to state planning was espoused for Wisconsin by

Philip Lewis, who identified "nodes of interest" in which the landscape was given high priority in planning.

The case for this position is clearer in more-developed than in less-developed countries. In the latter one often finds soils yielding four crops a year or a landscape of beautiful rolling hills abutting on the growing city. It seems sensible to preserve these, but the sacrifice of landscape may be necessary in the interests of the greater number. When population pressures set in, the rolling hills are the first to be pre-empted by squatters, as in Caracas or Ankara. The fertile land is often too valuable as building plottage and is needed to house thousands of home-hungry families. In these cases one cannot be doctrinaire and give nature automatic priority. (See CONSERVATION; ECOLOGY, HUMAN; ENVIRONMENT.)

piece of the action   Active participation in transactions or programs with the same opportunities for money-making as are available to the other participants. The term is used in various senses. Allowing blacks a piece of the action means not only to provide them with jobs but to enable them to become owners or stockholders entitled to share in the profits. Giving a piece of the action to an insurance company means not only borrowing the money from it but giving it a share of the deal as well. The insurance company will then advance more than it would have done simply as a lender. The financing arrangements in the new towns of Columbia and Reston are illustrative of this joint arrangement.

place   A Bureau of the Census term referring to an area with a population concentration. Usually places are incorporated political units, but certain unincorporated centers also qualify if they meet census criteria. An urban place is one that is incorporated and has a population of 2500 or more. Incorporated places with fewer inhabitants and unincorporated places with a density of at least 1000 persons per square mile may also qualify if they are located on the fringe of large urban areas. All others are rural places.

plan. See GOAL.

planned-unit development (PUD)   A residential development in which the subdivision and zoning regulations apply to the project as a whole rather than to its individual lots (as in most tract housing). Densities are calculated on a project-wide basis, permitting among other things the clustering of houses and provision of common open space. A main requirement is that over-all density not exceed that laid down in the guide lines. PUD facilitates a more comprehensive land-use plan along principles similar to the medieval village or New England town. Potential advantages include: an improved site design, free of standard lot pattern limitations; lower street and utility costs made possible by reduced frontages; more useful open space due to reduction or elimination of the unusable side and front yards required by traditional zoning; greater flexibility in the mixing of residential building types; the possibility through its greater freedom in design of increasing over-all densities without loss of essential amenities. (See ZONING, CLUSTER.)

planner Anyone who plans—for example, a city planner, an economic planner, a public health, transportation, or social planner. The term is more often employed to describe those engaged in environmental planning, which is most often called "city planning" and covers a variety of tasks.

City planning is as old as cities and might count among its earliest functionaries Cain, whose client was God; God himself, who oversaw the creation of numerous towns and the destruction of some unsuccessful ones; and Romulus, planner of Rome. But though they might be called planners, they were more in the nature of sponsors or entrepreneurs. It was Hippodamus (born 480 B.C.), planner of the ports of Athens and Rhodes, who was the earliest recorded professional. He is, in fact, credited with being the father of the gridiron plan.

City planners today are not all planners of cities in the Hippodamian sense but are planners or replanners of neighborhoods, zoning specialists, urban-renewal and housing specialists, or executors of the numerous tasks connected with spatial or environmental planning. In 1968 it was possible to list at least twenty different kinds of city planners, and the list is by no means final. Some take on multiple tasks and are skilled in more than one discipline, but there has been a growing trend toward specialization on the one hand and expansion of scope on the other. The specialist is finding that he must know more about his own specialty at the same time as he is being called upon to undertake more than he knows or can do alone. No sooner has he learned the intricacies of one new program than new legislation with new types of programs confront him.

The generalist planner takes on the over-all task and organizes the job, hiring specialists as he needs them to fulfill his commitment. He may know a little of most relevancies and a great deal about one or two. He is a kind of organizer and may be part of a planning, engineering, or architectural firm, or in the upper echelons of a public agency.

The architect planner, or urban designer, specializes in actual design. He knows about design and physical details, which is important, but is usually short on politics, legislation, regional planning, sociology, finance, real estate, and other specialties. Most architect planners are interested in structures, not policy or the intricacies of investment and profit-making; a number, however, have branched out into more comprehensive city planning and highway design, hiring or associating themselves with specialists as needed.

The housing-specialist planner is a vital factor in urban-renewal and slum-clearance operations. That most federal urban programs in the United States are linked to housing gives him an advantage.

The transportation specialist specializes in roads, mass transportation, and traffic problems. Since new roads open up new neighborhoods, make wastelands of old ones, and vitally affect developments on the peripheries of cities, he is an important influence. Until recently, however, he was concerned more with the cement than with the concrete aspects of planning.

The regional planner should be distinguishable from the regional scientist, who is a "planalyst" rather than an active planner and is concerned with studies on industrial location, effects of transportation on industrial formations, and the like, more apt to advise planners than be an independent contractor. Theories and practices in this area are still evolving, and a good deal of the problem lies in the political sphere, which the regional planner too often subordinates to his theoretical lucubrations. Regional planners may be employed by regional planning agencies, states, citizens' organizations concerned with regional development, or by several communities engaged in some joint undertaking.

The underdeveloped-area planner, or development planner, has a virtually uncharted field. The problems are unique as well as varied, and unless the planner is sensitive to differences between countries he can make a mess of things—if, for example, he applies what he knows about England or the United States to Asia, Africa, or Latin America. He will most often be employed by an international agency or by a foreign government. There is a paucity of good development planners because there are few good teachers and because many economic theories and texts have given housing and city planning a low priority.

The sociologist planner specializes in the social or anthropolitical aspects of urban life. Sociology, however, presumes to cover such a broad gamut of social phenomena—from the origin and history of human society to the laws controlling the progress of civilization and the nature of human intercourse—that it is difficult to judge his competence for a specific task. He is generally a generalist, not a general. Specialization in urban sociology helps, though, and with the recent emphasis on survey and evaluation techniques he may be a good person to undertake a survey or consult on such problems as community participation, social welfare, and the like.

The educational planner worries about the design, distribution, and financing of educational facilities. More and more he is being asked to advise on their operation and curriculum as well.

The public-health planner emphasizes aspects of public health (including mental health) and sanitation (including the problems of pollution). He is often trained in public-health administration, and there is a trend favoring a joint education with city planning. Public-health planning for cities is still a frontier.

The lawyer planner drafts legislation and performs the many tasks associated with the legal and legislative aspects of planning. Lawyers have occupied an important place in planning ever since Baron Haussmann. The wide scope of the law's involvement helps to qualify the trained lawyer for a number of planning tasks. Dual training for law and city planning has begun in a few universities.

The engineer planner deals with public works and the numerous engineering aspects of urban development. Engineering firms are often retained for building dams or developing highway schemes in the United States and are dominant in public-works operations in the less-developed countries. Engineer planners are often good organizers of teams, but one of their limitations is their orientation to public works so that creation of a decent environment takes second place to highway and utility building and to "getting the job done."

The economic planner specializes in the investigation of the conditions and laws affecting production and consumption of goods and the material means of satisfying human wants, needs, and desires in the urban environment. Economists have made important policy decisions affecting planning and housing, but their decisions have often been based on outmoded teachings. They used to know little of urban land economics or the intricacies of real estate but have recently proved to be useful associates on planning teams, particularly when they have widened their outlooks to embrace political and other pertinencies.

The administrative planner is trained in the executive and administrative functions associated with planning cities or neighborhoods or in running a planning operation. He is in the nature of an administrative organizer or executive and is often a civil servant. Some are political economists, some are lawyers, and some are politicians who have learned the complexities of public life and how to deal with them.

The zoning planner was among the early planners, when planning was mostly zoning and land-use regulation. He is still influential, particularly in small or incipient communities, and is continuously benefiting from political encounters with vested and invested interests.

The rural planner is concerned with planning rural environments and in laying out economically viable farm areas. He may deal with villages in rural areas or in the social or economic aspects of undeveloped or uneconomic regions.

The research planner systematically investigates phenomena concerned with environment or with cities. He is often trained in statistics, in computer operation, and in preparing surveys and studies of urban problems. He may have training in economics or sociology, which makes him more useful. His research is not always "diligent and systematic inquiry"—it may also be propaganda embellished with figures and linguistic abstrusenesses.

The real-estate specialist is familiar with private real-estate operations and their involutions, particularly with the laying out of speculative subdivisions for a client. Since private developments create many new neighborhoods, he plays an important part in the creation of the urban environment, but often finds himself yielding his aesthetic sensibilities to the profit motivations of his employer. His skills and capabilities are often underestimated, his experience may be wider than is credited to him, and when harnessed to a program with social purpose he can prove practical and useful.

The advocacy planner is a recent specialist who represents the interests of a neighborhood or local group in any public action affecting it. Since the rise of the community-participation concept the advocacy planner has become more vocal, and though he has an important role in planning, he too often believes that his is the only frontier in the planning process. His idealistic approach is admirable, but his sense of realism and his biases should be carefully weighed against his experience. Community participation is a new arena with a growing community bureaucracy that can slow operations to a halt as often as it can effect community cooperation.

The landscape planner, also called landscape architect, arranges the effects of natural scenery over a given tract so as to produce a proper aesthetic effect in relation to the use to which the tract is to be put. He may also plan the layout of the building plots on the tract. Once a city planner, he has been whittled down to a specialist. Since nature is being consumed in the urban thrust he is a much-needed associate. Some landscape planners have proffered imaginative and comprehensive proposals for neighborhood improvement, and a few have branched out into wider planning arenas.

The geographer planner specializes in broader aspects of population and industrial distribution and some other geographical aspects of environment. He is usually a theoretician, teacher, or writer. His concern for land problems does not often touch on development or the practical aspects of land planning.

A planning assignment will usually call for the services of one or several of these specialists supplemented by consultation with others; together they compose a planning team. Other specialists may also be called upon. The growing complexities of the urban world and the widening scope of the planning process tend to obsolesce the planner's capacities quickly, and he must constantly keep abreast of innovations in techniques and programs or fall by the wayside. (See CITY PLANNING.)

planning. See CITY PLANNING; TRANSPORTATION PLANNING.

planning education   The act or process of imparting or acquiring knowledge required to plan or replan the environments in which people live—a difficult if not an impossible task. Comprehensive training involves a familiarity not only with design, but with sociology, economics, law, finance, administration and management, real estate, housing, population analysis, racial problems, statistical techniques, traffic and transportation, and a host of other disciplines. Education has become so specialized, however, that the teacher tends to stay within his own limited horizon. Yet only those familiar with the relevant disciplines are equipped to know what they do not know as well as to identify priorities, accord the proper emphasis to issues, and render more balanced judgments.

Planning curricula are never either uniform or complete. One reason is that planning is still subject to continuous cross-fertilization with other disciplines. There is a healthy trend toward teaching these older disciplines with planning, and creating joint degrees (as for law and planning, engineering and planning, architecture and planning, etc.).

The times call upon the planner to integrate, to combine in himself the talents of the Renaissance man and the *chef de cuisine;* to be at once savant, oracle, and Admirable Crichton. There are few such men, of course, and it is questionable in this age of specialization that their numbers will increase. Still, the city planner is blessed in the challenge, and there will always be a few who will rise to the occasion.

planology The study of planning. The word is of recent vintage and was coined in Holland, where planology is taught in the university. It is the Dutch term for what is in the United States city planning and in England town and country planning.

plat A map or chart of a city, town, section, or subdivision, indicating the location and boundaries of individual properties. Plats and platting are an important part of subdivision procedures.

A preliminary plat is presented to the planning authority with other supplementary data indicating the nature of the proposed subdivision. It is submitted only after preliminary conferences with the authority and exhibition of informal sketches showing contemplated traffic arteries, boundaries, streets, topographical information, transport lines, schools, churches, shopping centers, park and industrial locations. After this preliminary conference, "the feeler" for the official reaction, the authority calls a hearing on notice to the subdivider and nearby owners. It may, after the hearing, require changes and then give conditional approval.

Thereafter the subdivider obtains his permits and puts in the land improvements.

The final plat conforms with the preliminary plat and is filed after completing the improvements, accompanied by certifications that the improvements have been satisfactorily completed and are recorded.

plinth The lower square member of the base of a column or pedestal. More relevant to housing is its definition as the two or more rows of bricks, stone, or cement at the base of a wall immediately above the ground. In the simpler housing of underdeveloped areas, the area of the plinth, its composition, and its manner of building are important indicators of durability as well as of resistance to earthquakes, termites, and other natural visitations.

plot A parcel of land or an assemblage of contiguous parcels into a single unit; also a relatively small area of land. A builder to whom a small parcel of city land is offered might say, "It's not a plot, it's too small and won't work out." By this he means that the number of potential units do not warrant investment in a new building. The cost of elevator installation or the maintenance cost, for example, might be too substantial to leave a sufficient operating profit. A larger plot might be "workable."

A plot plan indicates the location and boundaries of individual properties or plots for development or sale. It is sometimes called a ground plan.

points; discount At a mortgage closing, the agreed discount deducted from the principal given to the borrower. Points are a recent device for increasing the effective interest charge above the rate prescribed in the mortgage. In a tight money market, for example, a bank can often put its funds out in other investments at higher rates than might be allowed on home mortgages. In the case of a home purchaser wishing to borrow $50,000 on a first mortgage at $7\frac{1}{2}$ per cent, the bank might insist on deducting, say, 2 per cent ("two points" in the terminology of lenders) from the face value of the mortgage at the closing. Thus the borrower gets only $49,000 though he owes, and will be paying interest on, the full $50,000. Meanwhile the bank's return on the money it has actually invested rises above $7\frac{1}{2}$ per cent. The Federal National Mortgage Association deducts points for mortgage purchases, and institutions have adopted the practice on their mortgage loans. The point-deduction practice generally operates during periods of rising interest rates. (See INTEREST; MORTGAGE.)

police power The state's inherent right to regulate an individual's conduct or property to protect the health, safety, welfare, and morals of the community. Though the power is old, the term was not used until 1827, when it received its christening from Chief Justice John Marshall. In the United States the power must be used "reasonably" and with due process, but unlike the exercise of eminent domain, no compensation need be paid. During the nineteenth century the courts struck down considerable social legislation as unconstitutional, but with the development of a social conscience, their decisions showed more restraint and even some eloquence. They sustained laws compelling the installation of running water for each family, better fire protection, and even moratoria on foreclosures. As Judge Cardozo put it in upholding New York State's 1926 Multiple Dwelling Law: "Most of all it is a measure to eradicate the slums. It seeks to bring about conditions whereby healthy children shall be born and healthy men and women reared in the dwelling of the great metropolis. The end to be achieved is more than the avoidance of pestilence or contagion. The end to be achieved is the quality of men and women. If the moral and physical fibre of its manhood and its womanhood is not a state concern, the question is, what is? Till now the voice of the courts has not faltered for an answer."

In *Block v. Hirsch* (1921) the Supreme Court held housing a "necessary of life. All the elements of a public interest justifying some degree of public control are present. The only matter . . . open to debate is whether the statute goes too far."

It is whether a statute goes "too far" that the courts still take upon themselves to determine. What is "reasonable" or "unreasonable" depends upon the facts of each case. Though courts uphold a city's power to zone, each particular zoning ordinance may undergo scrutiny, and decisions will vary with the times and the judges. The right to zone for aesthetic motivations long divided the courts of the various states, but the Supreme Court in 1954 seemed to have settled the issue by asserting that beauty was a public concern and that zoning to maintain it was "reasonable." Rent-control was upheld because "the state may regulate a business, however honest in itself, if it is, or may become, an instrument of widespread oppression . . . and the business of renting houses in the City of New York is now such an instrument and has, therefore, become subject to control by the public for the common good."

The federal government has no police power as such, this being the province of the states, which have always been recognized as the "original sovereignties." The states, say the courts, did not delegate this power to the limited federal sovereignty they created. But a constructive federal police power seems to have been spun by judicial expansion of the various enumerated constitutional powers, the welfare power in particular. Health, welfare, morals, and safety are now regulated by federal agencies as an incident of one federal power or another, and, if reasonable, the laws have been upheld. The interstate commerce power now embraces regulation of drugs, securities, and other commodities. Invalidation of either state or federal laws aimed at the citizen's protection, though frequent before 1937, would be the exception today.

Yet the courts still stop short when laws go too far. Thus when the Central Savings Bank challenged a New York State law empowering the city to make repairs where the owner refused and recover its outlay through a first lien on the property, the law was invalidated as going "too far."

What is reasonable in one period may be unreasonable in another. There are no precise yardsticks for "reasonable" or "due process." The law of each age is what that age thinks should be the law, and the courts are not above cocking the judicial ear to the attitudes of the times. Practical judgment rather than judicial precedent most often determines the rule.

The distinction between the police power and eminent domain depends mainly on whether "the thing is destroyed or is taken over for public use." No compensation is paid when a right is sacrificed by regulation, but if it is taken for public use or benefit, compensation must be paid. (See EMINENT DOMAIN; POWER PLANT.)

polis The Greek word for "city." The root word in "metropolis" and "megalopolis," it is used to form names or nicknames of cities—*e.g.*, Cottonopolis (Manchester, England), Porkopolis (Cincinnati and Chicago), and Leatheropolis (Northampton, England). It is also good game for the urban neologists—*viz.*, necropolis, tyrannopolis, dynopolis. Lewis Mumford contributed parasitopolis and psychopatholopolis—a city ruled by a mad tyrant like Nero. (See CITY.)

pollution   The fouling of the air, water, or soil by the introduction of injurious or corrupting elements. Any material adversely affecting the natural environment is a pollutant. Noise and transgressions on aesthetics have also been included within the category of pollutants. The city dweller's nose and eyes warn him of dangers that lurk in the air, and the prohibitive rates of amoebic dysentery, cholera, typhoid and paratyphoid fevers in underdeveloped countries are a warning of the dangers lurking in water. The main water pollution hazard in the United States occurs where sewage and industrial wastes are discharged into a river or lake without proper treatment.

Air is polluted primarily by the combustion of fuels and the burning of refuse. Automobiles, power plants, factories, and houses are the principal culprits, with the automobile by some measures producing more air pollution than all other sources combined. Remedies for air pollution include exhaust controls, fuels that produce less soot and fly ash, or a new technology such as the atomic-power plant, provided its radioactive by-products are found to be less hazardous than fossil-fuel by-products.

Air pollution contributes to illness, disability, and death from chronic respiratory diseases. Sickness and death rates from such diseases—especially pulmonary emphysema, bronchial asthma, and chronic bronchitis —are higher in urban than in rural environments. An air-pollution catastrophe in London took an estimated 3500 to 4000 lives from December 5 through December 9, 1952, and there have been similar episodes elsewhere.

Increasing urbanization, industrialization, and use of fuel-powered machines for transport have intensified the dangers of both water and air pollution throughout the world. Weather modifications are one consequence, and some scientists say that the sensitive balances of the elements essential for man's existence are being threatened; unless immediate correctives are applied atmospheric and other changes will destroy the validity of the earth as an environment for human survival. (See CONTAMINATION; ENVIRONMENT.)

poly-nucleated city. See CITY, POLY-NUCLEATED.

population   The total number of people living in a given locality; also, the body of inhabitants of a country, region, city, or other area. The civilian population is a term used by census authorities for the non-military population normally resident in a studied area, *i.e.,* all people exclusive of those in the armed forces. (See BIRTH RATE; CENSUS; COHORT-SURVIVAL METHOD; DEMOGRAPHY; MORBIDITY RATE; MORTALITY RATE.)

population explosion; population implosion   Population explosion is the world-wide, dramatic increase in population. Population implosion refers to the increase in population within countries. Both will be felt mostly in the world's cities. The urban population of Africa is expected to grow from 58 million in 1960 to 294 million by the year 2000; that of Asia from 559 million to 3444 million; and that of Latin America from 144 million to 650 million. The world had no more than 250 million people at the time of Christ, and it took the following 1650 years to add another quarter billion; it then added a billion in the next 200 years, a second billion in the following century, and a third billion in the next 30 years. It is now expected that three more billion will be added by the end of the century. By then, at present rates, population will be increasing 1 billion every 8 years.

In contrast, the annual growth of per-capita income in Latin America and East Asia is only about 2 per cent; in Africa only 1 per cent; and in South Asia only about $\frac{1}{2}$ per cent. At these rates, a doubling of per-capita income in East Asia would take almost 35 years, in Latin America more than 40 years, in Africa almost 70 years, and in South Asia nearly a century and a half.

Overpopulation can be checked by either birth-control or death-decontrol. Birth-controls operate in the animal and insect world. With reduced access to food or crowding, for example, male rats fight duels to the death for the females, sex drives lessen, infant mortality increases, meals are made of the young, and other biological processes set in to curb growth. Similar controls have been found to exist in fish, birds, deer, and other living things, including human cannibals.

Man's success in reducing death rates has been undercut by his inability to limit births. Starvation no longer operates as it did in Ireland's potato famine, bubonic plague is rare, genocide has been universally declared immoral, while birth-control has been declared sinful for Catholics. The automobile helps to hold down some population growth by killing 60,000 Americans a year, but medicine, surgery, and sanitation save many times that number annually. The blessings of antibiotics, insecticides, inoculations, and vaccinations have held down mortality in

Asia and the Near East, Africa and Latin America, which contain 69 per cent of the world's grownups and (thanks to decreases in the infant death rate) 80 per cent of the children. Sociologist Kingsley Davis notes that in 20 years, life expectancy increased in Taiwan from 43 to 63 years, a rise in expectancy that the white population of the United States took 80 years to achieve. (See BIRTH RATE; CAPILLARITY, LAW OF; LEBENSRAUM; MORTALITY RATE.)

population, farm   All persons living in rural territory on places of less than 10 acres yielding agricultural products that sold for $250 or more in the previous year, or on places of 10 acres or more yielding agricultural products which sold for $50 or more in the previous year. They need not actually be engaged in agriculture. The definition is that of the Bureau of the Census in 1960. The non-farm population includes all persons living in urban areas and rural persons not on farms.

port   A place to which ships come and go for loading or unloading cargo or for embarkation of passengers; also, a city possessing such a harbor. The term "port" now embraces airports, carports, and hover ports, but only settlements accessible to ships qualify as port cities. It is their port facilities to which most great cities owe their greatness.

postal savings   A system for savings at post offices. It functions in many countries (efficiently and inefficiently), including areas where there are no banking facilities for the people. The postal-savings system in the United States functioned for a long time but lost considerable deposits owing to its low interest rates and poor management. Under the political pressures of private banks it was finally abandoned.

It has been often urged that postal-savings deposits be used to finance housing for workers, particularly where mortgage financing is either non-existent or at a premium. But, somehow, government policy has never quite assessed its housing-development potential.

poverty   The lack of purchasing power sufficient to maintain a socially acceptable minimum standard of living. It is to be distinguished from "destitution," which implies poverty so extreme that the very means of subsistence such as food and clothing are lacking, and from "indigence," which is not so extreme but implies straitened circumstances and a lack of the comforts one has or should have. There is no poverty of poverty terms: there is collective poverty of a whole nation or people; individual poverty, resulting from the person's misfortune; cyclical poverty, implying a periodic or temporary condition. Primary poverty, or lack of sufficient income, is distinguished from case poverty or secondary poverty (individuals suffering from mental or health problems, drink, ignorance, etc.), and insular poverty describes the poverty of those living in backward rural or depressed areas.

In the United States the poverty line has often been drawn at a certain income per year, below which a household is said to be in poverty. Manifestly, however, figures such as these must vary with the times, family size, age, and geography. Still another definition of poverty sees it in a relative sense, to be measured by comparison with the population as a whole. If the relative poverty line is taken at 50 per cent of median family income, poverty in the United States actually increased in the two decades preceding 1968.

Since the mid-twentieth century poverty has become associated with the city dweller, the black, and the elderly. The redistribution of people facilitated by the automobile and suburb has caused a shift of the middle class and the better-heeled from central cities to suburbs. The Negro simultaneously moved into the cities to better his condition, while the elderly poor as well as the indigent whites remained because their choices were limited. As the sources of the city's revenues declined, so did its capacity to support its poor and the greater were the pressures exerted on the federal government for assistance. Social-security programs have helped but not enough. The Poverty Program was a federal acknowledgment of the inadequacy of previous efforts, but though it helped, it fell far short of eliminating poverty. The violence that kept erupting in black ghettos highlighted the failure to deal with the Negro's poverty and the consequences of the default.

power plant (*of government*)   The three powers of government that enable it to act in relation to its economic and social purposes—*i.e.*, the police, eminent-domain, and tax powers. The tax power includes the spending power, though some view it as a fourth independent power.

It is in the way these powers are used that a government's political complexion can be identified. If there is a lenient employment of the three powers, laissez-faire capitalism will be indicated, while excessive employment of the police power suggests authoritarianism. An excessive exercise by government of eminent domain may suggest a trend toward socialization. Taxation when too burdensome will discourage capitalism, and when confiscatory will destroy it, but the tax power can also be used to encourage private enterprise by giving proper tax incentives.

Civilization has engrafted a coating of ethics upon the power plant that includes reasonableness in regulation, equality and justice in the dispensation of benefits, measuring ability to pay in the levy of taxes, and just compensation when property is taken for public use. There is, however, no universality in the application of the powers, and often official generalizations conceal individual injustices. The public power plant is the weatherglass of political life, and studying its actual exercise is a better way of judging the political winds than debating political abstractions. (See EMINENT DOMAIN; GENERAL WELFARE; POLICE POWER; TAX.)

PPBS (planning-programing-budgeting system) A planning and decision-making tool that attempts to organize information and analysis so that the consequences of alternative policies are clearly revealed and fully comparable. PPBS, which first gained fame in the Pentagon under Secretary Robert McNamara, was ordered instituted in each cabinet agency by President Johnson in 1966. In PPBS practice, programs having the same purpose are grouped together under the same category and compared to see which represents the best use of the government's money. As things stand, programs pursuing safety, health, education, and numerous other broad social purposes are scattered among many agencies and departments, and without some sort of new budgetary system there is no way to know just how *much* money the government is spending on a particular problem or goal, to say nothing of determining how *well* it is being spent. PPBS endeavors to display the allocation of resources in terms of the function; to gather hard, quantitative information on the actual results of programs; and to analyze the cost of the various efforts to achieve similar ends and rank them in terms of their effectiveness per dollar.

Enthusiasts hoped that PPBS would be so revealing that it would help officials set priorities among general governmental objectives, but this has proven to be both technically and politically naïve. Much of the time there is little data on what programs actually achieve, little agreement on what is a fair measure of "effectiveness," and difficulty in putting results into quantifiable and comparable terms. And even with all the information at hand, how does one choose between a program training a man for a job and one preventing a case of tuberculosis?

PPBS has proved of some use, however, in discriminating among different programs pursuing the same goal. For example, in a study of alternate means of averting deaths from motor-vehicle accidents, the Department of Health, Education and Welfare found that encouraging the use of seat belts had a lower cost ($87 per death averted) than a particular program for reducing driver drinking ($5300 per death averted). There are many questions to be asked of such an analysis—for example, provision of emergency medical services had an even higher cost per motor-vehicle death averted, but the planners had to take into account that such services were also useful to other injured or ill persons. Still, PPBS does point the way to more resourceful use of resources in both public and private spheres. (See COST-BENEFIT ANALYSIS; GOAL, OPERATIONAL.)

pre-existing use. See USE, PRE-EXISTING.

prefabrication   A term with many connotations, commonly applied to the precasting and assemblage of parts for houses and other structures. Parts have been precast ever since brick was baked for the Tower of Babel. Since a house is only a composite of numerous items prepared on the site or elsewhere, each of which is only a small fraction of total cost, the lure of the assembly line has long beckoned. The federal government has been induced to pour many millions into experimentation; the "Lustron steel house" drew some $40 million from the federal treasury but only a few rows of Lustrons ever rose to adorn the American suburb.

Prefabrication's difficulties have included, among others, consumer resistance, building codes, the difficulties of fitting precast units to varying terrains, high transportation costs, opposition by unions, and underfinancing. Simultaneously, skilled mass production of homes on the site with standardized parts and operational efficiency has provided a competitor for the packaged product and outpaced it. But advances have been made in prefabricating. There are more standardized bathroom units, walls, floors, roofs, windows, and door sections; apartment houses have been put up in the USSR and Europe out of sections manufactured in factories; on-site factories for prefabricated multiple dwellings have begun to be built in the United States. In Jamaica and Puerto Rico prefabrication coupled with mass on-site production has effected economies estimated at about 15 per cent of construction cost. Exteriors of many office buildings in the United States have been put up out of precast products. The infant prodigy, however, seems to be the mobile-home manufacturer, who has been taking the field by storm and is now moving from mobile to more traditional units.

Prefabrication has been tried by less-developed nations with small success and sometimes near-disaster. In Ghana in 1952 precast concrete walls were hauled from Holland across the seas to Accra's promontory, lowered to rocking canoes, and paddled precariously by intrepid natives over pitching breakers to the distant shore, where they were set up miles away to compose a few lonely monuments to the industrial age. In Beersheba, where Elijah once sought refuge from Jezebel's vengeance, a Tourneau-layer crane shaped tons of cement in a huge iron maw; the hardened slab was then carried by crane to the site, only to demonstrate its high costs and imperfections. In Karachi small aluminum prefabs were expanded by additions of adobe and discarded wood to compose the first prefabricated slums.

In the less-developed world, where labor is cheap and plentiful and where standards and materials are simple, the precast house is unessential and premature. Despite the glib sales-talk of prefab peddlers from abroad, the handicraft product is still cheaper, more expandable, and more realistic. Precast shells and mass-produced walls, roofs, pipelines, doors, and windows can help reduce costs, but the prefabricated package is still a long way off, except perhaps for the oil companies, to whom price is less important than quick accommodations for their labor. (See ASSEMBLY LINE; HOUSE, CONVENTIONAL; MOBILE HOME.)

preferential treatment. See COMPENSATORY TREATMENT.

prejudice   A judgment formed before due consideration or examination; a prejudgment. The word has had a number of meanings, one of which was a "precedent" or "previous decision." In its more frequent application it is a bias or leaning toward or against a person or thing in advance of, or not based on, actual experience. "To prejudice" means to impair one's right or affect injuriously, as when a newspaper article prejudices someone who is to be tried for a crime.

Thomas De Quincey wrote: "When a prejudice of any class whatever is seen as such, when it is recognized for a prejudice, from that moment it ceases to be a prejudice. Those are the true baffling prejudices for man, which he never suspects for prejudices."

The feeling against a group or individual may be favorable or unfavorable, but prejudice generally refers to a hostile attitude toward the group or to an individual belonging to the group, on the assumption that he has the objectionable characteristics attributed to the group.

Prejudice as a human reaction is not always illegal or always unjust—a person has a right to his own prejudices as part of his privacy, and prejudice has persisted throughout the ages. But when the prejudice is unjust it may be the prelude to discrimination, and when it is activated into discrimination or oppression affecting the rights of others it may become affected with a public concern. Prejudice becomes discrimination when pride, prestige, status, or property is directly challenged or fears are aroused about the loss of values or the impairment of neighborhood associations and amenities. It takes a more dangerous form when the discrimination is by a whole group or the majority of the citizenry. The neighborhood is the most sensitive area of prejudice; once activated there, prejudice may take its toll in a mass exodus by the inhabitants or in a concerted effort by them to exclude the stereotyped group.

Prejudice activated into oppressive discrimination has resulted in the exclusion of minorities not only from jobs but from advancement. Such discrimination has been practiced by unions, employers, and employment agencies.

A major challenge to minority rights arises when private prejudice is incorporated into the public ethic and becomes part of the public policy. Abuse of the zoning power to exclude minorities, use of the expanding police power to harass them and of eminent domain to oust them, have manifested themselves in the United States and elsewhere. Legislation barring aliens from buying land and unfair immigration restrictions are other discriminatory devices.

Social progress is achieved when the government makes affirmative efforts to educate people against unjust prejudices and when it moves from indifference toward affirmative action barring discrimination. But only a few countries have as yet moved in that direction. (See CIVIL RIGHTS; DISCRIMINATION; INTEGRATION.)

premature subdivision. See SUBDIVISION, ABORTIVE OR PREMATURE.

prestige architecture. See ARCHITECTURE, PRESTIGE.

price-no-object architecture. See ARCHITECTURE, PRICE-NO-OBJECT.

primogeniture An exclusive right of inheritance belonging to the first-born. In English law the right belongs to the eldest son; in the absence of lineal descendants, the property goes to the eldest male in the next degree of blood, to the exclusion of all female and younger male descendants of equal degree. The aim was to keep land from being fragmented. The practice was common in Europe until Napoleon abolished it, and it was one of the first practices to be banned in the American colonies. (See ENTAIL; LAND FRAGMENTATION.)

principal The amount due on a mortgage or other indebtedness as distinguished from the interest that accompanies it; also, the assets of an estate. Principal obligation is the amount of mortgage debt a borrower owes. (See AMORTIZATION; INTEREST; MORTGAGE.)

private property The exclusive right to the possession, use, or disposal of property or goods. Private property is the creation of man in society, and in turn the bundle of rights extended by society to man guarantees him its possession, use, and disposal subject to such intrusions upon it as society requires for the general welfare. James Madison put it succinctly: "The personal right to acquire property, which is a natural right, gives to property, when acquired, a right to protection, as a social right." The right shrinks or expands with the nature of the particular political system and the exertions of its police, tax, and eminent-domain powers.

Private property can be real property—*e.g.,* land and the buildings fixed on it; or personal property—that is, movable property. When a house is movable it is personal property, but when it is anchored to the land it is real property. Personal property in turn may be tangible (a cow or a painting), or intangible (stocks, bonds, money, patents, or claims).

It is intangible personal property that has come to dominate the capitalistic world, which has become a world of paper, each piece of paper standing for a fractional share in a mammoth enterprise or for a claim for a specific sum. The paper may be freely exchangeable, like money.

Land, once the dominant form of wealth, has been subordinated in importance to the intangibles. (See BUNDLE OF RIGHTS; LAND TENURE; OWNERSHIP; PUBLIC-LAND OWNERSHIP.)

program, project. See GOAL.

property tax. See TAX, PROPERTY.

protective association   An association one of whose purposes is to protect a neighborhood against "undesirable intrusions." The associations have varying names—"neighborhood improvement association," "civic association," "taxpayers' league," "property owners' association," "home-owners' association," "home-owners' foundation," or "chamber of commerce." They have long existed for the purpose of improving neighborhoods or maintaining their dignity, pressing for parks, lower taxes, better schools, and strict zoning; but the migration of minorities prompted many of these organizations to mobilize against minority intrusions. The racial restrictive covenant, now illegal, has been replaced by more subtle devices, such as required club membership for residents and other schemes. Another device favored by these associations is zoning, which, though illegal as a racial restrictive device, is written and enforced stringently to exclude the "wrong" people and relaxed for the "right" people. Use of eminent domain for parks and even urban renewal are urged upon local officialdom by the associations to grab up land threatened by a minority breakthrough. (See COVENANT.)

public bond. See BOND, PUBLIC.

public corporation   A corporation set up by a government to conduct, build, or administer an enterprise, function, or service in the public interest. The public (or government) corporation facilitates political autonomy and release from cumbrous legislative and other popular controls; autonomy in personnel selection by granting freedom in whole or in part from civil-service requirements; administrative autonomy, or greater freedom from the usual executive controls; and financial autonomy, or freedom from dependency upon periodic legislative appropriations and from auditing and budgeting controls.

Objections to the public corporation are that its freedom of action is not subject to control by the electorate's officials, thus encouraging it to be arbitrary; that it builds up surpluses that should go to the taxpayer; and that it can float tax-exempt bonds at higher rates than on direct public obligations. Another criticism is that the device is being used more and more for private purposes under the public cloak.

The degree of operational freedom of such corporations depends on the limitations the creating government imposes upon them, but as their number has increased, so have the pressures to impose more controls. As more controls have been imposed, the advantages of the corporate form have shrunk, and it has often begun to resemble the ordinary administrative agency. The Tennessee Valley Authority is perhaps the outstanding example of the effort to escape excessive supervision (by the federal Controller-General) and to maintain operational flexibility. Its dependency upon congressional appropriations has limited its freedom to proceed with its plans, but on the whole it has been relatively efficient.

The public corporate form saw its most impressive expansion in Europe after World War I, when railroad administration was reconstituted in Germany, Austria, Switzerland, Hungary, Rumania, Belgium, Poland, and Greece. In Great Britain the Central Electricity Board, the British Broadcasting Corporation, and the London Passenger Transfer Board are examples. In East Africa railroad and other vital functions are operated by international government corporations, and the nationalistic trends in these countries have not affected them in their operations across borders.

In the United States the First and Second Banks of the United States were early examples, while a spate of public corporations appeared during World War I—the Emergency Fleet Corporation, the United States Shipping Board, the United States Grain Corporation, the Sugar Equalization Board, the War Finance Corporation, and the United States Housing Corporation. The Reconstruction Finance Corporation, the United States Housing Authority, TVA, the Federal Housing Administration, the Federal Home Loan Banks, and the Federal Deposit Insurance Corporation were depression examples.

At the state and local levels, public corporations have also proliferated. The most notable local agency is the local housing authority, which issues its own bonds and operates housing projects under the corporate garb. Independence of the authority was sought by staggering the terms of members and by authorizing it to borrow independently, while freedom from political interference was thought to be assured by making the authority membership honorary and non-salaried. But in the more than thirty years of its operations the authority mechanism has been drawing steadily toward mayoral control. The power of appointment and removal has proven itself the abiding force.

The public and quasi-public corporate form is still in the developmental process. The public-private Communications Satellite Corporation (Comsat), in which stock is freely traded and quoted on the New York Stock Exchange, is a relatively new form. So is the reorganized Federal National Mortgage Association. At the local level the Philadelphia Housing Development Corporation, operating under private charter but financed by a city appropriation of $2 million, exemplifies a new kind of private but publicly financed corporation organized to build housing with virtually no legislative check on its operations. (See CORPORATION; METROPOLITAN SPECIAL DISTRICT; MUNICIPAL PRIVATE-DEVELOPMENT CORPORATION; SPECIAL DISTRICT.)

public domain   In the United States, all the lands owned at any time by government and subject to sale or other transfer or ownership under its laws, exclusive of land owned by individuals or other private interests. The federal or national domain is the total area under the operational jurisdiction of the United States government.

The federal government acquired sovereignty over the nation's present land area of 2 billion acres through a number of international agreements and treaties, but title to some of this acreage has always rested in individual states or their subdivisions or in private hands.

The federal domain, which once totaled 1.8 billion acres—nearly all of the country—has now dwindled to some 750 million, roughly half of it in Alaska. The zeal with which the United States added to its holdings has been paralleled only by the efforts it has made to rid itself of land. Historically there has been little support for planning to develop or sell the public lands for their best uses. A good way to pay off the federal debt, it seemed, was by selling off land, which would simultaneously satisfy the need for private development. Thus federal land policy was originally shaped partly by financial, partly by political and social considerations. Men of all classes tore through the primeval wilderness to reach the new lands, many of them taking possession without formality of title, while other more cautious buyers purchased from the government. Land speculation ran riot, and almost every landowner became an actual or potential speculator. Many bought land sight unseen only to discover, after they had journeyed weeks or months, that they were the owners of a sterile mountain or swamp. Rapid turnover of land and farms became the rule, and the whole economy of land became a thing of the market with the virgin soil traded much like any other commodity.

In defense of this seemingly profligate policy, one might ask whether the nation's unprecedented development would have occurred without it. Planless and reckless as it was, one might ask whether the roots of American democracy would have set without a land distribution that gave the little people quick access to what most of them had been deprived of in the Old World. It is possible (if not probable) that the Constitution alone, with all its fine libertarian rhetoric, would not have sufficed to establish democracy in the absence of the widespread ownership of land made possible by this policy.

In underdeveloped countries in which land has not been distributed the proletariat are seizing it. What has not yet been effected is a rationalization of land policy for our new urban world that will satisfy the yearning of the masses for a piece of land of their own while simultaneously planning the land so that it will be the site for something better than slums, frustration, lawlessness, and chaos. (See LAND POLICY; PUBLIC-LAND OWNERSHIP; SQUATTER.)

public housing. See HOUSING, PUBLIC.

public-land ownership The proprietorship of land by the state. It has been urged as the best means of planning-control and as the best preventive of land exploitation. The theory that all land should be state-owned found strong advocates in the agricultural world and has found equally strong proponents in the urbanizing world. Land, they contend, is not the product of human ingenuity or industry but the free gift of nature. Its value grows because of population growth and because of public improvements due to no exertions by the landowner. He is being unjustly enriched by the unearned increment, which should therefore accrue to the state and to its beneficiaries, the people.

The theoretical basis for land nationalization is to be found in the writings of Malthus, Ricardo, Mill, Spencer, and Henry George. To Malthus, the world's population increased in geometric ratio while the food supply from land increased only arithmetically—the remedy therefore was chastity and repeal of the Poor Laws. Ricardo thought rent would continuously rise. Mill saw landlords growing "richer, as it were, in their sleep without working, risking or economizing." Spencer mused that if landowners had a valid right to the land, "landless men might equitably be expelled from the earth altogether." Something, it was felt, had to be done before the landowner swallowed up all profit and ruled the world. George carried the theory over to urban land, attributed slum crowding to private land ownership, and pressed for a single tax on all land to confiscate the increment.

The USSR's ownership of all land has hardly proved itself the recipe for happiness. After the extinction of millions who would not conform to the decrees of the new owner, the Soviets grudgingly made some concessions: the occupants of rural land, while still not the fee owners, are assured of tenure and have been given inheritance rights. If their property is taken for public use, they are promised just compensation in money or equivalent land. Cooperative ownership of apartments is growing rapidly in the cities and is preferred to public housing by those who can afford it. If all land is still owned by the state, major modifications are being made, and other Communist states have by no means copied the USSR's earlier formula.

Adherents of the nineteenth-century theories, Fabians, and some influential British planners still plug for public ownership, particularly of the land in new towns. Their influence has worked its way into international reports and has been making inroads in land policy in some developing countries. The trouble is that what may be good for England may not be good for less-experienced regions. The average Britisher has been accustomed to tenancy ever since William the Conqueror and has known very little else. At the beginning of the twentieth century, half the territory of the United Kingdom was still in the hands of only 7400 individuals, with the other half divided among 312,500 people. Englishmen became accustomed to building on leaseholds or depending on the landlord's grace for continued occupancy, and since the landlords were of good blood the tenants felt fairly secure that it would not run cold when renewal time came around.

Even if the blood is not so blue among the landlords of other countries, public ownership may not necessarily be the better alternative, for in cases where the state is landlord there is little evidence that things have improved. In Jamaica, a former British colony, defaults in rent to the government landlord totaled more than 70 per cent; in Barbados, another former British colony, 90 per cent; in Venezuela 70 per cent. If these three countries are indicative of the consequences of public-land ownership, a world-wide move toward government landlordism could invite a world-wide default and a collapse of government-aided programs.

In most underdeveloped nations, moreover, fee title is a long-standing custom as well as a strong human desire, and tenants will neither build nor improve their dwellings unless they own them or have ownership's near-equivalent in a very long lease. Finally, there is the problem of the expiring lease irrespective of its original term. No one should be expected to make extensive repairs when his lease may soon expire. Agreements to pay the value of improvements upon expiration of the long lease would help, and there are doubtless other possible compromises with fee ownership, but outright public ownership, which British planners are recommending to the world, is not the universal answer.

What another Englishman, Arthur Young (1741–1820), said is still relevant: "Give a man the secure possession of a bleak rock, and he will turn it into a garden; but give him a nine years' lease of a garden and he will convert it into a desert." (See BETTERMENT; OWNERSHIP; PRIVATE PROPERTY; TAX, INCREMENT; TAX, SINGLE.)

public purpose; public use   Objects for which public powers or funds may be employed for the benefit of the public; public purpose and public use are now used interchangeably to express this criterion of public benefit. What is a public use or purpose may be determined by either the executive, the legislature, or the courts, depending on laws and procedures. In general it involves public benefit, utility, or advantage. Public money may not be spent or public powers applied for private advantage. A use is public if it affects the public generally or any part of the public, as distinguished from benefiting an individual or a few special individuals. The determination is important, for eminent domain can be exercised only where the use or purpose is public or benefits the public. This does not mean that the agency employing the eminent domain power cannot be private—it is the use or purpose that is determinative, and the legislature may confer the power on private parties such as railroads or utility companies if the purpose is public.

The rule on public use has been stated by Nichols:

It is a public use for which property may be taken by eminent domain, (1) to enable the United States or a state or one of its subdivisions to carry on its governmental functions, and to preserve the safety, health and comfort of the public, whether or not the individual members of the public may make use of the property so taken, provided the taking is made by a public body; (2) to serve the public with some necessity or convenience of life which is required by the public as such and which cannot be readily furnished without the aid of some governmental power whether or not the taking is made by a public body, provided the public may enjoy such service as of right; (3) in certain special and peculiar cases, sanctioned by ancient custom or justified by the requirements of unusual local conditions, to enable individuals to cultivate their land or carry on business in a manner in which it would not otherwise be done, if their success will indirectly enhance the public welfare, even if the taking is made by a private individual and the public has no right to service from him or enjoyment of the property taken.

The one ethic with a claim to universality has been that the property of one individual may not be taken solely for the purpose of turning it over to another. This ethic comes close to being violated in urban-renewal policy. The principle is preserved, however, by the presence of slum clearance as the public purpose ("slums menace health"). Yet there is more justification in the United States for a liberal use of the eminent-domain power and a liberal construction of public purpose because here land lacks the unique quality it possesses in countries where it is in short supply or where the opportunities for investment in other types of property are lacking. In the United States land is a commodity of the market and is freely convertible into cash. The only victims of such a liberal policy are the tenants evicted without compensation, and this should be remedied by provisions to make them whole, at least financially. In public acquisitions, at least, there has been some progress in this direction.

A distinction between public purpose here and in England is that what Parliament declares a public use or purpose is not reviewable by the judiciary, whereas in the United States the courts are the final arbiters and may overrule the legislative determinations.

A superior public use is one which by statutory authorization takes precedence over another public use. In assembling large parcels of land, there is often existing property owned by public or private corporations which is in public use, such as streets, railroad tracks, or public utilities. To avoid litigation between the two interests, the legislature may designate that a particular use has priority over another. The statute under which Stuyvesant Town in New York City was authorized contained such a designation which allowed the taking by eminent domain of a subsidized limited-dividend housing project on the site. (See EMINENT DOMAIN; URBAN RENEWAL.)

public utility A private enterprise so essential to the public interest as to justify an exclusive franchise in return for submitting to regulation and the obligation to serve its consumers without discrimination. The most common examples are gas, electric, railroad, and telephone companies; others are oil pipelines, buses, ferries, and taxi companies. Rates and standards are usually controlled by a public-service commission or other agency.

The public-utility concept has been the subject of controversy and judicial dialectic, with certain enterprises once clearly private in character now embraced within the public-utility category. The most controversial type of property is land and housing, which have been called monopolistic and therefore subject to profit regulations, rent control, non-discrimination laws, and other restrictions. Though the concept has not been fully accepted in theory, the restrictions over land and housing in a city like New York have grown to the brink of the public-utility classification.

public works. See PUMP-PRIMING.

pucka. See CUTCHA.

PUD. See PLANNED-UNIT DEVELOPMENT.

pump-priming The expenditure of public funds for public works, housing, or other activities to increase employment and purchasing power and stimulate economic activity, particularly during economic slumps. Pump-priming was initiated during the New Deal era with the passage of the National Industrial Recovery Act, which created a Public Works Administration authorized to build bridges, dams, public housing, and similar works. The bridges and dams took too long to plan and build, while too little money went into labor and too much into steel. Housing was thought to be more suited to the task, and the United States Housing Act of 1937 was enacted partly as a social measure and partly to increase jobs. Other housing stimuli were initiated, including the Home Owners Loan Corporation and the Federal Housing Administration. When the pump wheezed and faltered, a Works Progress Administration (WPA) was set up and money was doled out for hundreds of projects designed less for their contributions to the environment than for putting people to work.

In the late 1960s massive federal public-works projects were once again being advocated as an antidote for joblessness, particularly among blacks and young people—with the emphasis on urban revitalization and cleaning up the environment. But these would not be for pump-priming so much as for cutting welfare rosters and keeping social peace. (See BOONDOGGLING.)

quick take   The acquisition by a public authority of title to property immediately upon commencement of eminent-domain proceedings. Quick takes must be authorized by statute. In the absence of the quick-take procedure the litigation may drag on for years while the property continues in private ownership and the improvement is delayed. Under the quick-take method, title vests in the public agency upon the filing of a "declaration of taking." The authority can immediately begin to demolish and improve. The value as of the date of the taking is thereafter fixed at a trial or hearing.

An alternative, but not so efficient, procedure is for the public agency to apply to the court for possession after commencing eminent-domain proceedings. The law may allow the agency to enter upon and improve the property after paying the owner a specified interim sum. The owner receives the balance when the court or jury determines the value. (See EMINENT DOMAIN; URBAN RENEWAL.)

quiet enjoyment Literally, peaceful pleasure, but in legal usage a covenant in a lease, express or implied by law, that the lessee will remain undisturbed in his possession of the premises. Disturbance may be by force, odors, vermin, noise, a leaky roof, or a yodeling neighbor. If life becomes intolerable he is "constructively evicted" and may break the lease or sue for damages. A covenant of quiet enjoyment may also be contained in a deed, in which case the seller guarantees the buyer a valid title. (See DEED, FULL COVENANT AND WARRANTY; NUISANCE; PRIVATE PROPERTY.)

quota system A device for limiting the number of persons entering a country under the immigration laws; by extension, a method of limiting the entry of a particular minority group into a college, resort, or other place.

A "benign quota" is a seeming contradiction in terms, for it is always unbenign to exclude people solely on account of race, creed, color, or national origin. The term has nevertheless found its way into the language as meaning an honest effort to integrate minorities into housing, schools, or other places that are either segregated or threatened with segregation. Well-meaning efforts to *include* rather than *exclude* have been unjustly called quotas, and in a few instances they have been held to be illegal.

Good faith in the administration of laws should be a relevant consideration in passing on the actions of a public agency dealing with the race issue. Motive should also be part of the guiding criteria in the effort to find a way out of a legal dilemma. It is relevant in zoning and in passing judgment on other legal devices used to exclude or include minorities. Devices known as "quotas" will be employed by the ill-intentioned to exclude and by the well-intentioned to include, and the good or bad motivations should be relevant in determining whether these should be struck down or sustained. (See CIVIL RIGHTS; COLOR-BLINDNESS; COVENANT; SEGREGATION; TIPPING POINT.)

Rachmanism The practice of driving out white tenants by harassment so as to make room for home-hungry minorities, and then exploiting the latter in turn. It derives its name from Peter Rachman, a British landlord who was charged with engaging in such practice. Rachmanism occurs particularly in areas threatened with a racial change in occupancy. (See BLOCK-BUSTING; GHETTO.)

racial polarization The lasting establishment of a society segregated by race. It refers particularly to the existence of a predominantly black society in American central cities and a predominantly white society in the suburbs.

The trend toward polarization can be halted by constructive federal action. More vigorous enforcement of anti-discrimination laws would help. Making the cities a better place to live would help even more. This would require a realistic assumption by the federal government of responsibility for better education, greater safety, health, and welfare. Racial polarization can also be avoided by a movement of blacks into suburbia similar to the mass migration of blacks into cities—which will happen only if the barriers to entry are lifted and black income is elevated sufficiently to qualify them for suburban housing, or, alternately, if such housing is brought within their means.

rack rent. See RENT, RACK.

Radburn planning Planning for a new community, one of the main objects of which is the complete segregation of automobile traffic from pedestrians. The idea was espoused after World War I by Lewis Mumford, Henry Wright, and Clarence Stein. Stein first put it into effect in his planning of Radburn, New Jersey. Superblocks were ringed by roads from which cul-de-sac service roads led to the interior, while all paths and walks linking the blocks and the business district passed either under or over the roads. The new towns of Vallingsby, Sweden, and Cumbernauld, Scotland, among others, have followed the principle. (See CUL-DE-SAC.)

radial street pattern A design in which the streets run from a center outward or from the circumference inward along a radius. The Arc de Triomphe in Paris, for example, has fourteen converging avenues on a radial pattern; the Capitol in Washington, D.C., has eleven. (See LINEAR SYSTEM.)

Radiant City A vertical garden city conceived by Le Corbusier. Tall buildings in a landscaped area would absorb the city's population, leaving substantial open space for other uses. "Suppose we are entering the city by way of the Great Park," wrote Le Corbusier. "Our fast car takes the special elevated motor track between the majestic sky-scrapers: as we approach nearer, there is seen the repetition against the sky of the twenty-four sky-scrapers; to our left and right on the outskirts of each particular area are the municipal and administrative buildings; and enclosing the space are the museums and university buildings. . . . The whole city is a Park." As Le Corbusier envisioned it, the population density at the core would be 1200 persons to the acre, but 95 per cent of the land would be open. There would be underground streets for vehicles and deliveries. The high-income families would live in low-rise luxury housing. "The garden city," said Le Corbusier, "is a will-o'-the-wisp. Nature melts under the invasion of roads and houses and the promised seclusion becomes a crowded settlement." He proposed his "vertical garden city" as the alternative *ville contemporaine.* It has never been built.

real estate; realty Real estate or realty means property in houses and land. The legalistic definition is "land, tenements, and hereditaments." The derivation of "real" is from "royal" and "realty" from "royalty," the land in England having belonged to the King, whose subjects were his tenants. Realty once also meant sincerity and honesty, but that definition seems to have obsolesced.

realtor A copyrighted word defined as "an active member of a local board having membership in the National Association of Real Estate Boards, an organization incorporated in 1908, for the advancement of the interests of real-estate brokers and the protection of the public from unprincipled agents or brokers." "Realtor," according to NAREB counsel, "is not a word, but a trade right coined and protected by law." According to H. L. Mencken, there was an outcry when Sinclair Lewis referred to Babbitt as a realtor. In 1924 the *Realtors' Bulletin* of Baltimore reported that foes of the profession were claiming that "realtor" was derived from the English word "real" and the Spanish *tor,* meaning "bull," or *real bull.* Mencken reports that a hint from the board's alert general counsel was probably enough to stop it.

Until about 1950 NAREB's official code of ethics barred a realtor from "introducing into a neighborhood a character of property or occupancy, members of any race or nationality, or any individual whose presence will clearly be detrimental to property values in the neighborhood." The clause has since been eliminated by the Board, though discrimination by many of its member boards continues. (See BROKER.)

reapportionment The reassignment of legislative seats and the realignment of election districts in states, counties, or other governmental subdivisions to reflect more accurately the number of voters in each. More specifically, the term is used to refer to a 1964 Supreme Court decision holding that the urban areas of every state must be represented in the state legislatures in direct proportion to their populations—*i.e.*, "one man, one vote." "Legislators," said Chief Justice Earl Warren, "represent people, not trees or acres. Legislators are elected by voters, not farms or cities or economic interests. . . . Full and effective participation by all citizens in state government requires, therefore, that each citizen has an equally effective voice in the election of members of his state legislature. Modern and viable state government needs, and the Constitution demands, no less."

The court's decision was a response to what in the new urban society had become a political absurdity. Rural backlands had as much representation as teeming counties. In Dade County, Florida, one-fifth of the state's total residents had only one of thirty-eight state senators and three of ninety-five representatives, while thirty-seven of the smallest counties with half of Dade's population had fourteen times Dade's votes in the state senate and twelve times its votes in the lower house. In 1964 there were thirty-nine states in which both legislative houses were controlled by the representatives of less than 40 per cent of the electorate.

The political reaction to the decision was bitter wherever the decision threatened to disturb rural hegemony. In many states implementing laws were enacted but were as often struck down by the courts as not complying with the mandate. In other cases reapportionment was complied with but only when it favored the new suburban populations or did not substantially threaten the *status quo*. In 1964 the Senate adopted a compromise resolution which in effect approved judicial reapportionment in those states whose legislatures failed to act promptly after courts had held their existing systems invalid. It asked the courts to be liberal in giving them time to act.

recreation Any activity voluntarily undertaken for pleasure, fun, relaxation, exercise, self-expression, or release from boredom, worry, or tension; that which is physically or psychologically rejuvenating because it is apart from the essential routines of one's life.

Urbanization has localized the recreational pattern; three out of four Americans travel less than fifty miles from home to enjoy a day's outing. Much of our recreation has gone indoors, but the principal federal agency for recreation is an Outdoor Recreation Resources Review Commission, which gives little attention to the much-needed indoor forms.

Recreation has become big business. It holds about eighteenth place among the nation's industries. The movie, dance hall, and night club compete with the television set for control of the indoor diversions. The restaurant, which in France and Greece is a recreational retreat for workers, has given way in America to the lunch counter, where turnover is more important than customer comfort. A meal must be wolfed down in ten minutes or the restaurateur loses money. What is leisurely lingering abroad is loitering in America.

Though European countries have state-supported opera, music, theater, and ballet, such institutions depend on hard-won contributions in America. The publicly sponsored Tivoli Gardens in Copenhagen appears in America only when a Walt Disney launches it on a paying basis. The city street abroad is a meeting place and boulevard, but in America it has either become dangerous to walk on or been appropriated by the automobile. The peripatetic has become a waning breed, and the word "pedestrian" is used mainly to describe the dull, commonplace, and unimaginative.

Costly parking and traffic jams are other impediments to in-city recreation. Urban recreation and urban entertainment would be enhanced by the creation of urban recreation commissions that would give the same encouragement to urban and indoor recreation that have been accorded to publicly subsidized outdoor forms. (See LEISURE; URBAN ESCAPE HATCH.)

redevelopment company   A corporation organized under the Redevelopment Companies Law in New York State, under which property can be compulsorily acquired by a city for its projects and tax exemptions given on the improvements on condition that the company limits the return on its investment to a fixed percentage.

The law was specially tailored to accommodate the Metropolitan Life Insurance Company, which organized and controlled the Stuyvesant

Town Corporation. Although Stuyvesant Town provided low-rent housing and was tax exempt, tenants did not have to have low incomes, and
many with high incomes benefited from the huge tax-exemption subsidy.
Had the city made a gift of the land to the company without cost and
taxed the project, it would have recovered the cost of the land from the
increased taxes in about five years. The formula was clearly defective
when employed to benefit families other than those of low income. The
formula simultaneously proved unhappy for Metropolitan, which despised regulation of any kind and had to apply to the city for a rent increase each time its yield went below 6 per cent. The continued opposition of the tenants to increases did not help matters. Metropolitan also
encountered public opposition when it announced that it would not accept Negro tenants although it was benefiting from the city's eminent-domain power and tax exemption.

Stuyvesant Town did demonstrate that renewal schemes are sound in
sound sections and can be profitable when the city assembles the land,
clears the site, and sells it at use value to a redeveloper. It also suggested
that the proper formula for renewal was not tax exemption for high-income families but assemblage of the land coupled with a write-down in
land costs. In this respect it laid the groundwork for the urban renewal
formula of the 1949 Housing Act. Stuyvesant Town also demonstrated
(after accepting some Negroes as tenants following enactment of an anti-
discrimination ordinance) that the presence of blacks does not necessarily drive out the whites or endanger the developer's investment. (See
URBAN RENEWAL.)

refinancing Obtaining a new mortgage in place of an existing one or
borrowing fresh capital to pay off an existing debt. Housing authorities
refinance where they have borrowed temporary capital. Cities and public
agencies as well as private corporations refinance when a loan is pre-
payable and a lower interest rate may be obtained. They may also refinance when a loan is about to mature. (See FINANCING, PERMANENT.)

region A portion of the earth's surface defined and distinguished from
adjacent areas by some homogeneity in its natural features, its climate,
people, interests, involvements, or administrative controls. There are natural regions and created regions. Those created often follow the natural
features; sometimes they are arbitrarily imposed by legislation or fiat.
There are at least six types of regions:

(1) A jurisdictional unit such as a county, state, prefecture, or province.

(2) A large metropolitan complex such as the London or New York regions, embracing cities and suburbs.

(3) A group of municipalities trying to resolve common problems through the creation of an integrating unit.

(4) The creature of two or more states, cities, or other jurisdictions to which powers are delegated to handle an area's common problems, such as port administration or water supply.

(5) An area whose common physiographic resources (such as a river) make it desirable to view it as a region and harness the natural resources for the common interest (*e.g.,* the TVA region).

(6) An area linked by fear, by the need for common defense against a potential disaster or an enemy, or for the common advantage of trade, freer passage of goods or people.

Another type, identified as far back as the year 1704, is the "Regions of the Air," which might have been ignored except for the recent concern over rockets indiscriminately being fired off to circle in orbit. This has stirred demands for some sort of atmospheric regional planning to demarcate the emerging spheres of stratospheric influence.

A micro-region is one focused on the influence of a minor urban center. In England it would correspond generally to a "district."

A nodal region is one in which activities are concentrated, as in an intensively developed metropolitan area.

regionalism Partiality to one's own region as expressed in loyalty or in devotion of one's interests to it; also, the principle or practice of dividing a country or part of one into separate administrative areas, as well as the advocacy of such a principle. Regionalism is a counter-movement to centralism. Its manifestations appear as a result of geographical isolation, independent regional traditions, racial, ethnic or religious concentrations, or regional economic and class interests.

regional planning The planning of activities and facilities for an area larger than a single community and smaller than a nation. The regional planner is mostly concerned with the rational distribution of major economic activities, a settlement pattern consistent with this distribution, the provision of channels of movement between them, and the proper allocation of open space.

Regional planning is also the integration of economic activities of a number of communities or nations aimed toward achieving a more coordinated and a more advantageous system of tariffs, movement of labor and capital, and joint and reciprocal policies on labor, social welfare, agriculture, transport, and foreign trade. Regional plans can be advisory, restrictive, coordinative, developmental, or any combination of these.

Advisory regional planning bodies may be either official or unofficial. Since they do not have executive powers their function is largely to provide inspiration, on the notion that what should be will be. *The Regional Plan of New York and Its Environs* and *The Second Regional Plan,* for example, have been sponsored by the Regional Plan Association, an unofficial, privately supported organization trying to guide some fourteen hundred jurisdictions in three states by illustrating where it thinks the highways, universities, residences, commercial districts, industries, transit facilities, airports, parks, parkway systems, and civic centers should be. The Association and its plan have had some influence upon the ultimate improvements. An advisory association may also serve a political purpose (where there are powerful opposing interests) by bringing the issues into the open or by "running interference" for cautious officials unwilling to carry the ball.

A restrictive regional plan suggests compulsory powers to prevent unwise industrial settlement, deforestation, deruralization, or misplaced developments of one sort or another. It presumes that if you establish what cannot be done, you help bring about what should be done. Zoning, permission to develop or locate industries, and subdivision controls are some of the tools available. The tax power may also be manipulated as a restrictive device by imposing heavier levies on some areas or types of development than on others.

A coordinative plan attempts to rationalize the projects of a number of affected jurisdictions. It is used by cities in developed areas where expansion has made cooperation essential. But whether coordinative plans win the consent of the constituent government units usually depends on how great the pressures are and how critical the needs. If, for example, there is not enough water or there is a critical drainage problem, coordination will more readily be agreed to. Coordination requires consent, and consent usually follows out of self-interest, fear, crisis, and, in rare cases, a concern *pro bono publico.*

The most important (and potentially the most constructive) regional plan is the developmental plan providing for a major improvement that brings inevitable consequences in its wake. The Tennessee Valley development is one example. The harnessing of the Volta River in Ghana will make it possible not only to turn bauxite into aluminum, but also to alter the lives and ways of a rural-tribal society, disenthrall its economy from its dependency on cocoa, inspire secondary industries, shipping, and trade, improve health, and speed a migration from unredeemingly depressed areas to cities—which in turn will spur the need for housing, utilities, and amenities. Regional planning works best when it is part of a broad national development program. (See CITY PLANNING.)

rehabilitation The restoration or improvement of deteriorated structures, public facilities, or neighborhoods. It is more than a repair or remodeling, less than a conversion or reconstruction, and close to a reconditioning. Nevertheless it has come to be used to describe any substantial improvement in a building.

Rehabilitation may be an aided or unaided private undertaking or a public operation. Private rehabilitation is common in cities and will be undertaken when projected new rents justify the outlays. There has been a surge of federally aided rehabilitation programs designed to upgrade the existing residential inventory, but these have been less successful than anticipated because of the high rents resulting from the improvement cost and the inability of families to pay them. Also, as has belatedly been discovered, rehabilitation cost has often been excessive compared to the cost of new private construction.

Rehabilitation should be part of any housing program, but it involves the careful distinction between buildings that will respond to economic rehabilitation and those that should be consigned to the wrecking crews. It is always a risk to break plaster—one never knows what troubles lie behind it. There is no magic formula equally applicable to all structures, all cities, or all neighborhoods, but the following are general guides.

Rehabilitation should be undertaken by a private investor only when the projected net income compensates for the capital outlay, trouble, and risk.

The attractive shell of an old building is a great investment seducer, but its value represents only a fraction of total rehabilitation cost. The smaller gamble is a house in which interior walls can remain and additional amenities can be installed without substantial structural changes. Scottish baronials boasting the rugged virtues of Caledonia and alcazars with overgenerous hallways and heraldry-ridden porticoes are a headache for the architect and a money trap for his client.

Existing amenities in old structures may be invaluable. Some well-designed old buildings are replete with built-in antiques. High ceilings, large rooms, fireplaces, French windows, storage basements, woman-size kitchens and man-size toilets, backyards, gardens, bay windows, or skylights may draw customers from the new minimum-standard multiples and set off the spark that makes prospects glow. Old masonry walls leak fewer decibels than the skimpy partitions of new houses.

The cost of alterations sometimes exceeds the cost of a new house. The latter can be estimated more accurately and may be a better investment.

A venture in rehabilitation often means gambling more on the neighborhood than on the structure. The character of a neighborhood and its amenities are vital elements. Rehabilitating for families entails consideration of such factors as good schools, play spaces, and safety.

City regulations may spell the difference between success and failure. Obsolete or complex building codes that no one can interpret, finicky inspections, rent controls, overrigid zoning, and occupancy restrictions can make rehabilitation an expensive chore. Just as regulation can prove a nuisance, city cooperation can prove a boon. Subventions in the form of tax abatement or tax remission can make the difference between a solvent and an insolvent undertaking.

A low purchase price is deceptive—it costs about the same to alter a house in a high-rental as in a low-rental section, but the profit differential may more than justify paying more for the shell in the better area.

Income taxes are important in the rehabilitator's calculations. The investment, for example, can be written off in a short term against income. In some cases part of the outlay can be deducted from taxable income as a repair.

Good mortgage conditions are a prime factor not only in spurring rehabilitation but in increasing the net return on the cash investment.

The presence of minorities in an area is not an inevitable invitation to financial disaster. Ethnic formations may add spirit and value to adjoining sections.

In public operations, social and planning objectives may often out-
weigh economic criteria. High cost may be justified in refurbishing the
one or two structures blighting an otherwise sound block. (See
ALTERATION.)

rehabilitation, instant   A demonstration project in New York City for
speedy and economical rehabilitation of old-law tenements by combining advanced engineering techniques with the use of preassembled components. The idea was proposed in 1965 by the engineering firm of
T. Y. Linn and Associates, and the subcontract was subsequently assigned to Conrad Engineers. In its initial planning stages, forty-eight
hours and a $5000 cost per unit were set as targets. The venture turned
out to be the longest and most expensive instant on record. It was also
the most publicized venture of its kind when it began and the least publicized when it failed.

New York City's Rent and Rehabilitation Administration was the
prime mover behind the project, and the federal government was the
financier for a non-profit corporation, which was the recipient of the
grant. The instant rehabilitation had all the earmarks and gadgetry of the
new technology—prefabricated parts and critical-path scheduling to assure coordination of all the steps. Tenants were moved out for several
nights and moved right back in. Kitchen and bathroom units fabricated
off-site were lowered into the building by a crane through holes made in
the roof and floors.

Instead of $5000 per unit the final construction cost came to $22,000,
or about $45 per usable square foot. A comparable rehabilitation project
using traditional methods ran to about $14 per usable square foot. Worse
still, the cost of $22,000 per "instant" unit was the actual construction
cost attributable to building; it omitted such costs as experimentation,
testing, etc.

relocation   Settlement of households or businesses in new locations, particularly as applied to persons displaced by governmental action. It has
been often referred to as the Achilles heel of urban-renewal programs
and is now the bane of the interstate-highway program.

Before a federal loan or grant is made for urban renewal, the local renewal agency must present a "feasible plan to relocate the families in the

renewal site" and also demonstrate that good housing within the means of the displaced families is being provided. But local renewal agencies, eager to get on with their programs, have not all been scrupulous in accommodating their displaced families. Relocation programs have been criticized for the inadequacy of the compensation, the unavailability of good housing, the increased rents, the lack of social services, the poor quality of the advisory services provided, the poor treatment of the families by the authorities, and the poor timing of the aids given. For these reasons relocation, which is more often dislocation, has met with considerable resistance from both residential and commercial tenants.

Urban-renewal programs, however, have been neither the only nor the main displacer of poorer families. Code-enforcement, highway, and other government programs displace more. Moreover, urban renewal was the first program to accept responsibility for the people it displaced and to break precedent with the rule that gave no compensation to a monthly tenant or lessee who had waived his right to an award (the common practice in leases).

Some improvement in displacement procedures has occurred—including a solatium to displaced owners, greater uniformity in displacement compensation, and more rigid federal supervision over local malpractices. But the poor tenant family and the small businessman continue to bear more than their share of the cost of public improvements. (See EVICTION; SOLATIUM.)

rent A payment made periodically by a tenant to a landlord for the use of land, buildings, a residence, or other property. Alfred Marshall defined it as the income derived from the ownership of land and other free gifts of nature (meaning by this primarily the proceeds from agricultural land). From the sixteenth to the eighteenth century "rent" also meant the interest on a loan. It is also used to describe the amount paid by contract for the use of a commodity or property of any kind (including real estate).

Additional rent is the rent added to the fixed rent as prescribed by a lease. It is usually based on the percentage of gross receipts of a commercial property and becomes payable when the percentage of the receipts exceeds the fixed rent. Additional rent may also be prescribed for an increase in taxes on the property or a rise in the cost-of-living index.

Graduated rent is a rent rising at different periods of the lease, in accordance with its terms. (See LEASE; SUBLEASE.)

rent-control   The regulation of rents, the prohibition of evictions, and the control of the landlord-tenant relationship by legislation and regulation. Rent regulation is generally brought on by housing shortages and the need for preventing mass evictions or oppressive rent increases. The practice exists in many countries; it was employed nationally in the United States as part of price-controls during World War II, and at this writing still prevailed in New York City and a few other cities in New York State.

Ceilings on rent do not bring roofs overhead. They are easier to impose than to remove. When imposed, controls should be viewed as an emergency measure and as part of a housing program designed to eliminate the controls by easing the shortage that necessitated them. When controls linger on beyond their time, evasions, gaping rent differentials between dwellings of the same value, disrepair, and even abandonment are the consequences. Occupants hold on to dwellings they do not need, and relationships between landlord and tenant harden as both look to the law instead of the contract for their rights and privileges. Under no circumstances should rent-controls be imposed on private new construction, except, perhaps, in publicly aided building. They frighten mortgage lenders and tend to inhibit the very building that can relieve the shortage and eliminate the need for controls. The best way to ease the housing shortage is to build more housing, not impose more controls, and when rent-control exists or is threatened, a crash housing program is needed with all the possible inducements to build.

rent, economic   The amount of rent sufficient to cover all costs of operating and maintaining a building, including debt service on the mortgage over the building's economic life. Thus the economic rent of a public-housing unit is the rent that would be payable without the subsidies.

In early economics it referred to that portion of the earth's produce paid to the landlord for the use of the "original and indestructible powers of the soil"; also, the excess of the produce or return from a given piece of cultivated land over and above the cost of production.

rent, ground   The rent payable on the land as distinguished from rent payable on the building. Ground rents are still common in Baltimore,

Maryland, where the land is let at 6 per cent for long term. They are also common in England. Valuable land is still leased in the United States, with costly improvements being made by the lessee, but in smaller transactions the freehold seems to be winning its way. (See FEE SIMPLE; FREEHOLD.)

rent, peppercorn   A nominal rent paid to establish a legal landlord-tenant relationship. In the Middle Ages rent was frequently paid in the dried berries of black pepper, thus the name. When squatters invade privately owned land, owners sometimes try to induce them to pay a nominal rent so as to establish landlord-tenant relationship. This forestalls a claim by the squatter that he has a legal right to the land (other than the tenancy), while it puts the owner in a better position to terminate the tenancy when the agreed rental period expires. The same practice may be resorted to by public agencies faced with a stubborn squatter invasion.

rent, rack   Rent equaling or nearly equaling the entire value of landed property or the products produced on it; hence an excessive or unreasonably high rent. Great Britain's Public Health Act of 1875 fixed rack rent at "not less than two-thirds of the full net annual value of the property out of which the rent arises." To "rack-rent" is to exact the highest possible rent.

reparcelation   Pooling of uneconomic or fragmented plots (mainly rural) to achieve a workable holding. Reparcelation was employed in France to rationalize the strip or ribbonlike plots that were the consequence of the abolition of primogeniture under the Napoleonic Code. The law prescribed that ownership of all the lots in a given area could be compulsorily pooled on the application of a majority of owners. The property holders received an ownership interest in the area proportionate to their prior holdings, and after redevelopment was effected, lots were redistributed accordingly. After World War II reparceling was employed for the reconstruction of devastated areas. Owners were organized into a cooperative association with a public representative and special powers, to be dissolved after redistribution was effected. (See LAND FRAGMENTATION; LEX ADICKES; PARTITION ACTION; PRIMOGENITURE; URBAN RENEWAL.)

repercussion effects. See EXTERNALITIES.

replacement cost The cost of replacing an asset such as a factory or apartment house with a new one of equal value and utility. It is synonymous with "reproduction cost." It is relevant as evidence of value in eminent-domain proceedings, in tax-assessment hearings, and in appraisals of value. (See APPRAISAL; VALUATION, PHYSICAL; VALUE.)

revenue bond. See BOND, REVENUE.

revenue financing; "pay as you go" financing" The financing of developments or improvements out of current revenues, as distinguished from borrowing against future income. Financing through bond issues has become common practice among cities and other governmental agencies, particularly to launch capital improvements. Frequently, however, money is also borrowed on long term to finance current expenditures, and this, it is argued, is indebting the future generation for the present generation's obligations. Revenue financing often also refers to revenue-bond financing. (See BOND, PUBLIC; BOND, REVENUE.)

reversion The return of real estate to the grantor and his heirs after the period of the grant is over or because of a violation of the terms of a grant or deed providing for such a reversion upon default. In the United States reversion for a default is generally frowned upon by the courts. (See DEFAULT.)

ribbon development An urban extension that takes form in a single depth of houses along roads radiating from the city. Visually offensive, destructive of the countryside, and costly to provide with utilities and services, ribbon development was made illegal in England under the Town and Country Planning Act of 1947; attempts to deal with its earlier development included the Restriction of Ribbon Development Act of 1935. In American parlance, ribbon, or strip, development usually refers to the garish commercial stretches lining highways, particularly those leading into and out of major urban areas. Little has been done on this side of the Atlantic to curb it.

right-of-way Legal right to pass through the grounds of another. It may be acquired through accepted usage or by contract. Also, the strip of land on which a highway, railroad, or transit line runs. In securing a pathway for a transportation facility, public agencies and utilities usually acquire a width in excess of that actually needed for the improvement in order to provide for expansion and to protect against the encroachment of adjacent uses. (See CHANNELS OF MOVEMENT.)

riot Temporary but violent mass disorder. It is officially defined by the Civil Rights Act of 1968 as a public disturbance involving an act or acts of violence by one or more persons part of an assemblage of three or more persons creating a clear and present danger of actually injuring a person or property; or a threat of violence by one of an assemblage of three or more persons having, individually or collectively, the ability of immediate execution of such threats, where the performance of the threatened acts of violence would constitute a clear and present danger of, or would result in, damage or injury to an individual or to property.

Riot is to be distinguished from insurrection or rebellion in that it involves no effort to bring down the government. The riots among blacks in the late 1960s were not rebellions: they aimed to secure greater participation in the existing order, not to overthrow it. Rioting, however, may be the prelude to rebellion, as it was prior to the French and Russian Revolutions.

Rioting is generally the result of some underlying social disturbance that erupts after an incident has heated up passion or anger, stirred boldness in a leader or leaders, and turned a crowd into a mob. The unconscious gains the upper hand, a variety of emotions and temperaments attains homogeneity, and the mob moves like a single body in one direction toward a particular target.

Riots have punctuated history since its dawn. They erupted in the class wars of the Greek city-states and in the Roman Empire; they appeared in the form of peasant uprisings, brawls between families, May Day celebrations, gang and labor riots, draft protests, and anti-alien and anti-Jewish demonstrations. They originate in economic, political, religious, and racial antagonisms. There have been Negro riots in the United States and anti-Negro riots; riots in India and Pakistan that shed the blood of millions; organized and spontaneous riots; riots that followed from scandals and those spawned by mere rumors; there have been summer riots and winter riots, contained riots and epidemic riots that spread like the plague.

As defined by state laws, riots have the following elements: the presence of three or more persons in one place (in some states two are sufficient); a common purpose that is unlawful; the setting into motion or execution of the purpose; an intent to aid one another by force against anyone opposing them; force or violence that will alarm at least one person of "reasonable firmness and courage."

Riot laws are far from uniform over the world, and the laws in the United States are generally milder in their penalties than those of England, where the first Riot Act was prompted by the widespread violence that followed the crowning of George I.

Among the most serious riots in the United States were the Draft Riots during the Civil War, when casualties in New York City matched those of some battles in the war itself—four days' fighting claimed two thousand dead and about eight thousand wounded. Virtually every man on the city's police force was said to be injured, and fifty soldiers lost their lives. The rioters hanged eighteen Negroes, and some seventy others were reported missing. About eleven thousand stands of arms and several thousand bludgeons were captured.

Of a different order were the riots in black ghettos of many American cities in the 1960s. They were not riots in the accepted sense of the term but "unusual, irregular, complex, and unpredictable social processes," in the words of the National Advisory Commission on Civil Disorders.

And, indeed, the most significant and most horrifying aspect of the outbreaks was their spontaneity and extensiveness. A local "tension-heightening incident" was no longer needed to initiate the violence, nor were the exhortations of a leader. The generating incident could be an assassination, a riot two thousand miles away, or a hot afternoon. (See CIVIL DISORDER; CROWD.)

Riot Act An English statute of 1715 providing that if twelve or more persons assemble unlawfully and riotously, to the disturbance of the public peace, and refuse to disperse upon proclamation, they shall be considered guilty of a felony. To read the Riot Act is to command the cessation of an activity under threat of penalties. According to an early judicial decision in England, the Riot Act had to be read as a whole—the omission of the words "God Save the King" at the end of the reading was enough to invalidate the charge made against the alleged rioters.

riparian rights   The rights accruing to a landowner on the bank of a natural watercourse, lake, or ocean to enjoy access to it for power, fishing, irrigation, swimming, skating, or building piers or wharves.

Riparian rights vary with state laws, as they do with the rights conveyed or reserved in deeds. A riparian owner's rights cease at the water's edge, and he may not interfere with its use by others offshore. A riparian owner may develop water power and has the right to use the natural fall in a river brought about by a difference in a stream's levels where it first touches his land and where it leaves it, but he may not alter the level of the water or pollute it. On navigable streams, power rights are subordinate to public rights such as navigation.

The rights in underground water also vary between states. In California the doctrine of "correlative right" exists—*i.e.,* the owner has the right to use the water fully if the supply is adequate; if not, each landowner is entitled to a reasonable share. In New Mexico the right to underground water belongs to the public. Under common law the owner of the surface has full rights to the water running under his land.

ripe   Ready for use. The word is used to designate land that is ready for development and can be sold, rented, or developed for a particular purpose. An area may be ripe for redevelopment when it has exhausted the economic life of its existing use and could be more economically developed for another use.

road   Any improved line of communication for passage or travel between different places that is wide enough for vehicles and possesses a reasonable length. (Originally, the act of riding on horseback as well as a journey on horseback.) The "rule of the road" was the fixed custom regulating the side to be taken by vehicles in progressing or in passing each other.

An access road is one giving direct access to the land and premises on one or both sides.

A bypass road takes traffic around a congested area and thereby facilitates through movement.

A distributor road is an intermediate link between local streets and major arteries and does not necessarily have direct access to the properties fronting it.

A ring road (beltway) is a circumferential highway that avoids the core of an urban area, permitting through traffic to bypass the center and local traffic to distribute itself to various points around the center.

road hierarchy The classification of thoroughfares by their varying sizes and purposes. The following are generally accepted categories, according to purpose, type of access control, and other features:

Free Access

Local Street: a facility providing access for pedestrians and vehicles to properties that front on it; it is not intended for through traffic.

Collector: a facility designed to bring traffic from local streets to major channels; it has few restrictions on entrances, and traffic control is usually by stop sign.

Restricted Access

Major Street, Secondary Road, Minor Arterial: a street feeding major channels with no access from individual driveways and with limited entrances (at approximately 1500-foot intervals); traffic control is usually by street light.

Arterial, Major Road, Major Arterial: a preferential through facility designed to move larger volumes of traffic on intracity trips; entrances are at restricted locations and intersections are channelized.

Limited Access

Expressway: a divided multi-lane road designed to move large volumes of through traffic from one part of an urban area to another; grades are separated at important intersections, although there may be some grade crossings; it has a minimum number of traffic signals.

Freeway, Turnpike, Thruway: a divided multi-lane road with full grade separation, total control of access, and buffers along the sides; it has no need for ordinary traffic signals and is basically designed for intercity and interstate traffic.

Parkway: an expressway or freeway intended for passenger cars and non-commercial traffic only; as the name implies, such roads are often located within a park or a ribbon of parklike development.

roll-back The fixing by law or order of a price or rent retroactively applicable to a prior date. Thus a roll-back of rents entails cancellation of rent increases and compulsory retreat to previous levels. (See RENT-CONTROL.)

roof loans Loans made to persons putting up the four walls of a house to cover the cost of their roof. Ghana adopted a roof-loan scheme on the recommendation of a United Nations Mission in 1954 and provided government loans to defray the cost of the roof, doors, and windows. The mission recommended that the loans be made to societies or councils formed of the elders and householders of a village. The societies and councils in turn would make smaller loans to their individual members. If the societies or councils failed to repay the loans, further advances would be curtailed. As a result of the scheme thousands of houses were constructed—and constructed more substantially. The societies generated other activities as well; members met to discuss local problems, build better roads, improve sanitation, and often to advance their educational status. The scheme also sparked the organization of benevolent societies fashioned on the roof-loan society formula; there were a thousand such societies by 1960.

One of the lessons learned was that out of the ancient cooperative aspects of the tribal and village system a new device could be forged that would not only produce many new homes but also stimulate other improvements, achieve greater cooperative effort, consolidate community life, and develop social and communal responsibility. (See HOUSE, CORE; HOUSING, SELF-HELP; MUTUAL-AID CONSTRUCTION.)

roofscaping Decorating a roof or penthouse with landscaping; putting a bower on a tower. Roof gardening is the Jeffersonian vine and fig-tree concept applied to the penthouse. It has its hazards not only for the plants but for the structure, if their weight is more than the roof can bear. Literature exists on the proper architectural features—*i.e.,* wall fountains, pools, sculpture, tile, paving, etc. Trees like ailanthus will thrive almost anywhere, but albizzia, Burford holly, willows, Japanese cherries, and apple and pear trees will grow only for those who care and who have faith that they will survive the rigors of city life. (See URBAN ARBORICULTURE.)

room An interior space within a building enclosed by walls or separated from other similar spaces by walls or partitions. If the definition of a room were that uniform, there would be no room for doubt. But a bathroom is not a room in the accepted sense though it meets the dictionary definition. Neither is a closet. In the effort to circumvent congressional limitations on room costs, government agencies have invented their own definitions. So have builders. Kitchenettes, breakfast nooks, entry platforms, porches, spaces separated by room-dividers, balconies, and other odd spaces, enclosed or unenclosed, are often counted as rooms or half-rooms. The room count has become so confusing that one tends to describe one's apartment by the number of bedrooms rather than rooms.

rural-urban fringe. See URBAN FRINGE.

sampling   The technique of testing or examining a representative portion of an aggregate on the supposition that it will be a reasonable approximation for the whole. Sampling, or sample surveys, are employed to determine housing conditions, trends in the cost of living, a candidate's prospects, and popular opinion of a particular soap.

satellite city. See CITY, SATELLITE.

scenic easement. See EASEMENT, SCENIC.

schedule. See GOAL.

scheme. See GOAL.

school busing. See BUSING, SCHOOL.

school, exemplary. See EXEMPLARY SCHOOL.

section; district A distinct part of the country or a city distinguished by its location, people, or features—a slum section, the financial section, etc. In most of the United States west of Ohio it also describes one of the thirty-six numbered subdivisions, each one mile square, of a township as laid out by the federal government at the time of settlement. A quarter section is a tract of land half a mile square containing 160 acres.

sector theory A theory of urban growth that holds that classes of residential uses tend to be arranged in wedge-shaped sectors radiating from the central business district along major transportation routes. Developed by Homer Hoyt in his study of residential areas in the 1930s, the theory holds that high-rent residential areas are prime shapers of city growth and that there is a decline in desirability and value in all directions from them. Different income groups of a city segregate themselves residentially in sectors and then migrate within the same general sector but away from downtown as the sector grows. The middle-income groups attach themselves as closely as possible to the upper-income areas, which usually have the highest and best land, the most prestigious residents, and the best access to other parts of the city. The theory has been criticized by Lloyd Rodwin, who said that Hoyt's conclusions were based on questionable assumptions and on an *ad hoc* theory of class structure. It assumed that locations were selected for class attractiveness while it ignored other considerations such as the functional adequacy of established environments. (See CONCENTRIC ZONE THEORY; GRESHAM'S LAW OF NEIGHBORHOODS; MULTIPLE NUCLEI THEORY.)

security Money deposited to guarantee performance of a contract, particularly a lease. It may compensate the owner for his damages or if the agreement so provides be forfeited. Depending on the terms, security may draw interest for the depositor, be held in trust, be applied to the last month's rent, or be repaid in installments as the lease draws to its close. Under some statutes failure to repay security when due is a criminal offense.

seed money The initial nominal capital required to sow a business or building operation. The remaining capital may be raised by borrowing or by securing the interest of other investors. Seed money, like seed, is small and its anticipated fruit is profit.

Seed money is also the initial working fund required by non-profit housing sponsors to have preliminary architectural plans drawn, make site surveys, purchase options, pay legal fees and closing costs. This is non-risk capital, which is ultimately refundable under city, state, and federal housing programs, but since no government agency will approve a project or advance monies without some evidence of feasibility, a certain amount of start-up cash is indispensable. Herein lies a great dilemma for many non-profit groups—to get money for these expenses they must have a developed project and to develop a project they must have some money. Pre-seed money—for renting an office, hiring a staff, organizing tenants—is also hard to come by and is generally not reimbursable. In some cases the builder can be persuaded to assign part of his profits to the group for their efforts. The Office of Economic Opportunity, foundations, and a parent organization (such as a church or union local) are other sources. For want of "seeding" more than a few housing projects have been frustrated. (See EQUITY; FRONT MONEY.)

segregation   The separation or isolation of a group by either law, social pressure, or custom. When enforced by law, public agencies, or social sanctions it is compulsory segregation. It is voluntary segregation when people choose to live with their own kind either because of a common language or race or because they feel comfortable that way. The distinction is important because there are those who argue that all ghettos should be demolished, including voluntary ghettos. This would violate the right to be left alone. It is when compulsion appears in any form that segregation becomes invidious, and when the segregation is in public institutions, practiced by public agencies or with the use of public funds, the segregation is unlawful. In the classic case of *Brown v. Board of Education* (1954) the Supreme Court, citing the social harm of compulsory segregation to children, said: ". . . in the field of public education the doctrine of 'separate but equal' has no place. Separate educational facilities are inherently unequal." The schools were ordered to desegregate. (See APARTHEID; COLOR-BLINDNESS; CULTURAL PLURALISM; DISCRIMINATION; GHETTO; HOUSING, OPEN-OCCUPANCY; INTEGRATION; PHASE PROGRAM; QUOTA SYSTEM; "SEPARATE BUT EQUAL.")

selective law enforcement   Policing or prosecution that uses a strong hand against some groups and winks at violations by others. Selective law enforcement may favor whites in the South and bear down on blacks; in Northern black ghettos, on the other hand, the police might ignore petty crimes through fear of stirring violence while making arrests for similar crimes in white areas. Selective law enforcement is unequal protection under the law but most often affords its victim no remedy.

self-help housing. See HOUSING, SELF-HELP.

"separate but equal" A term used in the case of *Plessy v. Ferguson* (1896), which gave judicial approval to segregation provided the segregated accommodations for Negroes were equal in quality to the white accommodations. The Supreme Court held in this case, which involved a Louisiana statute requiring the separation of Negroes and whites on trains, that the law was "powerless to eradicate racial instincts or to abolish distinctions based on physical differences"; that the states were constitutionally justified in classifying citizens on the basis of race in the use of state facilities and public utilities. But, said the court, "Laws permitting and even requiring [separation of the races] in places where they are liable to be brought into contact do not necessarily imply the inferiority of either race to the other, and are generally, if not universally, recognized as within the competency of the state legislatures in the exercise of their police power. The most common instance of this is connected with the establishment of separate schools for white and colored children, which have been held a valid exercise of the legislative power even by courts of states where the political rights of the colored race have been longest and most earnestly enforced."

The doctrine was overturned in *Brown v. Board of Education* in 1954. (See EQUALITY; SEGREGATION.)

septic tank A tank plus a leaching pit or trenches in which waste matter is purified and decomposed through bacterial action. Unlike cesspools, septic tanks are acceptable sanitary systems for low-density development. The stage of development at which they must be replaced, to preserve health standards, by a full-scale sewer system varies, depending on soil conditions and lot sizes. (See CESSPOOL; SEWER SYSTEM.)

service trades Activities providing services rather than producing goods. This is the fastest-growing sector of the American economy. It is not always simple to distinguish between the two. Repair shops for automobiles, shoes, or electrical appliances, for example, are regarded in the United States as service industries, while British legislation classifies them as factories.

setback regulations   The requirements of building laws that a building be set back a certain distance from the street or lot line either on the street level or at a prescribed height. Their aim is to allow more room for the pedestrian or to reduce the obstruction to sunlight reaching the streets and lower stories of adjoining buildings. (See ZONING, HEIGHT.)

settlement house   A community center offering social, educational, and recreational facilities at nominal or no charge to the residents of less-privileged neighborhoods. Its origins are in London's Toynbee Hall, founded in 1884. The idea spread to American cities—Hull House in Chicago was established, and the Henry Street Settlement, Greenwich House, Hudson Guild, Madison House, and others in New York City. The settlement houses taught immigrants English, prepared them for citizenship, and laid the groundwork for adult education; and they worked to improve housing and environmental conditions. Some of the movement's leaders fought the sweatshops, child labor, and labor exploitation.

The type of settlement house born of the needs of European immigrants does not meet the needs of the blacks in-migrating to American cities. In fact, many black neighborhoods are devoid of settlement houses and settlement workers. Where they do exist the trained white workers are often viewed with suspicion. Trained black workers have been few, and alienation has made rapport more difficult. Government-aided programs, however, have supplanted some voluntary programs, and the church and Negro organizations have become vortices around which black interest revolves. Government-assisted programs are being looked to for the solution of neighborhood problems and the easing of neighborhood tensions. (See COMMUNITY CENTER; PECKHAM CENTRE.)

sewage   Liquid or water-borne wastes generated within residences, business establishments, institutions, and industrial buildings or as by-products of any residential, commercial, industrial, social, or municipal activity.

Domestic or sanitary sewage is composed of human bodily discharges carried by flush water, soiled water from washing and laundering, and other water-borne material discarded as a by-product of regular household and human sanitary operations. For purposes of planning and waste management, sanitary sewage is distinguished from liquid industrial wastes.

Storm sewage is that resulting from rain or snowfall.

sewage treatment   The artificial removal of pollutants from sewage, their transformation into an inert state, and the altering of the objectionable constituents by controlled physical, chemical, or biological processes. One or more of the following steps are involved:

Primary Treatment: a series of mechanical treatment processes that remove most of the floating and suspended solids but have limited effect on colloidal and dissolved material.

Secondary Treatment: a series of biochemical, chemical, or mechanical treatment processes that remove, oxidize, or stabilize non-settlable, colloidal, and dissolved organic materials.

Tertiary Treatment: any purification process capable of removing more than 98 per cent of the pollutants from sewage.

(See CESSPOOL; CONTAMINATION; EFFLUENT; LATRINE; PACKAGE PLANT; POLLUTION; SEPTIC TANK.)

sewer system   Man-made physical devices intended for the collection, removal, treatment, and disposal of sewage generated within a given area, usually consisting of a collection network and a treatment facility. A sewage system is the unappreciated blessing of more-developed cities, and its absence is a bane. Lagos, Nigeria, for example, gave a higher priority to slum clearance and turned down a loan offer from the World Bank to build a sewage system; the result is that human feces are still collected in buckets (if at all) with the accompanying odors, discomforts, and dangers. (Some 85 per cent of the schoolchildren suffer from parasites, and dysentery is one of the major causes of death.) A strike by the bucket collectors can paralyze the city and sometimes does.

A fully developed sewer system will generally include:

Branch Sewers, which receive flows from house connections and laterals.

Combined Sewers, which are single conduits to remove both sanitary sewage and storm water run-off from developed areas.

House (or *Building*) *Connectors,* pipes leading from a building's internal plumbing system to a communal or public sewer.

Interceptors, major sewers collecting flows from a number of main and trunk sewers and carrying the discharge to a treatment or disposal facility.

Lateral Sewers, minor sewers receiving flows from house connectors only.

Main Sewers, which serve as collectors for sizable districts.

Out-fall Sewers, used to transport effluent from a treatment facility (or raw sewage when no treatment plan is available) to a point of final discharge.

Sewage Treatment Plant, the collection terminal.

Storm Drains, intended exclusively for removal of storm water, surface run-off, and street wash.

Trunk Sewers, major sewers collecting flows from a large area.

A sewer collection network is a system of sewers carrying sewage from points of generation to a treatment or disposal facility, consisting of house connections, laterals, branch sewers, interceptors, out-fall sewers, manholes, and other sewer hardware.

shackery A settlement of shacks, or groups of shacks.

sharecropping. See METAYAGE.

shelter A place where one dwells, as distinguished from "home," which is not only the family seat but the center of domestic affections. As Robert Frost defined it, "Home is the place where, when you have to go there, they have to take you in."

There is a marked difference between what an owner in a developed land expects of a home and what he expects in an underdeveloped area, where the urban habitation serves three main purposes: to protect against the elements, to store possessions, and as a place to reproduce the species. In more developed countries shelter becomes, as well, a means of self-expression, a place for card-playing, cocktail parties, exhibition of one's art and honorific belongings, the children's study center, a television auditorium, and a retreat from urban civilization; the variety of activities depends primarily on its size and the initiative and talents of the female.

Urbanization has shaken the foundations in both areas. Some 35 million people move every year in the United States, and the surge of the mobile home as one of the dominant forms of shelter highlights the growing rootlessness of American life. In less developed countries, the massive descent of poor people on the cities has seen vast squatter invasions of land in which continued possession hinges on the whims of the police and on the mass resistance the squatters can offer.

For many families in both developed and underdeveloped areas, land which once was the fixed base of family life and development is moving toward becoming a temporary anchorage. Transience and uncertainty have begun to beset the neighborhood scene and what were once communities may become mere agglomerations of people whose houses pass in the night. (See DOMICILE; DWELLING; HOUSE.)

shelter, emergency Retreats in the event of aerial bombardment, radiation, chemical or bacteriological attack. They are either built as shelters (though hardly insurance against extinction) or located in indicated places in subways, cellars of office buildings, and other underground or underutilized places.

shophouse A structure combining store and dwelling for the occupant's use. This combined use is prevalent in Far Eastern cities, where the ground floor may be used either for the sale of goods, light manufacture, or even the growing of bamboo shoots. With space at a premium, the combined use saves money as well as travel time.

shopping center A group of commercial facilities built primarily for retailing the principal goods required by a household. These centers are generally, though not always, built on the outskirts of cities on sites readily accessible by automobile, with parking provided. There are local shopping centers and regional shopping centers, each defined by its size, the volume of goods it merchandises, and the extent of the area from which it draws its clientele. Department stores and large chain stores that attract trade make the center viable for the smaller tenants. (See TENANT, KEY.)

side effects. See EXTERNALITIES.

sidewalk café A sidewalk adjunct to a restaurant in which refreshments are served. In Europe, where it first appeared, the refreshments were primarily beverages and there were no structural changes made to the sidewalks to accommodate the customers. For many it has become symbolic of the good life, urban style, and was felt to be an important missing ingredient in American cities. In the 1960s, the sidewalk café, American style, came into vogue, particularly in New York City.

It is said that the first thing a reform mayor does is pull in the streetwalkers, after which he gives away the streets. This appears precisely to have happened in New York City, where the Lindsay administration permitted the erection of substantial brick structures on the walks. Sidewalks thus become full-fledged restaurants, some of them covering half the width of the walk and often containing more seats than the original establishment itself. Between curb cuts and cafés, one can no longer trip the light fantastic on the sidewalks of New York without tripping over one obstruction or another.

simulation In planning, the imitation of real world processes either through a mechanical analog or model, through the operation of a computer process, or through a planning game. (See MODEL.)

single-room occupancy. See SRO.

single tax. See TAX, SINGLE.

site A plot of land intended or suitable for development; also the ground or area upon which a building or town has been erected.

Site value is the allocation to the site of its worth in relation to the worth of the improvement.

sit-in Organized and unlawful occupation of property as a form of protest or as a means of gaining an end. Occupation may be of seats in a restaurant, a bus station, or the site of a controversial public improvement. Sit-ins have been staged by Negroes as part of an effort to end exclusion or segregation practices. They succeeded in highlighting unfair practices that stubbornly resisted change.

The practice has worked its way into protests of other sorts, including rent strikes and organized resistance to eviction from city halls, armories, parks, and other public places. Student sit-ins in university buildings have been a recent addition in a number of countries. Sit-ins are trespasses but, though illegal, have often brought progressive social or political change. At other times they have sparked public resentment and reactionary trends. (See SQUATTER.)

"608" A section of the Housing Act of 1942 originally devised for war housing and revived in 1946 to stimulate postwar rental projects through a liberal administration of FHA insurance. Under Section 608, FHA officials told builders they need have "no risk capital or permanent capital investment" and that they could get back whatever money they invested "before one spade of earth is turned." FHA officials also told builders they could inflate their cost estimates, their land prices, their architectural and other fees. Builders did not hesitate to oblige. Some made dummy leases between themselves and wholly owned subsidiary corporations at a spurious rent for ninety-nine years. FHA would then insure a mortgage on the leasehold and upon default would have to pay the fictitious rent for the duration of the lease.

In 80 per cent of 543 projects examined by a Senate committee in 1954, the mortgages were higher than the costs. In 437 projects scrutinized, mortgage proceeds exceeded total costs by more than $75 million. The promoters appropriated the difference although the law stated that mortgages were not to exceed 90 per cent of estimated cost.

When builders told the Senate committee that the country would not get rental housing unless they could bail out without any investment, Chairman Homer Capehart called this "a great disappointment to a committee whose members believe so completely in private enterprise." Section 608 was reluctantly repealed. (See FEDERAL HOUSING ADMINISTRATION.)

sketch plan A quick and incomplete plan drawn early in the planning process after only limited observation and study. Its purpose is to test out preliminary ideas, capture hunches and first impressions on paper before they fade, elicit response from a client or collaborator, and guide subsequent stages of the work.

sketch, preliminary A rough drawing or design for a building or project giving the essential features of the proposed improvement without the details. The builder requests it of the architect or planner to help him approximate the nature of the improvement, the allowable land coverage, and other preliminary information from which he can make quick estimates and evaluations without committing himself to the cost of more detailed plans and specifications.

skid row The area of a city frequented by unattached and homeless men, spotted with cheap lodging houses, saloons, missions, barber colleges, and other establishments catering to these men. Skid-rowers occupy old flophouses in which finding a bed is often a gamble. Some sleep on the streets or in hallways or pile up on the floors of a city shelter, if there is one. They are a miscellaneous lot—semi-settled or settled panhandlers, homeless workingmen, chronic alcoholics and ex-criminals, the elderly, the disabled, and the unemployed. Many pensioners and ordinary workers find in skid row the cheapest and often the only accommodations available to them; and welfare and social agencies send older or disabled clients there for the same reasons. Lodgings are cheap because they are cramped, deteriorated, and often vermin-infested; many are firetraps. In skid row the sensitive poor can spend less for clothing and personal care without social embarrassment.

Though skid row is generally looked upon as the most sterile and extinguishable part of town, it is often a labor center for agricultural, unskilled, and semi-skilled workers who can be recruited for work in isolated areas.

No big city has ventured a complete solution for this problem or for its homeless men on or off skid row, although a few are playing with the idea. Few cities provide a public shelter and either look to urban renewal as the "solution" or press the skid-rower to move elsewhere.

Skid row is sometimes called "skid road," "hobohemia," or "the Bowery"—after the street that is the heart of this section in New York City. (See URBAN NOMAD.)

slum A building or area that is deteriorated, hazardous, unsanitary, or lacking in standard conveniences; also, the squalid, crowded, or unsanitary conditions under which people live irrespective of the physical state of the building or area. The latter definition is a deviation from the standard meaning, which puts emphasis on physical conditions. At three persons per room, however, even sound housing is a slum. A neighborhood may be physically sturdy, but if it is devoid of good transportation (as in Watts, Los Angeles) it could be classified as a slum. If the neighborhood school is a disgrace, the best cosmetic treatment of the housing will not eliminate its slum aspect.

The word "slum" is a piece of cant of uncertain origin, little more than a century old. Its derivation may be from "slump," meaning "swamp," or it may be a fortuitous blend of "slop" and "scum"; it also carries with it the cadence of "slob," "slush," "slovenly," "slut," and other derivatives of the *sl* combination. Slum reveals its meaning the moment it is uttered. Abhorrence of slums has often led to reckless destruction and more than once contributed to severe housing shortages. (See BLIGHT; GRAY AREA.)

slum clearance   The removal of a slum by demolishing it, altering it, or correcting the conditions causing it. The word "clearance" should not mean slum destruction only; a slum can be cleared by rehabilitation, by providing better schools and social facilities, and by removing those conditions of life that bring hopelessness, helplessness, and haplessness to its residents. (See BLIGHT; SPOT CLEARANCE; URBAN RENEWAL.)

slum demolition   Removal of a slum by tearing it down. The term is often used interchangeably (though incorrectly) with "slum clearance." Slum demolition, though legally and judicially authorized, can aggravate slum conditions by crowding the displaced slum dwellers into the residual slum inventory. Since crowding is one of the most harmful aspects of slum life, a slum surplus is often to be preferred to a slum shortage. Slum demolition should not be undertaken unless and until ample alternative accommodations are available. (See DEMOLITION; HOUSING SHORTAGE; RELOCATION; URBAN RENEWAL.)

slum, planned   A slum formation deliberately planned as part of a program for creating shelter that is improvable as time and funds permit. Such slums are not as evil as the term implies but may in fact be a first step toward better housing. In the less-developed areas where wholesale squatting is taking place with its inevitable chaos and crowding, planned slum programs would allow the settlers to build anything they wish on land laid out in plots by the public authority and provided with minimum utilities (or with allowance made for their future installation). If the initial layout is sound, and the settlers are given security of tenure and some financial help, the slum dwellings would gradually improve and the area would take on the attributes of a sound community. Unplanned, the dwellings would become irremediable slums. (See URBAN RENEWABILITY.)

slum reclamation The restoration of a slum to a better or more livable condition by rehabilitation and improvement of services and amenities. It implies that a particular slum area has values that should be identified and built upon rather than consigned to the bulldozer. The program should include liberal rehabilitation, some new buildings where necessary, facilitation of home-ownership, installation of playgrounds and social facilities and of good schools that will help stem the exodus from the area and reclaim the neighborhood.

slurb A California term denoting suburban slum formations. It contracts "sluburb" into a single-syllabled descriptive neologism. In California one giant urban complex is forming in the north from Sacramento to Monterey Bay, and another in the south from Los Angeles to San Diego. New subdivisions carved out of agricultural land are linking these two complexes. Three million acres of productive land and much of the state's great natural landscape will be turned into building lots. If current trends continue, before the turn of the century all the farmland in this area will be gone and even the untrod lands will become victims of the bulldozer. It is this fear that has spurred a California crusade to prevent slurb by planned building as well as planned conservation. (See SPRAWL; SUBURB.)

SMSA. See STANDARD METROPOLITAN STATISTICAL AREA.

socialism A word of many meanings, including public ownership of the means of production; but it has also been applied to political systems where only some enterprises are publicly or cooperatively owned; it may describe a Fascist, Nazi, or Soviet type state; or it may be a hate word for any system seen as threatening the existing capitalist order. In the United States, where "private enterprise" has been a popular theme, mortgage insurance has been socialized in the name of encouraging private enterprise; while in Europe, where the word "socialism" is semantically palatable, subsidization of private enterprise has often been effected in the name of socialism. Socialism has had almost as many varieties as Christianity.

Christian socialism was a movement based upon Christian principles begun in the mid-nineteenth century as a protest against the hardships of the working class; it fostered small self-governing workshops at one stage and cooperatives at another.

Utopian socialism embraced the notions of Robert Owen, Charles Fourier, and Louis Blanc; it was essentially communistic and was implemented through colonies such as New Harmony (1825).

Guild socialism was the social ownership of the means of production, with industrial operations managed by the workers organized in associations patterned after the medieval guilds but federated into national guilds and represented in a guild congress.

State socialism (often used interchangeably with state capitalism) was a loosely defined system for moderated change—encompassing nationalization of primary industries and curbing monopolies; also, a system with broad social-welfare legislation and progressive taxation to redistribute wealth.

Fabian socialism, an English theory, was a system based on socialistic principles but rejecting the class struggle in favor of evolutionary changes ("the inevitability of gradualism") and compromising with other political parties working for reform.

Municipal socialism encompassed public ownership and operation of local utilities such as water supply, gas, and electricity.

The word "socialism" (formed from the Latin *socius,* or "comrade," which is how socialists and communists often address each other) was first used to describe certain doctrines of Robert Owen, some of which were communistic rather than socialistic. Karl Marx, the architect of modern socialism, at first called his program "communism" and only later "socialism." Today socialism and communism are often used interchangeably, with some devotees of communism calling socialism the initial stage or entering wedge into communism. The latter is definable as the ownership by the government or the community of all wealth, with production by each according to his ability and consumption according to his need.

Economic systems cannot be categorized easily. In the first place they are changing rapidly to accommodate themselves to experience and to pressures, particularly those of urbanization. They are also often a blend of systems rather than pure systems. Thus though the Soviet system confiscated land, forbade petty trade, and turned independent farmers into wage-workers for the state, popular pressures have forced modifications. People enjoy the ownership of houses and cooperative apartments, which are guaranteed against expropriation without compensation; inheritance rights are recognized, savings are encouraged, and sale of truck-farm products by the farmer for profit is allowed. Incentives have also begun to play a part in factory management. In Poland, which nationalized its larger industries, a 1947 statute assisted private builders with land grants, freed all new buildings from rent controls, exempted them from taxation for five years as well as from income tax, and sought to attract "new capital in private hands" by promising black marketeers that if they invested their gains in building they would not be questioned as to how they came by their money.

In the United States the widespread ownership of corporate stock by the public, a tax system that takes as much as 72 per cent of an entrepreneur's annual profit, the socialization of housing for the poor and other private operations, the subsidization of some enterprises and the removal of stake and risk from others, the ever-growing regulation of enterprise, the nationalization of great power plants, such as the Coulee Dam and the Tennessee Valley, are all modifications of the old capitalist formula.

Systems are tending to balance forces and meet pressures by accepting a cut of socialism here and a dash of capitalist enterprise there. It is less important to label the system than to know that it provides the necessary incentives for human growth and improvement, provides equitably for the have-nots, is flexible enough to meet change, and respects the essential freedoms. There are dangers and imperfections in all modern systems. What is called socialism is not always successful. Nor does it inevitably emanate from the political left—it may steal in from the right as well, in socialization of entrepreneurial losses, in the removal of stake by private enterprise with government footing the bill, and in the conversion of corporate investment from risk-taking to guaranteed investment. Federal mortgage guarantees were one of the early forms; the supersonic transport is a later one. The issue that may well have to be resolved is not whether there shall be socialism or capitalism, but socialism for whom.

Cui bono? (See CAPITALISM; COMMUNISTIC SETTLEMENTS; MIXED ECONOMY.)

socialization of losses   The take-over by government of a private deficit operation; also, the absorption of losses on a private venture by government. Socialization of losses has occurred when government has taken over railroads, as in Germany, and when the New York Port Authority was forced to take over the bankrupt Hudson Tube. (See WELFARE STATE, BUSINESS.)

software programs.   See HARDWARE PROGRAMS.

solatium   An additional payment made to an owner whose property is taken by eminent domain (compulsory purchase) to afford him "solace" for the taking. Though the policy was long untried in the United States, solatia of 10 per cent have long been paid in England for property taken by railroads. In India, British-drawn legislation set the solatium at 15 per cent above market value. In the United States and in most other countries market value has usually been the compensation paid, but there is a growing feeling that this does not adequately compensate for all the losses. It does not compensate the owner for his moving costs, the costs of his lawyers and valuation experts, or for the premium he must often pay for a new house bought under pressure, to say nothing of the emotional and psychological costs. Moreover, in the United States the owner must pay a tax on his profit, which he would not have had to pay had he not been forced to sell. Congress sought to remedy this by not requiring the owner to pay the tax if he buys another house within a year, but this has helped only those who buy; it is of no value to those who cannot find a suitable purchase within a year or those choosing to rent. In a tight money-market the inequities are further highlighted when owners with houses bearing older mortgages at 5 or 6 per cent interest find themselves paying $8\frac{1}{2}$ per cent or more for the mortgages on their new houses.

The pressures for solatia increased as more and more houses were acquired for urban renewal, highways, and other government programs. Tenants also, for whom existing federal legislation authorized only moving expenses, made increasing demands, and even here the amounts paid varied from one federal program to another. The tenants felt that they were also entitled to solatia of some kind to compensate them for their inconvenience and the increased rents they were forced to pay after their displacement. In response to these pressures and following the example set by the State of Maryland, the Housing Act and the Federal-Aid Highway Act of 1968 authorized solatia for home-owners in an amount up to $5000. The laws also broadened benefits to tenants. (See RELOCATION.)

soul-brother   A term for a brother-in-spirit, used by blacks to denote their membership in a common in-group with a group solidarity that means respect for one other and one another's property. During Negro rioting "Soul-Brother" or "Negro Soul-Brother" was marked on homes and shops to denote that they were black-owned and therefore should not be targets of violence or vandalism. During the Detroit riot in 1967 virtually the only properties deliberately destroyed or damaged were white-owned or operated, and whatever Negro property was affected was adjoining or down-wind of the burning white property.

Soul City   A city built for and inhabited by Negroes. The idea was sponsored by Floyd McKissick, who proposed building a city for 20,000 people in Warren County, in North Carolina's black belt. It is one of the by-products of the drive by some Negro leaders for self-segregation. Unless Soul City is open to all families, irrespective of race or color, the proposal would meet the same constitutional objection as the building of an all-white city. This objection could be met, however, by agreeing to accept applications from such white families as would apply for housing in what is intended to be a community solely or predominantly for black families.

special assessment. See ASSESSMENT, SPECIAL.

special district   A local public agency set up for a single purpose, such as building a school, sewer, or water system. The district may float tax-exempt bonds for the improvement, repaying them from assessments or other earmarked revenues. It is the device employed by small unincorporated areas and by two or more jurisdictions making a common improvement. The number of special districts in the United States has grown rapidly.

If the special district has its uses it also has its abuses. The freedom with which they can be formed has made them a favorite tool of land speculators, who will set them up to take advantage of the tax-exemption privilege and raise cheap money for their personal private adventures.

It took only two voters, both representing a private California land-owner, to approve a tax-exempt bond issue of $178 million to fill in land in Redwood City, California, on which no one lived. The taxes on the property from the future home-owners would pay off the bonds, they hoped. Seventy million dollars in bonds for reclamation will be secured by land in the district assessed for tax purposes in 1964 at only $354,450. The legality of the bond issue was upheld by the courts.

In California, too, millions of dollars in tax-free bonds have been floated by special districts representing pint-size communities to build cableways for skiers and restaurants that are leased to private entrepreneurs after they are built. A brochure recently offered the public a tax-exempt bond that could be converted into the stock of a private company that wanted to build a factory in one of these midget communities. The bond-buyer was given two licks at possible profit—the community's tax-exempt security or, at his future option, the speculative shares of the company.

California, Texas, and Nevada have been the most liberal states in allowing special districts to flourish. Like the industrial-development bond, the special district is a recent device for immunizing wealth against federal tax liability and raising cheap money for private operations at the expense of the taxpayer. (See BOND, INDUSTRIAL-DEVELOPMENT BOND, PUBLIC; METROPOLITAN SPECIAL DISTRICT.)

speculation The practice of buying and selling land, stocks, or other property in order to profit by the rise or fall in their market value, as distinct from occasional trading or investment. It implies engagement in an enterprise of a venturesome or risky nature, offering the chance of substantial or unusual gain based on a gamble. The line between speculation and investment is thin, and one might say that a speculator is an investor who takes greater risks for larger profits. One of the speculations most inveighed against by reformers has been land, which was once the principal asset one could speculate in, but represents today only a minor part of speculative operations. Profits are often exaggerated, and often overlooked is the fact that holding raw land deprives the owner of the interest he might have earned had he not bought the property or converted it into cash. Also forgotten are declines in the value of the dollar, the detrimental impacts of restrictive zoning that might be imposed, and the real-estate taxes paid on the land while it is ripening. If loss of interest and other costs are considered, land must double in value every ten to fifteen years for the owner to break even. (See OPERATOR; PUBLIC-LAND OWNERSHIP; RIPE; TAX, INCREMENT.)

speculative architecture. See ARCHITECTURE, SPECULATIVE.

speculative building. See BUILDING, SPECULATIVE.

spillovers. See EXTERNALITIES.

sponsor The person, public body, or organization that originates or assumes responsibility for a program or project; also, one who backs another for a job or enterprise. A non-profit sponsor assumes responsibility without expecting a profit; its corporate charter may forbid a profit or it may be stipulated in the contract. A university, for example, is often the sponsor of a grant from the government or a foundation. It may receive its overhead, but no more. A variety of federal programs with special incentives are available to non-profit bodies willing to build housing, train or upgrade workers, and undertake various other socially useful tasks. (See ENTREPRENEUR; SEED MONEY.)

spot clearance Demolition and removal of single structures or comparatively small groups of structures from substandard areas, leaving the rest of the area untouched. Spot clearance is poor policy when the clearance leaves a dreary void that becomes the neighborhood dump. It is good policy if the clearance removes an abomination that is promptly replaced with something that gives a lift to the area. (See SLUM CLEARANCE.)

spot zoning. See ZONING, SPOT.

sprawl The awkward spreading out of the limbs of either a man or a community. The first is the product of bad manners, the second of bad planning. Sprawl is the by-product of the highway and automobile, which enabled spread of development in all directions. As builders scramble for lots to build on, the journey to work is lengthened and green spaces are consumed by gas stations and clutter.

Hardly any urban areas have a solvent plan for accommodating increased population. The future environment will be a chaos of sprawl or scatteration, with long stretches of potential "tobacco roads" punctuated by sad little houses cut off from the main road. "Planned sprawl" is an effort to guide the inevitable sprawl wherever possible so as to minimize its consequences and perhaps salvage some ribbons of open space in the process. It was considered as one of the alternatives in the "year 2000 plan" for the Washington, D.C., metropolitan area. (See AGGLOMERATION; CONURBATION; RIBBON DEVELOPMENT; SLURB; SUBURB.)

squatter One who settles on the rural or urban land of another without title or right. Allied terms are "squattage" and "squatment," meaning the holding occupied by the squatter; "squatterism," or the practice of acquiring land by squatting; "squatterdom," or the collective body of squatters; and "squatters' rights," a verbal contradiction implying that some legal or moral color of right has been acquired by the squatter. A squatter has no rights except what he may acquire by pressure or by statute.

Urban squatting is one of the most perplexing dilemmas facing underdeveloped countries. In the mid-1960s squatters made up about half the population of Ankara, Turkey, and more than a fifth of Istanbul's. In Venezuela they were more than a third of Caracas' population and about half of Maracaibo's. Cali, Colombia, had a squatter contingent amounting to about a third of its total population, while a quarter of the residents of Santiago, Chile, were squatters. Singapore, Kingston (Jamaica), Delhi, Karachi, and other cities of the developing world all have substantial squatter populations, and the squatter problem appears to be only at its beginnings.

Equivalent terms for squatters are: *favelos* (Brazil), *rancheros* or *conqueros* (Venezuela), *paracaidistas* ("parachutist," Mexico), and *gecekondu* (Turkey). Squatter communities are sometimes referred to in colorful and more often in contemptuous terms: "witch towns," *barrios piratas, callampas, bidonvilles,* and *arrabates.*

There are various types of squatter. The *owner squatter* owns his shack (though not the land), which he erects on any vacant plot he can find. He is the most common variety. The *squatter tenant* is the poorest class, does not own or build a shack, but pays rent to another squatter. Many new in-migrants start this way, hoping to advance to ownership. The *squatter holdover* is a former tenant who has ceased paying rent and whom his landlord fears to evict. The *speculator squatter* is usually a professional to whom squatting is a business venture. He squats for the tribute he expects the government or the private owners to grant him sooner or later. He is often the most eloquent in his protests and the most stubborn in resisting eviction. The *store squatter* or *occupational squatter* establishes his small store on land he does not own, and he may do a thriving business without paying rent or taxes. Sometimes his family sleeps in the shop. A citizen of Davao, in the Philippines, can get a dental cavity filled by a squatter dentist, his broken leg set by a squatter surgeon, or his soul sent on to a more enduring tenure by a squatter clergyman. The *semi-squatter* has surreptitiously built his hut on private land and subsequently come to terms with the owner. Strictly speaking, he has ceased to be a squatter and has become a tenant. In constructing his house he usually flouts the building codes. The *floating squatter* lives in an old hulk or junk, which is floated or sailed into the city's harbor. It serves as the family home and often the workshop. It may be owned or rented, and the stay may be temporary or permanent. In Hong Kong there are so many thousands of junks and sampans in one area that one is no longer aware of the water on which they rest. The *squatter "cooperator"* is part of the group that shares the common foothold and protects it against intruders, public and private. Its members may be from the same village, family, or tribe, or may share a common trade.

Motivations for squatting vary and include rural privation, oppression, fear, the attractions of the city and its better income and employment opportunities, opportunism, speculation, and mass expulsions. The squatter population includes not only poor people and workers needing housing but professional people, policemen, and civil servants.

Squatment building is the main contributor to the shelter supply in most developing countries. It is mostly poor, unsanitary, a fire and health hazard. But with proper planning and programing it can become a constructive contribution to community formation. Distribution of public land to the urban in-migrant will usually witness better building. Improvement of rural conditions to hold down the exodus to the cities, loan programs for building materials, better transport, firm action to curb speculation in squatments, and a housing or land and utilities program are all among the policies that can help. But no uniform program can be applicable to all places and circumstances since conditions vary, even within the same country.

Two things, however, seem clear: unless a policy is made, respect for law and property will disappear (the new clarion call might well be "Squatters Unite—you have nothing to lose but your claims"); not all squatters should be treated as lawbreakers and summarily ousted— squatting is often a trespass of desperation, the inevitable consequence of housing famine and human privation. Constructively tackled, it can often be converted into an asset and be the primitive forerunner of working urban communities.

If land is designated for squatting, if it is planned and elementary utilities are provided, makeshift houses will be built at first; if, thereafter, ownership is assured to the squatter, he will improve his dwelling and a tolerable community will eventuate. (See OWNERSHIP.)

SRO   Single-room occupancy. In New York City the "Essaro's" are considered one of the worst types of slum. Often whole families are crowded into the single space at a weekly or monthly rent far in excess of what the limited space deserves. Services are limited, and family life so crowded and degraded that the city has vacated most of them as a menace to health. The problem has always been to find suitable relocation housing and maintain a sufficient supply of SRO's for legitimate singles, particularly the elderly. (See LIFE CYCLE.)

standard consolidated area   A Census Bureau term used to describe the larger metropolitan agglomerations that have recently come into being through the gradual merging of two or more standard metropolitan statistical areas. As of the 1960 count there were only two—New York–northeastern New Jersey, and Chicago–northwestern Indiana. (See STANDARD METROPOLITAN STATISTICAL AREA.)

standard metropolitan statistical area (SMSA)   As defined by the Bureau of the Census in 1960, a county or group of contiguous counties that contains at least one city of 50,000 inhabitants or more (or "twin cities" with a combined population of at least 50,000); also, contiguous counties essentially metropolitan in character and socially and economically integrated with the central city. In New England, the SMSA is defined on a town rather than county basis.

standard of comfort The degree of comfort that a person, group, or community desires or insists on having. It is what might be described as adequate, somewhere above a subsistence standard but below the luxury level. (See POVERTY.)

standard of living The measure of the necessities, comforts, or luxuries viewed as essential to maintaining a person or group in his or its customary or proper circumstances. When it is said that the American standard of living is high, this implies that most of the population has come to regard certain goods and services as essential, though the same goods in a less fortunate country might be enjoyed by only a very few. The standard of consumption differs from the standard of living in that it relates solely to consumer goods, whereas the standard of living embraces such things as working conditions, choices among a variety of consumer goods, and availability of leisure time.

story That part of a building that lies between any one finished floor and the ceiling above it. Synonyms are "floor" or "flight." The height of a story is the vertical distance from the finished floor to the finished floor next above it. The height of the topmost story is the distance from the top surface of the finished floor to the top surface of the ceiling joists.

stratification The hierarchical or vertical division of society along economic or social lines. Urbanization has reduced the old rigidity of the economic line and sometimes tended to dissolve the social hierarchy. An *Eta* in Japan, for example, can better conceal her origins in the bustle of Tokyo than in the tight village community in which caste, class, and origin are easily identifiable and traceable. Democratization has also helped dissolve some of the tyrannical social lines, while occupation and achievement have begun to play a more important role than birth in determining status. (See MOBILITY.)

straw man. See DUMMY.

street   A public way leading from the house to the world outside, serving a multitude of activities as well as housing all the underground equipment that is the city's intestines. In American cities the street is the palatinate of the automobile, but in the older cities of the world, particularly in Asia, it is the mass dining room for the family and the place where one gets one's oxygen amid the miscellaneous odors of culinary activity. It is the market, the display room for wares, the social meeting place and the recreational outlet, the source of livelihood for the peddler, rickshaw or trishaw man, and a theater of action in which every child, visitor, tradesman, and hawker and the thousands converging on the street are the players. In Europe and in a few older cities in the United States the street is still respected. It is inefficient for its many new tasks but still vital; it is often exasperating but it is a way of life.

A dead-end street is a roadway closed at one end.

The street line is the dividing line between the public street and the private lots.

A through street is a roadway or section of road on which the traffic has the right-of-way over traffic from intersecting routes.

street furniture   The accouterments of the street, such as lights, benches, signs, bus shelters, canopies, kiosks, plants, etc. With the advent of the automobile, city streets have often been widened at the expense of the walks, while the walks have become the emplacements for a growing stockpile of municipal equipment. Real furniture that might comfort the weary such as benches are generally not part of the inventory except when contributed by a resourceful merchant who offers comfort in return for a display.

street hardware   The outfittings of mechanical and utility systems on the street, such as parking meters, traffic signs and signals, utility poles, fire hydrants, overhead wires, direction signs, manhole and sewer covers, police and fire boxes, mailboxes, and transformers.

street sleeper   A homeless person who uses the street for living quarters; a mobile squatter without a house. If the climate and the authorities are clement the street sleeper continues bedding down in the streets until he can find a better cover and the means to pay for it. Others accept the pavement as their established abode.

There was considerable street sleeping in Europe during the early stages of industrialization, but it has been eliminated except for derelicts and vagrants. In the streets of London in 1904, for example, there were about 1700 adults and 50 children sleeping, compared with 129 adults on one cold November night in 1963. But in Calcutta in modern times an estimated 100,000 people sleep on the streets and at times the estimates have run up to 600,000. Some are part of generations of street sleepers spawned on the street and raised there. Census figures for Bombay in 1963 showed that 1 in every 66 persons was homeless, while another 77,000 people lived under stairways, in cattle sheds, on landings, or in similar spaces. Though some of these city dwellers can afford to pay for minimum shelter it is not always available. In Lagos, Nigeria, a street sleeper will watch a shop at night and keep away other street sleepers in return for the nightly use of a threshold. Many will seek a spot on the piers in the rat-ridden lagoon or scout around for an unguarded space on which to lay a straw mat. Street sleeping permits little family life, no privacy, no relief from heat, no escape from cold or rain, and no decent means for disposing of human waste. It is the way of the stray animal and the lowest form of human existence. (See SQUATTER.)

streetwalker   A pedestrian; a prostitute seeking trade. (See PEDESTRIAN.)

strip zone. See ZONE, STRIP.

subdivision   The process of dividing a given area of land into sites, blocks, or lots with streets or roads and open spaces; also an area so divided.

subdivision, abortive or premature   A subdivision that has miscarried because it was unsuitable for development. In the ill-fated Florida boom of the 1920s and in the years of the depression, many areas were subdivided only to end up in weeds or in the hands of the taxing authority. Subdivision is premature when there is still hope for its eventual development; it is abortive when it fails as a development and should not have been undertaken in the first place.

subdivision regulations   Regulations governing the development of raw land for residential or other purposes. They prescribe standards for the street improvements, lot sizes and layouts, procedures for dedicating private land for public purposes and other requirements. Procedures are also given for filing maps; for receiving the approval of the public engineer, planning commission, and other departments.

Subdivision regulations and the way they are implemented will condition the nation's future environment. Like zoning, however, control of this vital force is in local political hands and is manipulated more often to protect the vested interests of the few than to foster the interests of the many. (See ZONING.)

sublease   To lease property that has already been leased from another to a third party. The original landlord is the lessor; the lessee is then the sublessor, and the third party is the sublessee. The sublessor cannot sublet a greater estate than he has under his lease, and the sublessee's rights collapse in the event of the sublessor's default. The original lease may contain a covenant against subletting or against subletting without the lessor's consent.

Subrenting is the renting by a tenant of an apartment or other property without a lease, but the term is also used interchangeably with subletting. (See LEASE; RENT.)

subordination   Making a prior mortgage a lesser lien on real estate; also, allowing one's land to become subject to a mortgage as a condition of a sale or lease transaction. Subordinations and agreements to subordinate land are frequently made in real-estate transactions. Thus a landowner may permit a prospective builder-purchaser to raise a first mortgage on the property to help finance the building operation. Sometimes, too, a first mortgagee may permit his mortgage to become a second mortgage subject to a new first mortgage, for a consideration. The risk, of course, is increased by the subordination. (See MORTGAGE.)

subsidy   Any grant or aid extended for an undertaking to which a public interest is imputed. Originally it meant the reserve troops of the Roman army, and the word came to be applied to support generally, particularly financial support granted by Parliament to the King.

The term now includes those aids which promote private operations in trade, industry, or agriculture and those grants-in-aid which are made to assist other governmental units in their fulfillment of public purposes. Many government subsidies were prompted by economic or military considerations—such as the need to stimulate infant industries or promote self-sufficiency in time of war. One of the first subsidies given in the United States was to the codfish-salting industry. Subsidies currently support not only infant industries but senile industries as well (railroads and housing, for example). A growing proportion of subsidies is used to advance infant social services.

The varieties of subsidies include the cash subsidy (direct and aboveboard but the least popular politically); the interest or rent subsidy and the subsidy in the form of goods and services (the recipient enjoys them as a reduction in his costs rather than as a supplement to his means, as in the surplus food and public housing programs); the lending of superior credit through guarantee or insurance of mortgages or yields (a guarantee is always a potential subsidy, particularly where the true risk cannot be determined in advance, as in FHA mortgage insurance); the granting of land or the writing-down of land costs (as in the Homestead Acts or the Urban Renewal Program); the leasing or sale of public properties at terms that constitute a subsidy (this has occurred in the sale of government war-housing projects); tax exemption and abatement (easy to hide and therefore widely used).

The principles governing use of subsidies have never been adequately stated, and there is a tendency to employ them indiscriminately. The general principles are, though, that subsidies should serve a public purpose and be part of defined long-term objectives; should serve multiple purposes wherever possible (housing subsidies, for example, also stimulate building, which in turn primes economic activity); should be defined, not hidden, with their extent and costs fully revealed; should be dispensed impartially to the class served; should be administered by a public agency or be adequately controlled by the public if given to private agencies; should burden the taxpayer as little as possible and be amenable to practical administration.

Subsidy dispensation hinges on whether the particular government has the funds. In the United States the federal government has pre-empted almost two-thirds of all the revenues collected by the federal, state, and city governments. As late as 1932 local governments were collecting about half the taxes; by 1966 their share had shrunk to less than 20 per cent.

Subsidies in the United States are accommodating the pressures of influence rather than need. While the nation has become an urban nation with only 6 per cent of the population engaged in agriculture in 1965, the Department of Agriculture was receiving some $6 to $7 billion a year and paying some farmers subsidies amounting to as much as $2 million a year for not planting. Thanks to the highway lobby, federal subsidies for interstate highways have been 90 per cent of cost and run to more than $4 billion a year. (See CAPITAL GRANT; TAX EXPENDITURES.)

subsistence allowance   Money paid to a worker in addition to his salary to cover expenses not embraced in his wages. It might be paid in the form of a welfare allowance to a family with an inadequate income. It might also be required by law or wage agreement to compensate the worker for travel to work or for housing.

suburb   A district, usually residential, on the outskirts of a city. A suburb can be a village, part of the county, or a legal city. The distinction between the suburb and the city is comparable to the distinction between a satellite and the larger body around which it revolves, hence a satellite town is a suburb. A suburb cannot exist without an urb. But it can grow into an urb itself and in turn have satellites around it.

According to the *Oxford English Dictionary*, "suburban" means "having the inferior manners, the narrowness of view, etc., attributed to residents in suburbs." In seventeenth-century London it was often used to refer "to the licentious life of the suburbs." Neither definition can be applied to American suburbs today, which house the respectable middle class—the married couples with children, those who wish to own a home, have more access to trees, lawns, play space, and a better school. Racial exclusion is practiced in most parts of suburbia.

Since about 80 per cent of houses in the United States are being erected in urban areas outside the central cities, the future condition of the nation's environment is at stake, but up to 1968 there was little effective effort to control suburban sprawl. Whatever planning there was, was localized and shaped by the vested interests in each locality. The federal government remained virtually aloof, while FHA practices sanctioned local control and planning autonomy. (See CITY, SATELLITE; DIS-CRIMINATION; SLURB; SPRAWL.)

suburban matriarchy A social system, purportedly the result of suburban living, in which the mother is the kingpin in the family. Suburbia, it is claimed, makes the father more like a dormitory occupant and less a headman, parent, and peace officer. Herbert Gans, in his study *The Levittowners,* thinks this misreads the trend toward a general equalization of the sexes. He finds the husband still making the decisions though he concedes that man generally is relinquishing power to woman. (See URBAN PERSONALITY.)

suburban personality. See URBAN PERSONALITY.

superblock A consolidation of a number of smaller blocks and the interstitial streets into one large block, thus creating a much larger area free of through traffic; also, any very large block—or "square," in British usage. (See BLOCK.)

superstructure Any structure or part of one that is set above another; also, the portion of a building above the foundation.

survey A critical examination of facts or conditions to provide information on a situation, such as a survey of the housing in an area or a survey of living conditions.

A survey is also the delineation of the location, form, and boundaries of a parcel of land and the buildings on it by measuring the lines and angles, the encroachments of buildings and fences on the street and adjoining property, as well as encroachments by others on the property surveyed. A survey of vacant land is generally made to indicate the land on which one is to build or to show the purchaser the precise land he is buying.

A windshield survey is an inspection by automobile of an area to give one a quick general impression. It is a view taken through a pane, not a painstaking survey. The more careful surveys follow later. (See LAND-USE SURVEY.)

sweat equity. See EQUITY, SWEAT.

syndicate A group associated for the special purpose of investing in or underwriting an undertaking. This usually calls for putting up capital or assuming a risk that the members are unwilling to undertake individually and that a syndication enables them to share. Syndicates have become common in large real-estate developments. In a properly drawn syndication agreement, each individual can deduct his proportionate share of taxes and interest for income-tax purposes and pay a capital gain in the event of sale. In real-estate syndications the syndicate's manager or organizer takes a fee or larger share of the profits for his efforts.

Real-estate syndicates flourished during the boom of the 1950s, paying as much as 12 per cent on capital to their participants, but as deals yielding such returns narrowed, the managers bought more speculative property and a number of syndicates collapsed, tarnishing the syndicate image. One of the shortcomings of syndicate operations in real estate is the general inability to enforce assessments against the participants when additional capital is needed. The operation must carry itself, and deficits usually spell default.

Syndicated stock underwritings are also common among Wall Street investment houses, who also bid for housing-authority, bridge, sewer, and similar bonds. These have involved hundreds of millions of dollars in underwritings. After the issue is awarded, the bonds are sold to the general public.

system A word with at least sixteen definitions, embracing human bodies, political bodies, heavenly bodies, the whole organization of society, and the formula for breaking the bank at Monte Carlo. It now enjoys frequent usage in planning, architectural, and engineering circles in combinations such as systems approach, systems building, systems planning, and systems design. The general definition in the *Oxford English Dictionary* is as good as any for its general meaning—*i.e.,* "a set or assemblage of things connected, associated, or interdependent, so as to form a complex unity; a whole composed of parts in orderly arrangement according to some scheme or plan." The *OED* notes that the word is "rarely applied to a simple or small assemblage of things."

systems planning, systemic planning A means of organizing elements into an integrated decision-making procedure to achieve the best possible results. Systems planning is a comprehensive, rational, and precise approach to problem-solving. It focuses on the organization and interrelationships in a complex system like a city, rather than on the individual parts, and can be amplified by numerous mathematical, operations-research, and decision-making techniques, as well as simulation models, where appropriate.

None of its many definitions is clear or final despite the plethora of verbiage that has issued from the managers on what systems planning really is. One commentator says that "a clear definition would only confuse." At a meeting of the Operations Research Society of America, definitions ran the gamut from "helping administrators ease decision-making when faced with multi-directional functional alternatives," to "presenting a synthesis of a very diverse network of homogeneous complexities"—all of which inspired a *New York Times* comment that "jargon came into its own that day." At least half of today's systems programs do not accomplish their full objectives, and the publicity record has far outstripped the record of achievement.

The systems approach is a new name, with advanced techniques, for the ancient practice of building a house and assembling its proper parts into a whole or of running a hardware store in which the storekeeper's mind operates his homely "system."

In city planning the systems approach is analogous to "comprehensive planning." Both have failed when all the relevant elements were not included or their respective impacts weighed. Not the least of the obstacles are the widening nature of the city-planning process, the multiple disciplines involved in understanding the life of cities, the identification of all the elements that require integrating, and the priorities. Political wisdom cannot be put through a computer, nor can the philosophy that should underlie a planner's decision be systematized. Trained instincts will always play a part. Systems planning can help the expert think more inclusively, but he will still have a long way to go to solve the world's urban problems or give man the good life. (See COST-BENEFIT ANALYSIS; PLANNER; PPBS.)

take-out Long-term financing that pays off the temporary financing for an improvement. Temporary financing is secured to pay for the improvement as it proceeds, while permanent—or, more accurately, long-term —financing is a long-term mortgage based on a proportion of the value of a completed structure. To secure the temporary financing, assurance must often be given the lender that the temporary loan will be repaid upon the improvement's completion—in other words, that there is a take-out. The commitment of a bank to make the long-term loan is called a "take-out commitment." (See BAIL OUT; FINANCING, PERMANENT; LOAN, CONSTRUCTION; MORTGAGE.)

target. See GOAL.

task force A committee or group of experts appointed to investigate and report on a specific problem. It was originally a military term referring to a temporary grouping of units under a single commander, formed to carry out a specific mission.

Non-military task forces proliferated during President Lyndon B. Johnson's administration. They were assigned to work on noise, air pollution, American Indians, violence, housing, oceanography, cities, beauty and open space, the sonic boom, and the racial problem. In addition, there were task forces designated by congressional committees, by government departments, by states, and by cities. A super-task force to identify the linkages among all the reports of the federal task forces and establish some common objectives would have been salutary.

Not all task-force reports get reported—the task-force study on American Indians made to President Johnson went underground because it recommended spending money while the war was on in Vietnam. Not many reports are translated into legislation. Some of them are propaganda with political rather than legislative purposes. In the effort to get a consensus, compromises are often made and pointed recommendations blunted. Often a report represents the viewpoint more of the hired staff than of the big-name members. Some reports are nevertheless good studies, have had impact, and brought change. Some compare in quality to the British white papers, others are quickies gotten up to meet the political necessities of the moment.

tax A levy on the income, property, or sales of individuals and of corporations for the support of government and public services. Some taxes are designed to discourage particular activities. In such cases the success of the tax would be inversely related to the amount of revenue raised.

tax abatement; tax remission The forgiveness or relinquishment of taxes. The two terms differ from tax exemption in that taxes remitted or abated would normally be due and they are forgiven or canceled rather than excepted from future levy. Though taxes in general are more likely to be increased than forgiven, a tendency to exempt, remit, or abate them has become noticeable in slum-improvement operations.

tax, ad valorem A tax based on a property's value, as distinguished from a tax on income, sales price, etc. The value taxed by local governments is not always or even usually the market value but only a valuation for tax purposes. In some cases the rate is high and the valuation low; in other cases the rate may be low and the valuation high, low, or near the market level.

The ad valorem tax on real estate in the United States was originally a general property tax on land, buildings, and personal property, including cows, sheep, implements, and other personalty. As happened elsewhere, the personalty was easily concealed when the tax assessor came around; the tax thus gradually became a tax only on the realty. (The house was not yet mobile, as many are today.) More recent efforts to tax personal property ad valorem still experience trouble. It is either concealed or moved to another jurisdiction.

Ad valorem taxes can be challenged when the valuation is excessive or too high compared to valuations on comparable property. The issue is raised by a formal protest and thereafter by a certiorari proceeding asking the court to review the assessment.

tax, betterment   A tax on the increment in value accruing to an owner because of development and improvement work carried out by local authorities. Such a tax was included in Britain's Town and Country Planning Acts (1932 and 1947). Under the 1932 Act, 75 per cent of that increment could be collected by the local authority, but generally only when there was a change in the ownership or in the use of the land affected. The practical obstacle to any real recovery of betterment, however, lay in the authority's difficulty in proving that there was any increase in value, and if there was, that it was due solely to its works. The law, however, simultaneously provided for compensation when the owner suffered loss because of a local authority's action. Compensation therefore became due at once, while recovery of betterment was remote and difficult. The 1947 Act and later acts sought to remedy this difficulty, but betterment and compensation still remain a troublesome problem.

In the United States a kind of betterment tax is levied in the form of an "assessment for benefit," under which partial or total recovery of the cost of improvements (such as sewer installations) is effected through an assessment on the property, payable in installments. (See ASSESSMENT; BETTERMENT.)

tax deed. See DEED, TAX.

tax exemption   A grant by a government of immunity from levy. It is given by cities to churches, non-profit institutions, and some private operations, such as newly settling industries and slum-clearance operations. Exemption is freely given for public housing, which pays a fixed sum in lieu of taxes. A ten-year tax exemption on new housing in New York City stimulated new construction in the 1920s. Another local law not only granted tax exemption on the value of the new private improvements made to old-law tenements for a twelve-year period, but abated up to two-thirds of all the real-estate taxes that would be due on the property over a twenty-year period. The subsidy has helped stimulate some rehabilitation. That it has not done more than that has been due to administrative delays and the unwillingness of rent-control officials to elevate rents to acceptable levels. Another criticism has been that its benefits were often extended to upper-income or luxury units for which the subsidy program was not intended. (See SUBSIDY.)

tax expenditures Revenues not collected because of special deductions, credits, exclusions, exemptions, and preferential rates built into the income-tax laws. Economists have begun to treat revenues foregone as though they were monies expended, and some have argued that these constitute an unrecorded "shadow" budget affecting the actual budget just as though the government were spending the money directly. Economists in President Johnson's administration, for example, calculated that the "cost" of property tax and mortgage-interest deductions taken by home-owners would exceed the projected direct federal expenditures of $2.8 billion on community development and housing in 1970. Total tax expenditures for this same year were forecast at close to $50 billion.

tax incentives Favorable tax treatment to induce the beneficiary to do something he would not otherwise be likely to do. Some countries give industry tax exemptions (Ireland, for example), as do many states and cities in the United States. Exemption from federal taxation is given to purchasers of state and municipal bonds, although the federal government has always been chary of giving similar exemptions on its own paper. But the pressures are setting in. Social reform has always been the mask under which profits in new forms make their entry. The stage was set for this when slum clearance became a public purpose. If slum clearance is such, why should not big business investing in slum areas be given accelerated depreciation allowances—and thereafter other types of tax escapes?

The time seems not distant when social reform will be industry's most promising raw material. It adds public purpose to private profit, lends public support to entrepreneurial operations, and if in addition there will be tax incentives and tax escapes, investment might even become a riskless adventure in which all gross profit will be net profit. (See BOND, PUBLIC; DEPRECIATION; SUBSIDY; WELFARE STATE, BUSINESS.)

tax, increment A special tax on the increased value of land or its "unearned increment." The increased value is thought to be due to no labor or expenditure by the owner, but to natural causes such as the increase of population or the general progress of society. Thinkers as different in their views as Adam Smith and Karl Marx agreed that the landowner was a do-nothing who indolently sat on his hands and profited without any exertions of his own. Henry George carried these theories over to the urban scene. He saw acreage carved up into small city lots and laid the blame for urban overcrowding on private ownership of land: "Before anybody can build a house a blackmail price must be paid to some dog in the manger."

Though these theories have faded as truths they survive as emotions. For odd reasons, increases in land values are still viewed in some quarters as less deserving than increases by stock speculation or rises in the price of commodities. There is no land shortage for urban man. But there is a keen competition for the land in and around cities. Though such land may account for as little as 1 to 5 per cent of a nation's total land area, its price soars.

This is particularly true in the less-developed countries for the following reasons:

1. There is rarely a tax on the land, or it is nominal.

2. Land is virtually the only commodity in which money can be invested.

3. Population is pushing into the cities, intensifying the demand for the central lands.

4. Public improvements add to the land value with no effort made to recapture part of the gain through assessments-for-benefit.

5. People put their money into land as an inflation hedge or because land investment is deeply rooted in tradition.

6. Inadequate efforts are made to open transportation routes to land surrounding the city so as to increase the accessible land supply or to supply adequate transport facilities on routes that have been opened.

The need in these cases is to tax the land though not necessarily the increment itself, and to force the land into use by the threat of levy where it is withheld from use and is not developed according to an approved master plan.

The main trouble with the argument for the tax on unearned increment is its moral overtones and the tendency of its advocates to urge it universally—even when land is already taxed on its value as in the United States, and even where increases in land value are no greater than those in other commodities. In these instances the increment tax smacks of the doctrinaire and the cult. It leaves personalty—by far the greatest beneficiary of unearned increment (especially in developed countries)—immune from its strictures. The tax on land increment (often called the single tax) also ignores the fact that the investor loses interest on his capital and must pay taxes during his possession and that land value in countries like the United States must double every ten to fifteen years for him simply to break even. This is not to say that land speculation is not a problem for almost all nations, but the main trouble is that land is too often held out of use and that when it is used for development it does not always serve the best needs of the community. Land socialization offers no solution for this problem; public ownership will only invite more squatting in the less-developed countries, more bureaucratic stultification and political beadledom elsewhere, and generally more headaches than reasonably regulated, reasonably taxed private ownership. A tax on land value to induce development has merit; taxing away the increment no longer makes either moral or fiscal sense. (See BETTERMENT; SPECULATION; TAX, SINGLE; TAX, USE.)

tax lien   A charge against property for unpaid taxes. When taxes on real estate are unpaid the tax lien may be foreclosed like a mortage.

taxpayer   A property composed of stores, generally one story in height. It may not be intended as the ultimate improvement for the site but be designed to yield enough revenue to offset some of the accruing charges, particularly real-estate taxes, pending development for its highest and best use. Sometimes the taxpayer remains the final improvement (as in areas where the stores rather than any improvement above them yield the best returns for the site), but it is still called a taxpayer. The advantage of building a taxpayer is that there are virtually no operating charges, almost all of the gross rent above taxes and mortgage charges representing net return.

A taxpayer is also a person who pays taxes or is subject to a levy. A taxpayer's action is a lawsuit brought by a taxpayer to restrain a city or state from spending money wastefully or illegally. (See USE, HIGHEST AND BEST.)

tax, payment in lieu of   An annual payment made by a local public-housing agency to the taxing jurisdictions in which its projects are located. Such payments on federally aided projects were long fixed at about 10 per cent of annual shelter rent. Since statutes exempt public housing from the payment of taxes, the "in lieu" payment aims to compensate the city for some of its services. Because it would be unreasonable to tax the projects on the basis of their cost, the agreed payment based on rent provides a sensible alternative. (See HOUSING, PUBLIC.)

tax, property A levy on the owners of real property. It is the main source of revenue for local governments in the United States and affects nearly everyone, including the propertyless, who pay it indirectly through their rents. (See TAX, AD VALOREM.)

tax rate, effective The actual real estate tax rate as calculated on market value. Some cities have a low tax rate and a high assessed valuation while others assess low and tax at a higher rate. The effective tax rate is determined by multiplying the actual assessment by the tax rate, as:

Community A:	assessment as per cent of value	40 per cent
	tax rate	5 per cent
	effective tax rate	2 per cent
Community B:	assessment as per cent of value	80 per cent
	tax rate	2.5 per cent
	effective tax rate	2 per cent

Thus jurisdictions with widely divergent tax and assessment rates may in fact have closely comparable effective taxes. (See ASSESSMENT RATIO.)

tax remission. See TAX ABATEMENT.

tax, single A tax on land value and other natural resources as the sole source of public revenue. Single-tax theory still has a few orthodox adherents whose well-intentioned misconceptions have occasional influence. It can be vaguely identified in proposals for land reform, such as the differential tax on land and buildings, and for land socialization.

Before the rise of intangible personal property as the dominant form of wealth and when land represented the almost exclusive form, the single-tax theory might have had some validity. But today land can no longer produce all or even a substantial fraction of the necessary revenues for governments.

The single-tax theory was based on the concept that the earth is the heritage of all mankind and that no individual has the moral right to usurp its fruits. "Suppose that there is a kind of income," said John Stuart Mill, "which constantly tends to increase, without any exertion or sacrifice on the part of the owners: those owners constituting a class in the community, whom the natural course of things progressively enriches, consistently with complete passiveness on their own part. In such a case it would be no violation of the principles on which private property is grounded, if the state should appropriate the increase of wealth, or part of it, as it arises. . . . It would merely be applying an accession of wealth, created by circumstances, to the benefit of society. . . . I see no objection to declaring that the future increment of land should be liable to special taxation."

In this suggestion of a "special tax" lay the germ of Henry George's more drastic theory of the single tax. The remedy seemed simple—by shifting all taxation to land alone, land values would be depressed, private ownership would cease being profitable, and land would ultimately revert to the public to whom it properly belonged.

A reasonable tax on land is justified as any reasonable tax on property would be. Soaring values in less-developed regions—where land is being held out of use and is appreciating because of population growth, public works, and limited transportation—certainly justify a land tax. But all this is a far cry from a single tax, and even George's most ardent followers no longer take his proposals literally. There are separate land levies in Scranton and Pittsburgh, Pennsylvania, and Jamaica (West Indies), and there are modified forms elsewhere in areas now or formerly within the British orbit, but the single tax as distinguished from the normal tax on real property is defunct as an economic theory and extinct as a political device. (See RENT, ECONOMIC; TAX, INCREMENT; TAX, USE.)

tax, use A tax on land aimed primarily at enforcing its use or improvement. A use tax was recommended in legislation drawn up for Pakistan in 1957 by a United Nations mission. As adopted by the government, land designated as ripe for development but not developed within three years after notification would be valued as though developed and taxed at the rate of 3 per cent until developed.

In less-developed countries where values have been rising, particularly those that inherited the British tradition of freedom from taxation on undeveloped land, the problem is often not land speculation *per se* but land refrigeration—*i.e.,* holding land vitally needed for the nation's development out of use. By making a master plan for an area, scheduling the enforced improvement of the land, and levying an appropriate tax if it is not improved in accordance with the plan, three benefits are gained: land is comprehensively planned before development begins; there is strong incentive to bring the land into use in line with the plan; substantial revenue is brought into the public treasury even if the land is undeveloped.

The UN mission found later that a similar tax had been invented three centuries earlier. Pressed by overcrowding, the Council of New Amsterdam in 1658 ordered all owners of vacant lots within the Henry Hudson stockade either to improve them, pay a special tax to retain them unimproved, or surrender them for public sale. (See LAND POLICY.)

temporary housing. See HOUSING, TEMPORARY.

tenant One who rents real property from a landlord by lease or other arrangement. There are various types of tenants, some of which are listed below.

Holdover Tenant, who remains in the premises after the expiration of his term.

Life Tenant, whose tenancy is terminable upon his death.

Monthly Tenant, whose tenancy is terminable by either the landlord or himself at the end of the monthly term, generally upon notice.

Statutory Tenant, who is protected by statute as under a rent-control law.

Tenant at Will, who remains at the pleasure of the landlord.

Tenant by Sufferance, originally having a lawful lease or permission to occupy but continuing in possession after his term has ended. At common law he is entitled to no notice to quit the premises.

Tenant for a year or term of years, whose term is fixed for a definite term of one year or more.

Tenancy has been the predominant form of tenure in Europe and other settled parts of the world, the tenant being at the constant mercy of the landlord, who could oust him at will, though custom often was a restraining force. Today the relations between tenant and landlord are more frequently governed by statute, and families are tenants either because they cannot afford ownership or do not want it. In the United States the rise of the single mortgage that finances the home-buyer up to as much as 100 per cent of cost has made ownership easier for many, and ownership has become the dominant form of tenure. (See OWNERSHIP.)

tenant, key A commercial tenant in a shopping center whose presence draws a large number of shoppers, thereby bringing trade to the other less-magnetic tenants. Major department stores, a Sears Roebuck or a Montgomery Ward, are considered key tenants, and the developers of shopping centers make every effort to sign them up. Once they do, there is little trouble in securing the secondary tenancies. The key tenant, knowing how indispensable he is, either pays a minimal rent (his proportion of interest and taxes without profit) or demands free land on which to erect his building. Smaller chain operations (like a Woolworth store) will follow the key tenant and pay a higher rental, but it is the minor chains and individual stores that will pay the highest rental for the privilege of becoming tenants and it is mainly their rentals that make the venture profitable. The developer makes rental concessions proportionate to the tenant's "draw" and looks for an over-all average rental that will give him the highest net profit. The promise of a key tenant or two will also assure him of the necessary financing for construction. (See 100-PER-CENT AREA; SHOPPING CENTER.)

tender; bid An offer by a contractor to perform specified work for a specified price. In England he may make his tender when he receives a "bill of quantities" or list of numbered items from the architect. The contractor usually enters his price opposite each item as well as the total, and the "priced bill" constitutes his tender or offer to do the work. In the United States the tender is called "a bid"; the bid may be due in a sealed envelope by a specified time and day, or informally delivered to the owner, architect, or general contractor.

"Tender" also has a legal connotation—*i.e.,* an offer fulfilling the terms of the law and of one's liability. Thus a tender may be made in money to discharge a debt or it may be in the form of a deed to real estate where the buyer claims the title is defective and the owner disputes it. In the latter case the tender usually precedes a lawsuit at which the feelings are far from tender.

tenement; tenement house A dwelling erected or used for the purpose of rental, especially one divided into separate flats. In large cities the term is applied to a building designed for multiple occupancy by poorer people.

Under New York State law it was defined as any building occupied or to be occupied as the residence of three or more families living independently of one another and doing their own cooking on the premises. This technically made the term applicable to most apartment houses irrespective of their rents, condition, or age.

There have been various types of New York City tenements.

Railroad tenements, an early type, were laid out as their name suggests, with the rooms running from front to back, requiring occupants to pass through every other room to get to the last. Interior rooms had no outside light or ventilation.

Dumbbell tenements, hailed as an improvement, were provided with airshafts between adjacent buildings, giving the structures their characteristic dumbbell shape and allowing the occupants to trade smells, noises, and intimate glimpses of family life. The term bears no relation to the designer and was the result of a competition in 1879, given by the publisher of the *Sanitary Engineer,* calling for the best plans for a tenement house on a New York City lot 25 x 100. The first prize, from among 206 plans submitted, was awarded to James E. Ware for the double-decker dumbbell tenement. Although considered a model tenement at the time, it actually made possible the crowding of a maximum number of dwelling units on narrow lots. In 1901 its future construction as well as that of other old-law tenements was outlawed.

Old-law tenement refers to housing built in New York City before the passage of the Tenement House Act of 1901. This would include some fine apartment houses built in that period, but generally the term applies to the six-story walk-ups that mushroomed in New York City to house immigrants. The old-law tenement was characterized by insufficiency of light and air and virtually complete coverage of the lot area; high danger from fire owing to non-fireproof materials; lack of separate toilet and washing facilities (only one toilet generally served four families even after backyard privies were eliminated); overcrowding and a high incidence of contagion due to absence of sunlight; foul and filthy cellars and courts; lack of family privacy and peace.

The Tenement House Act of 1901, based on the work of the New York Tenement House Commission of 1900, was an effort to correct most of these deficiencies, and tenements built in New York after the act's passage were known as "new-law tenements"—only a small improvement.

As of 1968 there were over forty thousand old-law tenements still standing in New York City. Some (in Greenwich Village and Yorkville, for example) have been remodeled into smaller studio units. All have had to comply with corrective legislation so that the vertical ladder fire-escapes are now at about 45-degree inclines; cellar ceilings and stairways have been fire-retarded; a toilet has been provided for each family; a scuttle allows escape to the roof; central heating has replaced the old coal stoves. The value of these costly improvements, however, has been offset by the deterioration that has affected the buildings, partly because of rent-control, partly because the low rents do not warrant any major expenditures, and partly because of lack of cooperation by the tenants. These tenements, moreover, once owned by responsible investors and mortgaged to responsible institutions, have gone over to a less dependable type of owner who either cannot afford or will not invest what the buildings require for preservation. With the properties often viewed as contraband, many of the owners treat their investments as such and expect the returns on their small capital which trading in contraband commands. Many owners are "quick traders" or people of low and moderate means seeking large profits on small capital, with much of the profit actually compensating for management, rent collection, and risk of fine or jail.

New-law tenements are multi-family dwellings built after 1901 but before 1929 and the Multiple Dwelling Law, which raised minimum requirements a bit further. The new-law tenements were more fire-resistant, covered less ground, had an enlarged interior court permitting more light and air, and included toilet facilities in each apartment.

Open-stair tenements were built as models by Alfred T. White following the model of the George Foster Peabody dwellings in London. These provided stairs between buildings open to the street.

Rear or backyard tenements were built behind tenements fronting on the street. These were thought to be among the worst, but some are now in better esteem for their freedom from street noises and traffic.

tenure. See FEUDAL TENURE; LAND TENURE.

terminal. See TRANSPORTATION TERMINAL.

tied house. See HOUSE, TIED.

time-contour map. See MAP, TIME-CONTOUR.

time zoning. See ZONING, TIME.

tipping point The point at which a housing project, neighborhood, or public facility heads toward becoming segregated by the entry of more members of a minority group than are acceptable to the majority of occupants. It has been said, for example, that a public-housing project will remain integrated and will resist segregation when the composition is about one-fifth black, but that when that proportion is exceeded the project will head toward all-Negro occupancy. White families will move and other white families will not apply for the vacant units. There have been instances where black families have sought to maintain the balance in a mixed neighborhood by urging white families not to take flight lest the "balance be tipped." The tipping point varies with the customs, social status, and economic positions of minority and majority, as well as with the school composition, the stability of the neighborhood, its size, and its particular characteristics. (See HOUSING, PUBLIC; QUOTA SYSTEM; SEGREGATION.)

title The legal right to property ownership. A title by occupancy is a right of property acquired by taking the first possession of a thing (or the possession of something which belonged to nobody) and appropriating it. (See DEED; LAND REGISTRATION.)

title, abstract of A condensed history of ownership, consisting of the various links in the chain of title, together with a statement of all liens, charges, or encumbrances affecting a particular property. The abstract is the buyer's or mortgage lender's guide to the title and its defects, if any. It is also a useful history of the property, something every owner should know. He may secure it from a title company or the lawyer who examined the title.

title, cloud on An outstanding claim, defect, or encumbrance that impairs the owner's or prospective owner's title. A cloud on a title may be a previous defective conveyance, a judgment against a prior owner during his tenure, a bankruptcy proceeding against a prior owner affecting his right to convey, a questionable disposition by will, or any other deficiency impairing the chain of conveyances. If unremoved, it authorizes the buyer's rejection of the title. In a large-scale assemblage of property there may be numerous defects that impair the achievement of contiguity, such as a strip or gore belonging to someone other than the owner. Public acquisition by eminent domain can clear such defects by making the claimants party to the proceeding; for this reason it is often undertaken even though all or most of the parcels in an assemblage have or could have been acquired through voluntary sale.

In less-developed countries clouded titles are common owing to shifts from tribal to individual tenures or because tribal customs governing sales were not technically complied with. Boundary disputes also complicate titles. These and failure to put registration systems into effect prevent orderly urban development and the growth of a mortgage system. (See LAND REGISTRATION.)

title insurance   A guarantee offered by a title-insurance company that the title to a property is clear or that it is clear except for specified defects that require curing. (See TORRENS SYSTEM.)

Torrens System   A system for registering titles, the marketability of which is then guaranteed by the government. It was first introduced into South Australia in 1857 by Sir Robert Torrens, then registrar of deeds, and has been adopted by that country, to some extent in Canada, in a modified form in South Africa and Central Europe, and in a number of states in the United States. In the United States title-guaranty companies also function to insure titles and look with competitive disfavor at Torrens titles. (See LAND REGISTRATION; TITLE.)

tourist cabins   A group of buildings, generally on main highways, erected separately or in rows, containing sleeping accommodations for transient occupants. (See MOTEL.)

town   In the United States, an urban settlement that is grander than a village or hamlet but falls short of being a city. In England, either a village that holds a market periodically or, more generally, a large well-populated place such as a borough or a city. In New England a town is a rural or urban unit of local government smaller than a city but functioning as a political subdivision of the state. Town might also be used to mean township. Colloquially, "going to town" means going to the big city. (See CITY; HAMLET; NEW TOWN; VILLAGE.)

town and country planning   Planning for development of communities that would preserve and make use of the natural advantages of sites, secure the most advantageous conditions of housing and traffic, and the most convenient locations for public buildings and spaces without marring the countryside. The term is of British origin and has no exact American counterpart, the closest being city planning. It is derived from the theory that farm and factory, houses and roads, churches and pubs could be so related to one another as to make country life possible and tolerable. "Then," as one English devotee of the green spaces put it, "the spirit of the countryside will return, and men and women will enjoy life and give vent to their joy in the true tradition of rural peoples."

The linkage between town and country has always been present in the minds of English planners, as exemplified by the creation of a Ministry of Town and Country Planning and by the numerous Town and Country Planning Acts. The regard for preserving country while planning the town has also been manifested in the white papers on planning and the passion for green belts and towns of limited population. Town and country planning has become one of Britain's principal exports. There has been little support for the idea in the United States, but the Department of Agriculture has shown some recent interest. (See CITY PLANNING.)

town-gown problem   The apparently universal conflict existing between an urban university and the neighboring citizens. Various reasons have been assigned for the problem's existence—the intellectual snobbery of the scholars and the anti-intellectualism of the townsmen; the expansion plans of the university that threaten neighborhood displacements; the built-in class antagonisms between students, who have been traditionally the scions of wealth, and the proletariat; the private university's tax-exempt status, creating the feeling that it is being publicly subsidized without public control; the partial immunity of students and faculty from civil law; the rowdyism and distinctive mores of a subcommunity of youth; the heretical or revolutionary ideas issuing from the university; the presence of aliens, foreigners, and outsiders in general, which is encouraged by the school and resented by the townsmen; and, particularly in the United States, the race problem when a university body predominantly white finds itself surrounded by a concentrated and often militant black neighborhood. Finally, the cause may be the crassness of the university establishment itself, which so often persistently ignores its neighbors and their problems, when in fact the surrounding district can be part of the learning process for its students and teachers and an area it can serve and help to improve through its educational and intellectual resources.

The views on the relationship of an urban university to its community vary, with one school of thought holding that the university's function is to teach and that it should do nothing more; another saying that its functions are to teach and undertake research (which is understandable, since much of the financial support for many universities now comes from research funds); a third holding that there are three functions—teaching, research, and service.

That service is part of an urban university's function has long been accepted in one area—the operation of hospitals by university medical schools. Without a hospital the medical school—not to mention its medical research facilities—would be of little value. But urban life has expanded the duties and opportunities of the urban university far beyond the hospital. The neighborhood and the city are the living laboratories where the school of social work, the teacher's college, the law school, the sociology department, the school of architecture and city planning, can find rich material for learning and for rendering service in the process. The neighborhood can be part of the classroom. The student can often learn more from action programs than he can in the lecture course.

town, dormitory A town composed primarily of residences and a few essential services while the places of employment for the bulk of its citizens lie in another area. (See CITY, SATELLITE; SUBURB.)

township In England, a parish or the division of a parish, but now a political entity free of clerical domination. In the United States it is usually a unit of local government that is a division of a county, with administrative control over its own schools, roads, and other local affairs. (See CITY, SATELLITE; SUBURB.)

traffic Vehicles and persons in motion or stopped because temporarily prevented from moving.

traffic assignment   The procedure used in transportation studies and simulation models in which calculated trips between two given traffic zones (as determined by the trip-distribution procedure) are placed on interlinked segments of existing or proposed roads between the two zones. The minimum-time path between the zones is loaded to capacity first, and when its capacity is reached the traffic is then assigned to the next shortest route.

traffic distribution   The procedure used in transportation studies and simulation models in which the number of trips generated by any given traffic zone are distributed to all other zones in the study area in proportion to their "attractive" strength—as expressed by square feet of employment space, number of workers, number of residents, etc. Generally trips are distributed by means of a mathematical model fed into a computer.

traffic-generation procedure   A procedure used in transportation studies and simulation models for calculating the number of trips originating in any given traffic zone on the basis of the zone's characteristics and those of its inhabitants, such as family size, income, car ownership, distance from work, etc.

traffic generator   The "push" or "pull" that moves people, vehicles, and goods. All traffic is generated by individual or organizational needs and desires; but, in analyzing mass movements of people, land use and the activity associated with it is a useful surrogate. When traffic is said to be "generated" by large shopping centers or factories it is because their activities are a magnet for people. Where households are said to "generate" a certain number of trips the focus is on the residential land use. In other words, the "generator" may be the home base of the persons or goods making a trip or the place that attracts them, depending on the purpose of the analysis. It is generally possible to isolate one or more characteristics of a traffic generator (square footage in a shopping center, number of members and number of vehicles in a household) and multiply it by a constant factor (empirically determined) and thereby get a rough estimate of the total number of daily journeys associated with it.

traffic flow; traffic volume   The number of individuals, vehicles, or animals passing a given point within a specified time. Unless otherwise indicated, the count includes the flow in both directions. The graphic presentation of vehicular and pedestrian movement at given streets and times is called a traffic-flow diagram. The width of lines representing the composite of all trips along the route indicates the traffic volumes to scale.

traffic management The manipulation of traffic movements within street systems by recasting the flows and controlling the intersections and the times and places for parking to achieve the most efficient movement.

traffic, tidal Traffic on a two-way road proceeding predominantly in one or the other direction according to the time of day or other recurrent circumstances. Rush-hour traffic is the most common example of tidal traffic.

traffic zone The smallest geographic unit for which trip behavior is calculated and analyzed in transportation studies. Traffic zones may be based on groupings of existing census tracts or arbitrarily created by laying out an area into a grid of one-quarter-mile or one-mile squares.

trailer. See MOBILE HOME.

transitional area An area in process of change from one use or type of occupancy to another, or from one racial or ethnic group to another. Sectional stability has never been characteristic of American neighborhoods. From the frontier days onward mobility and neighborhood flux have characterized the country's development. Sometimes flux and growth went hand in hand, at other times flux was the prelude to neighborhood degeneration.

Frequently the reasons for a neighborhood transition are: physical decay or improvement; obsolescence of structures or uses; impairment or improvement of transit, school, or other physical facilities; lack of safety, or change affecting an area's security, environment, or livability; an ethnic shift or a shift from a higher- to a lower-income population or *vice versa;* aging of the population; a public improvement such as urban renewal, public housing, a thruway, etc.; emigration of the job sources or the entry of new sources or any impairment or improvement of a city's economy affecting opportunities for livelihood.

The forty million people who move annually in the United States are one of the main spurs to area transition. The dynamic change in American neighborhoods contrasts sharply with European neighborhood stability and the ancient practice of handing down the land (sometimes including the family cemetery) from generation to generation. Land in the United States is more like a commodity, freely transferred from person to person and exchangeable like other commodities for cash. (See CONCENTRIC ZONE THEORY; GRAY AREA; TIPPING POINT; TWILIGHT ZONE; URBAN FRINGE.)

transition zone. See ZONE, TRANSITION.

transit, mass The act or means of conveying masses of people from place to place along a given right-of-way system; routes are usually prearranged, and service is operated according to prescribed schedules. In dense urban areas mass transit competes with the king-size automobile by taking advantage of human verticality for space-saving, thereby minimizing the problems of peak-hour travel, parking, and other by-products of the sprawling ignition age. Its wider use has been impeded by the dispersed patterns of cities, the slow speeds of operation, the relatively long transfer and waiting periods, the long walking distance to stops, and the fierce competition of the private automobile.

The terms "mass transit," "public transit," and "rapid transit" are commonly used interchangeably, but they are not strictly the same. Public transit refers to transportation services available to the public without restriction. As public transport, it may also be regulated as to its operations, charges, and profits. Rapid transit is mass transit with an exclusive right-of-way. It is intended to convey people as quickly as possible from point to point. Rapid transit need not always be rapid and often is not during rush hours. (See CAR POOL; JOURNEY TO WORK.)

transportation The act or means of moving tangible objects (persons and goods as contrasted with ideas or electric impulses) from place to place; it usually involves the use of some vehicle, whether automobile, dog-sled, rocket, or rickshaw.

transportation planning The process by which new transportation facilities (and improvements to the old facilities) are systematically designed, their adequacy tested, and their future construction programed. Proposed new facilities could include streets, highways, subways, terminals, parking garages, tunnels, etc. Improvements might include widened streets, better traffic signs, signals and control systems, and one-way streets. Comprehensive transport planning considers all modes—mass transit, automobile, air, rail, etc., and regards the total as a single system.

transportation terminal   A facility where transfer between modes of transportation takes place; also, any facility providing for one or more of the following: the arrival and embarkation of passengers; the receipt, dispatching, and temporary storage of goods; the termination point and temporary housing of vehicles. Railroad stations, airports, truck and trailer depots, and docks are among the varieties of terminal facilities. Parking lots and garages may also serve as terminals. (See PARKING.)

trip   A one-way journey that proceeds from an origin to a destination by a single type of locomotion. It is the smallest unit of travel for most transportation studies, and it is the sum of these daily excursions that makes up the complex movement pattern of the metropolis. Each change from one means of locomotion to another signifies a new trip. Thus a suburban commuter who drives from home to railroad station, then goes by train to a railroad terminal, and thereafter by subway to his office takes three trips. In everyday usage, however, a trip embraces all the "trips" as one—*e.g.,* a trip to Europe.

trystorium   A place where male and female can meet. The number of urban trystoria are few, and scant provision is being made for them, so courting in a city now challenges the most tenacious suitor. The automobile (for those who can afford it) has taken the place of the porch. In multiple dwellings the parlor has been taken over by family television; the fireplace that once warmed hearts has given way to the radiator that only heats rooms. Simultaneously, parks have often become dangerous to stroll in, and the growing lack of safety in some city areas has disqualified many existing meeting places. While the urban cinema survives, it hardly makes the best type of trystorium. (See CONVERGENCE.)

turnkey job   Any job or contract in which the contractor agrees to complete the work to a defined point or to completion (when he turns over the key) and to assume all risk. (See HOUSING, PUBLIC.)

twilight zone; old-town greys   An area designated by a public authority for improvement or clearance that deteriorates markedly while the improvement or clearance is pending. The term is of British origin, and the areas are also referred to as "old-town greys."

Twilight zones are a serious problem in the United States, where vast areas designated for urban renewal remain unimproved for as long as a decade or more. With the mere designation of the area for improvement, owners neglect repairs, mortgagors refuse to lend money, tenants gradually move out, storekeepers stop making improvements, and the vandals come in for the loot.

Some areas designated for renewal may never be renewed because a developer cannot be found to stake the necessary investment. Instead of clearing a slum the public agency in these instances has created one. Slum creation is not the consequence of the urban-renewal program alone—it has also occurred in areas designated for roads in which the routes have subsequently been abandoned. No damage suit for slander of title lies in favor of an injured owner because malice must be shown, and this is virtually impossible to prove. The remedy must be statutory—a law should allow damages. Public agencies should also be barred, for a prescribed number of years, from again taking an area for a public improvement where they have abandoned a project after having designated it. (See BLIGHT; GRAY AREA; SLUM; TRANSITIONAL AREA.)

tyrannopolis   A big city with a tyrannous system of political and financial administration under a rigid bureaucracy and exercising a repression that, says Lewis Mumford, "leaves no place for young initiative, or for those forms of cooperation which, to be wholehearted, must be voluntary."

untenanted hazard   An unoccupied structure that threatens the surrounding neighborhood because it is the target of vandals, a refuge for undesirables, or a breeding place for fires. (See ABANDONMENT; BUILDING, DERELICT.)

urban arboriculture Programs for planting and cultivating trees in cities. In the United States the tree won early respect with William Penn's plan for a "green Country Towne" (Philadelphia) in 1682 and Jefferson's dream of a vine and fig tree for every family. During the War of Independence poplars and other trees were planted "as symbols of growing freedom."

The tree has become an urban concern. But cities get caught between the pro-tree pressures of urban nature-lovers (whose zeal reaches its peak on Arbor Day) and the anti-tree pressures of utility companies (concerned about damage to their underground installations by roots). Only a few cities have tree commissions, and most of those with tree banks have insufficient funds. Cambridge, Massachusetts, plants street trees and maintains them without charge. Others charge extravagantly for the service. Berkeley, California, Washington, D.C., and old New England cities, among others, are well treed, while New York City's lonely ginkgoes and planes fight a continuous battle with the trailer truck and are watered more by dogs than by owners.

The official New York City attitude was exemplified at a hearing in the 1960s on an ordinance that would have compelled all owners to install trees on any block on which more than 50 per cent of the owners had planted or agreed to plant them. The bill was defeated after one councilman insisted that trees encourage juvenile delinquency ("muggers hide behind them"), another that trees break windows ("the growing branches"), and a third that the ordinance would violate due process of law. American cities have a long way to go before their streets equal those of London or Paris in arboreal appearance. (See GREEN BELT; ROOFSCAPING.)

urban architecture. See ARCHITECTURE, URBAN.

urban corruption Dishonesty of officials in administering urban affairs. Corruption is apt to be more rife in cities than in rural areas and will generally increase with city size. Lord Bryce classified the forms of corruption as follows: taking cash bribes; taking bribes in kind (shares of stock or an interest in a contract); promising contracts (*e.g.,* giving official advertisements to a newspaper) in return for favorable treatment; trading a legislative favor for a promise of campaign funds; appointing people to office who can favor the appointers with profitable rewards;

pledging to support bad legislation in return for votes or influence. Although he called the government of cities the one conspicuous failure in the United States, he found improvement in that "rogues are less audacious. Good citizens are more active." While party politics was still a mischief, he concluded that a stronger sense of civic duty carried hope for change. That was in 1895. Matters have measurably improved since then, although some corruption has continued in every one of his classifications. Disclosure, however, has become more frequent, and the public attitude toward venality is now less indifferent.

In developing areas urban corruption is comparable to what it was in developing America. The traditions of good public service are less matured, and civil servants must often look to other sources of income merely to maintain a decent living standard. The councilmen of Kumasi, Ghana, for example, complained about their having to work without pay because the council system was fashioned on the British model of unpaid service. (The only compensation to members was a nominal stipend per meeting so that at least eight or ten were called each month, helping to defray the £300 that had to be spent for election campaigning alone.) It was not surprising that some councilmen soon made the job profitable through other devices.

Among the other reasons for corruption in the developing areas is that the upper class does not yet look upon public service as either a public obligation or a mark of distinction, while the opportunist sees public service as a short bridge to affluence. Frequently business looks on graft as essential oil to lubricate officials when administrative delays and frustrations seem endless. Where permits are required for building or importing, there is an open black market in some countries. Nor is the party in power always chary of accepting contributions in return for favors or of using public funds for promoting its re-election. In nations where tribal custom is still powerful, bribery is not easy to distinguish from traditional gift-giving.

urban county A county given responsibility for providing urban-type services for incorporated or unincorporated areas within its borders. Transfer of functions to the county may occur sporadically, by statute or through a conscious desire to rationalize local government in metropolitan areas. Counties have traditionally been little more than administrative subdivisions of the state, assigned to carry on such state activities as election administration, law enforcement, and certain judicial functions, and there are often constitutional limitations on enlarging county powers, particularly the power to raise revenues sufficient to finance urban-type services.

California has been the most liberal in granting authority to counties; Los Angeles County supplies police, street, park, and recreational programs. It also makes cooperative agreements for a variety of services, such as enforcing health ordinances, running library services, housing prisoners, organizing elections, collecting taxes, etc. Dade County in Florida has responsibility for county-wide functions such as highway building, air, water, rail, and bus-terminal facilities, traffic control, air-pollution control, assessments, fire and police protection, housing and urban renewal, building and zoning codes, and the construction of integrated water, sanitary sewerage and surface-drainage systems. (See FEDERATION.)

urban design The discipline concerned with and the process of giving form to ensembles of structure, to whole neighborhoods, or to the city at large. Urban designers blend the skills of the architect and city planner in an effort to make an urban area comprehensible, functional, and aesthetically pleasing through articulation of its parts. (See PLANNER.)

urban escape hatch An entertainment section of a city affording escape from the sameness, tedium, or funlessness of other neighborhoods. It may be Greenwich Village, Times Square, or Coney Island in New York City, the Gaslight district of St. Louis, or an entire city like Las Vegas (which provides relief from Boulder City and California's suburbs). Coffee houses, bars, night clubs, amusement arcades, theaters, and specialty shops usually characterize the urban escape hatch, which is frequented by teen-agers, beatniks, browsers, the bored, hippies, suburbanites, salesmen in quest of a fling, and tourists looking for a good meal, a spurt of espresso, or a nightcap. Most escape hatches are not created, they grow; but artists and budding literati with informal behavior and a taste for variety often help give them an initial fillip. No two escape hatches are alike nor are their origins similar. Generally escape hatches include any area of recreation or entertainment that is a magnet for the masses looking for temporary release from life's treadmill. (See LEISURE; RECREATION.)

urban fringe   The area of mixed agricultural and urban land use lying beyond the suburbs of a city at the periphery of its developed areas; also called the "rural-urban fringe." Because they are at the cutting edge of development and often lack the political organization and planning tools needed to cope with an urban invasion, fringe areas often present a devastated landscape.

urbanism   The French word for city planning, *urbanisme,* has no one-word equivalent in the English language unless one accepts "ekistics," which means something more and in any event is still to be naturalized. The word "urbanist" has been grudgingly accepted by more recent dictionaries as meaning a city planner, but the term must be shared with the Franciscan nuns living under the rule of Pope Urban IV. Since there is already some acceptance of "urbanist," "urbanism" should be an acceptable English addition to the city-planning vocabulary. (See CITY PLANNING.)

urban nomads   A term applied to urban people uprooted or displaced against their wills from more than one dwelling in their lifetime. They are not nomads in the technical sense, for their movements are neither voluntary nor part of their way of life. Federal and local programs for public improvements have made tenure uncertain for a growing number of poorer families, who often scurry from one slum to another in advance of the ubiquitous bulldozer. Some have been "relocated" as often as three or four times in a few years. A 1954 study by the New York City Planning Commission of a site required for public housing showed that 49 per cent of the occupants displaced moved into sections mapped for future development. As displacements increase under government-aided programs, the habitations for these people resemble way-stations more than homes. A stable life for them is impossible. The term "urban nomad" can also be applied to real nomads who have entered the urban environment. (See NOMADISM; RELOCATION; SKID ROW.)

urbanologist   One who claims to be an expert on the woes of the urban problem and professes to have the answers; an ekistician—also one who has the answers. (See EKISTICS.)

urban pathology   The science of the origins, nature, and course of the afflictions induced by urban life and the urban environment. Studies have been made of the spatial impact of urban life on rodents and human beings, but urban pathology is still an unexplored field—even its name has not yet been certified. We know that crowding, insanitation, and slums are not the happiest of environments; we are investigating for the first time the effect of noise and air pollution on human beings. The relationship between poor environment and high death rates, illiteracy, juvenile delinquency, sex offenses, divorce, non-support cases, venereal disease, alcoholism, suicides, mental disorders, mental deficiencies, arrests, and poverty have been iterated and reiterated. But the public-housing program is virtually the only official answer, and that has not proven very therapeutic.

urban personality; suburban personality   That quality or collection of qualities which makes the urban person what he is, as distinct from other persons from other environments. That the urban environment affects personality is unquestionable. A dog or a cat in a city home will act differently from one released into the woods (or abandoned in an urban-renewal area). So, too, a human being, particularly a child, is conditioned by the urban world. The cultural world of the urbanite is a world devised by man. He works irrespective of climate or seasons. He lives in a complex scene in which the tempo is faster and the machine sets the pace; he is more intensely stimulated by what goes on about him; he is group-oriented. He strives more intensively for social prestige and financial success; his life and future are more affected by personal contacts; he moves more often; his skills are specialized. Although the rural person in the United States has recently come closer to the city's action there are still differences, as there are personality differences between an urban Southerner and an urban Northerner.

The future impact on personality of suburbia is still to be determined. The suburb is part of the city though a distance from its core, and the suburbanite has not lost his city contacts. The long-term impact will probably be less intense than some writers have judged. Herbert J. Gans, in his study of Levittown, has found that the move to the suburbs "changes some people, but not in uniform ways," and that the most frequently reported changes are not caused by the suburbs but were reasons for going there in the first place. He finds that the new house and home-

ownership create more change than the new community. (See
DETRIBALIZATION.)

urban planning. See CITY PLANNING.

urban population   All persons living in urbanized areas or in places of
2500 inhabitants or more outside urbanized areas, as defined by the Bureau of the Census in 1960. All other residents are considered "rural."

urban redevelopment   The earlier word for urban renewal. Defined
broadly, it meant the programs, policies, and actions designed to eliminate urban blight and improve the urban environment and its institutions so as to produce a more wholesome life for a nation's urban people.
(See URBAN RENEWAL.)

urban renewability   The capacity of an area to respond to urban renewal, when the time comes. Planning areas so that they will have urban
renewability is a poor country's alternative to comprehensive planning,
based on the premise that the pressure of population will inevitably result in slum formations. If, however, the land on which the housing is
built is properly laid out into plots in advance, it will be easier and less
costly to build something better on it in the future, utilizing the existing
layout and utility pattern. Utilities can be minimal at first, but their later
installation should be provided for. It is the layout of roads, houses, and
utilities that has the greatest influence on replanning, and there should
therefore be less concern and less expenditure for the housing than for
land acquisition, planning, and utilities. (See SLUM, PLANNED.)

urban renewal   The improvement of urban environments through public
initiative and assistance in demolishing slums, rehabilitating or conserv-
ing existing structures, providing for better housing, commercial, industrial, and public buildings, as well as greater amenities pursuant to comprehensive plans and workable programs.
   While the term "urban renewal" is of American origin, the program is
no more novel than is the building of new cities. Earlier efforts to do
what is currently contemplated in urban-renewal schemes include Baron
Haussmann's program in Paris, Dublin's performance during the reign of
Charles II (1660–1685) and again during the reigns of Queen Anne

(1702–1714) and George I (1714–1727), and the wave of rebuilding schemes in Europe during the second half of the nineteenth century. Glasgow's formula in 1866 was virtually the same as the modern American version: the whole of the ancient town was rebuilt by a program under which Parliament not only authorized purchase and demolition of slum property and laying out of new streets, but sold the property to private parties for rebuilding. Relocation of the occupants was also included, and model tenements were built and later sold off. Similar projects were undertaken in Swansea, Wolverhampton, Derby, Nottingham, and Newcastle-upon-Tyne.

By 1970 urban-renewal programs were being undertaken not only in the United States but throughout Europe and in parts of Asia and Africa. In the United States the program was part of a broader objective to provide "a decent home and a decent environment for every American family." Private enterprise was to be encouraged to serve as large a part of the need as possible, and slums and blighted areas were to be cleared and low-income families rehoused. To provide the sites, local public agencies (housing authorities or renewal agencies) were authorized by state laws to acquire the necessary land and buildings by eminent domain. The land was then written down from acquisition cost to reuse value, with the local government providing a third of the write-down loss and the federal government two-thirds (a one-quarter/three-quarter division was made possible in special circumstances).

The American program underwent some unanticipated changes as it proceeded through the hundreds of urban mills in which it was tested. At first, slum clearance and rehousing were the predominant motivations. Because the program was slow in getting under way the problem of dealing with the families to be displaced did not seem serious: when it did get under way, it came face to face with the fact that the slum and the ghetto had become synonymous and that about three-quarters of the families that had to be displaced were black. A good portion of the rest were poor elderly folk. At best, public housing plus all the other public measures could accommodate no more than a fifth of those the renewal program evicted.

Another problem was site selection. Though urban renewal was to be primarily a slum-clearance measure, the private renewal investor could not be expected to stake time and money in slums where he could not recoup his investment or make a profit. Thus only where the sites were prime or semi-prime (gray areas) did investors bid at all—and in most cases they showed interest only where they could obtain federally backed financing for all or most of the capital needed.

A third problem came with site designation. Whenever a site was marked for renewal, repairs stopped, mortgage money withdrew, investment ceased, and people moved out in anticipation of the bulldozer. Since it took an average of a decade from designation to completion, designation became one of the most efficient means of slum creation. Worse still, of the 27,000 acres bought by cities between 1949 and 1965, 7400 acres were in 1965 still uncleared and another 3308 were cleared but lacked a sponsor.

Despite these troubles the urban-renewal program has had some constructive by-products. It enabled assemblage of plottage for much-needed improvements—the Southwest project in Washington, D.C., Philadelphia's Society Hill, San Francisco's Western Addition, and New Haven's downtown reconstruction. It spurred civic interest, as in New York City's Lincoln Center, and spawned cultural developments elsewhere. It induced some industries to stay put and provided much-needed land for university expansion. It built some high-rent housing, and because this displaced many poorer families, public-housing appropriations that Congress would probably not otherwise have agreed to were approved.

A program diffused among so many localities can be properly assessed only in terms of its parts. In many cities the program can be accounted a success, in others a failure. This is inevitable in a nation with a diversity of conditions and situations.

The main weakness is that the program has assumed that rebuilding a few slum or blighted areas would automatically make a city sound. The city in the United States, however, is at bay for reasons other than the slum problem. With middle- and upper-income families deserting it, with tax sources diminishing at the same time as the city becomes host to new waves of the nation's poor, a few reconstructed areas in or near its central business districts cannot make it whole. The American city needs massive federal assistance to build a better school system, to assure greater safety to its citizens, to improve its health programs, support its poor, and prop up its solvency. If urban renewal is to prove effective in relieving the ills of cities, it has to be one small part of a much bigger bundle of aids. Instead it is proffered as a specific. There is little purpose in rebuilding sections of cities that people won't live in or that are destined for oblivion. There is a purpose in saving those that are salvageable. Only when all the relevant national objectives for an urban society are known, stated, and accepted can urban renewal find a constructive place among them. (See ASSEMBLAGE; EMINENT DOMAIN; LAND FRAGMENTATION; PARTITION ACTION; TWILIGHT ZONE.)

urban servitude A right possessed by one person either to use another's building or land or to prevent certain uses of it. It is in the nature of an easement. The right to light and air over another's property is an urban servitude, as is the right to limit a neighboring property owner against building higher than a defined limit. (See EASEMENT.)

urban sociology The sociology of urban communities, or the study of the organization, history, development, and problems of people living together in cities with a view to determining the interaction among them and its effects on behavior, and the devices that might best help adjustment to the complexities of urban life. It is the science of human groups as they function in the urban orbit and the laws governing their behavior in such groups.

The seventeen-volume work of Charles Booth, *Life and Labour of the People in London* (1889), spurred interest in urban studies, which thereafter gained considerable impetus in the 1920s from the urban ecologists at the University of Chicago.

urbicide The death of a city at the hands of its own people through the misguided efforts of its officials or the indifference and neglect of its citizens. Since decline and decay are usually blamed on the suburbs, the state, the federal government, or some other outside agent, it is a difficult crime to substantiate and one perpetrated more commonly than is thought. A rational plan for a national population distribution and regional development would probably entail the mercy killings of certain marginal urban centers and the development of some form of municipal euthanasia, but urbicide is usually an unpremeditated and painful way to go. (See CITY HATRED.)

urbiphobia A dread of the city; it may also imply a dislike or aversion to the city. The growth in the number of urbiphobes has recently far exceeded the number of urbiphiles, particularly since the accelerated movement of blacks to the cities. The city, especially the big city, is viewed as the nest of crime and mobs, of insalubrity and degradation. Sometimes the urbiphobe stays and wants the city's destruction; more often he runs off to sub- or exurbia where he can safely berate it. The American variety of urbiphobe, however, often reverts to normality in the presence of a quaint European city such as Florence or a crowded one such as Paris or London. It should be added that a few suburbiphobes have begun to appear on the scene. (See CITY HATRED.)

use   A planning term denoting the specific purpose for which land or a building is designed or occupied. It is also the root word of other planning terms dealing with land—*i.e.,* abuse, non-use, disuse, misuse, and reuse. (See LAND USE.)

use, accessory   A use incidental or subordinate to the principal use of a building and located on the same lot. (See BUILDING, ACCESSORY.)

use district   A section of a city designated by a zoning ordinance that prescribes the use of its land and the type and characteristics of the structures that may be placed on it. (See ZONING.)

use, highest and best   The use of land to its maximum permissible development, one that will bring maximum profit to the owner. It is the use that would justify the highest payment for the land if offered for sale. There is a tendency for each site to be developed to its highest and best use through the competition of entrepreneurs, but often land may be developed temporarily for a lower use. A parking lot or a taxpayer may, for example, help pay carrying charges and taxes pending a later more comprehensive improvement. Not every site, of course, can support a Rockefeller Center or a Macy's. The highest and best use for most land is agricultural or residential. Usually only in central areas and along transportation corridors are higher uses possible. (See 100-PER-CENT AREA.)

use, mixed   A variety of land uses in a section as distinguished from the isolated uses and planned separatism prescribed by many zoning ordinances. Urban critic Jane Jacobs has made the most eloquent plea for mixed uses in cities. "Streets or districts which do have good primary mixtures and are successful at generating city diversity should be treasured, rather than despised for their mixture and destroyed by attempts to sort out their components from one another." This might be called the "Ashcan School of City Planning," which could have as much influence in breaking some of the old planning icons as the Ashcan School of Artists has had on painting. There has been much criticism of Mrs. Jacobs, some of it justified, but when one builds an abattoir for sacred cows, some beefing should be expected. The value of her contribution is not in the fact that she is right in all she says, but that she has put in issue some planning illusions that have become vested.

Though most zoning laws still foster sectional homogeneity, the need for revenues is softening attitudes, particularly in suburbia. Devices for controlling smoke, fumes, and odors, noise-deadening techniques, landscaping, and better architecture are making more industrial buildings acceptable there. Many an exclusive suburb is now seen scouting around for a watch factory, while a fine spray of ivy, an attractive design, and a fountain have often sublimated even a Coca-Cola bottling plant.

use, non-conforming   A building or use that is inconsonant with a district's zoning regulations. If erected after the enactment of the ordinance it may be ordered removed. If in being before the enactment it may continue in use, but a new non-conforming or different non-conforming use may not be substituted. Nor is its extension or enlargement permissible if the ordinance so provides. Many ordinances permit the rebuilding of the non-conforming premises when destroyed by fire. Once the use is abandoned, however, the right to its restoration falls, and the future use of the premises must conform to the zoning. Some states allow for the abatement of such uses at the end of a prescribed and usually lengthy period of time. (See ZONING, TIME.)

use, pre-existing   A land use that does not conform to a zoning ordinance but that existed before the enactment and that therefore may not be banned until its abandonment. Sometimes the pre-existing use, if a nuisance, can be abated by court action. In some jurisdictions pre-existing uses have been banned after the lapse of a reasonable period equivalent to a prescribed "depreciation period" or amortization of its use. (See ZONING, TIME.)

use tax. See TAX, USE.

use value. See VALUE, USE.

usury   The lending of money at exorbitant rates or at rates forbidden by law. The line between legal interest and unethical usury has always been a fine one, but despite the freedom of contract characterizing transactions in many national economies, the term "usury" has acquired a distinct unethical connotation. Jeremy Bentham demanded the same freedom for money trade as existed in commodity transactions. The law that aims to aid the poor by restricting the interest rate, he argued, excludes them simultaneously from the source of credit. It is also contended that interest restrictions bring a capital shortage and a consequent increase in the cost of credit.

While economic liberalism caused the abandonment of anti-usury statutes in many countries, they persist in the United States, ostensibly to protect the consumer against his own unwisdom. The exceptions and evasions, however, are many. Corporations may be charged any interest rate, so small businesses often incorporate in order to borrow. Exemptions from usury penalties are given to regulated lending institutions and finance agencies. Mortgages and notes acquired at discounts are not subject to penalties, so that the actual interest rates in these instances may far exceed the statutory maximum. Sales prices for installment purchases frequently carry premiums that boost the price of the articles far above the cash price and many times the legal interest rate.

The usury laws make no sense when prime interest rates are high and legislatures are slow to increase the allowable rates. Nor do usury laws make sense on risky ventures such as second-mortgage loans, on which the legal rates are required to be the same as are charged on the safer first mortgage. The tax laws and tax exemptions on public bonds make the interest restrictions completely senseless. One who lends to a builder at 12 per cent—a risky venture at best—will retain as little as 4 per cent after paying income taxes, while in 1969 he could buy a riskless tax-exempt bond at 5 or 6 per cent!

The only instances in which restrictions on lending practices might make sense are those of the professional racketeers who charge as much as 100 per cent. Yet even here the real objections to their practices are primarily their methods of collecting, their threats, and their subterranean operations. A free interest rate and a law requiring full disclosure of all loans and the interest rates charged would have a more wholesome effect. (See MORTGAGE; POINTS.)

Uthwatt Report   A 1942 British report on land and development policy, by a committee headed by Justice Uthwatt; its main recommendations were national planning; a ceiling on values as a deterrent to speculation; public purchase of property in war-devastated areas; public acquisition of development rights; collection of betterment from urban land by means of a quinquennial levy. The unique recommendation was the public acquisition of development rights. The compensation was to be paid to owners out of a "global sum." The ownership of the property would thereafter continue in the owner, but he would no longer possess the right to develop it without permission.

The Uthwatt Report followed the Barlow Report on the distribution of the industrial population (1940), which dealt with the situation up to the outbreak of World War II. The Barlow Report emphasized the need for planning and research and for decongesting the overgrown cities. Another report, by the Scott Committee, complemented the Barlow Report and emphasized the importance of agriculture and country life and the need to provide for their preservation in the national plan.

The "global sum" fixed by the Uthwatt Report to meet the claims against the government for taking the development rights was £300 million. If the owners elected to develop they had to pay a "development charge," the sum total of which would help reimburse the government for the compensation it would have paid for the development rights. Local governments were required to file general plans to which proposed private developments would have to conform.

The proposal was incorporated in the Town and Country Planning Act of 1947. The plan and the legislation were later substantially modified after encountering delays and frustrations. According to one authority, after nearly five years of operation the Act brought neither justice nor an equality of injustice to the landowners and created as many new problems as it attempted to solve. (See BETTERMENT; PUBLIC-LAND OWNERSHIP; TAX, BETTERMENT.)

utilities   The basic service systems required by a developed area—water supply, sanitary and storm sewers, electricity, gas, and telephone service.

Sometimes public transportation and garbage collection are added to the list. Ordinarily these services are provided by the public or a publicly regulated agency. (See INFRASTRUCTURE; PUBLIC UTILITY.)

utopia   An imaginary island enjoying the utmost perfection in law and society; thus any place, state, or system of ideal perfection. Utopias are social romances that have usually appeared during some period of disaffection or crisis which turned minds to an imaginary "Nowhere Land" in which the social ideal could be achieved. The *Republic* of Plato, Lord Bacon's *New Atlantis,* and Sir Thomas More's *Utopia* were such idealizations, and there have been many before and since. Utopia (Greek *ou,* meaning "not," and *topos,* "a place") received its name from More, on whose imaginary island everything was perfect. "Utopian" is now an adjective applied to any transcendent but impractical scheme.

Utopias not only critically transcribe the social ideas of the period but also compare what might be to what is. They most often mythicize proposals the writers dared not state openly. Thus Plato's *Republic* hoped to elevate the prevailing social attitudes and counteract the greed of egotism. Abolition of private property seemed logical. Sir Thomas More veiled his criticism, thereby hoping to avoid the wrath of a wrathful Henry VIII. Some of the utopian dreams have been realized, such as More's reduction of the working day to six hours, Bacon's romanticization of travel, and Plato's two houses for every family. But there will probably always be at least one new discontent for every old utopian hope realized.

There are a variety of derivative terms, including:

Anti-utopia—the antithesis of utopia, a place that lacks all the good things of utopia. There have also been anti-utopian novels, such as Aldous Huxley's *Brave New World* and George Orwell's *1984.*

Cacotopia—the imagined seat of the worst government—a nonceword coined and used by Jeremy Bentham in 1818 to denote the opposite of the best state imaginable. "Caco" is derived from the Greek and means "bad" or "evil," as in cacophony ("bad noise") or cacosomnia ("bad sleep"). It was used again by Patrick Geddes in 1913 and latterly by Lewis Mumford, who used it as a synonym for hell.

Dystopia—an evil place. (See CITY, IDEAL.)

vacancy   A housing unit that is not occupied.

vacancy rate   The ratio between the number of vacant units and the total number of units in a project or in an entire city. The gross vacancy rate counts every empty unit. The actual or available vacancy rate excludes units rented or sold but not yet occupied; units off the market (not for rent or sale); and seasonal and dilapidated housing.

An actual vacancy rate of about 3 to 5 per cent in every cost classification is considered desirable, since this would keep the housing market fluid and allow prospective buyers and renters a fair selection from which to choose. A lower rate usually represents a housing shortage and is likely to drive up shelter costs. A higher vacancy rate may keep rents and costs down, but it tends to inhibit new construction and may lead to abandonment and vandalism. Needless to say, for the owner of any housing development or apartment building the only desirable vacancy rate is zero per cent.

Vacancy rates in cities are no longer accurate indices of housing availability because of the lack of safety in certain neighborhoods and because of vandalism. A vacancy spotted by a census-taker today may be unlivable tomorrow. The statisticians need to revise their definitions of vacancy rates and condition their findings to accord with the realities.

valuation. See APPRAISAL.

valuation, physical   The use of the replacement cost of property as a basis for calculating the investment on which public-utility companies are entitled to a reasonable return. Physical valuation also guides the regulating agencies in the fixing of utility rates. (See REPLACEMENT COST.)

value   The worth of a thing in money or goods at a particular time—or, as the jingle puts it, "the worth of a thing is the price it will bring." In this sense it is synonymous with market value, or what a willing buyer would pay to a willing seller in a free market. The economists have therefore tried to distinguish between value as a convertible object of wealth and a measure of utility. "Nothing," said Adam Smith, "is more useful than water, but it will purchase scarce anything; scarce anything can be had in exchange for it. A diamond, on the contrary, has scarce any value in use, but a very great quantity of other goods may frequently be had in exchange for it." Today, of course, the city man pays for his water and his wife may put far less value on diamonds because they are an invitation to burglary. Smith's thought, however, is essentially correct. Value may mean worth in the market or worth to the owner. A university library building, for example, would bring only a small knockdown price if offered for sale, but its value to the institution is incalculable. So, too, its replacement value would be many times its sale value, which at best would be equal to just about its salvage value.

Thus, as we begin to discuss value, we are ineluctably drawn into sub-classifications of value that include the following:

All-cash value—the value on an all-cash basis as distinguished from a sale on terms with small down payment.

Appraisal value—the value as fixed by an appraiser.

Book value—the value carried on the owner's books.

Condemnation value—value as determined by the court in a condemnation proceeding.

Depreciation value—the value of a property to a particular taxpayer whose income taxes it reduces by virtue of its depreciation base.

Insurable value—the amount at which an insurance company will carry a risk.

Landmark value—the worth of the property because George Washington slept there.

Liquidation or forced-sale value—what the property will bring in a forced liquidation as distinguished from a sale at leisure.

Mortgage value—the value put upon it by a mortgagee who would lend on it.

Potential value—the hypothetical value based on a property's projected income in the future or on the basis of some improvement to be made.

Prestige value—the value for the prestige it confers on the owner or occupant.

Salvage value—the value of the material less the cost of demolition and sale.

Sentimental value—the value placed on it by the emotions.

Use value—value to a user.

Value for assessment—the value placed upon it by the tax assessor, which calls for comparing the valuation with other assessed property in the taxing jurisdiction.

One might now also add gift value, or the value a thing has for the purpose of a gift to a tax-exempt organization and the tax benefit it brings the giver. There are other kinds of value, and more will be born as systems put values on things or reduce them. In a utopian society people will probably put a value only on values and not on things. (See APPRAISAL.)

value, market   A hypothetical figure, used in appraisal, condemnation proceedings, and assessments for taxes, which a willing buyer presumably would pay to a willing seller in a free market. It is when the market is not "free" that the determination of value becomes an exercise in legerdemain. In judicial proceedings to determine property value, the opinions of the public and private appraisers under oath are sometimes so far apart that the bewildered judge either selects a value somewhere in the middle or arrives at some figure based on a valuation theory of his own.

value, use   The value ascribed to a property based on its worth to the user. An old industrial building may be of no value to anyone but the present owner, and were he to vacate there would be little or no salvage value. A vacant site in a slum area may have no use value for a private developer but may have for a public-housing agency. Written down to use value, some vacant renewal sites might find a redeveloper. Use value is also called "user value," or value to the user as distinguished from market value. The concept becomes important in properties known as "specialties," such as an old club, monastery, mansion, schoolhouse, power station, or armory. When occupied, they have substantial value for the user. When they are vacated, they are called a "drug on the market." The seller may make a fortune if he can find someone who can use the building as is, but if he cannot, its value is only the land value minus the cost of demolition. Valuation of these specialties in tax or eminent-domain proceedings is difficult. The owner claims the value on the basis of replacement cost, while the condemning authority alleges it has no value as a building at all. The court or jury is usually hard put to find a clear answer but may render an award that favors the owner or strike a figure somewhere between the two valuations. (See APPRAISAL; URBAN RENEWAL.)

variance; exception The granting of relief from the terms or conditions of a building or zoning law by a public agency vested with the power to authorize it. It may be given when the application of the law creates unnecessary hardship; where equally safe methods or materials may be used; where there are practical difficulties in meeting the existing requirements literally; or where the deviation or exception would not affect substantial compliance with the regulations and not threaten health or safety. It may also be granted to the political worthy and denied to the little fellow. The power to grant the relief may be vested in the existing building or zoning agency or in a separate body, such as a Board of Standards and Appeals.

An exception (or special exception) is also a deviation from standard zoning practice, but it is anticipated within the zoning ordinance and provisions for exceptions are made within the text. A private school, for instance, would not ordinarily be permitted in an area zoned exclusively residential; yet, since this might be a perfectly desirable and acceptable place for a school, allowance for the exception, subject to close scrutiny by the zoners, will be pre-established on the books. (See ZONING.)

vest-pocket housing. See HOUSING, VEST-POCKET.

vest-pocket park. See PARK, VEST-POCKET.

vigilantes A group self-appointed to maintain order or what it views as justice in an imperfectly organized community. Vigilante groups have operated in the South to "keep blacks in their place" and have recently cropped up in cities where violence has threatened. The term has also described some of the less muscular, self-appointed guardians of a cause, such as those who resist official efforts to convert a park into a building plot or demolish a monument; in these cases political pressures, picketing, or lying down before a bulldozer are the techniques.

village   A settlement that is larger than a hamlet but smaller than a town and not yet truly urban. Definitions vary, but an upper population limit of 2500 is commonly used. (See CITY; HAMLET; TOWN.)

visibility   The state of being identifiable by race, color, mannerisms, speech, features, or other characteristics. The Negro is said to have a "higher visibility factor," thus activating categorization by the white observer and accentuating ethnocentrism (or consciousness of race) and the prejudgments allied with it.

A "visible Negro" is a Negro employed by an enterprise or institution primarily because he is black. His may be only a token appointment to demonstrate freedom from discrimination or because his manifest presence may enhance trade with black consumers and elevate the employer's reputation with a community or group.

wattle and daub   A framework of woven rods and twigs plastered with clay or mud; also, a wall made with upright stakes with withes or twigs twisted between them and then plastered over. Wattle and daub is one of the oldest forms of building and is still used in the less-developed areas. The Egyptians used the stems of maize for the uprights, and Vitruvius mentions it in his works.

welfare state, business   A society dedicated to the theory that the general welfare can best be served by advancing the welfare of private enterprise; or, as one official once put it, "What is good for General Motors is good for the nation." Therefore public policies should be directed toward bigger and better profits. In line with the theory there has been a tendency to have private enterprise rather than public agencies carry out public programs, on the premise that they are more efficient and conform to the new business-welfare ethos. The growing store of subsidies would be allotted to corporations, with more tax incentives to boot. In the end corporations, rather than government, would meet public as well as private needs.

If the theory has virtues, it also has vices and dangers. Private enterprise may be more efficient and less bureaucratic than government, and business ethics have improved; there is indeed room for private enterprise to undertake operations for government agencies, such as basic research, construction of public housing for sale to local authorities, building of government installations, and so forth. The vice is in carrying the policy too far. Lush contracts dispensed by government spawn vested interests that are soon translated into powerful political pressure groups pushing for more of the same. The highway lobby is an example. A society that gives over public operations in too many fields is bound to subordinate the public to the private welfare and create a hegemony of private interests whose power will be difficult to curtail.

In the business welfare state, corporations seek escape from federal levy and the removal of investment and risk from their operations. Federal insurance of mortgage loans, diminution or elimination of risk capital, and easy liquidity through the Federal National Mortgage Association have cut down or eliminated risk. At the local level, where tax exemptions are freely given, the blue-chip companies have had cities and even hamlets build plants for them through the issuance of local tax-exempt bonds running into the hundreds of millions. Thus far the federal government has not extended the same exemptions on government bonds. But the argument is being made that, given the proper tax exemptions and incentives, business will not only prosper but also solve social problems in the slums and elsewhere. The price tag is big, for the hidden subsidies in tax exemptions are incalculable. If given headway, the burden of taxation will ultimately shift from those who can most bear it to those who can least bear it. Simultaneously, with the investments guaranteed and the risk removed from enterprise, profits will continue flowing in while losses will tend to be socialized. (See TAX INCENTIVES.)

white backlash A reaction by whites against protests or riots by blacks or against black efforts to achieve social and political advances. It may manifest itself emotionally at the polls, in pressures on legislators to vote against civil-rights legislation, or in violent action. Following the Black Power movement and the Negro riots of 1967 and 1968, there was a white backlash in the form of anti-civil-rights legislation in California, in anti-Negro movements elsewhere, and in the third-party movement in the presidential election of 1968. (See RACIAL POLARIZATION.)

write-down   A capital subsidy that reduces the price of land in urban-renewal projects from the public authority's acquisition cost to the use value for the purpose of redevelopment. The theory of the write-down is that only by cutting land cost will the site be attractive to the private redeveloper. In 1968 the write-down was shared by the federal government, which contributed two-thirds (up to three-quarters in some cases), and the local government, which contributed a third. A write-down may also refer to a subsidy of capital cost or building cost where so authorized. There was a write-down formula for public housing before the passage of the United States Housing Act of 1937, when it was replaced by an annual subsidy. (See CAPITAL GRANT; URBAN RENEWAL; VALUE, USE.)

yard   The open, unoccupied space on a building lot between the lot line and the extreme front, rear, or side wall of a structure. In common usage it refers to the space in the rear of a building. There have been numerous efforts to consolidate residential rear yards in cities so as to provide common contiguous spaces as "private parks." (See BLOCK INTERIOR.)

"year 2000 plans"   Development plans projected for the year 2000. Among the most notable are the plans for Paris and, in the United States, those of the National Capital Planning Commission for the region of the nation's capital. In the former there will be two parallel belts of development along the Seine, which can be extended if population pressures make it necessary. There will also be "zones of deferred development" in which speculative construction will be restricted.

The planners for the Washington region hypothesized a variety of possible forms, which included one of restricted growth (this was discarded because people would not accept it and because the population increase could not be contained by restrictive measures); planned or guided sprawl; dispersed cities under which new cities offering most of the advantages of a big city would be built ten or more miles beyond the presently developed areas; a "ring of cities" pattern in which the new towns would be a good distance from the Capitol (the new towns would be in a circle and would be separated from the center by a green belt); "peripheral communities," which would put the new towns closer to the center and linked to it with diagonal and circumferential freeways (this was thought to be too compact a plan); a "radial corridor" plan, under which new development would be concentrated in six corridors running outward from the city, between which corridors would be extension wedges of countryside (these would be controlled open spaces). The last-mentioned plan was favored because it would provide good access to the center, be best suited for mass transportation, and would preserve the countryside.

In both the Paris and Washington plans the main problem is maintaining the integrity of the plans against the pressures for quick development, particularly private. Green belts are not sacred. As long as there are people needing homes, developers will try to buy land to accommodate them, and it is the open land reserved for the green belt or the land closest to the big city's center that will be sought for the developments. (See GREEN BELT.)

zone, buffer   A strip established to separate and protect one type of land use from another; for example, as a screen to objectionable noise, smoke, and visual aspects of an industrial zone adjacent to a residential area.

zone, floating   A zoning district that has been established but not mapped in a specific location. A city may decide, for example, to permit industrial uses but feel the time is not yet ripe to fix the spot. This means that many areas are definitely excluded from development. If, however, a developer can assemble anywhere within other unrestricted areas a tract of sufficient size and meeting certain other requirements, the floating zone can be moored and the area designated. The floating zone is a tricky device which has been abused as often as not, but it is a praiseworthy attempt to put flexibility into overrigid zoning practices.

zone, strip   A long, narrow zone usually commercial and usually found along highways or other major thoroughfares. It is often no more than a lot deep and is frowned upon by zoning experts as "reflex" zoning and an invitation to blight. Nevertheless, strip development is found all over the United States, in both zoned and unzoned communities, and renders American roadways among the ugliest in the world.

zone, traffic.   See TRAFFIC ZONE.

zone, transition   A zoning designation intended to guide the orderly conversion of an area from one predominant use to another, usually residential to higher-density residential and commercial. As the downtown expands, transition zones are often created at the margin of central business districts where large old single-family homes are being converted to apartments, businesses, or professional offices.

zoning   In general, the demarcation of a city by ordinance into zones and the establishment of regulations to govern the use of the land (commercial, industrial, residential, type of residential, etc.) and the location, bulk, height, shape, use, and coverage of structures within each zone. (See LAND USE; POWER PLANT; SUBDIVISION.)

zoning, aesthetic   The regulation of property by zoning in the interest of beauty. Zoning, which once had difficulty in justifying its exercises for sheer beauty's sake, seems to have won the right. "It is within the power of the legislature to determine that the community should be beautiful as well as healthy," said Justice Douglas in delivering the majority decision in *Berman v. Parker* (1954). That the interpretation of beauty may not always be entrusted to officialdom is exemplified by the American Institute of Architects' choice of the best builder's house of 1950—it was denied mortgage insurance by FHA. Similarly, the Veterans Administration imposed a $1000 design penalty on an architect-designed house in Tulsa,

Oklahoma, which *House & Home* had displayed proudly on its 1954 cover as a beautiful house. (See BEAUTIFICATION.)

zoning, airport The regulation or limitation of the height or type of structures in the path of moving aircraft. The reasonableness of the regulation hinges on the prevailing character of the neighborhood. In neighborhoods in which higher residential structures or businesses or industrial buildings are the appropriate uses of the land, airport zoning must respect the existing uses. Restriction of towers, wires, and flagpoles, however, would probably be held by the courts to be reasonable. While in earlier cases courts enjoined interference by airports with private property, later decisions have recognized the rights of the public in airport building and maintenance and have upheld zoning restrictions against building in take-off and approach areas as being "for the greater good of the greater number."

Not all communities, however, are willing to pay the cost of airport noise. Some cities have been able to alter the flying pattern and divert the noise to neighboring suburbs, only to face the threat of the affected suburbs to enact similar ordinances that would send the noise elsewhere. Since no flight pattern will satisfy everyone, some authority must take superior jurisdiction if the issues (as well as the planes) are not to remain up in the air.

zoning, cluster A form of zoning that allows a developer to reduce his minimum lot size below the zoning ordinance's requirements if the land thereby gained is preserved as permanent open space for the community. Cluster zoning also facilitates continuous control of over-all dwelling density in an area. The builder will try to offer as "cluster land" the land he cannot build on—*i.e.,* the rugged or difficult terrain in his plottage, or the land he might have left open anyway. (See PLANNED-UNIT DEVELOPMENT.)

zoning, Euclidean Zoning of the type adopted by the city of Euclid, Ohio, and made famous in 1926 by the United States Supreme Court decision in *Village of Euclid v. Ambler Realty Company,* upholding the nation's first comprehensive zoning ordinance.

Once accommodating the lake trail of Indians, Euclid's Euclid Avenue later became the "millionaire's row" that accommodated John D. Rockefeller, Sr., and other tycoons. The Euclid zoning ordinance aimed to preserve the dignity of such settlements. It restricted the location of trades, industries, apartment houses, two-family houses, single-family houses, the lot area to be built upon, the size and height of the buildings, etc. The court found these restrictions neither "unreasonable" nor "arbitrary." Since that time the term has come to describe the most common form of zoning in the United States, in which "use districts" are designated (*i.e.,* light manufacturing, commercial, single-family residential) and only the permitted use or a "higher" one is allowed. Thus in an area zoned for heavy industry, all other uses would theoretically be permitted (though there are some exceptions to this under the principle of exclusive zoning), whereas in an area of single-family residences, no other uses are likely to be permitted.

zoning, height Regulations setting the maximum heights of buildings in specified areas or districts. Height limitations for one- and two-family residences in residential districts generally limit size up to 35 feet, or two and a half stories. In apartment districts they may run as high as fifteen or more stories, while commercial or office districts may reach skyscraper altitudes. Minimum-height limitations have been frowned on by the courts. In some cities setbacks from lot lines may be rewarded with a corresponding increase in height, resulting in the wedding-cake appearance of some downtown buildings. Height limitations often result in lowering room heights to gain the maximum number of stories, which frequently fails to improve aesthetics while curtailing needed construction. (See MOCK-UP, ECONOMIC; SETBACK REGULATIONS.)

zoning, performance standard Regulations providing general criteria for determining the acceptability of certain industries, land uses, and buildings as distinguished from specification standards or detailed requirements. This type of zoning does not bar an industry or use by name but admits any use, provided the particular requirements set for admission are met. Instead of grouping industries in ordinances under the headings "light," "heavy," or "unrestricted," technological measurements are made. For the terms "limited," "substantial," "objectionable," and "offensive," specified measurements are provided to determine the rating of a particular use. Such performance standards are usually written for the following: noise and vibration, smoke, odor, dust and dirt, glare and heat, fire hazards, noxious gases, industrial wastes, transportation and traffic, aesthetics, and psychological impacts.

Performance standards are also being employed for subdivisions; here, instead of specifying the width of a roadway or right-of-way, the performance regulation sets forth the required number of moving lanes, pedestrian ways, and parking facilities. Similarly, population density might fix over-all density requirements, such as six dwelling units per acre with a minimum lot area of 4500 square feet. This might afford opportunity for more original design and innovation than the rigid regulation and allow freer expression to technology, future as well as present.

Performance standards have not won general acceptance or achieved perfection. They may be subject to over-liberal interpretations under political pressures; technical know-how is not always available in small places; they often emphasize minimum rather than desirable standards. But the more detailed specification also has its problems, and performance standards have provided an experimental frontier pointing the way to a new form of land and building regulation that might season subdivision formations with something better than more of the same. (See ARCHITECTURE, LEGISLATIVE; PLANNED-UNIT DEVELOPMENT.)

zoning permit An official finding that a planned use or structure complies with the zoning regulations or is allowed by the granting of an exception or variance. No new development or substantial change of use can occur until such a permit is issued. (See CERTIFICATE OF OCCUPANCY.)

zoning, spot The designation of an isolated parcel of land for a use classification harmful to or inconsonant with the use classification of the surrounding area so as to favor a particular owner. The courts have held such zoning to be "unreasonable" and "capricious." To avoid judicial invalidation, zoning of small areas can be enacted only when it is in furtherance of a general plan properly adopted by, and designed to serve the best interests of, the community as a whole. This does not mean that an entire city or county must be zoned at one time, but there must be uniformity in the class or type of building to which the zoning applies.

zoning, time Restricting an existing non-conforming use to a specific period, upon the expiration of which it becomes illegal. Sometimes referred to as "amortization of the use," it is presumed to afford the non-conforming owner a reasonable number of years within which to recover his investment under the existing use. Some of the restrictions apply to billboards, garages, gas stations, and junkyards; others are more inclusive; some require abandonment in as little as two years, some as long as twenty. The validity of such restrictions has not been uniformly upheld in all jurisdictions, and while a one-year period was sustained in a Louisiana case, the rulings were elsewhere described as "Cossack interpretations of Muscovite ukases." Generally the elusive terms "reasonableness" and "administrative discretion" will rule the waves and permit waiving the rules. Zoning remains one of the most manipulable devices in the political kit of local officialdom. (See USE, NON-CONFORMING; USE, PRE-EXISTING.)

INDEX OF TERMS

abandonment
abortive subdivision / subdivision, abortive or premature
abstract of title / title, abstract of
acceleration clause
accessibility
accessory use / use, accessory
access roads / road hierarchy
activity rate / labor-force participation rate
ad valorem tax / tax, ad valorem
adverse possession
Aesopian covenant / covenant, Aesopian
aesthetic zoning / zoning, aesthetic
agglomeration
agora
airport city; jet city
airport zoning / zoning, airport
air rights
alienation
alley dwelling / dwelling, alley
alteration
amenities
amortization
annexation
annual contribution
annuity
anomie
apartheid
apartment
apartment, efficiency
apartment, garden
apartment, high-rise
apartment hotel
apartment house
apportionment
appraisal; valuation
appreciation
apprenticeship

arcade; galleria
architecture, legislative
architecture of discomfort
architecture, prestige
architecture, price-no-object
architecture, speculative
architecture, urban
assemblage
assembly line; mass production
assessment
assessment ratio
assessment, special
assignment
atomic energy
attic
authority / public corporation
automation

bail out
backlash / white backlash
basement
Bauhaus
beautification
betterment
betterment tax / tax, betterment
bid / tender
bikeway
binder
birth rate
black
black capitalism
black power
blight
block
block-busting
block interior
"blue-sky" laws
boarding house / house
bond, first-mortgage
bond, industrial-development

bond, public
bond, revenue
bond, surety
boondoggling; leafraking
borings
borough plan / federation
boycott
broker
Bronxification
brownstone
budget
buffer zone / zone, buffer
builder; developer
builder, operative
builder, tract
building
building, accessory
building and loan association
building area
building code / code, building
building, derelict
building, detached
building industry; construction industry
building line
building restrictions
building site
building, speculative
bulk regulations
bundle of rights
bungalow
business welfare state / welfare state, business
busing, school
bustee

cadastre
calibration
cantonment
capacity
capillarity, law of
capital budget
capital gain
capital grant
capital improvement
capital improvement program
capitalism
capitalization
car pool
CBD
cellar
cemetery
census
central business district / CBD
central city / city, central

central place theory
certificate of occupancy
cesspool
channels of movement
chattels
chawls
city
City Beautiful
city, central
City Efficient
city estate
city, floating
city hatred
city, ideal
city, linear
city manager plan; council manager plan
city planning; urban planning
city, poly-nucleated
city, satellite
cityscape
civic center
civic organizations
civil disorder
civil rights
civil service
client
closing
cloud on title / title, cloud on
cluster development / planned-unit development
cluster zoning / zoning, cluster
clustration
coalition doctrine
code, building
code enforcement
code, housing
cohort-survival method
collateral
color-blindness
color of right
commission
commission system of government
common law
communism / socialism
communistic settlements; communitarian societies
community
community center
community college
community control; neighborhood control
community development
community facilities

community organization
community participation
community property
commuter
company town
compensable regulations
compensatory treatment; preferential treatment
compound
comprehensive plan
compulsory purchase / eminent domain
concentric zone theory
concession
condemnation
condemnation, excess
condominium
confiscation
confrontation politics
congested district
conservation
conservation easement / easement, conservation
consolidation
constant-payment plan / level payments
construction industry / building industry
construction loan / loan, construction
contamination
contract
contractor
conurbation
conventional house / house, conventional
conventional mortgage / mortgage, conventional
convergence
conversion
conveyance
cooperative
cooperative housing / housing, cooperative
core house / house, core
corner influence
corporation
corporation, non-profit
corporation, public / public corporation
cost-benefit analysis
cottage
cottage, tied / house, tied
council houses
council manager plan / city manager plan
council of governments / metropolitan council
court

covenant
covenant, Aesopian
coverage
creative Federalism / Federalism, creative
critical-path method
crowd; mob
Crown Lands; Crown Estate
cubic contents; cubage
cubing
cul-de-sac
cultural pluralism
curb level
curtilage
cutcha

day-care center
daylight factor
debt limit
debt service
decentralization
decentrists
decision theory
dedication
deed
deed, full covenant and warranty
deed, quit-claim
deed, tax
default
deficiency judgment
delinquency
demography
demolition
denationalization / desocialization
density
depreciation
depreciation acceleration
depressed area
desegregation / integration
design-concept team
design contest
design speed
desire line
desocialization; denationalization
determinism / physiographic determinism
detribalization
developed area
developer / builder
development area
development plan
development rights
devise
discount points / points, discount

discrimination
discrimination, federal housing
discrimination in employment
district / section / congested district
   /metropolitan special district / special
   district
domicile
dormitory town / town, dormitory
doubling up
drafting
drafting, legislative
dummy; straw man
duplex
dwelling
dwelling, alley
dwelling, multiple
dwelling, seasonal
dynametropolis
dynapolis

earnest money
easement
easement, conservation
easement, scenic
ecology
ecology, human
economic base
economic life
economic rent / rent, economic
economy house / house, economy
economy, mixed / mixed economy
ecumenopolis
educational park
efficiency apartment / apartment, efficiency
effluent
ekistics
emergency shelter / shelter, emergency
eminent domain
enabling act
encroachment
encumbrance
endogenous; exogenous
entail
entrepreneur
environment
equality
equity
equity insurance
equity of redemption
equity, sweat
equivalent elimination
escheat
escrow

establishment
estate
Euclidean zoning / zoning, Euclidean
eviction
exception / variance
excess   condemnation / condemnation,
   excess
exemplary schools; magnet schools
exogenous / endogenous
Experimental City
expropriation
external economics
externalities; side effects; spillovers; repercussion effects
extraterritorial powers; extraterritoriality
exurbanite
exurbia

Fair Deal
fair housing laws
fall-out
family
FAR / floor-area ratio
farm population / population, farm
feasibility study
Federal Housing Administration (FHA)
federalism, creative
federation; borough plan
fee
feedback
fee simple
fee tail
feudal tenure
FHA / Federal Housing Administration
filtering
financing, permanent and temporary
flat
floating city / city, floating
floating zone / zone, floating
floor area, gross
floor-area ratio (FAR)
foreclosure
Fourierism
freehold
friction of space
frontage
front money
full covenant and warranty deed / deed,
   full covenant and warranty

galleria / arcade
game theory
garden apartment / apartment, garden
garden city; green-belt town

general welfare
geomorphic
gerrymander
ghetto
ghetto housing / housing, ghetto
givens
GNP / gross national product
goal; objective; plan; program; project;
  schedule; scheme; target
goal, operational
grade
grade separation
grading
grandfather clause
grant-in-aid
grant reservation
grantsmanship
gravity model
gray area
Great Society
green belt
green-belt town / garden city
Gresham's Law of Neighborhoods
gridiron plan
gross national product (GNP)
ground rent / rent, ground
groupers
guaranteed annual wage
guide lines

halfway housing / housing, halfway
hamlet
hardware programs; software programs
Haussmannization
headway
height zoning / zoning, height
heliport
high-rise / apartment, high-rise
highest and best use / use, highest and
  best
hinterland
hippies
hire purchase
holdout
holistic
home
home, mobile / mobile home
home rule
homestead
hostel
house
house, conventional
house, core
house, economy

household
houser
house, tied
housing
housing association
housing authority
housing code / code, housing
housing, cooperative
housing, ghetto
housing, halfway
housing, in-fill
housing, leased public / public housing,
  leased
housing, limited-dividend
housing, low-cost (low-income, low-
  rent)
housing, luxury
housing market
housing-market analysis
housing-market area
housing, open-occupancy
housing project
housing, public
housing, self-help
housing shortage
housing, substandard
housing, temporary
housing unit
housing, vest-pocket
housing, war
HSB
human nidology
human scale

ideal city / city, ideal
igloo
imageability
improved area; improved land / land,
  improved
improvement
improvement trust
income
income property
increment tax / tax, increment
industrial park; industrial estate
in-fill housing / housing, in-fill
infrastructure
installment construction
installment contract
instant rehabilitation / rehabilitation, instant
integration; desegregation
interest
intergovernmental agreements

interlocal cooperative agreements
intersection; interchange
invasion and succession
investment guaranty program

jerry-building
jet city / airport city
joint development
journey to work
justiciable

key money
key tenant / tenant, key
"key to the corner"

labor-force participation rate; activity
   rate
laissez faire
land
land bank
land development
land fragmentation
land hunger
land, improved
landlord
land, marginal
landmark
land-office business
land, parcel of
land policy
land poor
land, raw
land reclamation
land registration
land tenure
land, underemployed
land use
land-use plan
land-use survey
lane
latifundium
latrine
laundromat; washateria
leafraking / boondoggling
lease
lease back
lease, net
lease, percentage
Lebensraum
legibility
legislative architecture / architecture,
   legislative
leisure
level payment; constant-payment plan

leverage
Lex Adickes
license
lien
life cycle
limited-dividend housing / housing, limited-dividend
linear city / city, linear
linear programing
linear system
linkage
liquidity
listing
loan, construction
loan servicing
loan-value ratio
lobby
local public agency (LPA)
location theory, industrial
lot
lottery
low-cost (low-income, low-rent) housing / housing, low-cost
LPA / local public agency
lunch
luxury housing /housing, luxury

managing agent
map, base
map, official
map, reference
map, time-contour
market value / value, market
mass production / assembly line
mass transit / transit, mass
master plan; city plan; comprehensive
   plan; general plan
mayor-council plan
megalopolis; megapolis
melting pot
metayage; sharecropping
metes and bounds
metropolis
metropolitan area
metropolitan council; council of governments
metropolitan special district
migration
milkability
mixed economy
mobile home; trailer
mobility
mock-up
mock-up, economic

modal split
mode of transportation
model
monument
moratorium
morbidity rate
mortality rate; death rate
mortgage
mortgage, balloon
mortgage, blanket
mortgage, chattel
mortgage, conventional
mortgage-insurance premium
mortgage market
mortgage, open-end
mortgage, straight-term or standing
motel
"Mrs. Murphy"
multiple dwelling / dwelling, multiple
multiple nuclei theory
municipal corporation
municipal private-development corporation
municipality
mutual-aid construction
mutual savings bank

necropolis
neighborhood
neighborhood control / community control
neighborhood unit
neotechnic period / paleotechnic and neotechnic periods
net
New Deal
new town
new-town-in-town
noise
nomadism
non-conforming use / use, non-conforming
non-profit corporation / corporation, non-profit
non-white
nuclear complex / nuplex
nucleation
nuisance
nuplex; nuclear complex

"O and D" survey / origin-destination survey
objective / goal
obsolescence

occupancy rate
old town greys / twilight zone
100-per-cent area
open-occupancy housing / housing, open-occupancy
open space
operational goal / goal, operational
operator
optimum
option
origin-destination survey ("O and D" survey)
overcrowding
overspill
ownership

package plant
paleotechnic and neotechnic periods
parameter
parcel of land / land, parcel of
park
park, educational / educational park
park encroachment
parking
park, vest-pocket
partition action
party wall
paths, edges, districts, nodes, landmarks
patio
"pay as you go" financing / revenue financing
payment in lieu of taxes / taxes, payment in lieu of
peak hour
Peckham Centre
pedestrian
peppercorn rent / rent, peppercorn
percentage lease / lease, percentage
performance standard zoning / zoning, performance standard
phase program
physiographic determinism
piece of the action
place
plan / goal
planned-unit development (PUD)
planner
planning / city planning; transportation planning
planning education
planology
plat
plinth
plot

points, discount
police power
polis
pollution
poly-nucleated city / city, poly-nucleated
population
population explosion; population implosion
population, farm
port
postal savings
poverty
power plant (of government)
PPBS (planning-programing-budgeting
system)
pre-existing use / use, pre-existing
prefabrication
preferential treatment / compensatory
treatment
prejudice
premature subdivision / subdivision,
abortive or premature
prestige architecture / architecture, prestige
price-no-object architecture / architecture, price-no-object
primogeniture
principal
private property
privy
program, project / goal
property tax / tax, property
protective association
public bond / bond, public
public corporation
public domain
public housing / housing, public
public-land ownership
public purpose; public use
public utility
pucka / cutcha
PUD / planned-unit development
pump-priming

quick take
quiet enjoyment
quota system

Rachmanism
racial polarization
rack rent / rent, rack
Radburn planning
radial street planning

Radiant City
real estate; realty
realtor
reapportionment
recreation
redevelopment company
refinancing
region
regionalism
regional planning
rehabilitation
rehabilitation, instant
relocation
rent
rent-control
rent, economic
rent, ground
rent, peppercorn
rent, rack
reparcelation
repercussion effects / externalities
replacement cost
revenue bond / bond, revenue
revenue financing; "pay as you go"
financing
reversion
ribbon development
right-of-way
riot
Riot Act
riparian rights
ripe
road
road hierarchy
roll-back
roof loans
roofscaping
room
rural-urban fringe / urban fringe

sampling
satellite city / city, satellite
scenic easement / easement, scenic
schedule / goal
scheme /goal
school busing / busing, school
school, exemplary / exemplary school
section; district
sector theory
security
seed money
segregation
selective law enforcement
self-help housing / housing, self-help

"separate but equal"
septic tank
service trades
setback regulations
settlement house
sewage
sewage treatment
sewer system
shackery
sharecropping / metayage
shelter
shelter, emergency
shophouse
shopping center
side effects / externalities
sidewalk café
simulation
single-room occupancy / SRO
single tax / tax, single
site
sit-in
"608"
sketch plan
sketch, preliminary
skid row
slum
slum clearance
slum demolition
slum, planned
slum reclamation
slurb
SMSA / standard metropolitan statistical area
socialism
socialization of losses
software programs / hardware programs
solatium
soul-brother
Soul City
special assessment / assessment, special
special district
speculation
speculative architecture / architecture, speculative
speculative building / building, speculative
spillovers / externalities
sponsor
spot clearance
spot zoning / zoning, spot
sprawl
squatter
SRO
standard consolidated area

standard metropolitan statistical area (SMSA)
standard of comfort
standard of living
story
stratification
straw man / dummy
street
street furniture
street hardware
street sleeper
streetwalker
strip zone / zone, strip
subdivision
subdivision, abortive or premature
subdivision regulations
sublease
subordination
subsidy
subsistence allowance
suburb
suburban matriarchy
suburban personality / urban personality
superblock
superstructure
survey
sweat equity / equity, sweat
syndicate
system
systems planning; systemic planning

take-out
target / goal
task force
tax
tax abatement; tax remission
tax, ad valorem
tax, betterment
tax deed / deed, tax
tax exemption
tax expenditures
tax incentives
tax, increment
tax lien
taxpayer
tax, payment in lieu of
tax, property
tax rate, effective
tax remission / tax abatement
tax, single
tax, use
temporary housing / housing, temporary
tenant

tenant, key
tender; bid
tenement; tenement house
tenure / feudal tenure; land tenure
terminal / transportation terminal
tied housing / house, tied
time-contour map / map, time-contour
time zoning / zoning, time
tipping point
title
title, abstract of
title, cloud on
title insurance
Torrens System
tourist cabins
town
town and country planning
town-gown problem
town, dormitory
township
traffic
traffic assignment
traffic distribution
traffic-generation procedure
traffic generator
traffic flow; traffic volume
traffic management
traffic, tidal
traffic zone
trailer / mobile home
transitional area
transition zone / zone, transition
transit, mass
transportation
transportation planning
transportation terminal
trip
trystorium
turnkey job
twilight zone; old town greys
tyrannopolis

untenanted hazard
urban arboriculture
urban architecture / architecture, urban
urban corruption
urban county
urban design
urban escape hatch
urban fringe
urbanism
urban nomads
urbanologist

urban pathology
urban personality; suburban personality
urban planning / city planning
urban population
urban redevelopment
urban renewability
urban renewal
urban servitude
urban sociology
urbicide
urbiphobia
use
use, accessory
use district
use, highest and best
use, mixed
use, non-conforming
use, pre-existing
use tax / tax, use
use value / value, use
usury
Uthwatt Report
utilities
utopia

vacancy
vacancy rate
valuation / appraisal
valuation, physical
value
value, market
value, use
variance; exception
vest-pocket   housing / housing,   vest-
pocket
vest-pocket park / park, vest-pocket
vigilantes
village
visibility

wattle and daub
welfare state, business
white backlash
write-down

yard
"year 2000 plans"

zone, buffer
zone, floating
zone, strip
zone, traffic / traffic zone
zone, transition

zoning
zoning, aesthetic
zoning, airport
zoning, cluster
zoning, Euclidean

zoning, height
zoning, performance standard
zoning permit
zoning, spot
zoning, time